Social Order / Mental Disorder

Social Order/ Mental Disorder

Anglo-American Psychiatry in Historical Perspective

Andrew Scull

ROUTLEDGE

London

First published in 1989
by Routledge
11 New Fetter Lane, London EC4P 4EE

British Library Cataloguing in Publication Data

Scull, Andrew T.

  Social order/mental disorder.
  1. Man. Mental Disorders. – Sociological
    Perspectives
  I Title
  362.2′042
  ISBN 0-415-03636-4

Printed in the United States of America

1 2 3 4 5 6 7 8 9

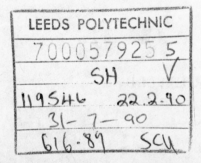

For Anna and Andrew Edward

CONTENTS

CONTENTS

ACKNOWLEDGMENTS

I feel fortunate that we no longer imprison debtors, for I have acquired far more obligations in producing these essays than I can hope to repay. A number of these are of the monetary sort: at various times in the past decade and a half, my work has been supported by the American Council of Learned Societies, the John Simon Guggenheim Memorial Foundation, the Commonwealth Fund, the American Philosophical Society, the Shelby Cullom Davis Center for Historical Studies at Princeton University, and the Faculty Senate at the University of California at San Diego. Such funding has been particularly crucial during the past ten years, when my residence in southern California has placed me at a considerable distance from the archives I regularly need to consult for my research. I am exceedingly grateful to all these institutions for their help, and hope they view this book as some (modest) recompense for their generosity.

My intellectual and personal debts are still more numerous, so much so that it is perhaps invidious to mention particular individuals. Still, I cannot entirely forebear. William Bynum, Roy Porter, and the staff of the Wellcome Institute for the History of Medicine have provided me with a home away from home, stimulating intellectual company, and access to the unrivaled riches of their library during my insufficiently frequent stays in London. Lawrence Stone was enormously helpful and supportive during my year at the Center he directs, notwithstanding his strong intellectual disagreements with some of my work; and Charles Rosenberg, Gerald Grob, and David Rothman have been similarly gracious over the years. Finally, having elected to call myself a sociologist, I have been lucky enough, over the past ten years, to find myself a member of a department that takes history seriously, one that has not held my burrowing around in the eighteenth and nineteenth centuries against me.

This volume is dedicated to my children, Anna and Andrew Edward, who have provided me with so much happiness and joy (not to mention distractions) over the years I have wrestled with a subject matter calculated to prompt the very opposite emotions.

LIST OF ILLUSTRATIONS

CHAPTER ONE

Reflections on
the Historical Sociology of Psychiatry

The history of the victors, for the victors, and by the victors is not only indecent, but also bad history and bad sociology, for it makes us understand less the ways in which human societies operate and change.

—TEODOR SHANIN,
Foreword to *The Agrarian Question and the Peasant Movement in Colombia*
by Leon Zamosc

Madness constitutes a right, as it were, to treat people as vermin.

—LORD SHAFTESBURY,
Diaries, 5 September 1851

"Well, in our *country," said Alice, still panting a little, "you'd generally get somewhere else—if you ran very fast for a long time, as we've been doing."*
"A slow sort of country!" said the Queen. "Now, here, *you see, it takes all the running* you *can do to keep in the same place."*

—LEWIS CARROLL,
Through the Looking Glass

For more than a decade and a half now, I have been preoccupied with understanding social responses to madness in Britain and the United States. Some of my work, dealing with the analysis of the origins and implementation of contemporary mental health policies, seems to fall within the conventional boundaries of sociology as the mainstream of the American profession defines them (though this is largely the result of intellectual accident rather than design). For the most part, however, as the contents of this volume reveal, my interests have been heavily historical, a choice that has quite consciously reflected both my intellectual conviction that an adequate sociological understanding is necessarily a historically grounded understanding and, to be candid, the great pleasure I find in rummaging about in the past.

Intellectual choices, of course, are not made in a vacuum, flowing in substantial measure from a complex interaction between biography and circumstance of which we are seldom fully aware. In largely unintended ways, I suspect that my formal education at Balliol and Princeton contributed to my initial interest in psychiatric history. (One's acquisition of a certain intellectual capital and the natural tendency to work over the

1

years on a set of interrelated problems makes one's early decisions of more moment than is generally realized at the time, so that in retrospect I can hardly be surprised at my continuing fascination with this subject matter.)

Undergraduates at Oxford are not allowed to take a degree in sociology, a peculiar prejudice that has doubtless been reinforced in the present reactionary political climate, given the (not wholly mistaken) notion that there is something inherently subversive about the sustained intellectual analysis of social institutions. The immediate consequence of this policy in my case was that I acquired a rather broad education in philosophy and in a range of social sciences, rather than the narrow indoctrination into a particular academic discipline more characteristic of English university instruction. Because I have always relished the freedom to trespass across established disciplinary boundaries, I think that among sociology's prime attractions for me was my sense of the capaciousness of the intellectual territory it sought to embrace.

This sense of the scope and ambition of the subject reflected the fact that the relatively small dose of sociology I had received at Oxford concentrated heavily on the work of Marx, Durkheim, and Weber, together with such atypical mid-twentieth-century sociologists as Barrington Moore and C. Wright Mills. Mainstream American sociology of the late 1960s, with its narrow, presentist bias, its crude scientism, and its preoccupation with method at the expense of substance, was infinitely less appealing. One might reasonably expect, therefore, that my passage into graduate school in the United States would have produced severe disillusionment. I was fortunate enough, however, to have chosen Princeton for my graduate training: fortunate in that, having cleared certain methodological and statistical hurdles, I (like the rest of my cohort there) was left almost entirely to my own devices, free to pursue my own intellectual whims and fancies.

While not without its hazards—virtually all my fellow students have disappeared without professional trace—this situation did have certain distinct advantages. In particular, when my reading of Foucault and Rothman had led me to an interest in matters psychiatric, no one was disposed to dissuade me from studying lunacy in the nineteenth century simply because the sociological audience for such work might prove vanishingly small. Soon I found myself fascinated by a whole set of interrelated questions about changing social responses to mental disturbance and the mentally disturbed and equally hooked on the pleasures of playing historical detective—a double addiction from which I have neither sought nor wished to escape.

There can be little question that, for many American sociologists, it must seem eccentric for one of their number to exhibit a persistent concern with such topics as eighteenth-century beliefs about madness, a lawsuit launched by an obscure and otherwise unmemorable middle-aged spinster in the late 1840s, the biography of a nineteenth-century alienist, the architecture of Victorian loony bins, and historiographic disputes about the interpretation of nineteenth-century lunacy reform. At the same time, only the most intellectually obtuse could avoid recognizing that a certified member of the sociological community is likely to be greeted with great wariness and suspicion by card-carrying professional historians, even if he somehow escapes being shot at by the border guards who so zealously patrol the artificial boundaries we have erected to distort the study of human society. Yet the intellectual rewards that can flow from resisting entrenched pressures to respect established disciplinary boundaries seem to me amply to justify a refusal to embrace conventional pieties about the territories that belong to the historian or to the sociologist.

One of the most pernicious, albeit widespread, views of the uneasy relationship between these two subspecies of *homo academicus,* while emphasizing that most historians and sociologists have better sense than to invade each other's ecological niche, suggests that when they do threaten to occupy the same social space, competition is reduced through a kind of division of intellectual labor. In the sociologist's version of this fairy tale, historians are portrayed as underlaborers for the queen of social sciences, engaged in the relentless pursuit of the particular without regard for its general theoretical significance, empiricists whose blind archival burrowings produce mounds of "facts," which then serve as the grist for the grander, *explanatory* science to ponder and process. As Joseph Gusfield puts it, "Historians tell stories without conclusions. [Historical] sociologists tell stories that are mostly conclusions."[1]

That this patronizing and, in my view, intellectually misguided set of claims has aroused considerable resentment in historical circles is scarcely surprising. Most historians, after all, quite rightly see themselves as engaged in the task of *explaining* and not simply reproducing the past and are disturbed at the crude and cavalier approach to the difficulties of reconstructing historical reality characteristic of most sociology of this sort. And, unfortunately but inevitably, there are plenty of examples of a "historical" sociology that eschews any but the most superficial acquaintance with the past and with the tools of the historian's trade, neglects (and even rejoices in an unconcern with) the difficulties and rewards of archival research, and blithely seeks either to cram the complexities of the past into a Procrustean bed of transhistorical "theory" or to reduce social reality to the banalities of lower mathematics, in the worst cases engaging in a little of both.

---

1. Joseph Gusfield, *Symbolic Crusade: Status Politics and the American Temperance Movement,* 2d ed. (Urbana: University of Illinois Press, 1986), 189.

But if there are—all too often—ample grounds for the historian's suspicion of the sociological imagination, there is also good reason for regret that this should be so. The distinction between the idiographic and the nomothetic, valuable enough if it refers to a tension embedded in all attempts to grapple with social reality and to the *relative* emphasis on the particular or the general to be found in any specific piece of scholarship, threatens to be quite pernicious if it is reified and taken to refer to a real *opposition,* a binary choice between two mutually exclusive approaches to the study of human society. To the contrary, while generalization based on third- or fourthhand acquaintance with historical reality (and often a superficial and highly selective encounter at that) raises grave questions about the ontological status of the proffered accounts, a resolute emphasis on the uniqueness of events, if taken at face value, simply dissolves into solipsism. Any attempt at description and explanation necessitates a resort to abstraction from the endless particularities of the individual case, a reliance on generalization and the use of analogy, and an explicit or implicit comparison of one set of events with another.

One may quite reasonably object to the grandiosity of much sociological generalization and to the absence of concern among all too many of its practitioners with the constraints and disciplines imposed by the richness of the historical record. One may sensibly take issue with the tendency to value, in Gusfield's terms, the conclusions over the story, heedless of the epistemological difficulties—to say nothing of the empirical distortions and inaccuracies—that such a preference invites. But neither of these arguments confers exemption from the dilemma confronted by all practitioners of the historical and social disciplines: that the ceaseless flux of social reality can be ordered, however provisionally, only by means of reasoned thought and comparison. And this process must of necessity rely on principles of classification imposed upon rather than drawn from that reality.[2] Historians are as subject to this imperative as sociologists because, ultimately, the distinction between the two disciplines is by and large an artificial and unfortunate one, however, entrenched it has become over the years in institutional structures and no matter how skillfully it is now rationalized by the self-interests of academic guilds.

Undesirable as the separation of history and sociology may be, still it constitutes, as Durkheim would say, a social fact, with whose ramifications one must necessarily come to terms. Responding, as they must, to a variety of factors—pressures to maximize the perceived distinctiveness of one's discipline; the consolidation and entrenchment, through the specialization and professionalization of scholarship, of different criteria

2. The last part of this sentence paraphrases some astute remarks in A. Salomon, "Max Weber's Methodology," *Social Research* 1 (1934): 157.

for evaluating intellectual merit; and the parochialism of contemporary academic life, which tends to create powerful linkages between one's nominal disciplinary affiliation and the type of work that is encouraged and recognized as legitimate—it should come as no surprise that historians and sociologists are frequently so much at odds, even (perhaps especially) when cultivating the same territory. But such squabbles are nonetheless regrettable, the more so since neither side possesses a monopoly of virtue.

Justifiably, historians complain that many sociologists neglect the first requisites of historical understanding. But in their eagerness to point out the motes in the eyes of the sociologists, they are all too ready to overlook the beams in their own. For a sensitivity to questions of evidence and inference must be combined with theoretical sophistication and vision, and understanding the particular necessarily depends on an ability to place one's findings within a broadly comparative frame of reference. All too often historians shy away from making their theoretical assumptions and interpretive frameworks explicit and regard comparative statements with ill-concealed suspicion and distaste—as if attending to such matters might contaminate the attempt "to understand the past on its own terms." To the contrary, this evasion leaves one's criteria of selection and relevance underdeveloped and unself-conscious, hence unchallenged and ill thought through; and it constricts one's vision, distorting the sense of perspective so as to leave in obscurity aspects of historical reality that acquire meaning only when placed in a larger contextual frame. The extent to which my own contributions to the history of psychiatry are distinctive is, I like to think, a result of my attempt to marry the traditional concerns of the historian and the sociologist: a willingness to do my historical homework, coupled with a concern with implicit or explicit comparison, with the more general significance of a given set of phenomena, and with issues that transcend the particularities of person and place.

Offering reflections on historical as well as contemporary issues, as I have done here and elsewhere, carries with it both risks and potential benefits. One's position on contemporary dilemmas may, of course, contaminate one's researches on the past, producing a narrow teleological history that abstracts both selectively and misleadingly from the record to provide a version of developments that neatly confirms one's current political prejudices. Gerald Grob and Jacques Quen have been bitterly critical of "revisionist" historians of psychiatry (most especially of David Rothman) on precisely these grounds, and their objections are not to be minimized, even though they apply with equal or greater force to those using them as a cudgel *pour épater les autres*. For whatever Rothman's deficiencies in this regard (an issue I discuss on occasion in other chapters), the much more common problem is precisely the reverse: the construction of versions of the past that serve (in ways generally obscured from those offering such accounts) to legitimate the activities of psychiatrists in the present.

This problem is scarcely unexpected, given that, until recently, much psychiatric history has been written by amateur historians, and a peculiar group of amateurs at that—psychiatrists themselves. Occasionally, as in the case of Richard Hunter and Ida Macalpine, this situation has produced work that, notwithstanding its obvious partiality, has been of lasting value. In the more usual case, however, the resulting distortions have fatally compromised the accounts offered.[3] Nor have psychiatrists-turned-historians been the only offenders in this regard, since the claims of the profession to rest its clinical practice on a scientific basis have led others to accord its activities a privileged ontological status, safe from even moderately searching critical scrutiny. Such "responsible" and sanitized history can expect a generally warm welcome, coinciding as it does with the received wisdom propagated by those whose claim to moral authority over the mad is sanctioned at once by law and by duly certified scientific expertise.

We know, of course, that history is always a matter of reconstruction through the filter of memory and that, to borrow Robert Castel's vivid phrase, all memory is built upon a foundation of forgetfulness (a forgetfulness, one must add, that is anything but random).[4] Furthermore, there is much in our societies' responses to madness, both past and present, that we are all too ready to consign to oblivion. Perhaps it is for this reason that one of the main functions of the history of psychiatry has traditionally been to provide a seemingly inexhaustible supply of images and exemplary tales documenting our passage from the barbarousness of the past into the enlightenment of the present: a movement from the dark period in which lunacy was not recognized as a condition requiring medical treatment, through a long struggle in which the steady application of rational-scientific principles produced irregular but unmistakable evidence of progress toward humane and effective treatments for those afflicted with mental alienation, to our present state of grace.

Within such a vision, we can persuade ourselves (as each generation before us has done) that we stand on the threshold of those discoveries that will finally banish the mysteries surrounding the etiology of madness, ushering in a Golden Age of understanding and practical treatment. It may well be, indeed, that it is precisely our repressed uncertain-

3. Splendid (or rather, sobering) examples include Gregory Zilboorg's *A History of Medical Psychology* (New York: Norton, 1941); and Franz Alexander and S. Selesnick's *The History of Psychiatry* (London: Allen and Unwin, 1967).

4. See Robert Castel, "Moral Treatment: Mental Therapy and Social Control in the Nineteenth Century," in *Social Control and the State: Historical and Comparative Essays,* ed. Stanley Cohen and Andrew Scull (Oxford: Basil Blackwell; New York: St. Martin's Press, 1981), 248–66.

ties about the limits of our current understanding (compounded by the natural anxieties that must attend the daily confirmation of our relative impotence in the face of the more serious forms of alienation) that account for the tenacity and fervor with which so many cling to the myth of progress. To recover the horrors of a prescientific past is to bolster the assurance of escape from darkness into light, an assurance clung to the more desperately the less securely it is anchored in one's mundane experience.

In the last analysis, of course, one's view of the past is necessarily conditioned by the present in ways both large and small, perceived and unperceived. Conversely, to assert that an understanding of the past somehow contributes to a firmer grasp of contemporary realities is to endorse what is too often a banality bereft of any substantive content. Yet the very intractability of the dilemmas we confront in endeavoring to respond to unreason, the peculiar and multiple interpenetrations of past and present that mark the psychiatric domain, the tendency (nowhere more evident and lamentable than here) for "progress" to mask repetitions at once both tragic and farcical, inescapably force historical echoes and parallels into our consciousness.

At the very least, for example, I would hope that those encountering our contemporary reformers and ideologues, who urge deinstitutionalization and praise the virtues of "community," may acquire a certain necessary skepticism from recalling how fervently their nineteenth-century counterparts once preached the gospel of retreat from the world and seclusion within the walls of the asylum.[5] Similarly, both those who urge liberty for the lunatic and those who on the contrary complain of patients "dying with their rights on" play out scripts with a long and checkered history.[6] And the metaphysical wager on a biologically reductionist account of mental disorder made by those who like to think of themselves as being on the cutting edge of modern psychiatry turns out to represent the latest twist on an oft-told tale—one whose full implications await a larger and more sustained analysis than has yet been provided.[7]

I began work on madness and its place in the social order in the early 1970s, the heyday of a romantic antipsychiatry that somehow attracted adherents ranging from the libertarian right to the self-consciously communitarian left. It would be disingenuous to pretend that this intellectual climate was somehow irrelevant to my own concerns and emphases.

5. See Chapter 13.
6. See the discussion in Chapter 12.
7. I plan to provide a history and analysis of the persistent resort to somatic treatments in my forthcoming *Desperate Remedies*. Elliot S. Valenstein's *Great and Desperate Cures: The Rise and Decline of Psychosurgery and Other Radical Treatments for Mental Illness* (New York: Basic Books, 1986) provides a useful survey of a portion of the terrain. There is further discussion of this issue later in this chapter.

For example, I largely concur with (and hope to develop in novel and defensible directions) the stress that this diverse literature places on the ways in which the recognition and response to mental disorder are inextricably culture-bound. Likewise, I have consistently argued that "madhouses, mad-doctors, and madmen" must necessarily be viewed in their sociological context, with much unavoidably remaining opaque and hidden from view till one penetrates the screens of ideology and makes sense of the impact of professional interests, changing social structures and relationships, and shifting forms of power. In my judgment, the usefulness of such claims is not to be demonstrated through abstract polemics, but through the examination and explication of concrete instances where these forces are at work.[8]

At the margin, what constitutes madness strikes me as fluctuating and ambiguous, indeed theoretically indeterminate, making its boundaries the subject of endless dispute and anxiety. Madness is, as Michael MacDonald has so felicitously put it, "the most solitary of afflictions to the people who experience it; but it is the most social of maladies to those who observe its effects,"[9] for its definitions, its boundaries, its meanings are but a distorted mirror image of the shifting social order. Moreover, those who claim the ability to decide for the rest of us where to draw the necessary moral and political lines continue to suffer from embarrassing intellectual vulnerabilities, to say nothing of an all-too-visible therapeutic impotence. My work, like that of the antipsychiatrists, is thus marked by a pronounced skepticism concerning psychiatry's self-proclaimed rationality and disinterested benevolence, a skepticism rooted in what is, on the whole, a dismal and depressing historical record.

On the other hand, I share with many of my fellow critics neither the perception that mental alienation is simply the product of arbitrary social labeling or scapegoating, a social construction *tout court*, nor the notion that psychiatry can be dismissed as merely a malevolent or cynical enterprise. I have never been comfortable with such romantic views of those incarcerated as crazy, which in my view elide and ignore the chronic demoralization and all-too-permanent incapacities that so frequently follow the descent into madness and grossly oversimplify their likely etiology. Nor do I find a simplistic portrait of psychiatrists as concentration camp guards or manufacturers of madness analytically helpful or substantively persuasive.[10] I have thus been increasingly troubled by the dis-

8. As I hope Chapter 7 (on John Conolly) demonstrates, this approach is valuable even at the level of individual biography. Old-fashioned histories of medicine focused all but exclusively on tales of the accomplishments of great men, wrenched from any broader historical or sociological context. My discussion of Conolly adopts a rather different approach to the life and work of one of the heroes of the pantheon.

9. Michael MacDonald, *Mystical Bedlam: Madness, Anxiety, and Healing in Seventeenth Century England* (Cambridge: Cambridge University Press, 1981), 1.

10. It is scarcely disputable that traditional asylums for much of their existence resembled cemeteries for the still breathing and that medical hubris has at times served to

position shared by such disparate figures as Thomas Szasz and R. D. Laing, Thomas Scheff and Erving Goffman, and Michel Foucault and his epigones to play down the degree to which behavior recognized as mad was (and is) genuinely problematic—to say nothing of their willingness either to ignore the enormity of the human suffering and the devastating character of the losses sustained by victims of this form of communicative breakdown or to lay the blame for whatever pathology they *do* acknowledge squarely and solely on the shoulders of a misguided or actively harmful profession. While I have argued elsewhere[11] that the sources of our current turn away from the asylum are not in the last analysis to be sought in an intellectual disenchantment with orthodox psychiatry and its works (indeed, I have contended that deinstitutionalization and the associated abandonment of the chronically insane has taken place with the active support and connivance of the mainstream of the profession), still the antipsychiatrists cannot escape their share of the responsibility for recent "reforms," if only for unwittingly providing an ideological figleaf with which to camouflage a policy of malign neglect.

The history and current state of both psychiatry and the objects of psychiatric attention are, of course, subjects of enormous complexity. And despite the increased attention they have attracted over the past decade and a half, our ignorance and uncertainties manifestly loom larger than those areas about which we can feel reasonably secure. Faced by such vast expanses of the unknown, the conventional historian seems to opt, on first instinct, for the narrowly circumscribed monograph, implicitly hoping that the accumulation of a whole series of these will ultimately, in Baconian fashion, provide the basis for the inductive con-

---

license dangerous, mutilating, even life-threatening experiments on the dead souls confined therein. (See, e.g., Andrew Scull and Diane Favreau, "'A Chance to Cut Is a Chance to Cure': Sexual Surgery for Psychosis in Three Nineteenth Century Societies," *Research in Law, Deviance, and Social Control*, vol. 8, ed. Steven Spitzer and Andrew Scull (Greenwich, Conn.: JAI Press, 1986), 3–39; Andrew Scull, "Desperate Remedies: A Gothic Tale of Madness and Modern Medicine," *Psychological Medicine* 17 [1987]: 561–77; and Valenstein, *Great and Desperate Cures*.) And only the sociologically blind would deny that psychiatrists are deeply and inextricably involved in the definition and identification of what constitutes madness in our world—in ways that render the notion that mental illness is a purely naturalistic category, somehow devoid of contamination by the social, a patent absurdity. Hence the polemical force of the analogy to concentration camps and of the assertion that mad-doctors "manufacture" madness. But to assent to these crude and unnuanced views as revealing the reality hidden behind the smokescreen of ideology is to commit an error as damaging in its way as its antithesis: the view of psychiatry as a straightforwardly and unambiguously humane and scientific enterprise. To examine psychiatry and its ministrations with a critical eye by no means entails the adoption of the romantic idea that the problems it deals with are purely the invention of the professional mind; nor does it require us to embrace the Manichean notion that all psychiatric interventions are malevolent and ill conceived.

11. See Andrew Scull, *Decarceration: Community Treatment and the Deviant—A Radical View*, 2d ed. (Oxford: Polity Press; New Brunswick, N.J.: Rutgers University Press, 1984).

struction of a picture of the larger whole. I have my doubts. The more likely result of ceding the field to those "who keep their noses buried in dusty files in the Public Record Office—or County Record Offices or libraries"—while resolutely shying away from broader questions or a broader context is that, for lack of a larger perspective, history will be reduced to simply one damn thing after another, that those noses will be lifted from the dust "only to tell us that they find the detailed process of interaction between the various individuals involved too complex to yield any overall patterns." [12]

During the 1970s, however, many of those working on the history of psychiatry quite decisively avoided any such narrowness and constriction of vision. If anything, the dominant tendency was to move in the opposite direction. For one of the side effects of the enormous influence of Michel Foucault's *Madness and Civilization,* with its grandiose attempt to offer a reinterpretation of Western Europe's encounter with unreason from the waning of the Middle Ages to the advent of industrial capitalism, was to provoke a number of other wide-ranging surveys of portions of this territory. These were ambitious studies in their own right even if they lacked some of the rhetorical ostentation and temporal sweep of the original. Books like Klaus Doerner's *Madmen and the Bourgeoisie,* David Rothman's *The Discovery of the Asylum,* Robert Castel's *L'Ordre psychiatrique,* and my own *Museums of Madness* forced a wholesale reexamination of the transformation of social ideas and practices vis-à-vis the insane during the eighteenth and the first half of the nineteenth century. In the process, they fostered heated debates and reassessments and opened up an array of provocative questions demanding further research. If, in the ensuing decade, peregrinations through the dusty archives have been pursued with a new vigor, they have at the same time been undertaken in an infinitely richer theoretical and historiographic context and, more often than not, have been motivated by the desire to refine or refute some of the assertions made in these larger surveys of the terrain.

The first generation of these more detailed studies are now beginning to see the light of day, first as doctoral dissertations and, increasingly, as articles and monographs. Anne Digby has recently provided us with a searching reexamination of the history of the York Retreat—along with

12. Quotations from David Philips, "'A Just Measure of Crime, Authority, Hunters and Blue Locusts': The Revisionist History of Crime and the Law in Britain, 1750–1850," in *Social Control and the State,* ed. Cohen and Scull, 68. This tendency is clearly observable in the work of Gerald Grob, most overtly in his historiographic essays (see, e.g., "Public Policy Making and Social Policy" [Paper, Harvard University, 1978]; "Rediscovering Asylums: The Unhistorical History of the Mental Hospital," *Hastings Center Report* 7, no. 4 [1977]: 33–41; and "Welfare and Poverty in American History," *Reviews in American History* 1 [1973]: 43–52), but also in his general histories of American psychiatry, *Mental Institutions in America: Social Policy to 1875* (New York: Free Press, 1973), and *Mental Illness and American Society, 1875–1940* (Princeton: Princeton University Press, 1983).

its symbolic antithesis, Bethlem, one of the two most famous institutions in the history of Anglo-American psychiatry.[13] Nancy Tomes and Charlotte MacKenzie have written model studies of nineteenth-century institutions, in the United States and England, respectively,[14] which concentrated on an upper-class clientele. With their restricted and privileged patient population, these are asylums whose history is in many ways quite different from that of the public hospitals in which the bulk of the insane were confined. But precisely *because* of the character of those they served, their archives are unusually rich and detailed, making possible, for instance, the reconstruction of the processes leading to commitment, the patients' families' views of mental disorder, and the daily routines of asylum existence in ways that the more voluminous but necessarily more superficial records of the public sector scarcely allow. Moreover, the examination of elite practice has, of course, its own special interest and significance, provided we remain constantly sensitive to the limitations on generalizing the findings.

Others have wrestled with institutions treating the opposite end of the social spectrum. In a splendid series of articles, John Walton has made use of the surviving records of the Lancaster County Asylum to explore how paupers were cast out of the community into the world of the asylum (and, more rarely, were brought back in); and he has exploited the opportunity offered by a more intensive examination of the history of an individual asylum to grasp the relationship of local developments to the broader national picture, as well as to question and, if necessary, to redraw, some portions of the larger portrait others have previously provided.[15] Ellen Dwyer has contributed a comparative study of the Utica State Hospital (original home of the *American Journal of Insanity*, now unfortunately renamed the *American Journal of Psychiatry*) and the Willard

13. See Anne Digby, *Madness, Morality, and Medicine: A Study of the York Retreat, 1796–1914* (Cambridge: Cambridge University Press, 1985).

14. See Nancy Tomes, "The Persuasive Institution: Thomas Story Kirkbride and the Art of Asylum Keeping, 1841–1883" (Ph.D. dissertation, University of Pennsylvania, 1978), published in revised form as *A Generous Confidence: Thomas Story Kirkbride and the Art of Asylum Keeping, 1840–1883* (Cambridge: Cambridge University Press, 1984), which deals with the psychiatric division of the Pennsylvania Hospital; Charlotte MacKenzie, "Social Factors in the Admission, Discharge, and Continuing Stay of Patients at Ticehurst Asylum, 1845–1917," in *The Anatomy of Madness*, 2 vols., ed. W. F. Bynum, Roy Porter, and Michael Shepherd (London: Tavistock, 1985), 2:147–74; and idem, "A History of Ticehurst Asylum" (Ph.D. dissertation, University of London, 1987).

15. See John Walton, "Casting out and Bringing back in Victorian England: Pauper Lunatics, 1840–1870," in *Anatomy of Madness*, ed. Bynum, Porter, and Shepherd, 2:132–46; idem, "The Treatment of Pauper Lunatics in Victorian England: The Case of Lancaster Asylum, 1816–1870," in *Madhouses, Mad-Doctors, and Madmen: The Social History of Psychiatry in the Victorian Era*, ed. Andrew Scull (Philadelphia: University of Pennsylvania Press; London: Athlone Press, 1981), 166–97; idem, "Lunacy and the Industrial Revolu-

State Hospital, a controversial institution set up to cope with New York State's overflow of chronic and incurable lunatics.[16] And focusing on a figure notable "not [for] his originality, but his very lack of it," Samuel Shortt has looked at the theory and practice of late-nineteenth-century psychiatry in a provincial Canadian asylum.[17]

Nor has the spate of new work been confined to the study of patients and institutions. The interaction between psychiatry and the law has always been the site of highly charged conflicts whose symbolic importance has far outweighed their apparent practical significance. While psychiatrists have repeatedly sought to remove their discourse to a plane where it would be accorded the objectivity of physical science, the legal system has exhibited persistent skepticism and doubts, remaining wedded to a commonsense schema wherein will or intention, the voluntary basis of action, assumed a central place; and, to the doctors' dismay, the law has periodically displayed considerable hesitations over the appropriate criteria and procedures for certifying someone as mad. Portions of this territory have now begun to receive close and epistemologically sophisticated attention.[18] In a very different vein, Nicholas Hervey has provided a meticulously researched examination of the most important nineteenth-century effort to regulate Victorian psychiatric practice and institutions, the English Lunacy Commission.[19] And, as I shall discuss at more length later in this chapter, a number of scholars have begun to examine the *content* of psychiatric theories and therapeutics in greater depth.

This voluminous outpouring of monographs has, quite naturally, presented us with a more nuanced and complex view of the history of madhouses, mad-doctors, and madmen (and even taught us something about

tion: A Study of Asylum Admissions in Lancashire, 1848–50," *Journal of Social History* 13 (1979–80): 13–18. Laurence J. Ray has also made use of the Lancashire records covering a somewhat later period: see his "Models of Madness in Victorian Asylum Practice," *European Journal of Sociology* 22 (1981): 229–64.

16. Ellen Dwyer, *Homes for the Mad: Life Inside Two Nineteenth-Century Asylums* (New Brunswick, N.J.: Rutgers University Press, 1987).

17. S. E. D. Shortt, *Victorian Lunacy: Richard M. Bucke and the Practice of Late Nineteenth-Century Psychiatry* (Cambridge: Cambridge University Press, 1986).

18. See especially Roger Smith, "The Boundary Between Insanity and Criminal Responsibility in Nineteenth Century England," in *Madhouses, Mad-Doctors, and Madmen,* ed. Scull, 363–84; idem, *Trial by Medicine* (Edinburgh: Edinburgh University Press, 1981); and Ruth Harris, "Murder Under Hypnosis: In the Case of Bompard—Psychiatry in the Courtroom in Belle Epoque Paris," in *Anatomy of Madness,* ed. Bynum, Porter, and Shepherd, 2: 197–241. For an ethnography of contemporary court proceedings on the question of mental competence, see Carol A. B. Warren, *The Court of Last Resort: Mental Illness and the Law,* with contributions by Stephen J. Morse and Jack Zusman (Chicago: University of Chicago Press, 1982). And see Chapter 12 below.

19. Cf. Nicholas Hervey, "The Lunacy Commission 1845–1860, with Special Reference to the Implementation of Policy in Kent and Surrey" (Ph.D. dissertation, Bristol University, 1987).

madwomen).[20] Almost without exception, though, the new work in the field remains marked by and in many ways deeply indebted to the earlier generation of revisionist studies. Mercifully, in consequence, we have been spared a return to a "public relations" history of psychiatry and have likewise not had to endure a revival of "historiographic nihilism or mindless empiricism."[21]

Recent scholarship hews to no consistent ideological line. That the so-called revisionist historians of psychiatry likewise did not constitute a unified counterorthodoxy scarcely requires demonstration. The historiographic essay that appears in Chapter 2 of this book was originally prepared for a conference on the meaning of nineteenth-century moral reform, at which David Rothman and I debated our sharply differing interpretations of the "discovery of the asylum."[22] Those who read even my half of the debate cannot harbor any illusions about the construction of a new revisionist consensus, even in an Anglo-American context, and the divisions between the Anglo-Saxons and the French are, if anything, still more marked.

In one sense, these divisions may seem odd, since all of us writing in the seventies and eighties owe multiple debts to the major figure of the French poststructuralist school, the late Michel Foucault. On the purely mundane level, it was surely the reception accorded to Foucault's work, and the stature he came to occupy in both the academy and café society, that played a major role in rescuing madness from the clutches of drearily dull administrative historians and/or psychiatrists in their dotage, giving the whole topic the status of a serious intellectual subject and thus attracting us to it in the first place. More broadly, whatever else he may have suffered from, Foucault did not lack for intellectual daring, and most of the best recent work in the field for the past fifteen or twenty years can be seen as responding, at least in part, to the intellectual challenges he threw down.

But Foucault was a very peculiar academic animal, in some ways suggestive of an escapee from the bizarre bestiary of Borges' Chinese encyclopedia, whose categories he himself reproduces with such relish at the

20. See Elaine Showalter, *The Female Malady: Women, Madness, and English Culture, 1830–1980* (New York: Pantheon, 1985; London: Virago, 1987); and my discussion in Chapter 11 below.

21. Bynum, Porter, and Shepherd, "Introduction" to their *Anatomy of Madness*, 1 : 5.

22. The papers delivered at this conference, whose other speakers were David Brion Davis and David Roberts, were subsequently published as a special issue of *Rice University Studies* 67, no. 1 (1981). Turnabout being fair play, interested readers may wish to consult this to see what Rothman has to say about me. His essay, "Social Control: The Uses and Abuses of the Concept in the History of Incarceration," can also be found in *Social Control and the State,* ed. Cohen and Scull, 106–17. For an empirical critique of the thesis Rothman advances in *The Discovery of the Asylum* (Boston: Little, Brown, 1971), see Chapter 5 below.

beginning of *The Order of Things:* "(a) belonging to the Emperor, (b) em-balmed, (c) tame, (d) sucking pigs, (e) sirens, (f) fabulous, (g) stray dogs, (h) included in the present classification, (i) frenzied, (j) innumerable, (k) drawn with a very fine camelhair brush, (l) *et cetera,* (m) having just broken the water pitcher, (n) that from a long way off look like flies."[23] Certainly he was not a historian in any ordinary sense of that term, and his work is marked by an audacious unconcern for the canons of histori-cal scholarship and a cavalier way with evidence never likely to command universal assent. Nor is his philosophical baggage such as to guarantee widespread acceptance, at least outside those avant-garde intellectual circles wherein the sun is presumed to rise and set on the Left Bank of Paris. And his labyrinth of language, self-consciously obscure and opaque, "in which," he confesses, "I can lose [even] myself,"[24] is notori-ously ambiguous and impenetrable. Perhaps it is not surprising, in these circumstances, that so many of the Anglo-American obeisances to Fou-cault involve ritual rather than substance and may be accompanied by complaints that his work is "too abstract, too angry, or too difficult to be of much use."[25] Yet besides these ritual acknowledgments (themselves a gesture of not inconsiderable significance), there are others who con-tinue "to regard him as a historian and often extract historical details from him."[26]

In reaching any balanced assessment of *Madness and Civilization,* we need to bear in mind that Foucault himself later repudiated much of the analysis he had presented there. In part, this turnabout reflected a major shift in his general perspective, involving a heightened emphasis on the inextricable interconnections of power and knowledge (the "power-knowledge spiral") and a stress on the *productive* effects of power.[27] In-

23. Michel Foucault, *The Order of Things: An Archeology of the Human Sciences* (New York: Pantheon, 1970), xv.

24. Michel Foucault, *The Archeology of Knowledge* (New York: Pantheon, 1972), 17.

25. H. C. Erik Midelfort, "Madness and Civilization in Early Modern Europe: A Re-appraisal of Michel Foucault," in *After the Reformation,* ed. B. C. Malament (Philadelphia: University of Pennsylvania Press, 1980), 252, referring to the responses of Gerald Grob, David Rothman, and Norman Dain.

26. Ibid., 249, 259. The dangers of treating Foucault as though he were indeed a histo-rian, in the conventional sense of that term, are perhaps suggested by his response to critics who have charged him with gross historical inaccuracies: to query him on such points, he sniffed, is misleadingly to pit "little true facts against big vague ideas" ("Débat avec Michel Foucault," in *L'Impossible prison,* ed. Michelle Perrot [Paris: Seuil, 1980], 29). As Robert Nye dryly comments, "That, of course, is exactly what the historian must do" (*Crime, Madness, and Politics in Modern France* [Princeton: Princeton University Press, 1984], p. 15).

27. See, in particular, the discussions in his *Archeology of Knowledge,* esp. 14–16, 47, 65, 157, 179; and in "Truth and Power," reprinted in *Power/Knowledge: Selected Interviews and Other Writings, 1972–1977* (London: Harvester, 1980). See also his *Discipline and Punish: The Birth of the Prison* (New York: Pantheon; London: Allen Lane, 1978), for his analysis of penality.

stead of the *repressive* activities of a psychiatry concerned to stifle and conceal the ultimate affront to bourgeois sensibilities, Foucault and his followers developed a portrait of a far more thorough-going Orwellian nightmare: a system of control and regimentation ("the carceral archipelago") that operated insidiously and all but invisibly, reaching out to encompass the normal, to snare them within an ensemble of "benevolent" interventions and a discourse of personal fulfillment, and in the process serving to manage and manipulate a universe of ever more "docile bodies."[28] But Foucault also grew increasingly scornful of one of the central features of *Madness and Civilization*, the attempt "to reconstitute what madness might be, in the form in which it first presented itself to some primitive, fundamental, deaf, scarcely articulated experience"; and he forswore what he had there "come close to admitting[,] an anonymous and general subject of history."[29]

English-speaking readers, thanks to an interesting variation on Gresham's Law (the appearance of a bad translation precludes the issue of a good one) have access only to a truncated version of Foucault's original argument. For reasons that remain obscure, what appeared in English was the abbreviated text of the French paperback edition, an abridgment that omitted at least 40 percent of the original version, as well as the bulk of the footnotes and references. (Perhaps Foucault did not object too strenuously, since in this version the transitions between madness in the medieval, the classical, and the modern periods seem much more mysterious than in the original, thus according with his later emphasis on the impossibility of explaining epistemological transitions or ruptures.)

On one fundamental issue, whether the reforms of the moral treatment era constituted a rupture with the past, I think Foucault is more correct than not. Roy Porter, in particular,[30] has recently sought to argue that, on the contrary, the activities of Samuel Tuke and Philippe Pinel exhibit fundamental continuities with earlier views and practices—a contention that, given historians' proclivity for emphasizing continuities

28. In addition to Foucault's own writings (including the works cited in the preceding note, see also *The History of Sexuality*, Vol. 1, *An Introduction* (New York: Pantheon, 1978). Some particularly important related books are Jacques Donzelot, *The Policing of Families* (New York: Pantheon, 1980); and Françoise Castel, Robert Castel, and Anne Lovell, *The Psychiatric Society* (New York: Columbia University Press, 1982). Useful, too, as an example of this later stress on "softer" forms of social control is Stanley Cohen, "The Punitive City: Notes on the Dispersal of Social Control," *Contemporary Crises* 3 (1979): 339–63.

29. Foucault, *Archeology of Knowledge*, 16, 47.

30. See Roy Porter, "The Rage of Party: A Glorious Revolution in English Psychiatry?" *Medical History* 27 (1983), 35–50. Porter has recently elaborated on this theme, and on his criticisms of Foucault, in his *Mind Forg'd Manacles: A History of Madness in England from the Restoration to the Regency* (London: Athlone, 1987). Compare also the comments in Midelfort, "Madness and Civilization," 258–59.

rather than drastic change, is likely to find a receptive audience. But, granted that Foucault's metaphysics leads him to adopt an overly schematic notion of a radical epistemological break with the past and that one can indeed uncover anticipations and adumbrations of moral treatment earlier in the eighteenth century, still I think he is right to insist on the importance of the *change* that moral treatment represents. My own reading of the evidence on this point is laid out in two related chapters in this book, one (Chapter 3) examining the shifting sense in which madness was seen as subject to domestication, the other (Chapter 4) focusing on the social roots of the altered perceptions that underlay the development of moral treatment.

Ironically, of course, in emphasizing the revolutionary character of moral treatment, Foucault appears to endorse one of the key tenets of the traditional triumphalist vision of psychiatric history. But for him, the revolution does not mark the liberation of the insane from their fetters of iron and shackles of superstition. On the contrary, it constitutes the imposition of an ever more thorough-going "moral uniformity and social denunciation"—the historical moment at which the medical gaze secures its domination over the mad, launching "that gigantic moral imprisonment which we are in the habit of calling, doubtless by antiphrasis, the liberation of the insane by Pinel and Tuke."[31]

Such ringing denunciations embody a rather complex set of assertions, some of which I think are defensible and correct, others quite dubious or wrong. To reduce moral treatment, for example, to a species of imprisonment, a more thorough-going form of repression, is to mask an important truth behind a screen of rhetorical excess. For moral treatment (like the larger reform it spawned) is Janus-faced: *pace* Foucault, it cannot be reduced to "the irruption of a bureaucratic rationalism into a preceding Golden Age of permissiveness towards insanity,"[32] and, from my perspective at least, there are good grounds for preferring the tactful manipulation and ambiguous "kindness" of Tuke and Pinel to the more directly brutal coercion, fear, and constraint that marked the methods of their predecessors; yet one must also recognize that in the not-so-long run, it was the other, less benevolent face of moral treatment that came to the fore. Its latent strengths as a mechanism for inducing conformity made possible the abandonment of the brutal and harsh methods of management that had previously been inextricably connected with the concentration of large numbers of lunatics in an institutional environment. And in placing far more effective and thorough-going means of control in the hands of the custodians while simultaneously re-

31. Michel Foucault, *Madness and Civilization: A History of Insanity in the Age of Reason* (New York: Pantheon, 1965), 259, 278 (*Histoire de la folie à l'âge classique*, new ed. [Paris: Gallimard, 1972], 514, 530).

32. Peter Sedgwick, *Psychopolitics* (London: Pluto Press; New York: Harper and Row, 1982), 138.

moving the necessity for the asylum's crudest features, the reality of that imprisonment and control simultaneously became far more difficult to perceive. So in a wider perspective, the major—if unintended—contribution of those who introduced the techniques of moral treatment was to make it possible, in a very practical sense, to manage and clothe with a veil of legitimacy the nineteenth- and twentieth-century museums for the collection and confinement of the mad.[33]

Similarly, the horrors of the nineteenth-century "loony bins" are real enough[34] so that there is no need to exaggerate their awfulness by conjuring up a contrast with the myth of a primal Arcady prior to the Fall produced by the advent of bourgeois reason. Yet it is precisely such a romantic counterimage that Foucault sees fit to invent, reaching back into the Continental equivalent of Merrie Olde England to draw a portrait of folly freed from pernicious social restraint. In medieval times, he informs us, "Les fous alors avaient une existence facilement errante. Les villes les chaissaient volontiers de leur enceinte; on les laissait courir dans des campagnes éloignées, quand on ne les confiait pas à un groupe de marchands et de pèlerins." More picturesquely still, the mad might find themselves on a perpetual voyage in search of their reason, on one of those ships of fools that supposedly haunted the medieval imagination. (Unlike all the other "vaisseaux romanesques ou satiriques," Foucault hastens to assure us, "le *Narrenschiff* est le seul qui ait en une existence réelle, car ils ont existe, ces bateaux qui d'une ville à l'autre menaient leur cargaison insensée.")[35]

What can one say? As Erik Midelfort has pointed out, the ship of fools (like Foucault's other striking image of the medieval leprosaria, waiting across three centuries, "soliciting with new incantations a new incarnation of disease, another grimace of terror, renewed rites of purification and exclusion," till they were populated by the mad)[36] is simply a figment of the latter's overactive imagination: "Occasionally the mad were indeed sent away on boats. But nowhere can one find reference to real boats or

---

33. Cf. the bitter comment of John Thomas Perceval, son of the assassinated prime minister and one of the founders of the Alleged Lunatics' Friend Society: "The glory of the modern system [of moral treatment] is repression by mildness and coaxing, and by solitary confinement" (*Letters to Sir James Graham . . . upon the Reform of the Law Affecting the Treatment of Persons Alleged to Be of Unsound Mind* [London, 1846], letter dated 1 August 1845, quoted in Nicholas Hervey, "The Lunacy Commission 1845–60, with Special Reference to the Implementation of Policy in Kent and Surrey" [Ph.D. dissertation, Bristol University, 1987], 338).

34. See the discussion in Chapter 8 and my more extended treatment of asylum conditions in *Museums of Madness: The Social Organization of Insanity in Nineteenth-Century England* (London: Allen Lane; New York: St. Martin's Press, 1979). The later chapters of Rothman's *Discovery of the Asylum* provide a useful comparative perspective on American state hospitals in the nineteenth century.

35. Foucault, *Histoire de la folie*, 19 (*Madness and Civilization*, 8).

36. Foucault, *Madness and Civilization*, 3 (*Histoire de la folie*, 13).

ships loaded with mad pilgrims in search of their reason."[37] Where the mad proved troublesome, they could expect to be beaten or locked up; otherwise they might roam or rot. Either way, the facile contrast between psychiatric oppression and an earlier almost anarchic toleration is surely illusory.

Foucault's history of madness allocates a central place to the classical age, the period, as he sees it, of the "Great Confinement." Beginning with the founding of the first *Hôpital Général* in Paris in 1657, the poor, the disabled, the deviant, and the morally disreputable—all those who displayed an incapacity for productive work—were swept up and confined. The mad formed only a tiny fraction of the total, yet Foucault's account portrays the whole episode as constituting a grand confrontation between "reason" and "unreason" that led to a profound shift in social sensibilities: "In the classical age, for the first time, madness was perceived through a condemnation of idleness and in a social immanence guaranteed by the community of labor. The community acquired an ethical power of segregation, which permitted it to eject, as into another world, all forms of social uselessness."[38] It was "the immorality of unreason" that prompted its segregation from public view, as an affront to bourgeois sensibilities.

Madness, it seems to me, is here accorded a much more significant place in comprehending the *ancien régime*'s resort to confinement than its quite marginal role actually warrants. Moreover, because he rejects any explanatory schema in which notions of central state power and the economic determination of action play a central role, Foucault neglects the instructive contrast between the Continental and English experiences in this period.[39] At the same time, he goes badly astray even in trying to account for the French policies, for, as Erik Midelfort points out, "the massive attempt to compel the poor to enter institutions originally set up on a voluntary basis . . . has more to do with absolutism and centralization than with bourgeois inspiration."[40]

Developments elsewhere likewise emphasize the central importance of attending directly to the political realm. In Ireland, for example, the pe-

37. Midelfort, "Madness and Civilization," 254. See also Peter Sedgwick *Psychopolitics*, 125–48.

38. Foucault, *Madness and Civilization*, 58.

39. See the sketch of some basic points of comparison in Scull, *Museums of Madness*, 20–22. Cf. also Klaus Doerner, *Madmen and the Bourgeoisie* (Oxford: Basil Blackwell, 1981). One particularly salient difference was the private "trade in lunacy." Cf. William Parry-Jones, *The Trade in Lunacy: A Study of Private Madhouses in England in the Eighteenth and Nineteenth Centuries* (London: Routledge and Kegan Paul; Toronto: University of Toronto Press, 1972). The problems of applying Foucault's picture of a "Great Confinement" to the English experience in the eighteenth century have recently received more extended attention in Porter's *Mind Forg'd Manacles*.

40. Midelfort, "Madness and Civilization," 256.

culiar quasi-administrative structure English imperialism imposed had far-reaching effects on the establishment and development of district asylums. Where the strength of localism in England ensured that lunacy reformers there faced a protracted and hard-fought battle to secure enactment of their schemes, in Ireland the conversion of a small governing group to the virtues of the asylum solution sufficed to secure the prompt passage of the necessary legislation, seemingly without much in the way of attention or debate. Subsequently, the authorities in Dublin Castle retained much greater powers over the size and operations of the system than were possessed by their counterparts in London, the lunacy commissioners. The United States presents a different pattern again, its federal structure leaving responsibility for coping with insanity to the individual states. As I analyze in Chapter 5, the continued intellectual dependence of the new republic on Europe profoundly influenced America's first experiments with the asylum; but thereafter the history of American psychiatry is indelibly marked by the dispersion of policy-making responsibility among the several states.[41]

If Foucault's analysis failed to present either a systematic discussion of politics or a serious dissection of economic structures, it also neglected to provide us with any coherent or persuasive account of how professional control over madness was secured by physicians. It is, he claims, "Tuke et Pinel [qui] ont overt l'asile à la connaissance médicale."[42] But Tuke was a layman, and the whole burden of his version of moral treatment constituted "a rather damning attack on the medical profession's capacity to deal with mental illness."[43] Moral treatment, at least in its English guise, was a *threat* to preexisting medical involvement in the mad business, and, as I discuss later, it took a concerted effort on the part of interested medical men to put down the challenge it posed to their emerging hegemony. And though Pinel was an eminent physician, his experience convinced him that medicine was all but useless in madness, and he concluded that the success obtained in applying exclusively a moral regimen "gives great weight to the supposition, that, in a majority of instances, there is no organic lesion of the brain nor of the cranium."[44] Jan Goldstein's detailed reconstruction of the circumstances surrounding Pinel's

41. Cf. Grob, *Mental Institutions in America*, passim. As Chapter 13 below demonstrates, this dispersion continues to be true today. The differing speed and character of current British and American efforts to deinstitutionalize the mentally ill must be understood, at least in part, as a reflection of the differences between the two political systems. Moreover, even within the United States, the marked interstate variations compel attention to the local political apparatuses.

42. Foucault, *Histoire de la folie*, 525 (*Madness and Civilization*, 271).

43. William F. Bynum, "Rationales for Therapy in British Psychiatry, 1780–1835," in *Madhouses, Mad-Doctors, and Madmen*, ed. Scull, 43.

44. Philippe Pinel, *A Treatise on Insanity*, trans. D. D. Davis (1806), facsimile ed. (New York: Hafner, 1962), 5.

"discovery" of moral treatment has demonstrated quite conclusively "its non-esoteric, lay origins—which Pinel [himself] so proudly and defiantly proclaimed."[45] By his own account, his contribution was to convert this "charlatanistic" technique developed by the lay *concierges* who had day-to-day charge of the insane "into a respectable tenet of official medicine," a scientizing project he accomplished through philosophical specification of the mechanisms of both cause and cure and through the application of statistical methods to measure and confirm quantitatively "the efficacy of the treatment."[46]

In Pinel's eyes, "the lay *concierge*, as diligent, perceptive, and talented as he might be, was inalterably the intellectual inferior of the *médecin-philosophe*. The latter would take the rough-hewn commonsensical knowledge of the former and transform it into something refined, scientific, and esoteric; the elite professional confraternity, at one moment threatened with dissolution by Pinel, was thus fundamentally—and quickly—restored by him."[47] But not always securely. As Dowbiggin has shown,[48] in France, too, moral treatment's implied or explicit denigration of the value of medical treatment on occasion threatened the legitimacy of the physician's presence in the asylum, a problem that long persisted and then recurred, much to the discomfort of later generations of alienists. So the role of Pinel and Tuke in ushering in the Golden Age of psychiatry[49] is at the very least far more complicated and indirect than the reader of *Madness and Civilization* might surmise.

45. Jan Goldstein, *Console and Classify: The French Psychiatric Profession in the Nineteenth Century* (Cambridge: Cambridge University Press, 1987), 72–119.

46. Ibid., 105 and 101.

47. Ibid., 77.

48. Ian Dowbiggin, "The Professional, Sociopolitical, and Cultural Dimensions of Psychiatric Theory in France 1840–1900" (Ph.D. dissertation, University of Rochester, 1986). On French psychiatry in the first half of the century, see also Jan Ellen Goldstein, "French Psychiatry in Social and Political Context: The Formation of a New Profession 1820–1860" (Ph.D. dissertation, Columbia University, 1978), now revised and published as *Console and Classify: The French Psychiatric Profession in the Nineteenth Century* (Cambridge: Cambridge University Press, 1987). As Goldstein notes, Pinel's protégé Esquirol was far more overtly and forcefully concerned with the maintenance and expansion of professional prerogatives. Compare his typically combative claim that

> The physician must be, in some manner, the vital principle of a lunatic hospital. It is he who should set everything in motion; he should regularize all actions, just as he has been called upon to be the regulator of all thoughts. . . . The action of the administration, which governs the material aspect of the establishment and supervises all the employees, ought to be hidden. Never should the administration appeal a decision made by the physician, never should it interpose itself between the physician and the lunatics or between the physician and the non-medical staff (*les serviteurs*). The physician should be invested with an authority from which no one is exempt (quoted in *Console and Classify*, 132).

49. Cf. Robert Castel, *L'Ordre psychiatrique: L'Âge d'or d'aliénisme* (Paris: Minuit, 1976) (English translation: *The Regulation of Madness: Origins of Incarceration in France* [Berkeley: University of California Press; Oxford: Polity Press, 1988]).

Chapter 6 represents an attempt on my part to examine these issues; it was, in fact, the first essay I published on matters psychiatric. Its focus only on events in the late eighteenth and nineteenth centuries is, I now feel, somewhat misleading. My subsequent researches into seventeenth- and eighteenth-century medical writings, some of which form the basis of the argument presented in Chapter 3 on the domestication of madness, made clear to me that I had underestimated the degree of interest in insanity some medical men displayed at that time. More generally, the passage from an eclectic fusion of the supernatural and the scientific— the religious, the magical, the social, the moral, and the medical—to a purely naturalistic and secular account is unquestionably more complex and convoluted than a narrow focus on nineteenth-century develop- ments would lead one to believe. Michael MacDonald, for example, has plausibly argued, in his splendid *Mystical Bedlam*,[50] that a preference for natural causation and a "hankering after the bare Mechanical causes of things,"[51] which entailed a disposition to reject demonological and super- natural accounts of madness, grew ever more widespread among the En- glish elite in the aftermath of the Restoration, in substantial measure as part of a conscious rejection of religious fanaticism and "enthusiasm."

At the same time, as MacDonald himself concedes, "ordinary men and women were reluctant to abandon beliefs that reinforced their view of the universe as a theatre of spiritual warfare between the forces of good and evil, and they continued to fear the power of Satan and malign spirits throughout the eighteenth century."[52] Thus (among other things) they remained disposed to see madness in more traditional terms. Fur- thermore, evidence that a large fraction of the English elite had come to embrace medical accounts of mental disorder during the course of the eighteenth century does not invalidate the claim that the ineffectiveness and scandals associated with medical treatment, in the context of the emergence of the lay vision of moral treatment, posed a potentially pow- erful threat to medical hegemony at the outset of the following century.[53] I continue to believe, in consequence, that the account I offer here of the cognitive and legal entrenchment of a medical monopoly over the treat- ment of madness retains much of its force and relevance.

Recent work has begun to examine in more extended contexts the sig-

50. Michael MacDonald, *Mystical Bedlam: Madness, Anxiety, and Healing in Seventeenth Century England* (Cambridge: Cambridge University Press, 1981). See also idem, "Religion, Social Change and Psychological Healing in England," in *The Church and Healing*, ed. W. J. Sheils (Oxford, 1982); idem, "The Secularization of Suicide in England, 1660–1800," *Past and Present* 3 (1986): 50–100; and, for similar arguments, Porter, "The Rage of Party."

51. Henry Halliwell, *Melampronea; or, A Discourse of the Polity and Kingdom of Darkness* (London, 1681), 77–78, quoted in MacDonald, "Secularization," 86.

52. MacDonald, "Secularization," 87.

53. For other commentaries on this point, see William F. Bynum, "Rationales for Therapy in British Psychiatry, 1780–1835," in *Madhouses, Mad-Doctors, and Madmen*, ed. Scull, 35–57; and Anne Digby, *Madness, Morality and Medicine*, esp. chaps. 2–6.

nificance of psychiatry's commitment to the somatic style, and this is likely to be a continuing focus of future research in the field. Reflecting the poverty of its cognitive accomplishments, its persistently dismal therapeutic capacities, and the social undesirability and disreputability of most of its clientele, psychiatry has enjoyed a perpetually marginal and unenviable position in the social division of labor—a profession always, so it seems, but a step away from a profound crisis of legitimacy.[54] Without question, its repeatedly successful defense of its tenuous social mandate has had multiple sources, many having little to do with its ideological presentation of self: the absence, for instance, of plausible rivals for its role; the continuing social utility of medical discourse as a rationalization for measures of intervention and control directed at the acute and persistent problems posed by the mad; and the real, if sharply circumscribed, impact of medical technology on the more florid manifestations of madness. Still, as a growing body of research repeatedly demonstrates, the organic metaphor, periodically reworked to bring psychiatric language into plausible correspondence with the reigning models of the somatic machine that characterize the medical mainstream, has been (as it continues to be) of quite central importance in establishing the psychiatrists' exclusive jurisdiction over the insane, their expertise as medical specialists, and popular acceptance (however grudging) of that expertise.

Stephen Jacyna, for example, has provided a detailed and searching examination of English psychiatric ideas in the mid-Victorian era,[55] pointing out the intimate connections between the rise of an aptly named "physiological psychology" and its polemical usefulness "to entrench and to enhance . . . professional prerogatives." Reflex models of nervous function had come to dominate British neuroscience by the mid-nineteenth century, and over the next decade and a half it was in terms of reflex action that British alienists increasingly couched their explanations of insanity. But the construction of these connections masked a huge gap between scientific pretensions and reality. The use of reflex theory was crude and casual. What masqueraded as inferences from the latest developments in neurology was in fact simply the restatement of "old doctrines in a novel idiom." For beneath "the thin veneer of modernity" provided by the appropriation of the language of neuroscience there lurked a continuing attachment to a vascular, inflammatory etiology of insanity.[56]

54. Cf. Charles Rosenberg, "The Crisis of Psychiatric Legitimacy: Reflections on Psychiatry, Medicine, and Public Policy," in American Psychiatry: Past, Present, and Future, ed. G. Kriegman et al. (Charlottesville, Virginia: University Press of Virginia, 1975), 135–48.

55. L. S. Jacyna, "Somatic Theories of Mind and the Interests of Medicine in Britain, 1850–1879," Medical History 26 (1982): 233–58.

56. Ibid., 241, 244, 248.

In an important series of papers,[57] focusing on the last third of the nineteenth century, Ian Dowbiggin has similarly sought to connect French psychiatry's precarious social and scientific standing to the question of theory choice in the discipline. His discussion demonstrates how, in a very different sociopolitical and scientific setting, the theory of morbid heredity and degeneration "offered a loosely defined yet appealing cognitive model through which psychiatrists could terminate the theoretical conflicts dividing their profession and simultaneously counter their declining image, gain intellectual legitimacy through identification with the more fashionable biological sciences, and accommodate themselves to a general pessimism that characterized nineteenth-century French currents of thought."[58] Particularly salient in the French context was the persistent threat posed by clerical interest in the problems of insanity,[59] hence one powerful and culturally specific source of pressures to reemphasize the centrality of the body. But, more generally, the profession's therapeutic impotence, the psychiatrists' own growing despair, the massive overcrowding of French asylums, and the low esteem, even outright hostility, with which psychiatrists were greeted by the French public made them a beleaguered group desperate to hang on to the threads of respectability. Not just the persistent inability to discover cerebral lesions in autopsies performed on the insane, but also the developing rejection of the doctrine of pathological anatomy among members of the Paris School of Medicine forced alienists to modify the basis of their claim that madness was rooted in disorders of the soma. Yet their conviction remained unshakable that insanity was brain disease. It was a proposition, for them, not intelligibly subject to doubt, for to question it was to challenge their claims to objectivity and to scientific status, the very basis of their privileged and authoritative role in the diagnosis and disposition of the lunatic.

But the persistent recourse to somatic theories of mental disorder has a much broader significance than its role in convincing political elites to legislate in favor of medical interests. As Roger Smith has rightly suggested, if we are to comprehend the "more subtle role played by belief as a cultural resource, and not just as a vehicle of professional advance-

---

57. See Ian Dowbiggin, "Degeneration and Hereditarianism in French Mental Medicine 1840–1890: Psychiatric Theory as Ideological Adaptation," in *Anatomy of Madness*, ed. Bynum, Porter, and Shepherd, 1:188–232; idem, "French Psychiatry, Hereditarianism, and Professional Legitimacy 1840–1900," in *Research in Law, Deviance, and Social Control*, Vol. 7, ed. Andrew Scull and Steven Spitzer (Greenwich, Conn.: JAI Press, 1985), 135–65; idem, "French Psychiatric Attitudes Towards the Dangers Posed by the Insane ca. 1870," in *Research in Law, Deviance, and Social Control*, Vol. 9, ed. Andrew Scull and Steven Spitzer (Greenwich, Conn.: JAI Press, 1988), 87–111.

58. Dowbiggin, "Degeneration and Hereditarianism," 189.

59. See the extended discussion in Goldstein, *Console and Classify*, passim, esp. 197–275 and 361–77.

ment," we must necessarily pay close attention to the detailed content of medical theories.[60] Much of the time, for example, psychiatry has derived, not only its mandate, but also its therapeutics from its metaphysical embrace of the body. Repeatedly, an emphasis on physical pathology has prompted the employment of physical treatments. Henry Maudsley articulated the logic of this position with characteristic bluntness: "That which . . . has its foundation in a definite physical cause must have its cure in the production of a definite physical change."[61] The alternative could be speedily and scornfully dismissed. "No culture of the mind, however careful, no effort of will, however strong, will avail to prevent irregular and convulsive action when a certain degree of instability of nervous element has, from one cause or another, been produced in the spinal cells. It would be equally absurd to preach control to the spasms of chorea, or restraint to the convulsions of epilepsy, as to preach moderation to the east wind, or gentleness to the hurricane."[62]

As Michael Clark has brilliantly demonstrated,[63] in this fierce rejection of psychological approaches to mental disorder, Maudsley was entirely representative of his generation. Moreover, his convictions were firmly anchored in the "deep structures" of Victorian psychiatric theory, notwithstanding that somatic-pathological approaches to insanity (borrowing, by now, from the French emphasis on degeneration and morbid heredity), embodied a double failure: they yielded little in the way of increased *scientific understanding* of the etiology and pathology of insanity; and, equally, they possessed no clear-cut or decisive *therapeutic advantages* over "moral treatment" or other purely empirical nonmedical methods when it came to curing the insane.

Though we lack a full-fledged study of comparable scope and sophistication for the United States in the same period, it is apparent that not just institutional psychiatrists, but also such emerging specialisms as neu-

60. Roger Smith, Review of *Museums of Madness, Isis* 71 (1980):257.

61. Henry Maudsley, *The Physiology and Pathology of Mind* (London: Macmillan, 1867), 83. Psychiatrists over the years have been equally enamored of the reverse proposition: that physical interventions cure or modify mental disorder is alleged as "proof" that the condition itself has a physical etiology.

62. Ibid., 83. Cf. John Gray, editor of the *American Journal of Insanity:* "If insanity be merely a disease of the mind, pure and simple, we can readily admit the all-sufficiency of moral means of treatment. Believing, however, that it is but a manifestation of physical lesion, . . . to which the psychical phenomena are subordinate or secondary, any other conclusion than that which makes medical therapeutics the basis of treatment involves an absurdity" ("Editorial," *American Journal of Insanity* 21 (1865):558.

63. Michael Clark, "The Rejection of Psychological Approaches to Mental Disorder in Late Nineteenth Century British Psychiatry," in *Madhouses, Mad-Doctors, and Madmen,* ed. Scull, 271–312. See also idem, "'The Data of Alienism': Evolutionary Neurology, Physiological Psychology, and the Reconstruction of British Psychiatric Theory, c. 1850–c. 1900" (D.Phil. dissertation, Oxford University, 1982).

rology and gynecology, competitors with the more established professionals for patients on the borderland of insanity,[64] evinced a similarly thorough-going materialism.[65] Much of neurological therapeutics, for example, from the elaborate shiny machines for administering static electricity to S. Weir Mitchell's famous "rest cure" (which involved isolation from one's family, rest, diet, massage, and absence of all responsibility), to our eyes depended for its efficacy largely on its psychological impact on the patient. But while acknowledging that individual suggestibility sometimes played a part in a cure, the neurologists remained deeply antagonistic, not merely to psychological *explanations* of insanity, but to any sustained or systematic attention to mental therapeutics. Mitchell himself, though he accepted that there were some similarities between his rest cure and the activities of exponents of religiously based "mind cures," insisted that the fundamental impact of his approach derived from its contribution to building up the patient's "fat and blood."[66] And when George M. Beard had the temerity to suggest that "expectation is itself a curative force,"[67] he met with furious criticism from his colleagues, who denounced him for descending "to the level of all sorts of humbuggery."[68]

There is ample scope for further interrogation of these nineteenth-century materials, but the work done to date has already opened up a number of further lines of inquiry, exploration of which is only just beginning. In the first place, the twentieth century provides perhaps the most startling examples of the psychiatric profession's predilection for physical treatments, ranging from malarial mosquito therapy through metrazol-induced seizures, insulin comas, electroshock treatment, and surgical treatments for focal sepsis (not to mention several more exotic, if less widely canvassed, forms of therapy). The list extends, of course, to encompass direct surgical intervention on the organ most often held to blame for the outbreak of madness, the brain, with lobotomy being one of only two psychiatric interventions held to warrant the award of the Nobel Prize in medicine!

One can easily comprehend why psychiatry might wish to envelop

64. On American neurology's conflict with psychiatry in the late nineteenth century, see Bonnie Ellen Blustein, "'A Hollow Square of Psychological Science': American Neurologists and Psychiatrists in Conflict," in *Madhouses, Mad-Doctors, and Madmen*, ed. Scull, 241–70.

65. For the gynecological example, see Scull and Favreau, "'A Chance to Cut Is a Chance to Cure.'"

66. S. Weir Mitchell, *Fat and Blood*, 3d rev. ed. (Philadelphia: Lippincott, 1884); idem, *Wear and Tear; or, Hints for the Overworked* (Philadelphia: Lippincott, 1871).

67. George M. Beard, "The Influence of Mind in the Causation and Cure of Disease: The Potency of Definite Expectation," *Journal of Nervous and Mental Diseases* 4 (1877):429–34.

68. William Hammond, in "Minutes of the American Neurological Association," *Journal of Nervous and Mental Diseases* 3 (1876):429–37.

these episodes in a veil of obscurity, but it is less clear why the rest of us should collaborate in this willful amnesia. For I suspect that their history can provide uniquely powerful insights into the interdependence of the intellectual and the social (a central theme of much of the best recent work in the field) and into the nature of the psychiatric enterprise as a whole. Strategically, too, the latest example of the fascination with facsimiles of more conventional medical therapeutics—the rise of psychopharmacology, associated particularly with the advent of the phenothiazines, the so-called major tranquilizers—appears to have been of quite major importance in the recapture of the commanding heights of psychiatric training programs by biological psychiatry[69] and in the interprofessional competition between psychiatry and the burgeoning numbers of lay psychotherapists, social workers, clinical psychologists, and the like. Its importance notwithstanding, we have as yet investigated only a small portion of this territory in any depth.[70]

Equally intriguing is the opposite line of investigation: how medical resistance to psychological approaches was, in different settings, at least partially overcome, permitting the development of dynamic psychiatry, particularly in its Freudian guise. Apart from the intrinsic interest that attaches to this question, it clearly has a vital and direct bearing on how and why twentieth-century psychiatry was able to expand and diversify the territory it was presumed competent to manage.

Not the least important factor was surely the continuing therapeutic and scientific barrenness of work based on pathological anatomy, and the growing recognition of this as the Victorian era drew to a close. Michael Clark has suggested that "it was an acute awareness of just how lowly, despised and vulnerable institutional psychiatry's existing social position was, and a desperate desire to escape its suffocating constraints

69. As Donald Light has noted, the increasing prominence of psychoanalysis in America in the years after World War II, was reflected, through the late 1960s, in the dominant role analysts began to play in the psychiatric training programs at major medical schools and in the successful "capture" of the brightest young residents by the analytic community during those same years. But the following decade saw a sharp reorientation "toward biology and physiology with a seriousness and depth that are neither cosmetic nor ephemeral . . . a basic shift in how psychiatrists are trained and go about their work" (Donald Light, *Becoming Psychiatrists* [New York: Norton, 1980], xi). One measure of the psychoanalytic decline is provided by a 1976 survey conducted by the American Psychoanalytical Association, which revealed that the average analyst had only 4.7 patients under treatment, as compared with 6.2 patients a decade earlier, a fall of more than 20 percent. (Figures cited in Anthony Clare, *Psychiatry in Dissent*, 2d ed. [London: Tavistock, 1980].) Given the social and scientific significance of these changes, it is somewhat surprising that they have yet to attract serious scholarly attention.

70. The most extensive analysis to date is Valenstein's *Great and Desperate Cures*. For a more limited analysis of the use of oral and abdominal surgery as a treatment for focal sepsis (and thus, so its proponents believed, for mental illness), see Scull, "Desperate Remedies."

and frustrations, rather than any more vaunting ambition, which drove later-Victorian psychiatrists to broaden and diversify their territory."[71] And, within their own professional circles, Americans quite openly made a similar diagnosis: "Our therapeutics," C. G. Hill complained, in his 1907 Presidential Address to the American Medico-Psychological Association, "is simply a pile of rubbish."[72] Two years later, in his address to his fellow neurologists, Weir Mitchell echoed Hill's analysis: "Amid enormous gains in our art, we have sadly to confess the absolute standstill of the therapy of insanity and the relative failure, as concerns diagnosis, in mental maladies of even that most capable diagnostician, the post-mortem surgeon."[73]

But this internal sense of crisis and malaise was clearly insufficient, by itself, to prompt more than public handwringing and lamentations. In the British context, both Elaine Showalter and Martin Stone have suggested that it was a powerful set of social pressures, "the exigencies of war and a mass epidemic of mental disorders"—shellshock among the troops—that constituted the necessary stimulus "to set the mechanism of psychiatric change in motion."[74] Unquestionably, World War I had similar effects in the United States. Here, however, the effects of wartime experience were to speed up a process that had already acquired considerable momentum in the earliest years of the new century. Once again, even with our present rather imperfect understanding of these changes, it seems clear that external developments were powerfully implicated in producing internal realignments of the profession. Most especially, the extraordinarily rapid proliferation of religiously based mental healing cults (of which Christian Science was the most notable) had prompted a growing "exodus of patients from the doctor's waiting room to the minister's study."[75] Faced by people voting with their feet for mental therapeutics, many physicians apparently concluded that patients must be saved from themselves, even if this meant that psychological medicine would have to abandon its traditional "antagonism to methods of treatment which appeal to other than physical means."[76]

71. Clark, "'Data of Alienism,'" 312.

72. Charles G. Hill, "How Can We Best Advance the Study of Psychiatry?" *American Journal of Insanity* 64 (1907):6.

73. Silas Weir Mitchell, "[Presidential] Address to the American Neurological Association," *Transactions of the American Neurological Association* 35 (1909):1.

74. Martin Stone, "Shellshock and the Psychiatrists," in *Anatomy of Madness*, ed. Bynum, Porter, and Shepherd, 2:242–71; idem, "The Military and Industrial Roots of Psychology in Britain" (Ph.D. dissertation, London School of Economics, 1985); Showalter, *Female Malady*, chap. 7.

75. Barbara Sicherman, "The Quest for Mental Health in America, 1880–1917" (Ph.D. dissertation, Columbia University, 1967), 269–70.

76. Edward Wyllwys Taylor, "The Attitude of the Medical Profession Toward the Psychotherapeutic Movement," *Journal of Nervous and Mental Diseases* 35 (1908):420. We need

At present, too, these are aspects of the evolving relationship between psychiatry and the larger social order that we can glimpse only in broad outline. If we are serious about grasping the unfolding effects of professional intervention in the lives of the mad and about understanding the complexities of the interrelationships between psychiatric power and knowledge, we obviously have a large agenda of research before us. The bulk of recent historical work in the field has concentrated on the eighteenth and nineteenth centuries,[77] and by contrast, our own century, even as it draws to a close, remains for the most part a dark continent in which merely a few prominent landmarks stand out. Only with respect to the last quarter century are things a little better, for this is a territory in which even an ahistorical sociology feels at home and about which it has had something to say.

Indeed, in some respects, sociology has been a *participant* in, rather than just an observer of, recent events. For the sociological critique of the mental hospital's pathologies, along with labeling theory's portrayal of stabilized mental disorder as ironically the *product* rather than the *object* of psychiatry's attentions, played a considerable role ideologically in underwriting the shift from institutional to community care and in prompting the constriction of the permissible grounds for certifying someone as so mad as to need confinement. At the birth of the asylum, reformers conjured up a mythological portrait of its virtues and its startling therapeutic effectiveness. Subsequently, alienists campaigned long and hard (albeit with at best limited success) to persuade the public of the need to adopt broad and easily satisfied commitment criteria: decision rules that would license swift commitment of incipient lunatics to their institutions, before minor eccentricities and mental imbalance passed over into permanent and chronic insanity. Our contemporary myths, embracing exactly the contrary set of assertions, have proved the more powerful since they can claim to constitute the findings of social "science."

One of the virtues of a historical perspective that extends beyond the ideas and events of the past quarter century is that it makes us properly

---

to recall that in both societies, even at the zenith of dynamic psychiatry's popularity, powerful elements in the profession remained unalterably opposed to any but somatic approaches and continued to stigmatize those who strayed from the path of scientific medicine as teetering on the brink of quackery. For a somewhat more extended analysis of these issues, see Andrew Scull, "The Social History of Psychiatry in the Victorian Era," in *Madhouses, Mad-Doctors, and Madmen*, ed. Scull, 19–23.

77. Among the obvious exceptions to this generalization, besides the somewhat tiresome sectarian squabblings about the history of psychoanalysis, are Gerald Grob's *Mental Illness and American Society, 1875–1940* (a useful, if somewhat plodding, administrative history of the American scene); David Rothman's *Conscience and Convenience* (Boston: Little, Brown, 1980), discussed at length in Chapter 10; and Martin Stone's still unpublished Ph.D. thesis, "Military and Industrial Roots of Psychology in Britain."

skeptical about claims of intellectual breakthroughs and the discovery of utopian solutions to the complex and extraordinarily recalcitrant problems we label mental illness. It also leaves us better placed to assess just how novel and original our current enthusiasms really are. Modern sociological critics of the "total institution" have remained blissfully innocent of the degree to which their findings reproduce observations first made a century and more ago.[78] And examination of nineteenth-century debates over what constituted adequate grounds for involuntary commitment to an asylum likewise disabuses us rather rapidly of the conceit that our generation has developed some privileged insight into the dangers of unchecked psychiatric authority over the commitment process.[79] If the social impact of such ideas and criticism turns out to vary sharply over time, it constitutes just one more reminder not only of the profound and inescapable mutual dependence of the social and the intellectual but also of the impossibility of gaining a proper understanding of one without knowledge of the other.

At various times during the past decade, I have been accused both of being viciously anti-institutional[80] and of wanting to reinstitutionalize the mad *en masse*.[81] While I take a certain sly pleasure in having simultaneously ruffled the feathers of the complacent souls who somehow continue to see mental hospitals as "the most blessed manifestation of true civilization"[82] and of the odd mixture of zealots and penny-pinching politicians who continue to call malign neglect "community *care*," I must respectfully decline both labels. Like the late Peter Sedgwick, my knowledge of what went on in the old "loony bins" makes me want to shout "Never again!" to the prospect of a return to an unreconstructed psychiatric Victorianism.[83] But this must not blind us to the appalling deficiencies of yet another generation of mental health "reforms" or prevent us from recognizing that, as a last resort, sheltered care must remain an option for coping with a minority of the mentally disturbed. Over the past century and a half, we have swung wildly from viewing the asylum as the universal panacea for the defects of the community to seeing the com-

78. See the discussion of nineteenth-century critiques of the asylum in Scull, *Decarceration*, chaps. 6 and 7.

79. In addition to the discussion in Chapter 12 below, see Nicholas Hervey's paper on the wonderfully named Alleged Lunatics' Friend Society of mid-Victorian England ("Advocacy or Folly: The Alleged Lunatics' Friend Society, 1845–63," *Medical History* 30 [1986]:245–75).

80. Seymour Mauskopf, review of *Museums of Madness* by Andrew Scull, *Journal of Interdisciplinary History* 11 (1981):726–29.

81. Cf. Leonard V. Kaplan, "State Control of Deviant Behavior: A Critical Essay on Scull's Critique of Community Treatment and Deinstitutionalization," *Arizona Law Review* 20 (1978):189–232.

82. George E. Paget, *The Harveian Oration* (Cambridge: Deighton and Bell, 1866), 34–35.

83. Cf. Sedgwick, *Psychopolitics*.

munity itself as a ubiquitous and uniformly desirable solution to the problem of what to do with the mentally defective. But, for all the rhetoric about community treatment, we remain as far as ever from solving the problems of "how to create the economic means of employment, the material apparatus of housing, the ethical structures of friendship and solidarity, for those who through various forms of mental disability cannot purchase these benefits as commodities in the marketplace."[84] Worse still, I fear the balance of political forces in Britain and the United States gives little prospect of major initiatives being undertaken to mitigate or eliminate the deficiencies of existing mental health policy.

Not just the present, but even the future for the chronically crazy strikes me as grimly unpromising. I wish it were otherwise. But, as Freud once taught us, reality, however harsh, is in the long run preferable to the childish consolations offered by a retreat into the realm of fantasy (appealing as the latter may sometimes seem).

84. Ibid., 241.

CHAPTER TWO

Humanitarianism or Control?
Some Observations on
the Historiography
of Anglo-American Psychiatry

In my experience, large academic conferences are often stupifyingly boring affairs. In general, they appear to have little to do with matters of intellectual substance, providing instead a platform for the posturing and preening of academic narcissists and/or the opportunity for graduate student supplicants to sell themselves to prospective employers. Smaller gatherings, however, sometimes escape this fate, and the conference at which the following paper was given proved to be one such occasion. In the winter of 1980, the Department of History at Rice University invited David Brion Davis, David Roberts, David Rothman, and me (they must have run out of Davids) to spend several days debating the origins and significance of nineteenth-century moral reform. Both the formal papers and some of the informal discussion were subsequently published as a special issue of *Rice University Studies.* Our disagreements were many, and over the three days, quarter was neither asked nor given. Still, the whole occasion proved to be a consistently stimulating and lively one, conducted on the friendliest of terms. For my part, I was grateful for the incentive to think systematically about the recent historiography of psychiatry and for the opportunity to debate some of the fundamental interpretive issues with David Rothman.

Pace the oddly obtuse readings of the more naive and indignant defenders of the liberal public relations theory of psychiatric history, there exists no unitary "revisionist" school of psychiatric historians. Certainly, Rothman and I had no difficulty uncovering some quite fundamental issues on which we disagreed, notwithstanding our shared skepticism about an earlier conventional "wisdom." Since this essay appeared, a number

Chapter 2 is reprinted from *Rice University Studies,* Winter 1981, pp. 21–41, by permission of the editor.

of others have sought to survey the historiography of Anglo-American psychiatry. I find the following particularly helpful and challenging: David Ingleby's "Mental Health and Social Order"; [1] John Walton's "Casting out and Bringing back in Victorian England"; [2] and Roy Porter, "Shutting People Up." [3] Joan Busfield's discussion in Part 1 of her *Managing Madness* provides a reasonably helpful overview. [4] Finally, Michael Ignatieff's "State, Civil Society and Total Institutions," while only tangentially concerned with matters psychiatric, still contains an interesting assessment of Rothman's work from a self-described "former, though unrepentant, member of the revisionist school"; [5] and his "Total Institutions and the Working Classes" provides a more general survey of the territory. [6]

Humanitarianism or Control?
Some Observations on the Historiography of Anglo-American Psychiatry

I

To judge by the increasingly strident tone of their mutual recriminations, historians of psychiatry have taken almost too much to heart J. H. Hexter's injunction that "in an academic generation a little overaddicted to *politesse*, it may be worth saying that violent destruction is not necessarily of itself worthless and futile. Even though it leaves doubts about the right road for London, it helps if someone rips up, however violently, a 'To London' sign on the Dover cliffs pointing south." [1] At times, the pro-

1. David Ingleby, "Mental Health and Social Order," in *Social Control and the State: Historical and Comparative Essays*, ed. Stanley Cohen and Andrew Scull (Oxford: Blackwell; New York: St. Martin's Press, 1981), 141–88.

2. J. K. Walton, "Casting out and Bringing back in Victorian England: Pauper Lunatics, 1840–1870," in *The Anatomy of Madness*, 2 vols., ed. W. F. Bynum, Roy Porter, and Michael Shepherd (London: Tavistock, 1985), 2:132–46.

3. Roy Porter, "Shutting People Up," *Social Studies of Science* 12 (1982):467–76.

4. Joan Busfield, *Managing Madness: Changing Ideas and Practice* (Wolfeboro, N.H.: Longwood Publishing Group, 1986).

5. Michael Ignatieff, "State, Civil Society and Total Institutions: A Critique of Recent Social Histories of Punishment," in *Social Control and the State*, ed. Cohen and Scull, 75–105.

6. Michael Ignatieff, "Total Institutions and the Working Classes: A Review Essay," *History Workshop Journal* 15 (1983):169–72.

1. J. H. Hexter, *Reappraisals in History*, 2d ed. (Chicago: University of Chicago Press, 1978), 138.

tagonists in the debate on the meaning of lunacy reform have given the impression of attempting to destroy, not just each other's work, but each other. On the one side, there have been accusations of attempts to "disguise contemporary social criticism and advocacy as history"[2] and of "destructively misleading" research marked by "errors, inconsistencies, unsupported assertions, and disparaging motivational assumptions" that, taken together, have produced "work that must be embarrassing to the professional historian."[3] And from the object of these assaults have come claims that their authors "rely on platitudes of historiography and straw men" and that the cries of villainy are a "stratagem to give novelty to findings that are now no longer novel."[4] Impelled by logic and evidence to swallow much of the revisionist case, even the opposition's "leading voice" apparently can do no better than resort to "shrillness" in an effort "to differentiate, in however marginal a fashion, his work from theirs. It is like putting a few touches of chrome on an automobile and saying that now a product differs from that of its competitors. Such a tactic may do well in the marketplace, but it has less relevance, one would hope, in the world of scholarship."[5]

Clearly, to venture into this fiercely contested territory is to take one's life (or at least scholarly reputation) into one's hands. Matters take a decided turn for the worse when one enters the combat zone with the conviction that it is not simply that neither side possesses a monopoly of virtue, but rather that both are wrong; for one is now without allies and susceptible to attack from either front or rear. And when the foolhardy intruder is a trespasser from an alien discipline, the risk is high that (like the fate of one who intervenes in a quarrel between husband and wife) the outcome will be an assault from both forces simultaneously. Thus, like the proverbial liberal, I suppose the best I can look forward to is matching lumps on each side of my head.

II

I think it is only appropriate to begin by acknowledging that the debate on the interpretation of lunacy reform, and more especially the work of

2. Gerald Grob, "Treatment vs. Incarceration: The Mental Hospital in Historical Perspective" (Paper delivered at the Philadelphia College of Physicians, December 1976), 24.

3. Jacques Quen, Review of *The Discovery of the Asylum*, by David Rothman, *Journal of Psychiatry and the Law* 2 (1974):119–20. See also Gerald Grob, "Welfare and Poverty in American History," *Reviews in American History* 1 (1973):43–52; and idem, "Public Policymaking and Social Policy" (Paper delivered at the Conference on the History of Public Policy, Cambridge, Massachusetts, November 3–4, 1978).

4. David Rothman, Review of *Mental Institutions in America*, by Gerald Grob, *Journal of Interdisciplinary History* 7 (1976):534.

5. Ibid., 536.

some of those in the revisionist camp,[6] has been the occasion for a signifi-cant advance in the historiography of psychiatry. As those who are ac-quainted with the work of Albert Deutsch on the situation in America or of Kathleen Jones on that in England will be aware, the picture of lunacy reform as on the whole relatively simple and straightforward progress toward enlightenment is far from being merely a straw man, erected solely to exaggerate the novelty and significance of a less simplistic al-ternative. Rereading even some of the best and most scholarly of more specialized accounts from this era (for example, Norman Dain's[7]) is suffi-cient to remind us vividly of how deeply embedded "progressive" as-sumptions were in this period. And a glance at the treatment accorded lunacy reform in such more general surveys of Victorian social reform as David Roberts' *Victorian Origins of the British Welfare State* demonstrates how widespread their influence once was. For proponents of this view-point, the direction of the line of march and the sources of the impulse to march were essentially unproblematic:

> The obstacles to the improvement of asylums had been not vested inter-est but public ignorance and apathy. For centuries [*sic*] that apathy had re-mained unchallenged, but when nineteenth-century humanitarianism joined with a more scientific understanding of insanity it diminished. Yet neither humanitarianism nor science would have availed much had not government officials investigated the abuses and had not Commons [*sic*] placed asylums under the surveillance of government inspectors.[8]

Whatever the excesses and inadequacies of the various revisionist ac-counts of lunacy reform (to which I shall attend shortly), one must surely be grateful to them for liberating us from the narrowness and naïveté of a vision that reduced the whole process to a simplistic equation: humani-tarianism + science + government inspection = the success of what David Roberts terms "the great nineteenth century movement for a more humane and intelligent treatment of the insane."[9]

We are now aware that such interpretations of social reform in gen-eral and lunacy reform in particular function more as intellectual strait-

---

6. Particularly Rothman and Foucault. Note that the labels *antirevisionist* and *revisionist* obscure as well as reveal. There are, in the antirevisionist camp, important differences of tone, emphasis, and sophistication between, say, Gerald Grob and those he himself identi-fies as his allies (Nathan Hale, John Burnham, Norman Dain, Charles Rosenberg, et al.), and, in the revisionist camp, perhaps still greater divergences between Rothman and Foucault on the one hand and the more historically and theoretically naive Thomas Szasz and Robert Perrucci on the other.

7. Norman Dain, *Concepts of Insanity in the United States, 1789–1865* (New Brunswick, N.J.: Rutgers University Press, 1964).

8. David Roberts, *Victorian Origins of the British Welfare State* (New Haven: Yale Univer-sity Press, 1960), 63.

9. Ibid., 62.

jackets than as means to insight and understanding. In the present instance, the sources of the movement and the reasons for its success are infinitely more complex, the humanitarianism and the science indisputably more ambiguous, and the intelligence and humanity of the regimen in the public museums of the mad inescapably more dubious than any explanation of this sort allows.

In what follows, I shall begin by discussing in a little more detail the work of David Rothman and Gerald Grob. The former is clearly the best-known American exponent of the revisionist, or social control, approach to lunacy reform; the latter, the most tenacious and sophisticated defender of a modified form of the more traditional wisdom. I shall point to some of the serious reservations I have with the accounts offered by each of them; and I shall then attempt to sketch some elements of an alternative perspective on this example of nineteenth-century humanitarianism (though my account will have reference to England rather than to the United States).

III

Despite their sharp and serious disagreements on both the sources of lunacy reform and their overall assessment of the movement, there is a curious formal symmetry in the work of Rothman and Grob. Both place major emphasis in their respective accounts on the stated intentions and more or less acknowledged motivations of the lunacy reformers themselves. But strikingly and significantly, they employ the words of the asylum superintendents and their allies to reach almost diametrically opposed conclusions. As Johnson had earlier suggested was true of the history of schooling, it turns out that "on the basis of this sort of evidence the enterprise may be represented as a quasi-coercive and essentially self-protective response or as the genuine outgrowth of humanitarian Christian consciences."[10]

Out of the arguments of moral entrepreneurs like Horace Mann, Dorothea Dix, and Samuel Gridley Howe and from the reports and other published writings of the less widely known medical superintendents and overseers of the earliest asylums, Rothman constructs an account of the discovery of the asylum that emphasizes its sudden eruption onto the nineteenth-century scene and its uniquely American origins and that locates the source of this transformation of social practices in an "effort to ensure the cohesion of the community in new and changing circumstances."[11] The United States in the second quarter of the nine-

10. Richard Johnson, "Educational Policy and Social Control in Early Victorian England," *Past and Present* 49 (1970): 99.

11. David Rothman, *The Discovery of the Asylum: Social Order and Disorder in the New Republic* (Boston: Little, Brown, 1971), xviii.

teenth century is portrayed as "a society that has slipped, for reasons that remain unclear, into a temporary state of disequilibrium," and the drive to institutionalize the deviant is itself seen as "a mysteriously diffuse movement toward equilibrium."[12] As Rothman himself puts it,

> The response in the Jacksonian period to the deviant and the dependent was first and foremost a vigorous attempt to promote the stability of the society at a moment when traditional ideas and practices appeared outmoded, constricted, and ineffective. . . . The asylum was to fulfill a dual purpose for its innovators. It would rehabilitate inmates and then, by virtue of its success, set an example of right action for the larger society. . . . The well-ordered asylum would exemplify the proper principles of social organization and thus ensure the safety of the republic and promote its glory.[13]

At the very outset of his analysis, Rothman rightly rejects a vulgar structural determinism that posits an automatic and inevitable linkage between urbanization/industrialization and the rise of the asylum. A few pages later, he insists that "institutions, whether social, political, or economic, cannot be understood apart from the society in which they flourished."[14] Admirable sentiments; and yet in the body of his work, there is never any serious and sustained or clearly articulated attempt to link ideas and changing social practices with underlying structures. Worse, when his reliance on the ideological level of analysis falters, Rothman tends to resort to the same quasi-magical incantations and invocations of demographic and economic developments that he had earlier stigmatized.[15] Throughout, there is a lack of perception of the fundamental divisions of American society and of the shifting basis and nature of social conflict through time, a deficiency closely related to his failure "to inquire into the group or class interest that institutionalization served" and his inability to see social control as "more in the interest of one social group than another."[16] Instead, there is his constant resort to that curious explanatory variable, "an imaginary homogeneous group labelled 'the Americans.'"[17]

One might well argue that, given Rothman's characteristic analytic strategy, the larger social and political order *necessarily* remains opaque,

12. Richard Fox, "Beyond 'Social Control': Institutions and Disorder in Bourgeois Society," *History of Education Quarterly* 16 (1976): 203.

13. Rothman, *Discovery of the Asylum*, xviii–xix. For a critique of the idea that the asylum was an American "discovery" and a demonstration that the first critical stages of the American lunacy reform movement involved a heavy dependence on ideas and examples borrowed from abroad, see Chapter 5 below.

14. Ibid., xvi, xix.

15. For example, ibid., 13, 57–58.

16. Fox, "Beyond 'Social Control,'" 204 and 203.

17. William Muraskin, "The Social Control Theory in American History: A Critique," *Journal of Social History* 9 (1976): 559.

since it is generally perceived only dimly and indirectly through the mediation of the perceptions of society's individual members. To the extent that people's ideas are used to demonstrate the existence of the underlying structures and that their *perceptions* of disorder are not kept analytically distinct from the reality of disorder (and Rothman is persistently inclined "to use the reformers' claims of social upheaval as his primary evidence for the existence of disorder"[18]), any attempt to relate ideology and social structure threatens to dissolve into mere tautology. And at the level of the ideas themselves, there is a striking tendency to take the claims made at face value—a failure to perceive the degree to which the talk of looming disorder, the promotion of the institution's reformatory functions, and so forth, were rhetoric (albeit significant rhetoric) designed by a particular social group for particular polemical purposes.

For example, Rothman's analysis neglects the obvious question of "whether it was in the professional self-interest of such reformers to exaggerate the extent of the upheaval in order to help loosen state legislators' purse strings."[19] Was not the anxiety about the stability of the social order the anxiety of a specific stratum, the response of the bourgeois and professional classes to the corrosive effects of capitalism on such traditional precapitalist social restraints as religion and the family? And does not Rothman's approach ignore the still precarious social status of the psychiatric profession, its members' strivings to build a strong institutional base for their profession, and their direct attempt to do so through "the legitimation of the asylum and their own position in it"?[20]

An inadequate attempt to come to terms with the nature of the social and political order is something Rothman shares with that school of sociologists by whom he appears to have been most influenced and among whom he has certainly been most influential—those committed to the labeling, or societal reaction, theory of deviance. Once again, his work demonstrates how this narrowness of vision inevitably leads to an analysis that depicts social control as arbitrary. As Richard Fox has put it, "The social control perspective flattens out . . . vital structural developments by positing an abstract conflict between a group of controllers and their victims, and then by moralistically upbraiding the controllers and their alleged inclination to dominate."[21]

18. Fox, "Beyond 'Social Control,'" 203–4.
19. Ibid., 204.
20. Nancy Jane Tomes, "A Generous Confidence: Thomas Story Kirkbride's Philosophy of Asylum Construction and Management," in *Madhouses, Mad-Doctors, and Madmen: The Social History of Psychiatry in the Victorian Era,* ed. Andrew Scull (Philadelphia: University of Pennsylvania Press; London: Athlone Press, 1981), 121–43; Andrew Scull, *Museums of Madness: The Social Organization of Insanity in Nineteenth-Century England* (London: Allen Lane; New York: St. Martin's Press, 1979), 90ff; and Chapter 6 below.
21. Richard Fox, *So Far Disordered in Mind* (Berkeley: University of California Press, 1978), 14.

IV

It is, in part, the very weaknesses and excesses of the work of Rothman and other revisionists that have prompted the revival, albeit in a more sophisticated and seductive modern guise, of the traditional meliorist explanation. Gerald Grob, who has been the major figure in this movement, for the most part rests his critique of Rothman on quite other grounds than those I have just outlined. Yet, in the first instance, it is the implicit moral condemnation of the reformers and asylum superintendents that provokes some of his most severe strictures on Rothman's work. Like Jacques Quen, he seems extraordinarily concerned to rescue the reformers' reputation for humanitarianism and benevolence.

Much of Rothman's animus against the reformers (so Grob and Quen allege) derives from his political stance vis-à-vis contemporary social policy in these areas, most notably a commitment to an explicitly anti-institutional position. There is, I think, a measure of truth to this claim (and certainly Rothman's nostalgic evocation of a preinstitutional Golden Age, the Paradise Lost with the advent of the asylum, has been eagerly embraced by the deinstitutionalization ideologues). But there is a tendency here to refuse to see in their own eyes the motes they are so eager to point out in his. For their interpretations, and those of the other scholars in the field who receive their imprimatur,[22] are equally evidently grounded in a fundamental acceptance of a vision of history most congenial to (because supportive of) the powers that be and in a largely uncritical adherence to orthodox liberal pieties.

Grob's own thesis is more deeply embedded in his materials than Rothman's, and thus less immediately apparent to the casual reader—as perhaps befits one who lays such stress upon "understanding the past on its own terms." After all, the more open one is about one's interpretive framework, the more vulnerable one is to the charge that one's conclusions have been allowed to shape the selection of data, rather than the other way around. But this is not to say that in Grob's work the past in some mysterious way speaks for itself or that no organizing intelligence intervenes here. To the contrary, Grob's vision of social process and his metahistorical assumptions continuously affect both his selection and his presentation of materials. Theoretical models are not absent, merely underdeveloped and unself-conscious—and hence underscrutinized.

Grob is scornful of those who attribute the growth of the mental hospital to the attempt by dominant elites to restrain "deviant groups or largely lower-class elements, thereby ensuring some measure of social control (if not hegemony)."[23] As he views it, "A few saw reform as a con-

---

22. Grob, "Treatment vs. Incarceration," 43 n. 2.

23. Grob, "Public Policymaking," 4–5. At times like this, Grob speaks as though the social control thesis can be equated with an explanation in terms of class interest. But this view is, I think, a mistake. David Rothman's analysis of the rise of the asylum is centrally

servative phenomenon in that it would diminish class rivalries and antagonisms and thereby preserve a fundamentally sound and moral social order. But many more were primarily concerned with uplifting the mass of suffering humanity and were not particularly aware of political or economic considerations."[24] In arguing for the contrary position, the social control theorists have confused "the by-product with the primary intention."[25] And they have persuaded others of the correctness of their position primarily by illegitimately attributing motives on the basis of the consequences of the reformers' actions.

The danger in this, as Grob sees it, is clear:

> It is, after all, extraordinarily difficult to infer motives from outcome without adopting a viewpoint that makes events the result of strictly rational, logical, or conscious behavior. Nor can we assume with any degree of confidence that undesirable consequences flowed from callous behavior or malevolent intentions, even though such elements were by no means absent.[26]

Yet even assuming that Grob has correctly judged which of these intentions were primary (and while the identification of human motivation is a peculiarly treacherous business, he presents no real arguments for this crucial assumption), and leaving aside the difficult issue of penetrating to unacknowledged but possibly powerful motives, he takes the content of their "benevolence" all too much for granted. And behind this there looms a still larger issue, to which I shall recur: "How far is it sufficient to comprehend [developments] in terms of the conscious purposes of contemporaries? Or should we not be concerned with the working out of unconscious function within some wider system of change?"[27]

If the origins of reform are here to be sought in benevolence (coupled with the pressures created by demographic change and the spread of new ideas about the treatment of mental disorder from France and England), what of its subsequent fate? Grob's answer is heavily conditioned by his view of nineteenth-century social policy as essentially incremental in character. Rather than being the result of conscious choices by legislators and officials, it represents the sum total of a series of unrelated

---

based on the notion of control—but not class interest. As we have seen, in his account the central factors are rather the fear *Americans* have about the stability of the social order and about the adequacy of existing institutions to meet the challenge of a fluid, mobile, expanding society, coupled with their sense that the asylum could restore the needed order and provide the very model of a new social equilibrium. This reference to Americans is in part a source of weakness rather than of strength, since it leaves us with no coherent account of who is worried about what, and why.

24. Gerald Grob, *Mental Institutions in America: Social Policy to 1875* (New York: Free Press, 1973), 109.

25. Grob, "Public Policymaking," 27.

26. Ibid., 30.

27. Johnson, "Educational Policy and Social Control," 98.

decisions.[28] Further, the absence of effective means of collecting and
analyzing empirical data "often led to the adoption of policies that in the
long run had results which were quite at variance with the intentions of
those involved in their formulation."[29] (Again, he sees this circumstance
as rescuing "nineteenth-century legislators and administrators" from
misplaced charges that they "were deficient in intelligence or malevolent
in character."[30])

Within this overall framework, Grob then points to a number of more
specific factors that he sees as linked to the collapse of the asylum's pretensions to cure.[31] The list is a long one: the growing size of the asylum;
the influx of the lower classes, and particularly of the Irish and other
ethnic groups; the consequent financial undernourishment of the system; the accumulation of chronic, incurable inmates; the difficulties associated with the "routinization of charisma," as one generation of asylum superintendents succeeded another; and the transformation of the
mental hospitals into "strictly welfare institutions as far as their funding
and reputation were concerned," thus solidifying "their custodial character."[32] All these developments, we are informed, "took place in several
distinct stages and without any particular awareness of the eventual outcome."[33] In this sense, he sees them as once more affirming one of his
central theses, the accidental and "nonmalevolent" character of reform.

28. Grob, "Public Policymaking," 13.

29. Grob, Mental Institutions, 87. As Michael Katz points out, Grob's analysis at this
point seems to embody the curious assumption "that the acquisition of scientific knowledge
automatically leads to rational, humanitarian solutions framed in the best interests of the
people to which they were directed" (Katz, "The Origins of the Institutional State," Marxist
Perspectives 1 [1978]: 12–13).

30. Grob, Mental Institutions, 86–87. I shall suggest later that malevolence, benevolence, or lack of intelligence are not really the central issues that theories of massive social
change ought to be addressing; and I shall indicate just how central I think they are as a
metaphysical underpinning of Grob's work.

31. Rothman has seized on this portion of Grob's analysis to argue that, for all the
bitterness of the latter's protests, he has been forced to swallow the revisionists' medicine
and accordingly, with some surface modifications, to "write a history of the mental hospital
that is linked to the issue of order among the dangerous classes" (Rothman, Review of
Mental Institutions, 535). The claim is surely overstated, particularly if one looks at Grob's
analysis in its entirety; but it is not without some limited merit, for at least on this more
specific issue, his account falls uneasily between the "proressive" and "social control" tradi-
tions in the history of American psychiatry. However, Rothman's further claim that "the
central question, for Grob as for others writing in this field, is to explain the decline of
mental hospitals into custodial warehouses" (ibid., 534) has a distinctly disingenuous ring
to it. It was not the central question of Rothman's own work: "The question this book addresses can be put very succinctly: why did Americans in the Jacksonian era suddenly begin to construct and support institutions for the deviant and dependent members of the
community?" (Rothman, Discovery of the Asylum, xiii); and except for its being the issue on
which the various contending parties are least deeply divided, there is little reason to accord it pride of place now.

32. Grob, Mental Institutions, 238.

33. Ibid., 259.

At this point, therefore, even Grob is driven to concede that, looked at without rose-tinted spectacles, Victorian lunatic asylums in many ways present a dismal and depressing picture. And yet, if the *results* can scarcely be applauded, or must be damned with faint praise, the benevolent *intentions* remain. Apparently, the history of lunacy reform records the efforts of a largely well-intentioned group of men (and the occasional woman) whose endeavors mysteriously always produced accidental and unintended unpleasant consequences. However unattractive, the institutions they founded were not "inherently evil." On the contrary, "mental hospitals were not fundamentally dissimilar from most human institutions, the achievements of which usually fall far short of the hopes and aspirations of the individuals who founded and led them."[34]

But this simply will not do. In the first place, conceptualizations that operate through individuals' decisions or behavior are simply incapable of adequately reflecting social reality, both because "the policy or action of a collectivity [is in many instances] not attributable to particular individuals' decisions" and because the form of the organization (or social system) may itself generate systemic effects. In particular, the bias of the system is not sustained simply by a series of individually chosen acts, but also, most importantly, by "the socially structured and culturally patterned behavior of groups, and practices of institutions, which may indeed be manifested by individuals' inaction."[35]

With outcomes viewed as the product of benevolence combined with an endless series of incremental changes, no one of which was decisive and each of which is entitled to virtually equal explanatory weight, even the most flagrant examples of misery and inhumanity can be portrayed as largely accidental, and in any event as in no way calling into question the fundamental goodness and legitimacy of the social system within which they occurred. A neat reconciliation is thus effected between apparently contradictory phenomena, in such a fashion that the myth of the social system's basic humaneness is further strengthened and supported. Hence, I take it, the shrillness with which Grob insists upon the primary, the virtually unqualified, hegemony of benevolent motives. For it is precisely the benevolence of the intentions that rescues the whole enterprise of "reform" from the insinuations of the revisionists and other critics, leaving us to ponder the ironies of unintended consequences and historical accident—even while, as Ignatieff puts it, "maintaining the state's reputation as a moral agent."[36]

On any number of levels, therefore, the view of reform as the product of the "accidental," malevolent distortions of a Manichean world represents a denial of, or a failure to come to terms with, the multiple ways in

34. Ibid., 342.
35. Steven Lukes, *Power: A Radical View* (London: Macmillan, 1974), 21–22.
36. Michael Ignatieff, *A Just Measure of Pain: The Penitentiary in the Industrial Revolution* (New York: Pantheon, 1978), 211.

which structural factors constrain, prompt, and channel human activities in particular directions. On a deeper level, consequences that appear unintended and "accidental" considered from the viewpoint of the individual actor remain susceptible to investigation and explanation. Such explanation will always involve some abstraction from the complexities and particularities of individual events, and thus inevitably will do some violence to the richness of the historical record.[37] But, as Lawrence Stone has pointed out, if we are to explain anything at all, we must inevitably risk generalization and the use of analogy; indeed, without them we cannot so much as describe what we have found.[38] To denounce such attempts as producing "oversimplification of complex social processes,"[39] to insist too resolutely on seeing events as "process"[40] or "one damn thing after another," is virtually to guarantee explanatory impotence—to reduce explanation to a banal mixture of individual intentions (which in the present context are for Grob almost universally "the best and most honorable of intentions"[41]) and inadvertent transformations (through a series of events, "many of which were unanticipated and unpredictable"[42]) that lead society in spite of itself in morally unfortunate directions.[43]

V

In some of my own work on lunacy reform, which looks at this movement in Victorian England and not in the United States, I have attempted to demonstrate that the genesis and subsequent development of specialized segregative techniques for handling the mad was neither fortuitous nor the product of the mere piling up of a series of incremental,

37. I am perhaps unusually sensitive to the dangers involved here, because this is an offense of which sociologists are notoriously guilty and about which they are notoriously insensitive. (But then, prudently, sociologists customarily avoid exposing their accounts to the slings and arrows of an audience of historians.)

38. Lawrence Stone, *The Causes of the English Civil War* (New York: Harper and Row, 1969).

39. Grob, *Mental Institutions*, 2–3.

40. Ibid., 176.

41. Ibid., 222.

42. Ibid., 176.

43. One possible objection to the position taken here that perhaps deserves some notice is the claim that the explanatory factors being adduced are not directly given to observation and are thus in some sense metaphysical (for which read nonempirical and not to be taken seriously). Notice, however, that while in one sense intentions, hopes, fears, and so on are "surface" phenomena, with concrete empirical referents, in another sense they remain just as difficult and inaccessible to any but indirect observation as are more structural forms of causality. In both areas, historical investigation provides us with (and can only provide us) with data at the level of appearances. But we are all aware that there is an underlying reality that produces those "appearances" and to which we must somehow penetrate if we are to explain anything satisfactorily.

ad hoc decisions bereft of any underlying dynamic or logic. The activities of the lunacy reformers, and the outcome of their endeavors, must be seen as intimately linked to a whole series of historically specific and closely interrelated changes in English society's political, economic, and social structure and to the associated shifts in the intellectual and cultural horizons of the English bourgeoisie. I shall not attempt to recapitulate the whole of that analysis here. Instead, I shall look at just two of the many issues that require discussion (albeit two rather important ones) and try to indicate the general directions in which I think we need to go if we are to resolve them.

Let us begin by considering the "choice" of the asylum. Anyone claiming, as I would, that the adoption of the asylum as a response to madness was powerfully constrained by structural factors implies that the agents involved in the process could have acted otherwise only with extreme difficulty, if they could have done so at all. The assertion or denial of such an account thus rests upon a counterfactual claim that some specified agent or agents could or could not have acted (i.e., had or did not have the ability and opportunity to act) differently. Merely to state things in this form is to emphasize that, in all cases of this sort, empirical evidence must necessarily be indirect and lacking certainty. But that the "evidence must always be indirect and ultimately inconclusive"[44] is not to say that no empirical investigation is possible or that we cannot reach a balanced judgment on these matters. Rothman is quite clear on this issue. Unfortunately, I think he is also quite wrong. As he puts it, "There was nothing inevitable about the asylum form" and it was "not the only possible reaction to social problems."[45] On the most general level, much of the plausibility of these claims seems to derive from the essentially intentional account he offers of the origins of the asylum. The presumption must be that, absent the fear of disorder and the sense that institutions to "control abnormal behavior promised to be the first step in establishing a new system for stabilizing the community, for binding citizens together,"[46] the asylum would not have been built. But if an explanation on this basis is defective (as I have argued it is), no such presumption exists.

At this point, Rothman could fall back on two related and more specific counterarguments he presents to a structural account. First, there is his brief discussion and curt dismissal of the claim that the asylum was the "automatic and inevitable response of an industrial and urban society" to deviance.[47] He appears, at first sight, to be on strong ground

44. Steven Lukes, *Essays in Social Theory* (New York: Columbia University Press, 1977), 29.

45. Rothman, *Discovery of the Asylum*, xiv, 295.

46. Ibid., 58–59.

47. Ibid., xvi.

here, for not only is this "explanation" implausibly crude and mechanistic, but it fails to meet even the simplest of factual tests. The economic and demographic developments to which it refers came for the most part *after* the birth of the asylum in England[48] and still more unambiguously in America;[49] and the dissemination of the institutional approach bore no clear-cut relationship to whether a region was rural or urban.[50] But the support this provides for Rothman's argument is illusory, for it rests upon the demonstrably false claim that the linkage to urbanization and industrialization is the only form a structural account of the origins of the asylum can take.

Rothman's second counterargument is in a sense derived from the first and appears downright curious, if only because on its face it seems so unhistorical. It consists essentially in the assertion that, since, "beginning about 1900, the asylum began to lose its centrality"[51] (a trend still more marked during the past two or three decades), its presence cannot have been structurally required in the nineteenth century. If the still more urbanized and industrialized twentieth century can abandon the institution, the nineteenth could have too, but for some failure of nerve, imagination, or whatever. Perhaps; but this argument will not suffice to show it. For the notion that American (or English) society in the twentieth century is just like its nineteenth-century predecessor (only more so) strains credibility. And if the nature of the beast has changed, who can be surprised if those changes permit/require changes in the characteristic shapes and forms of the social control apparatus?[52]

Considerable familiarity with lunacy reform in England and somewhat less acquaintance with it in America suggest to me that the very issue with which we began may be something of a red herring. For the notion of making a choice implies the perception and weighing of alternatives; and what is most remarkable when one examines the sources is that most reformers seem to have assumed from the outset that any changes they might introduce would retain the asylum as their basis. Even in England, where the reform movement proceeded largely by exposing abuses in existing madhouses, the question posed was not whether or not to employ the asylum to treat lunatics (the answer to that was usually taken to be self-evident), but rather how the asylum model could be modified so as to overcome the defects that had just been exposed.

It would be misleading to suggest that there was no opposition to the asylum. To the contrary, the reformers on both sides of the Atlantic

48. See Scull, *Museums of Madness,* chap. 1.

49. Rothman, *Discovery of the Asylum,* xvi.

50. Scull, *Museums of Madness,* 29–30; Rothman, *Discovery of the Asylum,* xvi–xvii.

51. Rothman, *Discovery of the Asylum,* xvi.

52. For an analysis of these interconnections, see Andrew Scull, *Decarceration: Community Treatment and the Deviant—A Radical View* (Englewood Cliffs, N.J.: Prentice-Hall, 1977; 2d ed., Oxford: Polity Press; New Brunswick, N.J.: Rutgers University Press, 1984).

often met with considerable resistance when they sought to build a network of public asylums, usually on the grounds of cost, but also (and especially in England) because their schemes threatened to provide a precedent for increased central control over local administration. But such opposition was essentially negative. It was not linked to any alternative approach to the management of the mad, and hence its effect was to retard but not to deflect the movement to establish the asylum system.[53]

If one looks diligently enough, however, one can uncover a handful of figures whose opposition to the asylum rested on other, less limited grounds. In England in the period 1810–40, the crucial phase of the lunacy reform movement, there existed a small subterranean tradition that insistently criticized the asylum as a response to insanity. The critics we can identify were all medical men, and their claims amounted to a fundamental assault on the very concept of institutionalization. In the words of George Nesse Hill, a provincial surgeon, "Asylums stand opposed to all rational plans of speedy and permanent cure of insanity, and from their very nature are the most unfavorable situations in which . . . lunatics . . . can be placed."[54] The separation from the sane influences that surrounded mad people in the outside world exacerbated their problems, and the unfortunate inmates of asylums tended to feed off each other's delusions. The consequence, in the words of the well-known London medical writer John Reid, was that "many of the depots for the captivity of intellectual invalids may be regarded only as nurseries for and manufactories of madness; magazines or reservoirs of lunacy, from which is issued, from time to time, a sufficient supply for perpetuating and extending this formidable disease."[55]

In 1830, these ideas were revived and extended by John Conolly, previously the medical inspector of the madhouses in Warwickshire, then professor of medicine at the new University College, London, and later to become one of the most famous figures in nineteenth-century English psychiatry. While conceding that in some circumstances lunatic asylums were "unavoidable evils," he insisted that they were pernicious places from which all but the distinct minority of the insane who could not otherwise be cared for ought to be kept. For two-thirds of the inmates, "confinement is the very reverse of beneficial. It fixes and renders permanent what might have passed away. . . . I have seen numerous examples . . . in which it was evident that . . . a continued residence in the

---

53. Moreover, the opposition to increased centralization was under assault from a variety of directions and during the 1830s was dealt a decisive defeat over the issue of reform of the Poor Laws. Thereafter, resistance to similar measures aimed at the insane came naturally to be seen as less important, indeed futile.

54. G. N. Hill, *An Essay on the Prevention and Cure of Insanity* (London: Longman et al., 1814), 220.

55. John Reid, *Essays on Insanity, Hypochondriacal and Other Nervous Affections* (London: Longman et al., 1816), 205.

asylum was gradually ruining body and mind."[56] The sanest among us would find it difficult

> to resist the horrible influences of the place;—a place in which a thousand fantasies, that are swept away almost as soon as formed in the healthy atmosphere of a diversified society, would assume shapes more distinct; a place in which the intellectual operations could not but become, from mere want of exercise, more and more inert; and the domination of wayward feelings more and more powerful. . . . [Patients] are subjected . . . to the very circumstances most likely to confuse or destroy the most rational and healthy mind.[57]

Indubitably, "the presence of a company of lunatics, their incoherent talk, their cries, their moans, their indescribable utterances of all imaginable fancies, or their ungovernable frolics and tumult, can have no salutary effect."[58] Quite the contrary, "the effect of living constantly among mad men or mad women is a loss of all sensibility and self-respect or care; or, not infrequently, a perverse pleasure in adding to the confusion and diversifying the eccentricity of those about them. . . . In both cases the disease grows inveterate."[59]

Such arguments raised the claim, one not unfamiliar to our own ears, that the defects of the asylum were inherent in its very constitution, and hence ineradicable. In the words of an anonymous fellow-critic, the institution itself was always and necessarily "an infected region" in which "healthy impressions" could not possibly be received.[60] The force, relevance, and importance of this critique are evident, even in my abbreviated presentation of it. Yet what is most striking is that, for all the impact these words had, they might as well have never been uttered. It is not just that they had no influence on social policy, or that they were met by counterarguments that seemed plausible at the time. Rather, their fate was to be greeted by silence, to be consigned to oblivion.[61]

One can suggest a number of reasons for this general lack of impact:

56. John Conolly, *An Inquiry Concerning the Indications of Insanity* (London: Taylor, 1830), 17, 20.

57. Ibid., 22–23.

58. Ibid., 26.

59. Ibid., 22.

60. "What," he asked his readers, "would be the consequence, if we were to take a sane person, who had been accustomed to enjoy society, and . . . were to lock him up in a small house with a keeper for his only associate, and no place for exercise but a miserable garden? We should certainly not look for any improvement in his moral and intellectual condition. Can we then reasonably expect that *a treatment which would be injurious to a sane mind, should tend to restore a diseased one?*" (Anonymous, *On the Present State of Lunatic Asylums, with Suggestions for Their Improvement* [London: Drury, 1839], 39 (emphasis in the original).

61. For very qualified exceptions to this general contemporary neglect, see "Esquirol on the Treatment of the Insane," *Westminster Review* 18 (1833): 129–38; Maximilian Jacobi, *On the Construction and Management of Hospitals for the Insane* (London: Churchill, 1841).

the critics' lack of numbers and organization; the conservatism induced by existing investments in the institutional approach; and the single-mindedness of the reformers, with their consequent lack of receptivity to alternatives to their chosen solution. But none of these seems sufficient, singly or in combination: a conclusion that is strengthened when one recalls that, during the 1870s and 1880s, bolstered by a half-century of evidence that made these claims seem prescient, they were revived on both sides of the Atlantic—in America by the newly emerging profession of neurology[62] and in England by such eminent medical psychologists as John Charles Bucknill, Lockhart Robertson, and Henry Maudsley[63]—with comparable lack of effect.

There is, I think, a deeper reason for the failure of the anti-institutional position to secure a hearing, and one that emphasizes just how deeply embedded in the structures of nineteenth-century society the shift to the asylum was. The most fundamental source of the critics' difficulty lies in a simple question: It was all very well to suggest that the cure in this instance was worse than the disease, but what was the alternative? Few of those concerned with the plight of the insane could contemplate with equanimity the prospect of leaving them in the sorts of conditions that commonly prevailed in the larger towns, where the squalor, disease, and misery endured by the *sane* members of the lower classes were quite sufficient to provoke expressions of disgust and horror in those of their betters who came into contact with them. (Most, of course, took pains not to.)[64]

After all,

millions of English men, women, and children were virtually living in shit. The immediate question seems to have been whether they weren't drowning in it. . . . Large numbers of people lived in cellars, below the level of the street and below the water line. Thus generations of human beings, out of whose lives the wealth of England was produced, were compelled to live

62. See Bonnie Blustein, "'A Hollow Square of Psychological Science': American Neurologists and Psychiatrists in Conflict," in *Madhouses, Mad-Doctors, and Madmen*, ed. Scull, 241–70.

63. Scull, *Decarceration*, chaps. 6 and 7.

64. Cf. Chadwick's remark that "the statements of the condition of considerable proportions of the labouring population . . . have been received with surprise by the wealthier classes living in the immediate vicinity, to whom the facts were as strange as if related to foreigners or the natives of an unknown country" (Edwin Chadwick, *Report on the Sanitary Conditions of the Labouring Population of Great Britain* [London: Clowes, 1842], 397). Or Disraeli's description of England as "two nations between which there is no intercourse and no sympathy: who are as ignorant of each other's habits, thoughts, and feelings as if they were dwellers in different zones or inhabitants of different planets; who are formed by different breeding, are fed by a different food, are ordered by different manners, and are not governed by the same laws" (Benjamin Disraeli, *Sybil; or The Two Nations* [London: Davies, 1927], 77). One is reminded of John Stuart Mill's acerbic comment that "one of the effects

in wealth's symbolic counterpart. And that substance which suffused their
lives was also a virtual objectification of their social condition, their place in
society: that was what they were.[65]

In the circumstances, those who sought to improve the lot of the
pauper insane but who were doubtful of the merits of the asylum confronted a painful dilemma. They could scarcely dispute MacGill's claim
that "the circumstances of the great body of mankind are of such a nature as to render every attempt at recovering insane persons in their own
houses extremely difficult, and generally hopeless."[66] And if they balked
at the idea of keeping lunatics in such surroundings, it was hard to see
how they could avoid concluding that the asylum was better than the
other option available, the workhouse.

What stood in the way of ameliorating the environment of the insane
still at large? To improve the living conditions of lunatics living in the
community would have entailed supplying relatively generous pension
or welfare benefits to provide for their support, implying that the living
standards of families with an insane member would have been raised
above those of the working class generally. Moreover, under this system,
the insane alone would have been beneficiaries of something approximating a modern social welfare system, while their sane brethren were
subjected to the rigors of a Poor Law based on the principle of less eligi-
bility. Quite apart from anything else, such an approach would clearly
have been administratively unworkable, not least because of the labile
nature of lunacy itself and the consequent ever-present danger that,
given sufficient incentive, or rather desperation, the poorer classes would
resort to feigning insanity.

In any event, suggestions of this sort would have had no political appeal whatsoever to England's governing classes. Among the latter, "there
had developed by the 1830s a sense of precariousness about society. This
was expressed in the form that there was a delicate balance between institutions and their operation, and the behavior of the labouring classes.
There was a feeling that any concession to idleness might bring about a
rapid and cumulative deterioration in the labourer's attitude towards
work. This produced a growing sensitivity towards the Poor Law"[67]—

---

of civilization (not to say one of the ingredients of it) is that the spectacle, and even the very
idea of pain, is more and more kept out of the sight of those classes who enjoy in their
fullness the benefits of civilization" (John Stuart Mill, *Essays on Politics and Culture* [Garden
City, N.Y.: Doubleday, 1963], 64–65).

65. Steven Marcus, *Engels, Manchester, and the Working Class* (New York: Vintage, 1974),
184–85.

66. Stevenson MacGill, *On Lunatic Asylums* (Glasgow: For the Glasgow Asylum Committee, 1810), 4.

67. S. G. Checkland and E. O. A. Checkland, eds., "Introduction" to *The Poor Law Report of 1834* (London: Penguin, 1974), 20–21.

and towards anything else that, by lessening the dependence of the laboring classes on market forces, might weaken the social fabric of Victorian society.

By now, an abhorrence of outdoor relief had been etched deeply into the bourgeois consciousness. In part this reflected the ideological hegemony of classical liberalism. For the logical consequence of that doctrine's insistence on one's freedom to pursue self-interest and on one's unique responsibility for personal success or failure, when joined with its dogmatic certainty that intervention to alter market-derived outcomes could only be counterproductive, was to render the very notion of social protectionism anathema.

These obstacles, I suggest, presented a virtually insurmountable barrier to the development of a plausible, alternative, community-based response to the problem of insanity. Only the asylum plan offered the advantage of allowing scope for the exercise of humanitarian impulses while remaining consistent with the imperatives of the New Poor Law. Significantly, not one of the critics of the asylum was ever able to suggest even the basis of an alternative program (a *sine qua non* of their objections receiving serious consideration), and many of them ultimately conceded the futility of their opposition. Certain critics, while damning the asylum as "a prison" in which "the want of society, the absence of all amusement and employment, both of body and mind, must tend to *increase* rather than to relieve the morbid irritation of the brain,"[68] had from the outset blithely declared that such a solution was perfectly satisfactory for paupers.[69] (In this vision, only the rich were to be spared the asylum's horrors. Perhaps only their sensibilities were sufficiently refined to notice them.) Others, possibly lacking the capacity to engage in such flagrantly jesuitic reasoning, responded by gradually widening the definitions of those for whom the evils of the asylum were "unavoidable"— till, in John Conolly's case, he switched sides and became a leading and zealous advocate of county asylums for paupers.[70] In the last analysis, therefore, even its staunchest opponents were led to concede the asylum's inevitability.

VI

At the core of the reformers' approach to the asylum was a dual perception: positively, of the promise of cure; and negatively, of the revulsion

68. Anonymous, *On the Present State of Lunatic Asylums*, 16, 41 (emphasis in the original).

69. For a discussion of similar arguments by American neurologists in the Gilded Age, see Blustein, "Conflict Between Neurologists and Psychiatrists."

70. See John Conolly, *The Construction and Government of Lunatic Asylums and Hospitals for the Insane* (London: Churchill, 1847). For an account of the remarkable convolutions of Conolly's life and thought, see Chapter 7 below.

against cruelty and inhumanity. The conjunction of these two elements was a source of the greater part of the moral energy and commitment that sustained the drawn-out campaign for reform. Throughout the asylum's history, one source of the drive to institutionalize the insane has been anxiety, fear of the threat the mad posed to life, property, and the orderliness of social existence. In and of itself, however, fear provided only a weak argument for institutionalization, one that applied, at best, to a fraction of the insane. What was distinctive in many ways about the lunacy reform movement was not only its newfound conviction about the redemptive power of the institution, but also its insistence on extending the benefits of treatment to an ever-larger proportion of the mad. Certainly, in these connections we need to understand the relationship and appeal of lunacy reform to the Evangelicals, Quakers, and Benthamites in England, and to the Quakers, New England Unitarians, and those influenced by the Second Great Awakening in the United States. But we need to move beyond this to look for the broader sources of the profound shift in moral sensibilities that underlies and lends coherence to their activities—a humanitarian sensibility that finds expression in such diverse yet clearly related endeavors as controlling crime, relieving the poor and schooling the young, and that transformed slavery "from a problematical, but readily defensible institution, into a self-evidently evil and abominable one."[71]

This view implies that we must take the "humanitarianism" of the reformers very seriously indeed, and not dismiss it (as does Foucault) as "so much incidental music."[72] Of course, taking something seriously is not at all the same thing as taking it at face value or neglecting to subject it to further analysis. Reactions to traditional approaches to the management of the mad are sometimes taken to be self-evident. These approaches were cruel and brutal on their face, so that mere knowledge of or exposure to the conditions under which lunatics were kept was "naturally" sufficient to provoke horror and revulsion and to prompt vigorous and sustained efforts on the part of those endowed with the requisite temperament, intestinal fortitude, and religious sense of mission to rectify the treatment of the insane. In turn, once the general public were relieved of their ignorance and roused from their apathy by the efforts of these activists, reform straightforwardly followed.[73]

But, in the first instance, the claim of ignorance simply will not survive scrutiny. Broadsheets and other printed ephemera of the eighteenth

71. Thomas Haskell, "Capitalism and the Origins of the Humanitarian Sensibility: An Alternative to the Social Control Thesis" (Paper delivered at the Institute for Advanced Study, Princeton, New Jersey, April 1979), 1.

72. Clifford Geertz, "Stir Crazy," *New York Review of Books*, 26 January 1978, 3.

73. Roberts, *Victorian Origins*, 62–63.

century often took as their subject the horrors of the madhouse.[74] Hogarth and his many imitators likewise contributed to making the image of the madhouse a staple of the popular imagination in this period, as did a whole literature of asylum exposés, running from Defoe through Cruden down to the gothic novels of the early nineteenth century and the commitment scares later in the century.[75] That madmen were chained, whipped, menaced, and half starved in asylums in the eighteenth century was well known at the time. Indeed, it could scarcely have been otherwise when, throughout the century, the inmates of Bethlem were exhibited before the impertinently curious sightseers at a mere penny a time, and when many a treatise on the management of the mad advocated such treatment. Even the king's mania prompted the use of intimidation, threats, shackles, and blows,[76] a fact of which his subjects were scarcely unaware.

Such practices, then, were not something of which people became conscious only after the turn of the century. Yet it was only then that protests began to be heard that such treatment was cruel and inhumane. Only then did practices that had formerly seemed entirely appropriate and that had been advocated by the most eminent physicians and cultured men of their day[77] lose their appearance of self-evidence. And the process was a gradual and halting one. Even major figures in the reform movement did not succeed at a stroke in freeing themselves from the past. Sir George Onesiphorus Paul, for example, the prime mover behind the original County Asylums Act (1808), continued to believe that chains and the inculcation of fear were the best means of managing madness; he repeatedly expressed his approbation, based on close personal inspections, of the regime at the York Asylum.[78] Within less than a decade, other reformers excoriated "the institution at York under the excellent management of Dr Hunter"[79] as the epitome of all that was

74. A number of examples of these may be found in the Norman collection in the library of the Institute of Living, Hartford, Connecticut.

75. Daniel Defoe, *Augusta Triumphans* (London: Roberts, 1728); Alexander Cruden, *The London Citizen Exceedingly Injured; or, A British Inquisition Displayed* (London: Cooper and Dodd, 1739); idem, *The Adventures of Alexander the Corrector, with an Account of the Chelsea Academies, of the Private Places of Such as Are Supposed to Be Deprived of the Use of Their Reason* (London: For the Author, 1754). See Peter McCandless, "Liberty and Lunacy: The Victorians and Wrongful Confinement," *Journal of Social History* 10 (1976):366–86.

76. Ida Macalpine and Richard A. Hunter, *George III and the Mad Business* (London: Allen Lane, 1969).

77. For example, William Cullen, *First Lines of the Practice of Physic* (Edinburgh: Bell and Bradfute, 1784).

78. Sir George Onesiphorus Paul, *Suggestions on the Subject of Criminal and Pauper Lunatics* (Gloucester: For the Author, 1806); idem, *Address to the Subscribers to the Gloucester Lunatic Asylum* (Gloucester: For the Author, 1810); idem, *Observations on the Subject of Lunatic Asylums* (Gloucester: Walker, 1812), esp. 28–37.

79. Paul, *Suggestions*, 8.

wrong with previous approaches to the mad. Beyond the reformers' ranks, the old "backward" attitudes persisted even longer, prompting not only some of the opposition to the reformers' schemes, but also episodes of blank mutual incomprehension, as conditions that one side viewed as unexceptionable were viewed by the other with shock and outrage.[80]

I think we must accept, therefore, that in this period an authentic shift in moral consciousness took place, whose outcome was the development of a new sensibility vis-à-vis the treatment of the insane. We can define, too, some of the central dimensions of this change. There is the movement away from a view of madness as "the total suspension of every rational faculty,"[81] and from an outlook that stressed the need to subjugate the madman, to employ external discipline and constraint to break his will—indeed, a sharp break with a conception of the lunatic as an animal, a brute stripped of all remnants of its humanity. There is, instead, a new emphasis on the susceptibility of the insane to many of the same emotions and inducements as the rest of us; an insistence that "madmen are not . . . absolutely deprived of their reason"[82] and a belief that, through a suitable manipulation of inmate and environment, the qualities the lunatic lacks can and should be recreated or reawakened, so that he may once again be restored to the world, a sober, rational, "self-determining" citizen. Fundamentally, to put it another way, there is an abandonment of external coercion (which could never do more than force the crudest and least stable forms of outward conformity) for an approach that promises to produce the internalization of the necessary moral standards, by inducing the mad to collaborate in their own recapture by the forces of reason.

There remains, of course, the extraordinarily difficult task of defining what were, in David Brion Davis' words, "the material considerations which helped to shape the new moral consciousness and to define its historical effects."[83] But that is too large an issue on which to trespass within the confines of this chapter.[84] I suggest that an answer is not to be sought

80. See Scull, *Museums of Madness*, 65–66.

81. John Monro, *Remarks on Dr. Battie's Treatise on Madness* (London: Clarke, 1758), 6. "Not only [imagination], but every other quality, which distinguishes a man from a brute, except a few unconnected, incoherent words seems totally obliterated" (ibid.).

82. G. De la Rive, *Lettre adressée aux rédacteurs de la Bibliothèque britannique sur un nouvel établissement pour la guérison des aliénés* (Geneva: For the Author, 1798), 29.

83. Quoted in Haskell, "Capitalism," 20.

84. I have attempted to sketch some elements of an answer to this question in Chapter 4. For a related approach to these issues as they relate to slavery, see Thomas Haskell's "Capitalism." As Haskell argues in this paper, David Brion Davis' *The Problem of Slavery in the Age of Revolution* (Ithaca: Cornell University Press, 1975) can also be seen as moving in the direction advocated here.

in some more or less crude reductionism, which seeks to unmask the material or economic interest that produces and shapes the "humanitarian sensibility." Though such elements are undeniably by no means absent, we need rather to seek a broader comprehension of how the ways people look at the world are conditioned by the nature of their activity in it, and, more specifically, of the manifold linkages between the changes in conceptions of insanity and larger changes in the conditions of social existence.

CHAPTER THREE

The Domestication of Madness

I was fortunate enough to spend much of 1982 in London, supported by a Guggenheim fellowship. Here, I was able to take advantage of the hospitality and unrivaled facilities of the Wellcome Institute for the History of Medicine and to spend many months exploring the English medical literature on madness. The timing of my stay was particularly advantageous, since it coincided with the launching of a year-long biweekly seminar on the history of psychiatry, organized by William Bynum and Roy Porter. This turned out to be a singularly well attended, consistently fascinating, and intellectually stimulating parade of performances, with the additional benefit that it rendered one's invisible college of fellow researchers temporarily visible and available for discussion and debate.

Just about the only price the Wellcome exacted in return for its largesse was a requirement that I deliver one of the seminar papers. William Bynum approached me quite early on in my stay, while I had my nose buried in eighteenth-century texts, and extracted my commitment, together with a title, one that I thought would not confine me unduly when I actually wrote something up. In fact, my choice of the term "domestication" came to seem prescient, for it captured what I have argued was a central shift in English views of madness from the eighteenth to the nineteenth century.

One of the most predictable, and, after a time, faintly alarming features of my months at the Wellcome was the regular arrival on my desk of a new essay by the prodigiously productive Porter. The paper that follows was originally framed as an attack on one of his bolder and more provocative pieces, an essay seeking to demolish the claim that the ad-

Chapter 3 is reprinted from *Medical History*, Volume 27, 1983, pp. 233–48, by permission of the editors.

vent of moral treatment at the close of the eighteenth century marked a distinct rupture or shift in English responses to insanity. In its published form,[1] the argument was toned down considerably, though it continues to offer an interpretation sharply at variance with that offered here. Obviously, Dr. Porter remains less than wholly persuaded by my arguments, and vice versa.

Most of the papers given in the Wellcome seminar series were subsequently revised and published as *The Anatomy of Madness*,[2] a third volume of which appeared in 1988. My own essay appeared in print rather more rapidly, in an issue of *Medical History*. Over the course of the year, however, I also completed work on a long-standing project on which I had been researching and reflecting for several years, a reassessment of the life and career of John Conolly, the most eminent English alienist of the early Victorian era. It was this paper (see Chapter 7) that ultimately appeared in the collection of seminar papers.

The Domestication of Madness

We use the term "domestic" and its cognates in at least two very different contexts. On the one hand, there is the contrast between the wild and the tame, the sense in which we refer to animals as "domesticated." And on the other hand, there is the reference to the private familial sphere, the environment of the home and one's intimate circle: domestic as contrasted with public life. In this paper I shall suggest that the changing social responses to madness from the end of the seventeenth to the early nineteenth century may be usefully looked at in terms of the metaphor of domestication, comprehending the transition from efforts to tame the wildly asocial to attempts to transform the company of the deranged into at least a facsimile of bourgeois family life.

During the early eighteenth century, most English medical writing on mental disorder was concerned, not with the Bedlam mad,[1] but with the various manifestations of that Protean disorder, the grand "English malady,"[2] to which ladies and gentlemen of quality (but especially ladies of

1. Roy Porter, "The Rage of Party: A Glorious Revolution in English Psychiatry?" *Medical History* 27 (1983):35–50.
2. W. F. Bynum, Roy Porter, and Michael Shepherd, eds., *The Anatomy of Madness: Essays in the History of Psychiatry*, 2 vols. (London: Tavistock, 1985).

1. As Sir Richard Blackmore acknowledged, the subject of madness remained "a wild uncultivated region, an intellectual Africa, that abounds with an endless variety of monsters and irregular minds" (*Treatise of the Spleen or Vapours* [London: Pemberton, 1724], 263.
2. George Cheyne, *The English Malady: or, A Treatise of Nervous Diseases of All Kinds* (London: Wisk, Ewing and Smith, 1733).

quality) displayed such a striking susceptibility. To be sure, there were some discussions of the seriously mad—furious or moping—to which I shall return shortly. But the main focus of concern was clearly the various "nervous" distempers—the spleen, hypochondria, the vapours, hysteria—to which the physicians' fashionable clientele, blessed with excessively refined sensibilities and exquisitely civilized temperaments (not to mention money), were apt to fall victim. Such speculations (and I use the word advisedly) as Thomas Willis and his epigoni ventured on the subject of lunacy itself reflected an intellectual fascination with the difficult problem of providing a rational explanation of the origins and characteristics of madness, coupled with a marked distaste for any close or continuing contact with those suffering from the disorder: a combination not unknown among later generations of academic psychiatrists, and one which led John Monro to remark with some asperity that "the person who is most conversant with such cases, provided he has but common sense enough to avoid metaphysical subtleties, will be enabled by his extensive knowledge and experience to excell those who have not the same opportunities of receiving information."[3]

And yet, while the utterances of a Willis, a Robinson, a Cullen on the etiology and treatment of insanity reflect a remarkably restricted clinical acquaintance with the condition, they do mirror quite well a broader cultural consensus about the meaning of madness and the nature of the response one should make to it. Moreover, it seems to me that the fundamental thrust of what they have to say undermines, or at the very least sharply limits, the validity of Michael MacDonald's recent claim that the eighteenth century was marked by a shift away from more traditional stereotypes of mad behavior, emphasizing irrational violence, furious raving, and incoherent bestiality.[4] And it likewise undercuts Roy Porter's attempts to play down the distinctiveness of the moral treatment introduced at the end of the eighteenth century and to suggest the essential continuity between the reformers' program and what had gone before.[5]

For whether one looks to theoretical medical texts, to works on the jurisprudence of insanity, to literary allusions, to popular pictorial representations, or to the practices of the despised madhouse keepers themselves, the dominant images are of whips and chains, depletion and degradation, the wreck of the intellect, and the loss of the mad person's very humanness; and madness's constant accompaniments are shit, straw, and stench. The traditional imagery is found in Shakespeare and in Elizabethan drama more generally:[6]

3. John Monro, *Remarks on Dr. Battie's Treatise on Madness* (London: Clarke, 1758), 35.

4. See Michael MacDonald, "Insanity and the Realities of History in Early Modern England," *Psychological Medicine* 11 (1981): 11–25.

5. Roy Porter, "The Rage of Party: A Glorious Revolution in English Psychiatry?" *Medical History* 27 (1983): 35–50.

6. For example, John Marston's *What You Will:* "Shut the windows, darken the room, fetch whips: the fellow is mad, he raves, he raves—talks idly—lunatic." Or James Shirley's

Love is merely a madness; and, I tell you, deserves as well a dark house and a whip as madmen do; and the reason why they are not so punished and cured is, that the lunacy is so ordinary that the whippers are in love too.[7]

These notions find renewed expression in the more excremental outpourings of Jonathan Swift, who enjoins the madhouse keeper thus:

> Tie them keeper in a tether,
> Let them stare and stink together:
> Both are apt to be unruly,
> Lash them daily, lash them duly,
> Though 'tis hopeless to reclaim them,
> Scorpion Rods perhaps may tame them.[8]

This sense of madness as a condition that required taming, as one might domesticate and thus render predictable the behavior of a wild beast, runs through any number of eighteenth-century discussions of insanity. "Madmen," warned Thomas Willis, "are still strong and robust to a prodigy, so that they can break cords and chains, break down doors or walls, one easily overthrows many endeavouring to hold him."[9] More extraordinarily yet, they "are almost never tired. . . . Madmen, what ever they bear or suffer are not hurt; but they bear cold, heat, watching, fasting, strokes, and wounds, without any sensible hurt; to wit because the spirits being strong and fixed, are neither daunted nor fly away."[10] By mid-century, Richard Mead had extended this set of immunities a step further: the mad, it appeared, were likewise immune to the ravages of bodily disease, a formulation that was to be repeated almost by rote into the nineteenth century.[11]

But such striking immunity to the infirmities to which human flesh is heir were purchased at a heavy price, for the descent into madness marked the divestment of "the rational Soul . . . of all its noble and dis-

---

Bird in a Cage, where the madhouse is referred to as "a house of correction to whip us into our senses." See generally, Edgar A. Peers, *Elizabethan Drama and Its Mad Folk* (Cambridge: Heffer, 1914).

7. William Shakespeare, *As You Like It*, act 3, sc. 2, lines 420–26.

8. Jonathan Swift, *The Legion Club* (London: Bathurst, 1736), 3:835–836. Note, too, that Tobias Smollett's *Sir Launcelot Greaves* concludes with both hero and heroine trapped in a private madhouse run by a Mr. Shackle.

9. Thomas Willis, *The Practice of Physick: Two Discourses Concerning the Soul of Brutes* (London: Dring, Harper, and Leigh, 1684), 205. See also William Salmon, *A Compleat System of Physick, Theoretical and Practical* (London: For the Author, 1686), 37, 56–61; and Zachary Mayne, *Two Dissertations Concerning Sense, and the Imagination, with an Essay on Consciousness* (1728), facsimile ed., ed. René Wellek (New York: Garland, 1976), 91.

10. Willis, *Practice of Physick*, 205.

11. Richard Mead, *Medical Precepts and Cautions* (London: Brindley, 1751), 79. See also Thomas Arnold, *Observations on the Nature, Kinds, Causes, and Prevention of Insanity*, 2 vols., 2d ed. (London: Phillips, 1806), 1:4–5 ("No fact in medicine is more completely established").

tinguishing Endowments."[12] If, as Foucault[13] has argued, the madman's very animality protected him from all sickness and pathology, the bargain was nevertheless a poor one. The melancholy lunatic offered, said Nicholas Robinson, "the most gloomy Scene of Nature, that Mankind can possibly encounter, where nothing but Horror reigns; where the noble Endowments of the reasonable Soul are often disconcerted to a surprizing Degree, and this lordly creature then almost debas'd below the brutal Species of the animated Creation."[14] Still more clearly was the maniac reduced in status, losing "that Power by which we are distinguished from the brutal Class of the animated Creation: 'til at last upon a Level, or rather beneath the Condition of a mere Brute."[15]

"There is," said Mead, "no disease more to be dreaded than madness."[16] Such views were an eighteenth-century cliché,[17] yet, like many commonplaces, serve to reveal a great deal about contemporary beliefs. Dragged down to a state of brutish insensibility and incapacity, the lunatic occupied a wholly unenviable ontological status:[18] he became virtually a nonentity, one whose "Promises and Contracts" were "void and of no force" and whose behavior could never attain the dignity and status of human action. Such a creature, "deprived of his reason and understanding," could expect a miserable and humiliating career: "to attack his fellow creatures with fury like a wild beast; to be tied down, and even beat, to prevent his doing mischief to himself or others: or, on the contrary, to be sad and dejected, to be daily terrified with vain imaginations; to fancy hobgoblins haunting him; and after a life spent in continual anxiety, to be persuaded that his death will be the commencement of eternal punishment."[19]

Small wonder that the belief that madness was a state "even more deplorable than death itself"[20] enjoyed widespread assent. After all, it brought "the mighty reasoners of the earth, below even the insects that crawl upon it."[21] Nor, until the latter part of the century, was the gloom alleviated by any very confident claims from respectable quarters about

12. Nicholas Robinson, *A New System of the Spleen, Vapours, and Hypochondriak Melancholy* (London: Bettesworth, Innys, and Rivington, 1729), 241.

13. Michel Foucault, *Madness and Civilization* (New York: Pantheon, 1965).

14. Robinson, *New System*, 243.

15. Ibid., 44, 50.

16. Mead, *Medical Precepts*, 74.

17. See, for example, Robinson, *New System*, 50; Henry Mackenzie, *The Man of Feeling* (London: Cadell, 1771), 73; Arnold, *Observations . . . on Insanity*, 2:320; William Pargeter, *Observations on Maniacal Disorders* (Reading: For the Author, 1792), 122, 139.

18. John Brydall, *Non Compos Mentis; or, The Law Relating to Natural Fools, Mad Folks, and Lunatick Persons* (London: Cleave, 1700).

19. Mead, *Medical Precepts*, 74–75.

20. Pargeter, *Maniacal Disorders*, 139.

21. Samuel Richardson, in *The World*, 7 June 1753.

the possibility of cure. Quacks like Thomas Fallowes, whose M.D. was awarded by himself, might advertise their "incomparable oleum cephalicum" as a sure cure for frenzy.[22] Their orthodox competitors, however, were generally distinctly less sanguine. Willis, for example, held that "such being placed in Bedlam, or an hospital for Mad People, by the ordinary discipline of the place either at length returned to themselves or else they are kept from doing hurt to themselves or others."[23] And Richard Mead lamented "this unhappy circumstance, that the disorder is very difficult to be cured."[24] Even John Monro, the physician to Bedlam and a man whose name was virtually synonymous with the mad-doctoring trade, thought "madness . . . a distemper of such a nature that very little of real use can be said concerning it; the immediate causes will forever disappoint our search, and the cure of the disorder depends on *management* as much as medicine."[25]

The madman remained, then, emblematic of chaos and terror, of the dark, bestial possibilities that lurked within the human frame, waiting only upon the loss of "that governing principle, reason" to emerge in their full awfulness. Once encounter a man "deprived of that noble endowment," warned William Pargeter, "and see in how melancholy a posture he appears. He retains indeed the outward figure of the human species, but like the ruins of a once magnificent edifice, it only serves to remind us of his former dignity, and fill us with gloomy reflections with the loss of it. Within, all is confused and deranged, every look and expression testifies [to] internal anarchy and disorder."[26] Notwithstanding the more hopeful portrayal of milder forms of mental disarray embodied in the early eighteenth-century textbooks on the spleen, the traditional view of Bedlam madness retained most of its old force and even its content. Toward the close of the century, mania still wore its earlier garb, finding expression in "a violent and inordinate desire to do mischief; fury, vociferation, impetuosity of temper, and indomitable turbulence and vehemence; an angry and wild staring look in the eyes, actions rashly attempted, and as suddenly relinquished, obstinacy, perverseness, immodesty," while its melancholic counterpart could be recognized "by sullenness, taciturnity, meditation, dreadful apprehensions, and despair."[27]

22. Thomas Fallowes, *The Best Method for the Cure of Lunaticks* (London: [For the Author], 1705).

23. Willis, *Practice of Physick*, 205.

24. Mead, *Medical Precepts*, 75.

25. Monro, *Dr. Battie's Treatise on Madness*, advertisement (i.e., preface). On this point at least, Monro agreed with the target of his polemic, William Battie. See Battie's *A Treatise on Madness* (London: Whiston and White, 1758), 68.

26. Pargeter, *Maniacal Disorders*, 2-3.

27. William Rowley, *A Treatise on Female, Nervous, Hysterical, Hypochondriacal, Bilious, Convulsive Diseases with Thoughts on Madness, Suicide, Etc.* (London: Nourse, 1788), 230.

But still, under suitably controlled conditions, the varied beasts confined in "the wild abodes of secluded misery"[28] formed an entertaining display; an ever-varied menagerie from which an audience made up of both provincial bumpkins and urban sophisticates could derive almost endless amusement. From Ned Ward's *London Spy* to Henry Mackenzie's *Man of Feeling*, Bedlam offered, for a mere penny a time, the opportunity to view "the clamorous ravings, the furious gusts of outrageous action, the amazing exertion of muscular force, the proud and fanciful sallies of imagination"—if not perhaps "the excessive propensity to venereal intercourse"—that mad-doctors assured the public were the common currency of lunacy.[29] And by the thousands they came, as many as 100,000 in a good year, to what "was commonly regarded less as a hospital than as a kind of human zoo, with a fine, permanent exhibition of human curiosities."[30] All in all, an obvious setting for Hogarth to conclude his moral tract on the wages of sin (Figure 1), and an inevitable occasion for one of those floods of tears that Mackenzie's *Man of Feeling* repeatedly inflicted on his readers. As they were brought within the gates,

> their conductor led them first to the dismal mansions of those who are in the most horrid state of incurable madness. The clanking of chains, the wildness of their cries, and the imprecations which some of them uttered, formed a scene inexpressibly shocking. Harley and his companions, especially the female part of them, begged their guide to return: he seemed surprised at their uneasiness and was with difficulty prevailed on to leave that part of the house without showing them some others, who as he expressed it in the phrase of those that keep wild beasts for show, were much better worth seeing than any they had passed, being ten times more fierce and unmanageable.[31]

A generation or two later, as professional conceptions of insanity began to change quite sharply, John Haslam complained that "to constitute madness, the minds of ignorant people expect a display of continued violence, and they are not satisfied that a person can be pronounced in that state, without they see him exhibit the pranks of a baboon, or hear him roar and bellow like a beast."[32] And his jibes were echoed by Thomas

28. Andrew Harper, *A Treatise on the Real Cause and Cure of Insanity* (London: Stalker, 1789), iii.

29. Ibid., 26.

30. Michael V. Deporte, *Nightmares and Hobbyhorses: Swift, Sterne, and Augustan Ideas of Madness* (San Marino, Calif.: Huntington Library, 1974), 3.

31. Mackenzie, *Man of Feeling*, 73–74. Compare Ned Ward's description of his visit, some seventy years earlier: "Such rattling of chains, drumming of doors, ranting, holloaing, singing, and rattling, that I could think of nothing else but Don Quevado's vision where the damned broke loose and put Hell in an uproar" (*The London Spy* [1698–1709; London: Folio Society, 1955], 48–51).

32. John Haslam, *Observations on Madness and Melancholy* (London: Callow, 1809), 77–78.

Figure 1. Bedlam. Engraving by William Hogarth, 1735, retouched 1736. The final episode of *The Rake's Progress*, with madness presented as the wages of sin. (Courtesy of the Wellcome Trustees.)

Bakewell, who described with some disdain the public reaction when a convalescent madman escaped from his Staffordshire madhouse: "The alarm this has excited has been very like what might be expected, were lion, or royal tiger, to escape from a caravan; and the censure upon my conduct has been such as would be cast upon a keeper of wild beasts, on such a terrific event."[33] But their complaints have a somewhat disingenuous air, and not just because of medicine's long history of promoting and reinforcing such stereotypes. For even as they sought to dismiss such images as the product of ignorance and superstition, as eminent a physician as Charles Bell was displaying graphic evidence of their survival in the highest professional circles in his *Essays on the Anatomy of Ex-*

33. Thomas Bakewell, *A Letter to the Chairman of the Select Committee on the State of Madhouses, to Which Is Subjoined Remarks on the Nature, Causes, and Cure of Mental Derangement* (Stafford: Chester, 1815), 87.

pression in Painting (Figure 2).[34] To his sketches themselves, he appended a vivid description of his effort to render madness as it appeared in nature, as "ferocity amid the utter wreck of the intellect . . . a most unpleasant and distressing subject of contemplation."[35] The essential requirement for the artist (to the neglect of which Bell attributed the romanticized images "we almost uniformly find given [to madmen] in painting") was "to learn the character of the human countenance when devoid of expression, and reduced to the state of lower animals; and as I have already hinted, study their expression, their timidity, their watchfulness, their state of excitement, and their ferociousness."[36]

Corresponding to these conceptions of the madman as beast were a set of therapeutic practices whose logic remained largely intact and unaltered over the course of more than a century. The madman's ferocity must be tamed by a mixture of discipline and depletion designed to put down "the raging of the Spirits and the lifting up of the Soul."[37] As Willis argued,

> To correct or allay the furies and exorbitancies of the Animal Spirits . . . requires threatenings, bonds, or strokes as well as *Physick*. For the *Madman* being placed in House convenient for the business, must be so handled both by the *Physician*, and also by the Servants that are prudent, that he may in some manner be kept in, either by warnings, chidings, or punishments inflicted on him, to his duty, or his behavior, or manners. And indeed for the curing of Mad people, there is nothing more effectual or necessary than their reverence or standing in awe of such as they think their Tormentors. For by this means, the Corporeal Soul being in some measure depressed and restrained, is compelled to remit its pride and fierceness; and so afterwards by degrees grows more mild, and returns in order; Wherefore, Furious Madmen are sooner, and more certainly cured by punishments and hard usage, in a strait room, than by *Physick* or Medicines.[38]

Not that the lunatics were to escape the more conventional weapons of the medical practitioner, for, unless they were numbered among those not furious but "more remissly Mad, [who] are healed often with flatteries, and with more gentle Physick,"[39] "Bloodletting, Vomits, or very strong Purges, and boldly and rashly given, are most often convenient [though for whom Willis does not say!]; which indeed appears manifest, because *Empericks* only with this kind of *Physick*, together with a more severe government and discipline do not seldom most happily cure Mad folks."[40] A misplaced caution and timidity were at all costs to be

34. Charles Bell, *Essays on the Anatomy of Expression Painting* (London: Longman, 1806).
35. Ibid., 155, 156.   36. Ibid., 155.   37. Willis, *Practice of Physick*, 206.
38. Ibid.   39. Ibid.   40. Ibid.

Figure 2. Charles Bell's representation of "the madman," a portrait that
purported to strip away the romanticized images prevalent among artists and
to provide a faithful copy of nature. From: Sir Charles Bell, *Essays on the
Anatomy of Expression in Painting* (London: Longman, 1806), 153.
(Courtesy of the Wellcome Trustees.)

avoided in favor of a vigorous trial of the full rigors of the Galenic therapeutics; for "it is Cruelty in the highest Degree, not to be bold in the
Administration of Medicine" in such cases.[41] One must rather, said Robinson, have recourse to "a Course of Medicines of the most violent Operation . . . to bring down the Spirit of the Stubborn Persons [and] to reduce their artificial Strength by compulsive Methods."[42]

Country clergymen, who dabbled in "physick" and found themselves
consulted in the cure of the mad, were not always so convinced of the
merits of coercing right thinking. Some indeed, like Southcomb, objected to "all those Means which tend to the giving of Pain and Un-
easiness . . . such as *Blisters, Seatons, Cupping, Scarifying,* and all other
Punishments of the Like kind," urging that such "tormenting Means"
often "rendered a very *curable* Disease, either incurable or [were] the Occasion of protracting the Cure longer than otherwise the Nature of the
Case would have required."[43]

For the most part, however, such pleas fell on deaf ears, at least as far
as the medical profession was concerned. True, men like Richard Mead
sometimes conceded that "it is not necessary to employ stripes or other
rough treatment to bring [the outrageous] into order."[44] But the objection was not to beating as such, only to its being superfluous, since "all
maniacal people are fearful and cowardly."[45] "Diversions" would often
suffice for those afflicted with "sadness and fear"; but "melancholy very
frequently changes, sooner or later, into maniacal madness," and then
one must once more have recourse to "chiding and threatening" and to
the various weapons in the physician's therapeutic armamentarium.[46]

Like his observation about the exemption of the mad from the ravages of other forms of disease, Mead's doctrine about the cowardliness of
the insane was to prove widely influential,[47] eventually underpinning
and giving legitimacy to some of the most characteristic late-eighteenth-
century responses to madness. As Sir George Onesiphorus Paul put it,
more than half a century later, mad-doctors had determined that their
patients "possessed a cunning and instinctive penetration, which makes
them apprehend consequences from acts, and indeed to fear them; for

41. Robinson, *New System,* 401.

42. Ibid., 400.

43. Lewis Southcomb, *Peace of Mind and Health of Body United* (London: Cowper, 1750),
cited in Richard Hunter and Ida Macalpine, *Three Hundred Years of Psychiatry, 1535 to 1860:
A History Presented in Selected English Texts* (London: Oxford University Press, 1963), 384.

44. Mead, *Medical Precepts,* 98.

45. Ibid.

46. Ibid., 98–99.

47. For example, David MacBride, *A Methodical Introduction to the Theory and Practice of
Physick* (London, Strahan, 1772), 592; William Falconer, *A Dissertation on the Influence of the
Passions upon Disorders of the Body* (London: Dill, 1788), 83; Joseph Mason Cox, *Practical
Observations on Insanity,* 3d ed. (London: Baldwin and Underwood, 1813), 34.

they are universally cowardly. It is by keeping up this apprehension on their minds that they are so easily governed in numbers by the modern system of treating them."[48]

"To superficial observers," remarked William Pergeter, "the conduct of maniacs . . . appears extremely daring and courageous; but in reality they are exceedingly timorous and are found to be easily terrified."[49] (As we shall see, this perspective did not restrain the medical profession from exercising considerable ingenuity to foment that terror.) To accomplish the management that both Battie[50] and Monro[51] had urged as the key to the cure of the mad, the physician should ensure that his first visit was by surprise. But he must then "employ every moment of his time by mildness or menaces, as circumstances direct, to gain an ascendancy over them, and to obtain their favor and prepossession."[52] Much depended here on the mad-doctor's skill at managing his presentation of self, since "he may be obliged at one moment, according to the exigency of the case, to be placid and accommodating in his manners, and the next, angry and absolute."[53] Consequently, as Joseph Mason Cox noted,

there are very few, whom nature has been so kind as to qualify for the practice; every man is not furnished with sufficient nerve, with the requisite features for the varied expression of countenance which may be necessary, with the degree of muscular powers, or stature, etc. [But all, at least, could recognize that] as the grand object in their moral management, is to make ourselves both feared and loved, nothing can so successfully tend to affect this as a system of kindness and mildness, address and firmness, the judicious allowance of indulgences, and the employment of irresistible control and coercion.[54]

Sometimes the coercion and control were quite straightforward. Bakewell, for example, relates an instance from his practice where "a maniac confined in a room over my own . . . bellowed like a wild beast, and shook his chain almost constantly for several days and nights. . . . I therefore got up, took a hand whip, and gave him a few smart stripes upon the shoulder. . . . He disturbed me no more."[55] Such techniques were generally expected to be efficacious since, as Falconer put it, "those who attend them . . . mostly find, that although generally irrational, they re-

48. Sir George Onesiphorus Paul, in House of Commons, *Report of the Select Committee on Criminal and Pauper Lunatics* (London, 1807), 16.
49. Pargeter, *Maniacal Disorders*, 61.
50. Battie, *Treatise on Madness*.
51. Monro, *Dr. Battie's Treatise on Madness*.
52. Pargeter, *Maniacal Disorders*, 49.
53. Ibid., 50.
54. Cox, *Practical Observations on Insanity*, 84.
55. Thomas Bakewell, *The Domestic Guide in Cases of Insanity* (Stafford, 1805), cited in Hunter and Macalpine, *Three Hundred Years of Psychiatry*, 705.

tain a great consideration for personal safety, and that threats will often compel them to speak and act rationally."[56]

But direct physical threats were not always necessary. "It is of great use in practice," said MacBride, "to bear in mind, that all mad people . . . can be awed even by the menacing look of a very expressive countenance; and when those who have charge of them once impress them with the notion of fear, they easily submit to anything that is required."[57] Indeed, "the eye" was perhaps the most dramatic technique that the late-eighteenth-century mad-doctor claimed to have at his disposal and was used most famously by Francis Willis in his treatment of George III.[58] Benjamin Rush even went so far as to claim that "there are keys in the eye, if I may be allowed the expression," that allowed the skilled practitioner to vary "its aspect from the highest degree of sternness, down to the mildest degree of benignity" and thus to secure minute changes in the patient's behavior.[59] And the growing clinical literature of the period is replete with case histories like this one, offered by William Pargeter.[60]

56. Falconer, *Influence of the Passions*, 83.

57. MacBride, *Theory and Practice of Physick*, 592.

58. Following George III's recovery from his attack of "mania" in 1788, a parliamentary committee, among whose members were Burke and Sheridan, inquired into the king's treatment. During the course of these inquiries, it was revealed that Willis had allowed the king to shave himself with a cutthroat razor. The other royal physicians criticized Willis about this. "Burke also was very severe on this point, and authoritatively and loudly demanded to know, 'If the Royal patient had become outrageous at the moment, what power the Doctor possessed of instantaneously terrifying him into obedience?' 'Place the candles between us, Mr. Burke,' replied the Doctor, in an equally authoritative tone—'and I'll give you an answer. There Sir! by the EYE! I should have looked at him *thus*, Sir—*thus!*' Burke instantaneously averted his head, and, making no reply, evidently acknowledged this *basiliskan* authority" (*The Life and Times of F. Reynolds, Written by Himself* [London: Colburn, 1826], 2:23–24). If necessary, Willis used more than just "the eye" to secure the measure of obedience he saw as indispensable. His reputation for using force and fear to cow his patients was such that when he was called in to treat George III, the queen was extremely reluctant to allow him to proceed: "It was known to her, that the first principle of Dr. W's practice is, to make himself formidable—to inspire awe. In these terrible maladies, those who superintend the unhappy patients must so subjugate their will, that no idea of resistance to their commands can have place in their minds. It was but too obvious, that the long and habitual exercise of high command must increase the difficulty of accomplishing this, in the present instance;—and an apprehension of the necessity of peculiar rigour gave all possible aggravation to the queen's distress." But Willis refused to modify his practice, insisting that "he might be permitted to act without control. He said that there was but *one method*, in that complaint, by which the lowest and the highest person could be treated with effect:—and that his reputation was too much concerned in the event, for him to attempt anything, if he might not be invested with unlimited powers." The queen capitulated (Anonymous, *Some Particulars of the Royal Indisposition of 1788 to 1789, and of Its Effects upon Illustrious Personages and Opposite Parties Interested by It* [London: Printed for the Editor by R. Taylor, 1804], 31–33).

59. Benjamin Rush, *Medical Inquiries and Observations upon the Diseases of the Mind* (Philadelphia: Kimber and Richardson, 1830), 173–74.

60. Pargeter, *Maniacal Disorders*, 50–51, also 58–59.

The maniac was locked in a room, raving and exceeding turbulent. I took two men with me, and learning he had no offensive weapons, I planted them at the door with directions to be silent and keep out of sight, unless I should want their assistance. I then suddenly unlocked the door—rushed into the room and caught his eye in an instant. The business was then done—he became peaceable in a moment—trembled with fear, and was as governable as it was possible for a furious madman to be.[61]

One must realize, however, that the excitement of fear and the infliction of physical suffering were forms of treatment resting on a more elaborate theoretical basis than I have yet demonstrated. Madness was essentially defined, indeed constituted, by the preternatural force with which certain irrational ideas dominated the mind, heedless of the ordinary corrective processes provided by experience and persuasion. Mad people's loss of contact with our consensually defined reality, their spurning of common sense, reflected how deeply the chains of false impressions and associations were engraved upon their system. There were differences in degree between mania and melancholia: "The distinguishing character of [the latter] is an attachment of the mind to one object, concerning which the reason is defective, whilst in general it is perfect in what respects other subjects"; whereas mania entailed "an irrationality on all subjects."[62] And these differences argued for the use of a greater caution in handling the melancholic. But in both forms of the disorder, the thought processes were trapped in erroneous pathways—a language that reified and referred them to an underlying disorder of a (somewhat variously conceived) physical substratum of thought, from whose grip they must somehow be shaken loose.

The very tenacity with which maniacs adhered to their false and mistaken perceptions testified to the weight and strength with which these were impressed upon the brain, and by implication required and justified the extremity of the measures adopted to jolt the system back into sanity. Given that *the mind when waking is always active and employed,* it followed that *we have no method of banishing one set or train of ideas, but by substituting another in its place.*[63] And in view of the entrenched position occupied by the opposing ideas, one could only hope "to eradicate the false impressions by others still more violent."[64] Thus were intimidation and forceful persuasion embodied in a variety of physical treatments, which simultaneously brought moral and physiological pressures to bear

61. John Haslam, incidentally, was as scathing about such stories as about other claims put forward by his fellow mad-doctors: "It has, on some occasions, occurred to me to meet with gentlemen who have imagined themselves eminently gifted with this awful imposition of the eye, but . . . I have never been able to persuade them to practice this rare talent *tête-à-tête* with a furious lunatic" (Haslam, *Madness and Melancholy,* 276).

62. Falconer, *Influence of the Passions,* 77, 82.

63. Ibid., 4.

64. Ibid., 82. Cf. also Cox, *Practical Observations on Insanity,* 45.

on the patient and aimed to break "the chain of ideas which possessed the mind," even—what a splendid choice of words—if possible to "exterminate" them.[65]

Sometimes not just the insane *ideas* were exterminated. Throughout the century, classical sources were drawn on for inspiration, as the search went on for a suitable means of inducing the appropriate degree of terror. But there was a veritable paroxysm of inventiveness at the turn of the century, as the techniques of the Industrial Revolution were adapted to the task at hand. Elaborate systems of plumbing were developed to deliver forcible streams of cold water to the head of a suitably restrained maniac (Figure 3). The suggestion by Dutch physician Hermann Boerhaave that near-drowning be employed for its salutary effects gave birth to a variety of ingenious devices designed to produce this effect: hidden trapdoors in corridors designed to plunge the unsuspecting lunatic into a "bath of surprise" as well as coffins with holes drilled in their lids, into which the patient could be fastened before being lowered under water. As Guislain put it, the two critical aims to be realized, in constructing such an apparatus, were to obtain complete mastery of the madman, and to avoid drowning him (in that order). Francis Willis' attempt to reconcile these imperatives struck him as imperfect, prompting him to offer an improved version of his own (Figure 4). As he describes it,

> It consists of a little Chinese temple, the interior of which comprises a moveable iron cage, of light-weight construction, which plunges down into the water descending in rails, of its own weight, by means of pulleys and ropes. To expose the madman to the action of this device, he is led into the interior of this cage: one servant shuts the door from the outside while the other releases a brake which, by this maneuver, causes the patient to sink down, shut up in the cage, under the water. Having produced the desired effect, one raises the machine again, as can be seen from the drawing attached.[66]

Generally, he continued gravely, the treatment could be applied only once to each lunatic, and, he warned, "Toute fois ce moyen sera plus ou moins dangereux."[67]

Some sought to improve instruments of restraint to ensure "all the tenderness and indulgence compatible with steady and effectual government."[68] Benjamin Rush, for example, who trained under William Cullen

65. Alexandre Brière de Boismont, *On Hallucinations: A History and Explanation* (London: Renshaw, 1859), quoted in Hunter and Macalpine, *Three Hundred Years of Psychiatry*, 1059.

66. J. Guislain, *Traité sur l'aliénation mentale et sur les hospices des aliénés* (Amsterdam: Hey, 1826), 43–44.

67. Ibid., 44.

68. Thomas Percival, *Medical Ethics* (Manchester: Johnson and Bickerstaff, 1803), 68–69.

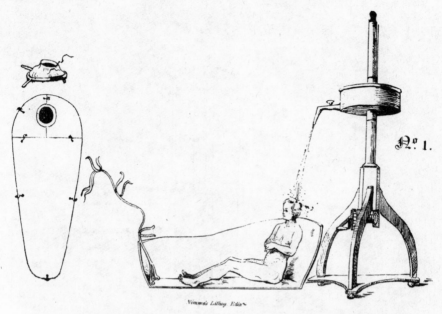

Figure 3. Immersion in cold water was an ancient nostrum for insanity. Aquatic shock treatment, otherwise euphemistically known as "hydrotherapy," here takes the form of the douche. From: Alexander Morison, *Cases of Mental Disease* (London: Longman and Highley, 1828). (Courtesy of the Wellcome Trustees.)

at Edinburgh (like so many mad-doctors of the late eighteenth century), designed an elaborate "tranquillizing chair," whose good effects in coercing a measure of good behavior from his patients he was not slow to advertise.[69] There was even a debate of sorts between those who preferred "the strait waistcoat, with other improvements in modern practice," on the grounds that they "preclude[d] the necessity of coercion by corporal punishment,"[70] and those who preferred "metallic manacles on the wrist; the skin being less liable to be injured by the friction of polished metal

---

69. As he wrote to his son, James, on 8 June 1810: "I have contrived a chair and introduced it to our [Pennsylvania] Hospital to assist in curing madness. It binds and confines every part of the body. By keeping the trunk erect, it lessens the impetus of blood toward the brain. By preventing the muscles from acting, it reduces the force and frequency of the pulse, and by the position of the head and feet favors the easy application of cold water or ice to the former and warm water to the latter. Its effects have been truly delightful to me. It acts as a sedative to the tongue and temper as well as to the blood vessels. In 24, 12, six, and in some cases in four hours, the most refractory patients have been composed. I have called it a Tranquillizer" (Rush to James Rush, *The Letters of Benjamin Rush*, ed. L. H. Butterfield (Princeton: Princeton University Press, 1951), 2 : 1052.

70. Percival, *Medical Ethics*, 69.

Pl. II. V 2.

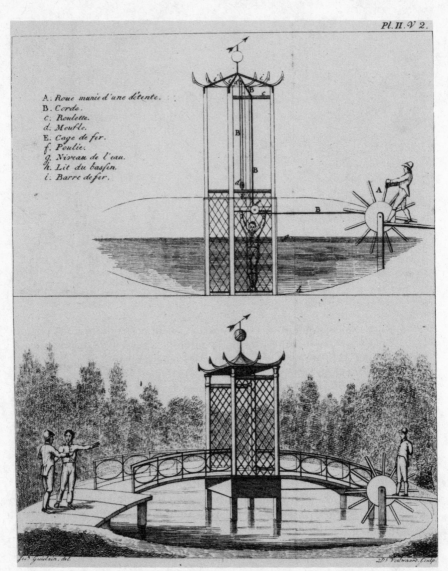

A. *Roue munie d'une détente.*
B. *Corde.*
c. *Roulette.*
d. *Moufle.*
E. *Cage de fer.*
f. *Poulie.*
g. *Niveau de l'eau.*
h. *Lit du bassin.*
i. *Barre de fer.*

Figure 4. A far more elaborate device for the application of water to the cure of madness, Guislain's so-called Chinese Temple. From: J. Guislain, *Traité sur l'aliénation mentale et sur les hospices des aliénés* (Amsterdam: Hey, 1826), vol. 2, Pl. 2. (Courtesy of the Wellcome Trustees.)

than by that of linen or cotton."[71] Paul Slade Knight endorsed the latter opinion, though he cautioned that "the clinking of the chains should be, by all means, prevented, for I have known it to impress lunatics with the most gloomy apprehension."[72]

Perhaps the most famous contrivance of all at the time was Joseph Mason Cox's swinging device (Figure 5). The idea for it had come from Erasmus Darwin, who in turn had derived it from classical suggestions about the value of swinging as a therapy.[73] But Cox was the first to develop a working model, and his book describing its construction and use[74] rapidly went through three English editions, as well as appearing in an American and a German edition; his device was recommended by Knight as "a machine that should be easily accessible in every asylum for Lunatics."[75]

Like Rush's tranquillizer, the swing acted simultaneously on both physiological and mental levels, allowing the physician to exploit "the sympathy or reciprocity of action that subsists between mind and body." In the application of this sovereign remedy, each became "in its turn the agent, and the subject acted on, as when fear, terror, anger, and other passions, excited by the action of the swing, produce various alterations in the body, and where the revolving motion, occasioning fatigue, exhaustion, pallor, horripilatio, vertigo, etc. effect [sic] new associations and trains of thought."[76] The "mechanical apparatus" provided the operator with the inestimable advantage of being able to regulate the whole process with extraordinary precision. One could, for example, vary its effects on the stomach so as to produce "either temporary or continued nausea, partial or full vomiting," and if necessary could secure "the most violent convulsions . . . the agitation and convulsion of every part of the animal frame."[77] Even the obstinate cases could not long resist its powers: if necessary it could be "employed in the dark, where,

71. Charles Dickens and W. H. Wills, "A Curious Dance Round a Curious Tree" (1852), reprinted in *Charles Dickens' Uncollected Writings from Household Words* (Bloomington and London: Indiana University Press, 1968), 2:382–83.

72. Paul Slade Knight, *Observations on the Causes, Symptoms, and Treatment of Derangement of the Mind* (London: Longman, 1827), 116.

73. Erasmus Darwin, *Zoonomia; or, The Laws of Organic Life*, 2 vols. (London: Johnson, 1796). Darwin's source was probably H. Mercurialis, *De arte gymnastica* (Amsterdam, 1672). For this reference I am indebted to Dr. Vivian Nutton.

74. Cox, *Practical Observations on Insanity*.

75. Knight, *Derangement of the Mind*, 63. See also William Saunders Hallaran, *An Inquiry into the Causes Producing the Extraordinary Addition to the Number of Insane* (Cork, Ireland: Edwards and Savage, 1810); idem, *Practical Observations on the Causes and Cure of Insanity* (Cork, Ireland: Hodges and M'Arthur, 1818).

76. Cox, *Practical Observations on Insanity*, 168–69.

77. Ibid., 143–44.

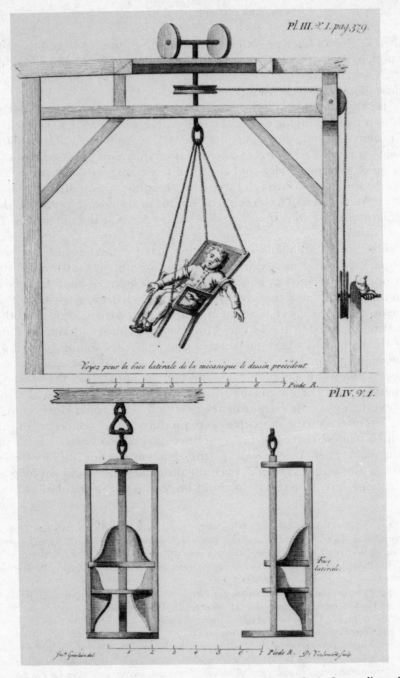

Figure 5. A rotary machine based on Cox's swing. A number of complicated variants on Cox's original design were developed in the early nineteenth century. This version was used in the Berlin Charite. From Guislain, *L'aliénation mentale*, vol. 1, Pl. 2. (Courtesy of the Wellcome Trustees.)

from unusual noises, smells, or other powerful agents, acting forcibly on the senses, its efficacy might be amazingly increased."[78] And by "increasing the velocity of the swing, the motion be[ing] suddenly reversed every six or eight minutes, pausing occasionally, and stopping its circulation suddenly: the consequence is, an instant discharge of the contents of the stomach, bowels, and bladder, in quick succession."[79]

The consequent "very violent shock both to mind and body" exhibited a wholly salutary "tendency to excite fear or terror."[80] Hallaran subsequently carried the whole process to a higher pitch of perfection, designing a seat that "supports the cervical column better, and guards against the possibility of the head in the vertiginous state from hanging over the side [sic],"[81] and placed the seat in an improved version of the apparatus so that now four patients could be treated simultaneously at speeds of up to 100 revolutions a minute. Elaborate case histories documented its immense usefulness as an agent of moral repression, reducing the most violent and perverse to a meek obedience.

Yet notwithstanding all such encomiums, the half-life of the gyrating chair proved exceedingly brief. By 1828, George Man Burrows was complaining that, despite his personal conviction of the swing's therapeutic value, public sentiment was such that he dared not make use of it, fearing lest, given "the morbid sensitivity of modern pseudo-philanthropy," any accident attending its use would leave him "universally decried, his reputation blasted, and his family ruined."[82] The authorities in Berlin and Milan had already banned its use, and it rapidly disappeared from English asylums as well.

Its demise formed part of a wider rejection of traditional modes of managing the mad (as well as the rationales underlying them) that spread ever more widely in the first half of the nineteenth century. The mixture of incomprehension and moral outrage with which formerly respectable therapeutic techniques came to be viewed was captured most vividly by Charles Dickens, who spoke scathingly of the mad-doctors' "wildly extravagant, . . . monstrously cruel monomania," their bizarre insistence "that the most violent and certain means of driving a man mad, were the only hopeful means of restoring him to reason."[83] "What sane person," he asked, "seeing, on his entrance into any place, gyves and manacles (however highly polished) yawning for his ankles and wrists; swings dangling in the air, to spin him around like an impaled cockchafer; gags and

78. Ibid., 140.
79. George Man Burrows, *Commentaries on the Causes, Forms, Symptoms, and Treatment, Moral and Medical, of Insanity* (London: Underwood, 1828), 601.
80. Cox, *Practical Observations on Insanity*, p. 170.
81. Burrows, *Commentaries on . . . Insanity*, 601.
82. Ibid., 606.
83. Dickens and Wills, "Curious Dance," 385.

strait waistcoats ready at a moment's notice to muzzle and bind him; would be likely to retain the perfect command of his sense?"[84]

It was not just the outwardly visible apparatus of physical restraint and coercion that began to lose its legitimacy (a process that culminated in Gardiner Hill and Conolly's triumphant claims to have secured the total abolition of mechanical restraint).[85] Rather, the very attempt to *tame* madness was increasingly viewed as seriously misguided. Samuel Tuke commented that by means of terror, lunatics

> may be made to obey their keepers with the greatest promptitude, to rise, to sit, to stand, to walk, or to run at their pleasure; though only expressed by a look. Such an obedience, and even the appearance of affection, we not infrequently see in the poor animals who are exhibited to gratify our curiosity in natural history; but, who can avoid reflecting, in observing such spectacles, that the readiness with which the savage tiger obeys his master, is the result of treatment at which humanity would shudder?[86]

Within the new orthodoxy, attempts to *compel* patients to think and act reasonably were themselves stigmatized as unreasonable:[87] "Intimidation and coercion may make or modify the symptoms of insanity, but can seldom produce permanently good effects."[88]

The nineteenth-century domestication of madness proceeded in a wholly different direction, reducing rage and despair to at least a simulacrum of moderation, order, and lawfulness[89] and transforming the imagery of confinement from the "pigstyes"[90] in which, as Wynter put it, the mad had been "hung from their fetters and chains on the wall like vermin chained to a barn door,"[91] to the peaceful Potemkin villages that were Conolly's and W. A. F. Browne's vision of what asylums "are and ought to be."[92] Here

84. Ibid. In similar language, Samuel Tuke had earlier condemned "those swingings, whirlings, suspensions, half-drownings and other violent expedients by which some physicians have sought to frighten the unhappy subject into reason, or at least into subjection" (Introductory observations to M. Jacobi, *On the Construction and Management of Hospitals for the Insane* (London: Churchill, 1841), 54.

85. Robert Gardner Hill, *A Lecture on the Management of Lunatic Asylums and the Treatment of the Insane* (London: Simpkin, Marshall, 1839); John Conolly, *The Treatment of the Insane Without Mechanical Restraints* (London: Smith, Elder, 1856).

86. Samuel Tuke, *Description of the Retreat: An Institution near York for Insane Persons of the Society of Friends* (1813), facsimile ed., ed. Richard A. Hunter and Ida Macalpine (London: Dawsons, 1964), 147–48.

87. John Conolly, in *Hanwell Lunatic Asylum Annual Report, 1840*, 55–56, 70.

88. T. Harrington Tuke, "On warm and cold baths in the treatment of insanity," *Journal of Mental Science* 5 (1858): 102.

89. Jacobi, *Hospitals for the Insane.*

90. House of Commons, *Report of the Select Committee on Madhouses in England* (1815), 21, evidence of Henry Alexander.

91. Andrew Wynter, *The Borderlands of Insanity* (London: Hardwicke, 1875), 85.

92. W. A. F. Browne, *What Asylums Were, Are and Ought to Be* (Edinburgh: Black, 1837).

calmness will come; hope will revive; satisfaction will prevail; . . . almost all disposition to meditate mischievous or fatal revenge, or self-destruction, will disappear; . . . cleanliness and decency will be maintained or restored; and despair itself will sometimes be found to give place to cheerfulness or secure tranquility. [This is the place] where humanity, if anywhere on earth, shall reign supreme.[93]

In the new iconography, madness was reined in amid the comforts of domesticity by the invisible yet infinitely potent fetters of the sufferer's own "desire for esteem," complemented by the benevolent authoritarianism of the asylum superintendent and the healthful influences of the new moral architecture.

A quasi-mythical scene recurs repeatedly: a maniac is brought to the asylum gates, frenzied, furious, exhibiting all the signs of dangerous and violent alienation, and in consequence laden with irons and chains. The alienist appears, and in the face of assurances from the man's captors that release will mean certain death for the bystanders, calmly orders that the bonds be discarded and leads the lamblike madman into dinner. "I treat them," said Thomas Bakewell, "exactly as I should do if they were not afflicted with that disease, and, in return, they almost uniformly behave as if nothing was the matter with them."[94]

"Language and actions" were once more to "become subordinate to a well-regulated will"[95] by inducing the madman to control himself. A person's madness was not to be reasoned with or refuted—a useless, even dangerous endeavor. Its content was ignored; its existence the lunatic had to be taught to suppress.[96]

93. John Conolly, *On the Construction and Government of Lunatic Asylums* (London: Churchill, 1847), 143.

94. Bakewell, *Domestic Guide*, 57. See also T. O. Prichard in *The Northampton Lunatic Asylum Annual Report, 1840;* and Tuke, *Description of the Retreat.*

95. Conolly, in *Hanwell . . . Report, 1840*, 70–71.

96. In Bakewell's words, "The effects of strong mental feelings are not to be counteracted by the conceptions of thought that arise from argument . . . in our endeavours to counteract the erroneous thoughts of lunatics we are not to expect anything but mischief, from the powers of argument, upon their particular hallucinations; all we can do is to promote a new train of mental images" (Bakewell, *Domestic Guide*, 38). Cf. Samuel Tuke's comment "No advantage has been found to arise from reasoning with them on their particular hallucinations. . . . In regard to melancholics, conversation on the subject of their despondency is found to be highly injudicious. The very opposite method is pursued. Every means is taken to seduce the mind from its favorite but unhappy musings, by bodily exercise, walks, conversation, reading, and other innocent recreations" (Tuke, *Description of the Retreat,* 151–52). In some respects, then, the proponents of moral treatment agreed with those wedded to more traditional approaches. For as we have seen, eighteenth-century physicians also thought that the successful treatment of madness was dependent on the therapist's possession of the capacity "of the artful association of ideas and of the art of breaking false or unnatural associations, or inducing counter-associations" (John Gregory, *A Comparative View of the State and Faculties of Man with Those of the Animal World* [London:

Central to the new approach, as I argue at more length in Chapter 4, was the internalization of control,[97] a goal that necessarily entailed a move away from a regime of undifferentiated restraint and fear. It required instead the recognition of the lunatic's sensibility and the acknowledgment (in a highly limited and circumscribed sense) of his status as a moral subject. Contrary to previous practice, the madman must not be addressed "in a childish, or . . . domineering manner,"[98] for this approach threatened to subvert the effort to rouse his "moral feelings," and to use these as "a sort of moral discipline."[99] As Bakewell put it, "Certainly authority and order must be maintained, but these are better maintained by kindness, condescension, and indulgent attention, than by any severities whatever. Lunatics are not devoid of understanding, nor should they be treated as if they were; on the contrary, they should be treated as rational beings."[100]

They were also to be treated in an environment that was self-consciously domestic in a more conventional sense. There was a tireless insistence that the inmates of an asylum were a family, and that the discipline to which they were subject "naturally arises from the necessary regulations of the family."[101] And this fictional domesticity was tenaciously maintained (linguistically at least) even after the thirty patients of Tuke's Retreat had become the 1,000 or more that swarmed into the burgeoning county asylum: Conolly moving among the hordes at Hanwell is described as "like a father among his children, speaking a word of comfort to one, cheering another, and exercising a kindly and humane influence over all."[102]

As this description suggests, the asylum regime in practice was no more than a grotesque caricature of the domestic circle: and the insis-

---

Dodsley, 1765], 186–88). What changed were notions about the *way* these goals were to be realized. (In view of the connection often made between the adoption of Lockean views on the nature and sources of insanity and the reliance on "mild" forms of treatment, it is perhaps worth noting that proponents of the older, heroic approach could with equal justice have defended their practices on Lockean grounds. For example, Locke's emphasis on the direct relationship between the strength of a particular sensation and the vividness of any given idea could be readily coupled with the notion that the cure of madness required the supersession of defective learned patterns of thought to legitimize the most extreme versions of therapeutic terror. The very existence of these diametrically opposed "implications" of Locke's ideas surely points up the limitations of any purely internalist account of changing responses to madness.)

97. Andrew Scull, *Museums of Madness: The Social Organization of Insanity in Nineteenth Century England* (London, Allen Lane, 1979). See also Chapter 4 of the present volume.

98. Tuke, *Description of the Retreat*, 159.

99. Bakewell, *Domestic Guide*, 59.

100. Ibid., 55–56. See also Benjamin Faulkner, *Observations on the General and Improper Treatment of Insanity* (London: Reynell, 1789), passim.

101. Tuke, *Description of the Retreat*, 141.

102. Wynter, *Borderlands of Insanity*, 108, quoting Forbes Winslow.

tence on the domestic imagery is the more ironic inasmuch as it coincides with the decisive removal of madness from family life.[103] But certainly insanity now assumed a more placid, less threatening garb, so much so that there were suggestions that "insanity has undergone a change, and that, whilst there is an increase in the number of cases of the disease, there is happily a marked diminution of its most formidable modification, furious mania."[104] Those running the asylums naturally preferred to see the change as an illustration of "the mildness and tractability of its forms under a humane and rational direction"[105] and to urge, with Conolly, that "mania, not exasperated by severity, and melancholia, not deepened by the want of all ordinary consolations, lose the exaggerated character in which they were formerly beheld."[106]

If cures swiftly proved beyond its reach in all but a small minority of cases, the asylum regime at least provided the public with symbolic demonstrations that the disturbing and dangerous manifestations of madness were firmly under control; that the disorderly could be rendered tranquil and tractable. Tuke's famous image of the inmates of the Retreat calmly sipping tea and exchanging social pleasantries found its echo in the county asylum reports of the mid-century. At Hanwell on the occasion of the Matron's birthday, 200 patients

> assembled in Ward Number 10, the decoration of which had previously afforded amusing occupation to some of them. They drank tea in the Airing Court, and were afterwards allowed to amuse themselves by dancing in the galleries, a piano having been removed thither for the purpose. It is impossible to image a more happy party. The utmost liveliness was combined with perfect good behavior. . . . Soon after eight o'clock they joined in singling the Evening Hymn, and returned, with perfect order, and many grateful expressions, to their respective wards.[107]

The mad could even be granted the consolation and the "indulgence of going to Chapel." Once again, they could be relied upon to preserve a perfect decorum. Indeed,

> so accustomed are the Patients to preserve their composure during the hour of service, that if, as sometimes happens, an Epileptic patient utters a loud scream, falls into a fit, and requires to be taken out by the keepers or nurses, very few of the Patients quit their seats; and those in the immediate neighbourhood of the person affected usually render what assistance they can, and then quietly resume their places.[108]

103. Scull, *Museums of Madness.*
104. Cited in *Northampton Lunatic Asylum Annual Report, 1840.*
105. T. O. Prichard, in ibid.
106. John Conolly, cited in Sir James Clark, *A Memoir of John Conolly* (London: Murray, 1869), 28.
107. Conolly, in *Hanwell . . . Report, 1840,* 79.
108. Ibid., 86–87.

Figure 6. A view of the Men's Gallery, Bedlam, in 1860. From: *The Illustrated London News* 36 (March 31, 1860): 308. (Courtesy of the Wellcome Trustees.)

Soon the public no longer had to take such portraits on trust. As they had been allowed in to view the menagerie at Bedlam a century earlier, so they were now invited (albeit under more restricted and controlled conditions) to move across the boundary wall of the asylum that divided the mad from the sane (Figure 6). And once inside, the question that most frequently occurred was, where were all the mad people?[109] In Elaine Showalter's words, "Madness was no longer a gross and unmistakable inversion of appropriate conduct, but a collection of disquieting gestures and postures."[110] Even the forces of sexuality had been successfully brought under control.[111] Mid-Victorian asylums usually enforced a

109. In Harrington Tuke's words, "The very type of the malady seemed to be changed; fearful, raving, desperate struggling, and maniacal excitement, heretofore the ordinary symptoms of mental disease, were now seldom seen. . . . The aspect and demeanor of the patients became so altered, that a foreign physician visiting the asylum, after seeing all its inmates, gravely inquired 'where all the real lunatics were confined?'" (Harrington Tuke, "Address of the President of the British Medical Association, Section of Psychology," *British Medical Journal*, October 1873, reprinted as a separate pamphlet, 4–5. See also, for example, *Athenaeum*, 1842, 65–66; *Illustrated Times*, 29 December 1859, quoted in Elaine Showalter, "Victorian Women and Insanity," in *Madhouses, Mad-Doctors, and Madmen: The Social History of Psychiatry in the Victorian Era*, ed. Andrew Scull (London: Athlone Press, 1981), 314; Dickens and Wills, "A Curious Dance."

110. Showalter, "Victorian Women and Insanity," 314.

111. As Wynter put it, "The decorous and regulated intercourse of the sexes is in itself a valuable lesson in self control" (Wynter, *Borderlands of Insanity*, 113).

Figure 7. A lunatics' ball at the Somerset County Asylum, with the superintendent, Robert Boyd, in the foreground. The "ballroom" is a converted kitchen. Reproduction of a lithograph by Katherine Drake (circa 1848). (Courtesy of the Wellcome Trustees.)

monastic segregation of the sexes. (The Lunacy Commissioners even complained when the "deadhouse" at the Cambridge County Asylum was shared by corpses of the opposite sex.[112]) But one exception to this policy was the lunatics' ball (Figure 7), a monthly (sometimes weekly) event in most asylums, and an event frequently used to display the asylum's achievements to outsiders:

> On the occasion of our visit there were about 200 patients present. . . . In a raised orchestra, five musicians, three of whom were lunatics, soon struck up a merry polka, and immediately the room was alive with dancers. . . . Had the men been differently dressed, it would have been impossible to have guessed that we were in the midst of a company of lunatics, the mere sweepings of the parish workhouses; but the prison uniform of sad coloured grey appeared like a jarring note amid the general harmony of the scene. . . . At nine precisely, although in the midst of a dance, a shrill note is blown and the entire assembly like so many Cinderellas, breaks up at once and the company hurry off to their dormitories.[113]

Madness domesticated (in my second sense) was madness tamed, and more effectively than the eighteenth century could ever have imagined.

112. *Commissioners in Lunacy Annual Report*, Vol. 25 (1861), 131.
113. 'Lunatic asylums,' *Quarterly Review* 101 (1857): 375–76.

CHAPTER FOUR

Moral Treatment Reconsidered

Traditional histories of psychiatry saw in moral treatment the first of a series of "revolutions" that transformed social responses to the mentally ill, rescuing them from viciousness and neglect and ushering in a humane and rational response to the problems posed by mental disorder. The work of modern revisionists, from Foucault onwards, has on one level exhibited a fascinating convergence with these old-fashioned directionalist histories, accepting that moral treatment represents a decisive epistemological break in the history of Western responses to madness. But, of course, the revisionists have evaluated this rupture very differently and have sought to comprehend its origins and analyze its nature in very different ways.

The initial polemical excesses of Foucault's own reassessment, which simply stood the traditional interpretation on its head (urging that one see moral treatment as a "gigantic moral imprisonment"),[1] have been succeeded by a more complex and balanced view: a perspective that can recognize why one might reasonably prefer the manipulation and ambiguous "kindness" of Tuke and Pinel to the "coercion for the outward man, and rabid physicking for the inward man" that were for an earlier generation "the specifics for lunacy,"[2] but a perspective that is nevertheless aware of moral treatment's less benevolent aspects and its latent po-

Chapter 4 is reprinted from *Psychological Medicine*, Volume 9, 1979, pp. 421–28, by permission of the editor and of Cambridge University Press.

1. Michel Foucault, *Madness and Civilization* (New York: Pantheon, 1965), 278.
2. Charles Dickens and W. H. Wills, "A Curious Dance Round a Curious Tree" (1852; reprinted in *Charles Dickens' Uncollected Writings from Household Words* [Bloomington and London: Indiana University Press, 1968], 2:382–83).

tential (all too soon realized) for deterioration into a repressive form of moral management.

The essay that follows represents my attempt, a decade ago, to grapple with a number of central and interrelated questions: How are we to make sense of traditional approaches to the mad, and in what do these consist? What, penetrating beneath the ideological accounts offered by the reformers themselves, are we to make of moral treatment? And, given the importance of the change it represents, how can we grasp its broader social roots and significance?

Since this paper appeared, Anne Digby has published a full-length study of the York Retreat, based on extensive and painstaking research in that institution's voluminous archives.[3] Her general assessment of the social origins, context, and significance of Tuke's version of moral treatment closely parallels (indeed is clearly indebted to) that offered here and in Chapter 3, though her subsequent analysis greatly broadens our understanding of the subsequent course of events at the Retreat and of the multiple ways in which the specifically Quaker character of the foundation influenced its unfolding history.

As I emphasize in what follows, even in an English context Tuke's was not an isolated achievement. Though it was the Retreat that made moral treatment famous in England, by the last years of the eighteenth century a number of madhouse proprietors were experimenting with generally similar approaches (just as, on the Continent, there were independent "discoveries" of the principles of moral treatment). Roy Porter, who has recently provided the first systematic synthesis of the history of madness in England from the late seventeenth to the early nineteenth century,[4] has cited the work of these other progenitors of moral treatment (among whom he numbers such figures as William Pargeter, John Ferriar, and Joseph Mason Cox) in support of a bold thesis: a rejection of the consensus (among traditionalist and revisionist alike) that "the eighteenth century was a disaster for the insane"[5] and a claim that Tuke's institution marked no radical switch in the handling of the mad, but rather exhibited substantial continuities with the practices of an earlier age.[6] Though I do not have the space to provide a detailed refutation here (and this is scarcely the occasion to do so), I think Porter is largely mistaken about

3. Anne Digby, *Madness, Morality, and Medicine: A Study of the York Retreat, 1796–1914* (Cambridge: Cambridge University Press, 1985); see also idem, "Moral Treatment at the Retreat, 1796–1846," in *The Anatomy of Madness*, 2 vols., ed. W. F. Bynum, R. Porter and M. Shepherd (London: Tavistock, 1985), 2:52–72.

4. Roy Porter, *Mind Forg'd Manacles: A History of Madness in England from the Restoration to the Regency* (London: Athlone, 1987).

5. Michael MacDonald, *Mystical Bedlam: Madness, Anxiety, and Healing in Seventeenth Century England* (Cambridge: Cambridge University Press, 1981), 230.

6. Ibid., 277 and passim.

these matters.[7] Still, his book provides us with the most provocative and wide-ranging survey of Georgian madness we are likely to see for many years to come.

Moral Treatment Reconsidered

What most sharply distinguishes a propagandistic from an ideological presentation and interpretation of the facts is . . . that its falsification and mystification of the truth are always conscious and intentional. Ideology, on the other hand, is mere deception—in essence self-deception—never simply lies and deceit. It obscures truth in order not so much to mislead others as to maintain and increase the self-confidence of those who express and benefit from such deceptions.

—ARNOLD HAUSER,
The Social History of Art

The glory of the modern system [of asylum treatment] is repression by mildness and coaxing, and by solitary confinement.

—JOHN THOMAS PERCEVAL,
Letters to Sir James Graham upon the Reform of the Lunacy Law

TUKE AND MORAL TREATMENT

We are all familiar with that traditional version of psychiatric history that celebrates it as a not always continuous, but ultimately triumphal procession toward the rational and humane forms of treatment presently practiced. In such accounts, the introduction of moral treatment always occupies a central place of honor: the legendary decision by Pinel to strike the chains from the raving maniacs in the Bicêtre; and the less dramatic but equally significant endeavors of William Tuke to provide humane care for insane Quakers at the York Retreat. It is with moral treatment that I shall be concerned in this essay. I shall try to explicate some of the central dimensions of its English version and to explore some of

7. To cite just one problem with his argument, Thomas Arnold, Thomas Bakewell, Joseph Mason Cox, John Ferriar, William Perfect, and others, whose writings he uses to demonstrate that the treatment of the mad in the *eighteenth* century varied from the portrait drawn by previous historians, were all active in the period from the late 1780s through the first decade and a half of the nineteenth century. They can tell us little about practice in the era before moral treatment or (come to that) about eighteenth-century responses to madness. And Porter's further claim that William Battie (who *did* practice in the 1750s and 1760s) propounded "(albeit in a rather schematic and theoretical guise) the key ideas of Tukean moral therapy" (Porter, *Mind Forg'd Manacles,* 276) is an example, to use his own words, of the historian playing "silly priority games" and anachronistically reading the future back into the past.

its broader social roots and significance. For I take it that one of the more important contributions that a sociologist can make to the history of psychiatry is to break down some of the parochialism that marks most treatments of the subject and to show some of its connections with larger social movements and processes.

Tuke's development of moral treatment was not, of course, an isolated achievement, even in England. A number of other practitioners in the "mad-business" were experimenting with essentially similar approaches by the end of the eighteenth century. John Ferriar of the Manchester Lunatic Asylum had become convinced that "the first salutary operation in the mind of a lunatic" lay in "creating a habit of self-restraint," a goal that might be reached by "the management of hope and apprehension . . . , small favours, the show of confidence, and apparent distinction," rather than by coercion.[1] And to cite just one other example, Edward Long Fox,[2] from whose Bristol madhouse Tuke recruited Katherine Allen (the Retreat's first matron), independently developed a system of classification and mild management that allowed the elimination of most of the "barbarous" and "objectionable" features found in most contemporary asylums. But it was Tuke's version of moral treatment that attracted attention, first from a stream of visitors, both English and foreign, and then from those Parliamentarians and others who had taken up the cause of lunacy reform. So it is to his work that I wish to give most of my attention, while recognizing that it forms part of a much broader shift in the methods used to comprehend and cope with madness.

TRADITIONAL APPROACHES TO MADNESS

From a number of perspectives, I think Tuke's admirers are quite right to stress that his approach marked a serious rupture with the past, rather than simply a refinement and improvement of existing techniques. They go astray, however, when they accept at face value the account that Tuke and his followers provide of their activities. The advent of moral treatment is both something more and something less than "the triumph of humanism and of therapy, a recognition that kindness, reason, and tactful manipulation were more effective in dealing with the inmates of asylums than were fear, brutal coercion and restraint, and medical therapy."[3] It will not do simply to assert that Tuke replaced *im*moral with moral therapy; or to attribute the reformers' achievements to their superior

1. J. Ferriar, *Medical Histories and Reflections*, vol. 2 (London: Cadell and Davies, 1975).

2. E. L. Fox, *Brislington House, an Asylum for Lunatics Situated near Bristol, Lately Erected by Edward Long Fox, M.D.* (Bristol: For the Author, 1806).

3. William F. Bynum, "Rationales for Therapy in British Psychiatry: 1780–1835," *Medical History* 18 (1974):318.

moral sensibilities, while consigning their opponents to the status of moral lepers, people devoid of common decency and humanity.

On the contrary, the perception that the traditional ways of coping with lunatics in madhouses (even such tactics as the use of whips and chains to maintain a semblance of order) were inherently cruel and in-humane is by no means as simple and self-evident a judgment as both the reformers and later generations came to believe. The practices of the eighteenth-century madhouse keepers seem so transparently callous and brutal that we tend to take this judgment as unproblematic, as imme-diately given to any and all who have occasion to view such actions. But cruelty, like deviance, "is not a quality which lies in behavior itself, but in the interaction between the person who commits an act and those who respond to it." [4] Consequently, whether or not a set of practices is per-ceived as inhumane depends, in large part, on the world view of the per-son who is doing the perceiving. Practices from which we now recoil in horror were once advocated by the most eminent physicians and cul-tured men of their day. That the mad were chained and whipped in asy-lums in the eighteenth century was well known at the time. How could it be otherwise when, throughout the century, the doors of Bethlem were open to the public and the inmates exhibited to satisfy the impertinent curiosity of sightseers at a mere penny a time, and when standard trea-tises on the management of the mad advocated such treatment? Cer-tainly, such practices were not something of which magistrates only be-came aware at the turn of the century. Yet it was only then that protests began to be heard that such treatment was cruel and inhumane.

To be sure, some of the treatment meted out to lunatics in private mad-houses was the natural product of an unregulated free market in madness—the consequence of the unchecked cupidity of the least scru-pulous, of the incentives to half-starve and neglect pauper inmates, of the temptation to rely on force as the least troublesome form of control. But there is more to it than that. Even in situations where such factors were obviously inapplicable, lunatics were treated in ways that later gen-erations were to condemn as barbaric and counterproductive and to find (as we do) virtually incomprehensible, almost by default attributing them to an underdeveloped moral sensibility, if not outright inhumanity.

The treatment of George III during his recurrent bouts of "mania" perhaps makes this point most dramatically and unambiguously. As By-num has pointed out,

> A great deal was at stake with this patient, and there is every reason to be-lieve that Francis Willis, his sons, and other assistants treated the king in a manner which (in Willis' considered opinion) would most likely result in

4. H. S. Becker, *Outsiders: Studies in the Sociology of Deviance* (Glencoe, Ill.: Free Press, 1963), 14.

the royal patient's recovery. Yet, as the Countess Harcourt described the situation, "The unhappy patient . . . was no longer treated as a human being. His body was immediately encased in a machine which left no liberty of motion. He was sometimes chained to a stake. He was frequently beaten and starved, and at best he was kept in subjection by menacing and violent language."[5]

Willis' approach was scarcely atypical. The eighteenth-century "trade in lunacy"[6] attracted a motley crew; but despite the heterogeneity of those engaged in the business, certain traditional approaches and techniques were widely employed—by medical and nonmedical men alike. As with the king, intimidation, threats, and outright coercion were commonly used to cow and subdue the madman, whose condition was viewed as a "display of fury and violence to be subdued and conquered by stripes, chains, and lowering treatments."[7] Most madhouse keepers operated on the assumption that "fear [was] the most effectual principle by which to reduce the insane to orderly conduct,"[8] on the grounds that it was "a passion that diminishes excitement . . . particularly the angry and irascible excitement of maniacs."[9] As eminent a man as William Cullen argued that it was "necessary to employ a very constant impression of fear, . . . awe and dread"—emotions that should be aroused by "all restraints that may occasionally be proper . . . even by stripes and blows."[10] Together with a more elaborate and sophisticated intellectual rationalization of these procedures, medicine simply provided its practitioners with a wider variety of tools for "coercing patients into straight thinking and accepting reason . . . 'vomits, purges, . . . surprize baths, copious bleedings and meagre diets.'"[11]

Within a few years of the Retreat's practices obtaining national attention, such treatment (or at least its open avowal) had come to seem unthinkable. The fundamental basis of this whole approach—the subjugation of the mad, the breaking of the will by means of external discipline and constraint, the almost literal battle between reason and unreason— had lost its former appearance of self-evidence and, indeed, was now

5. Bynum, "Rationales for Therapy," 319.

6. W. L. Parry-Jones, *The Trade in Lunacy* (London: Routledge and Kegan Paul, 1972).

7. Richard Hunter and Ida Macalpine, *Three Hundred Years of Psychiatry, 1535 to 1860: A History Presented in Selected English Texts* (London: Oxford University Press, 1963), 475.

8. Samuel Tuke, Manuscript memorandum of a visit to St. Luke's Hospital, 1812, reprinted in Daniel Hack Tuke, *Chapters in the History of the Insane in the British Isles,* (London: Kegan Paul and Trench, 1882), 90.

9. William Cullen, *First Lines of the Practice of Physic* (Edinburgh: Bell and Bradfute, 1784), quoted in Hunter and Macalpine, *Three Hundred Years of Psychiatry,* 478.

10. Ibid. Where such physical force was deemed necessary, he cautioned that stripes, "although having the appearance of more severity, are much safer than strokes or blows about the head" (ibid.).

11. Ibid., 475.

seen as wholly inappropriate. I would suggest that a necessary condition for the emergence of such a changed perspective (and of the moral outrage that did so much to animate the lunacy reformers' activities) was a change in the cultural meaning of madness. And I think that such a change can indeed be shown to have occurred.

If, in seventeenth- and eighteenth-century practice, the madman in confinement was treated no better than a beast, that merely reflected his ontological status. For that was precisely what, according to the prevailing paradigm of insanity, he was. One of the most notable features of the prenineteenth-century literature on madness is

> its almost exclusive emphasis on disturbances of the *reason*, or the higher intellectual faculties of man. Insanity was conceived as a derangement of those very faculties which were widely assumed to be universal to man; as a matter of fact, we sometimes find in the literature the presumed absence in animals of any condition analogous to insanity taken as proof that man's highest psychological function results from some principle totally lacking in other animals, that is, the soul.[12]

But this conception implied that in losing his reason, the essence of his humanity, the madman had lost his claim to be treated as a human being.

Intellectually, such notions did no violence to the dominant world view of the period. Indeed, they could be seen as a confirmation of perhaps its critical organizing principle—the idea of the continuity and gradation of nature in what Arthur Lovejoy has termed "the Great Chain of Being."[13] The very idea of a chain, with no discontinuities or gaps, implied that no rigid barriers existed between one part of creation and another, that there always existed intermediate forms. The division between apes and men was a permeable, not an absolute, one in eighteenth-century conceptions of nature, as attested by the denial of the concept of common humanity to a slave; the ready identification of apes and savages (even extending to speculation on fertile copulation between blacks and apes); the portrayal of criminals in animalistic terms; and the assimilation of the mad to the ranks of brute creation. As Bynum puts it, such notions were "built into the analytic tools with which eighteenth century Europeans classified man."[14] And in the case of lunatics, the apparent insensitivity of the furious maniac to heat or cold, hunger or pain, his refusal to abide clothing, and so on, were simply taken as confirmation of the correctness of the basic explanatory schema.

If a sociologist may be permitted to cite literary evidence in support of his case, it may be noted that Ophelia, in her madness, is described as

12. Bynum, "Rationales for Therapy," 320.

13. A. O. Lovejoy, *The Great Chain of Being* (New York: Harper, 1960).

14. William F. Bynum, "Time's Noblest Offspring: The Problem of Man in the British Natural Historical Sciences" (Ph.D. dissertation, University of Cambridge, 1974), 344.

Divided from herself and her fair judgement,
Without which we are pictures [i.e., no more than external facsimiles of
human beings] or mere beasts.[15]

In a similar vein, Pascal informs us, "I can easily conceive of a man without hands, feet, head (for it is only experience which teaches us that the head is more necessary than the feet). But I cannot conceive of a man without thought; that would be a stone or a brute."[16] "Expert" opinion concurs. John Monro, the physician to Bethlem from 1751 to 1791 and one of the two most eminent mad-doctors of the mid-eighteenth century, speaks of madness as involving "a total suspension of every rational faculty";[17] just as Andrew Snape, almost half a century earlier, had lamented "those unhappy People, who are bereft of the dearest Light, the Light of Reason."[18] In a revealing passage, Snape then goes on to say:

> Distraction . . . divests the rational soul of all its noble and distinguishing Endowments, and sinks unhappy Man below the mute and senseless Part of Creation: even brutal Instinct being a surer and safer guide than disturb'd Reason, and every tame Species of Animals more sociable and less hurtful than humanity thus unmann'd.[19]

Eminent mad-doctors of the early nineteenth century continued to adhere to this position, arguing that "if the possession of reason be the proud attribute of man, its diseases must be ranked among our greatest afflictions, since they sink us from our preeminence to a level with the animal creatures."[20]

I suggest that the resort to fear, force, and coercion is a tactic entirely appropriate to the management of "brutes." Thus, when we look at the treatment of the insane prior to "reform," we must realize, as Foucault points out, that

> the negative fact that the madman is not treated like a "human being" has a very positive meaning. . . . For classicism, madness in its ultimate form is man in immediate relation to his animality. The day would come when from an evolutionary perspective this presence of animality in madness would be considered as the sign—indeed the very essence—of disease. In

15. William Shakespeare, *Hamlet*, act 4, sc. 5, lines 85–86.

16. Blaise Pascal, *Oeuvres Complètes* (Paris: Gallimard, 1954), 1156.

17. John Monro, *Remarks on Dr. Battie's Treatise on Madness* (London: Clarke, 1758), 7.

18. Andrew Snape, *A Sermon Preach'd Before the Lord Mayor, the Alderman, Sheriffs and Gouvenours of the Several Hospitals of the City of London, April 16, 1718* (London: Bowyer, 1718), 15.

19. Ibid., 9–10. Elsewhere, he speaks of madmen who, with their "apish Gestures," prove that "something with a Human Shape and Voice may for many years survive all that was human besides" (ibid., 10).

20. Joseph Mason Cox, *Practical Observations on Insanity*, 3d ed. (London: Baldwin and Murray, 1813), ix.

the classical period, on the contrary, it manifested the very fact that *the madman was not a sick man*. Animality in fact, protected the lunatic from whatever might be fragile, precarious, or sickly in man. . . . Unchained animality could be mastered only by *discipline* and *brutalizing*.[21]

THE RUPTURE WITH THE PAST

It was this worldview that the nineteenth-century reformers and, indeed, society as a whole, were in the process of abandoning. Much of the reformers' revulsion on being exposed to conditions in contemporary madhouses derived from this changed perspective. For them, the lunatic was no longer an animal, stripped of all remnants of humanity.[22] On the contrary, he remained in essence a man; a man lacking in self-restraint and order, but a man for all that. Moreover, the qualities he lacked might and must be restored to him, so that he could once more function as a sober, rational citizen.

The beliefs that lie at the heart of the new approach to the insane— Tuke's moral treatment, as well as the much less well known equivalents developed by his contemporaries—differ so profoundly from those underlying traditional practices as to lend some credence to Michel Foucault's notion of a "rupture épistemologique." At the core of the eighteenth-century approach, as we have seen, was its view that the essence of madness was the absence, or the total perversion, of reason. "In the new system of moral treatment," by contrast, "madmen are not held to be absolutely deprived of their reason."[23] Tuke's whole system crucially depends upon "treating the patient as much in the manner of a rational being as the state of his mind will possibly allow"—a change so striking that it attracted much contemporary comment. In Sydney Smith's words, "It does not appear to them that because a man is mad upon one subject, that he is to be considered in a state of complete mental degradation, or insensible to feelings of gratitude."[24]

The emphasis on the lunatics' sensitivity to many of the same inducements and emotions to which other people were prone was associated, whether as cause or consequence, with other equally profound alterations in their treatment. What was seen as perhaps the most striking,

21. Michel Foucault, *Madness and Civilization* (New York: Pantheon, 1965), 66–69.

22. Cf. John Reid's complaint that in "either the public, or the minor and more clandestine Bethlems . . . such a mode of management is used with men, as ought not to be, although it too generally is, applied even to brutes," in *Essays on Hypochondriasis and Other Nervous Affections*, 3d ed. (London: Longman, 1823), 60.

23. G. De la Rive, *Lettre adressée aux rédacteurs de la Bibliothèque britannique sur un nouvel établissement pour la guérison des aliénés* (Geneva: For the Author, 1798), quoted in Kathleen Jones, *Lunacy, Law, and Conscience: The Social History of the Care of the Insane* (London: Routledge and Kegan Paul, 1955), 61.

24. S. Smith, "An Account of the York Retreat," *Edinburgh Review* 23 (1814): 189–98.

both at the time and subsequently, was the emphasis on minimizing external, physical coercion—an emphasis that has had much to do with the interpretation of moral treatment as unproblematically kind and humane. William Cullen articulated the eighteenth-century consensus when he contended:

> Restraining the anger and violence of madmen is always necessary for preventing their hurting themselves or others; but this restraint is also to be considered as a remedy. Angry passions are always rendered more violent by the indulgence of the impetuous notions they produce; and even in madmen, the feeling of restraint will sometimes prevent the efforts which their passion would otherwise occasion. Restraint, therefore, is useful and ought to be complete.[25]

Tuke's dissent from this position was sharp and unequivocal: "Neither chains nor corporal punishment are tolerated, on any pretext, in this establishment."[26] Less objectionable forms of restraint might be necessary to prevent bodily injury, but they ought to be a last resort and must never be imposed solely for the convenience of the attendants. As a routine policy, those running an asylum ought "to endeavor to govern rather by the influence of esteem than of severity." The insistence upon "the superior efficacy . . . of a mild system of treatment," together with the elimination of "gyves, chains and manacles,"[27] had a profound effect on contemporary reformers, who saw Tuke's success at the Retreat as proof that the insane could be managed without what were now seen as harshness and cruelty.

Tuke's approach was not kindness for kindness' sake. From its architecture to its domestic arrangements, the Retreat was designed to encourage the individual's own efforts to reassert his powers of self-control. For instead of merely resting content with the outward control of those who were no longer quite human (which had been the dominant concern of traditional responses to the mad), moral treatment actively sought to *transform* the lunatic, to remodel him into something approximating the bourgeois ideal of the rational individual. From this viewpoint, the problem with external coercion was that it could force outward conformity, but never the necessary internalization of moral standards. The change in aim mandated a change in means. Granted, "it takes less trouble to fetter by means of cords, than by assiduities of sympathy or affection."[28] But "the natural tendency of such treatment is, to degrade the mind of the patient, and to make him indifferent to those moral feelings, which, under judicious direction and encouragement, are found capable, in no small degree, to strengthen the power of self-

25. Cullen, *Practice of Physic* (1808 ed.), 2 : 312–13.
26. Tuke, *History of the Insane*, 141.   27. Ibid., vi. 171.
28. Reid, *Hypochondria*, 303.   29. Tuke, *History of the Insane*, 159–160.

restraint."[29] On purely *instrumental* grounds, then, "tenderness is better than torture, kindness more effectual than constraint. . . . Nothing has a more favourable and controlling influence over one who is disposed to or actually affected with melancholy or mania, than an exhibition of friendship or philanthropy."[30] Only thus could one hope to reeducate the patient to discipline himself. By acting as though "patients are capable of rational and honourable inducement" and by making use of the vital weapon of man's *"desire for esteem"* (which even lunatics were now seen as sharing), inmates could be induced to collaborate in their own recapture by the forces of reason. "When properly cultivated," the desire to look well in others' eyes "leads many to struggle to conceal and overcome their morbid propensities: and, at least, materially assists them in confining their deviations within such bounds, as do not make them obnoxious to the family."[31]

The staff played a vital role in this process of reeducation: they must "treat the patients on the fundamental principles of . . . kindness and consideration."[32] Again, this was not because these were goods in themselves, but because

> whatever tends to promote the happiness of the patient, is found to increase his desire to restrain himself, by exciting the wish not to forfeit his enjoyments; and lessening the irritation of mind which too frequently accompanies mental derangement. . . . The comfort of the patients is therefore considered of the highest importance in a curative point of view.[33]

Here, too, lay the value of work, the other major cornerstone of moral treatment, since "of all the modes by which patients may be induced to restrain themselves, regular employment is perhaps the most generally efficacious."[34]

By all reasonable standards, the Retreat was an outstandingly successful experiment. It had demonstrated, to the reformers' satisfaction at least, that the supposedly continuous danger and frenzy to be anticipated from maniacs were the consequence of, rather than the occasion for, harsh and misguided methods of management and restraint; indeed, that this reputation was in large part the self-serving creation of the madhouse keepers. It apparently showed that the asylum could provide a comfortable and forgiving environment, where those who could not cope with the world could find respite; and where, in a familial atmosphere, they might be spared the neglect that would otherwise have been their lot. Perhaps even more impressive than this was that, despite a conservative outlook that classified as cured no one who had to be readmitted to an asylum, the statistics collected during the Retreat's first fifteen years of operation seemed to show that moral treatment could restore a large proportion of cases to sanity.

30. Reid, *Hypochondria*, 303–4.   31. Tuke, *History of the Insane*, 157.
32. Ibid., 177.   33. Ibid.   34. Ibid., p. 156.

THE SOCIAL ROOTS OF THE NEW APPROACH

But if one must grant the importance of the changing conceptions of insanity and its appropriate treatment as an intervening cause in the rise of the lunacy reform movement, one must also recognize that ideas and conceptions of human nature do not change in a vacuum. They arise from a concrete basis in actual social relations. Put slightly differently, the ways men look at the world are conditioned by their activity in it. The question we must therefore address—albeit briefly and somewhat speculatively—is what changes in the conditions of social existence prompted the changes we have just examined.

In a society still dominated by subsistence forms of agriculture, nature rather than man is the source of activity. Just as man's role in actively remaking the world is underdeveloped and scarcely perceived—favoring theological and supernatural rather than anthropocentric accounts of the physical and social environment—so too the possibilities for transforming man himself go largely unrecognized and the techniques for doing so remain strikingly primitive. In a world not humanly but divinely authored, "to attempt reform was not only to change men, but even more awesome, to change a universe responding to and reflecting God's will"—to embark on a course akin to sacrilege.[35] And where the rationalizing impact of the marketplace is still weak, structures of domination tend to remain *extensive* rather than intensive; that is, the quality and character of the work force are taken as fixed rather than as plastic and amenable to improvement through appropriate management and training.

But under the rationalization forced by competition, man's *active* role in the process presents itself ever more insistently to people's consciousness. This development is further accelerated by the rise of manufacturing—a form of human activity in which nature is relegated simply to a source of raw materials, to be worked on and transformed via active *human* intervention. More than that, economic competition and the factory system are the forcing house for a thoroughgoing transformation in the relation of man to man. For industrial capitalism demands "a reform of 'character' on the part of every single workman, since the previous character did not fit the new industrial system."[36] Entrepreneurs concerned to "make such machines of men as cannot err"[37] soon discover that physical threat and economic coercion will not suffice: men have to be taught to *internalize* the new attitudes and responses, to discipline them-

35. H. Soloman, *Public Welfare, Science and Propaganda in Seventeenth Century France* (Princeton: Princeton University Press, 1972), 29–30.

36. S. Pollard, *The Genesis of Modern Management* (Harmondsworth: Penguin, 1965), 297.

37. Josiah Wedgwood, cited in N. McKendrick, "Josiah Wedgwood and Factory Discipline," *Historical Journal* 4 (1961):46.

selves. Moreover, force under capitalism becomes an anachronism (perhaps even an anathema) save as a last resort. For one of the central achievements of the new economic system, one of its major advantages as a system of domination, is that it brings forth "a peculiar and mystifying . . . form of compulsion to labour for another that is purely economic and 'objective.'"[38]

The insistence on the importance of the internalization of norms, the conception of how this was to be done, and even the nature of the norms that were to be internalized—in all these respects we can now see how the emerging attitude toward the insane paralleled contemporaneous shifts in the treatment of other deviants and of the normal. The new attitude coincided with and formed part of what Peter Gay has dubbed "the recovery of nerve"[39]—a growing and quite novel sense that man is the master of his destiny and not the helpless victim of fate; and it had obvious links with the rise of "the materialist doctrine that people are the product of circumstance."[40] "Is it not evident," said James Burgh (and certainly it *was* to an ever-larger circle of his contemporaries), "that by management the human species may be moulded into any conceivable shape?"[41] The implication was that one might "organize the empirical world in such a way that man develops an experience of and assumes a habit of that which is truly human."[42]

This faith in the capacity for human improvement through social and environmental manipulation was translated in a variety of settings—factories, schools, prisons, asylums—into the development of a whole array of temporally coincident and structurally similar techniques of social discipline.[43] Originating among the upper and middle classes, for example, there emerged the notion that the education and upbringing of children ought no longer to consist in "the suppression of evil, or the breaking of the will."[44] With the growth of economic opportunity and social mobility, the old system of beating and intimidating the child to compel compliance came to be viewed as a blunt and unserviceable technique, for it

38. M. Dobb, *Studies in the Development of Capitalism* (New York: International Publishers, 1963), 7.

39. Peter Gay, *The Enlightenment: An Interpretation,* vol. 2, *The Science of Freedom* (New York: Knopf, 1969), 6.

40. B. Fine, "Objectification and the Bourgeois Contradictions of Consciousness," *Economy and Society* 6 (1977):431.

41. J. Burgh, *Political Disquisitions,* vol. 3 (London: Dilly, 1775), 176.

42. Helvetius, quoted in Fine, "Objectification," 431.

43. Michael Ignatieff, "Prison and Factory Discipline, 1770–1800: The Origins of an Idea" (Paper presented at the Annual Meeting of the American Historical Association, 1976); Foucault, *Madness and Civilization;* idem, *Discipline and Punish* (London: Allen Lane, 1977).

44. J. H. Plumb, "The New World of Children in Eighteenth Century England," *Past and Present* 67 (1975): 69.

ill prepared one's offspring for the pressures of the marketplace. The child needed to be taught to be "his own slave driver," and with this end in view, "developing the child's sense of emulation and shame" was to be preferred to "physical punishment or chastisement."[45] John Locke, the theoretician of these changes, said:

> Beating is the worst, and therefore the last Means to be used in the Correction of Children. . . . The *Rewards* and *Punishments* . . . , whereby we should keep Children in order *are* of quite another kind. . . . *Esteem* and *Disgrace* are, of all others, the most powerful Incentives to the Mind, when it is once brought to relish them. If you can once get into Children a Love of Credit and an Apprehension of Shame and Disgrace, you have put into them the true principle.[46]

The essential continuity of approach is equally manifest in the methods and assumptions of the early-nineteenth-century prison reformers. Crime had been seen as the product of innate and immemorial wickedness and sin. Now, however, the criminal was reassimilated to the ranks of a common humanity. As Fine puts it, "The prisoner was to be treated as a person, *who possessed a reason in common with all other persons,* in contrast to animals and objects. However hardened the prisoner was, beneath the surface of his or her criminality an irreduceable reason still remained."[47] In consequence, as lunatics were for Tuke, they were "defective mechanisms" that could be "remoulded" through their confinement in a penitentiary designed as "a machine for the social production of guilt."[48] And for such purposes (again the parallel with moral treat-

45. Ibid., 67, 69.

46. John Locke, *Educational Writings* (London: Cambridge University Press, 1968), 152–53, 183. Note the stress on putting them *into* children. Locke's educational doctrines acquired an ever greater popularity among the upper and middle classes in the latter half of the eighteenth century. Plumb draws attention to the fact that "by 1780 John Browne could make one of the principal virtues of the expensive academy for gentlemen's sons that he proposed to set up a total absence of corporal punishment" (Plumb, "New World of Children," 70). (Interestingly, one of William Tuke's early philanthropic endeavors, prior to setting up the York Retreat, had been the establishment of Ackworth, a school for girls.) Seen in the context of these slightly earlier changes, Samuel Tuke's comment that "there is much analogy between the judicious treatment of children and that of insane persons" takes on a new significance (Samuel Tuke, *Description of the Retreat: An Institution near York for Insane Persons of the Society of Friends* [1813], facsimile ed., ed. Richard A. Hunter and Ida Macalpine [London: Dawsons, 1964], 150). In practice, the analogy was to extend even further. When Locke's doctrines (and their intellectual descendants) were modified to accommodate the children of the poor, they spawned the rigidities of the monitorial system: Andrew Bell's "steam engine of the moral world," and Joseph Lancaster's "new and mechanical system of education." When the techniques of the small, upper-class Retreat were adapted to the "requirements" of the mass of pauper lunatics, moral treatment was transformed into a set of management techniques for a custodial holding operation.

47. Fine, "Objectification," 429.

48. Michael Ignatieff, *A Just Measure of Pain: The Penitentiary in the Industrial Revolution in England* (New York: Pantheon, 1978), 213.

ment is clear) prison reformers plainly perceived that "gentle discipline is more efficacious than severity."[49]

The new practices, which had their origins in the wider transformation of English society, were shared, developed further, and given a somewhat different theoretical articulation in the context of the lunatic asylum. As in the wider world, so too in the lunatic asylum: one could no longer be content with the old emphasis on an externally imposed alien order, which ensured that madness was controlled, yet which could never produce self-restraint. Control must come from within, which meant that physical violence, now dysfunctional, became abhorrent.[50] The realization of the power that was latent in the ability to manipulate the environment and of the possibility of radically transforming the individual's "nature" was translated in the context of madness into a wholly new stress on the importance of cure. It represented a major structural support of the new ethic of rehabilitation. As the market made the individual "responsible" for his success or failure, so the environment in the lunatic asylum was designed to create a synthetic link between action and consequences, such that the madman could not escape the recognition that he alone was responsible for the punishment he received. The insane were to be restored to reason by a system of rewards and punishment not essentially different from those used to teach a young child to obey the dictates of "civilized" morality. Just as those who formed the new industrial work force were to be taught the "rational" self-interest essential if the market system were to work, the lunatics, too, were to be made over in the image of bourgeois rationality: defective human mechanisms were to be repaired so that they could once more compete in the marketplace. And finally, just as hard work and self-discipline were the keys to the success of the urban bourgeoisie, from whose ranks Tuke came, so his moral treatment propounded these same qualities as the means of reclaiming the insane.

49. J. Howard, *The State of the Prisons* (Warrington: Egres, 1778), 8.

50. Cf. Michel Foucault's comment on the attractions of the Panopticon to the bourgeoisie "It is not necessary to use force to constrain the convict to good behaviour, the madman to calm, the worker to work, the schoolboy to application, the patient to observation of the regulations . . . no more bars, no more chains, no more heavy locks" (Foucault, *Discipline and Punish*, 202).

CHAPTER FIVE

The Discovery of the Asylum Revisited: Lunacy Reform in the New American Republic

With the hubris so characteristic of graduate students, I originally intended that my dissertation would be a comparative study of changing responses to mental disorder in nineteenth-century England and the United States. Reason subsequently prevailed (or rather, my supervising committee, swamped with 700 pages on England alone, declared themselves ready to surrender). By this time, I had a rather extensive acquaintance with the existing secondary literature on the United States and had begun to burrow about in a variety of archives, most notably those at the Northampton State Hospital in Massachusetts and at the Institute of Living (formerly the Hartford Retreat), located charmingly enough (though in blatant contradiction of its managers' feeble attempt at euphemism) on Asylum Avenue, at some small remove from the Connecticut State Capitol. In substantial measure, I set this work aside once I arrived at the University of Pennsylvania, first concentrating my energies on a new topic more readily seen as legitimate among my sociological colleagues, a study of the disenchantment with and abandonment of the mental hospital in the third quarter of the twentieth century;[1] and then, when the passage of time rendered the task slightly less unpalatable, pruning my examination of the social organization of insanity in nineteenth-century England to a more manageable (and publishable) size.[2]

Chapter 5 is reprinted from Andrew Scull, ed., *Madhouses, Mad-Doctors, and Madmen: The Social History of Psychiatry in the Victorian Era*, 1981, pp. 144–65, by permission of the publishers, the University of Pennsylvania Press and the Athlone Press.

1. See Andrew Scull, *Decarceration: Community Treatment and the Deviant—A Radical View* (Englewood Cliffs, N.J.: Prentice-Hall, 1977; 2d ed., Oxford: Polity Press; New Brunswick, N.J.: Rutgers University Press, 1984).
2. Andrew Scull, *Museums of Madness: The Social Organization of Insanity in Nineteenth-Century England* (London: Allen Lane; New York: St. Martin's Press, 1979).

But I did not entirely lose touch with my earlier ambition to examine the parallel developments in the United States, and despite the competing distractions, I could not completely resist the temptation to nose around in the archives of the two very important pioneering American asylums that happened to be located in my new home town, the Frankford Retreat, and the psychiatric division of the Pennsylvania Hospital. A few years later, I was asked to present some general reflections on the historiography of Anglo-American psychiatry,[3] and in rereading David Rothman's influential *The Discovery of the Asylum*, was struck with how poorly his emphasis on the uniquely *American* character of the Jacksonian asylum accorded with the archival records I had examined. This finding seemed worth documenting with some care: hence the following chapter.

The Discovery of the Asylum Revisited:
Lunacy Reform
in the New American Republic

During the past fifteen years, with the possible exception of Michel Foucault's work, David Rothman's *Discovery of the Asylum* has attracted more attention than any other book on the history of our responses to insanity.[1] Like Foucault, Rothman has succeeded in reaching an audience far beyond the limited circle of historians who ordinarily concern themselves with social reform and administrative history. Indeed, he has even been widely read among sociologists, despite the well-known aversion of many of them to studying anything but contemporary America.

It is not difficult to suggest reasons for his success. At the very least, they include the following: the belated and welcome rupture with lingering Whiggish tendencies (still evident in many histories of psychiatry, though long since formally renounced in other areas of historical inquiry); the boldness and sweep of his argument, as well as his willingness (deriving in part from his acquaintance with the work of Goffman and others on "total institutions")[2] to seek similarities and connections be-

3. See Chapter 2.

1. Michel Foucault, *Madness and Civilization* (New York: Pantheon, 1965); David Rothman, *The Discovery of the Asylum: Social Order and Disorder in the New Republic* (Boston: Little, Brown, 1971).

2. Erving Goffman, *Asylums* (Garden City, N.Y.: Doubleday, 1961).

tween the rise of the lunatic asylum and the adoption of segregative responses to other forms of deviance; the intrinsic appeal of his subject
matter, given the newly fashionable interest in the poor and the powerless, in "history from below," bolstered in this instance by Rothman's claim
that attention to these apparently peripheral concerns could shed new
light upon so central an issue as the bases of social order and cohesion;
and the resonance of his implicitly anti-institutional, antibureaucratic,
antiexpert analysis, not just with the general intellectual climate of the
1970s, but (ironically enough) with the more particular ideology of a
contemporary "reform" movement seeking the deinstitutionalization of
the deviant.[3]

One further source of the book's popularity, I think, lies in its subliminal appeal to a certain sophisticated variant of cultural chauvinism.
English historians have long treasured and nurtured the myth of "the
peculiarities of the English,"[4] their American counterparts have been
equally enamored of the image of "the city on the hill," the unique and
special destiny of the American Republic. And, of course, the central element in Rothman's fundamentally idealist account of the rise of the asylum is his emphasis on the uniquely *American* properties of the new institutions and on their origins in a peculiarly Jacksonian mixture of angst
about the stability of the social order and utopianism about the solutions
available to meet the difficulty. As I have pointed out elsewhere, such an
account is vulnerable to the overwhelming evidence that, so far from
being a uniquely American phenomenon, the "discovery of the asylum"
was well under way in Europe long before the Jacksonian era began.
Furthermore, while Rothman's account persuasively *describes* the anxiety
and the vision of perfectibility, it neither explains the emergence of
these ideas nor analyzes the social location of those who espoused them.[5]

In this essay, however, I want to take this criticism a step further. For
it is not just a comparative perspective on parallel developments in England, France, and elsewhere that undermines Rothman's argument.
Rather, in his insistence on the domestic character of the changes he describes, he gives scant attention to evidence that the lines of influence
were precisely the *reverse* of those he implies, to intimations that the first
critical stages of the American lunacy reform movement involved a

3. On this last point, see Andrew Scull, *Decarceration: Community Treatment and the Deviant—A Radical View* (Englewood Cliffs, N.J.: Prentice-Hall, 1977; 2d ed., Oxford: Polity
Press; New Brunswick, N.J.: Rutgers University Press, 1984).

4. The latest, and perhaps oddest, example of this school is the anthropologist turned
historian, and former specialist on Nepal, Alan Macfarlane. See his *Origins of English Individualism* (Oxford: Basil Blackwell, 1978).

5. See Andrew Scull, "Madness and Segregative Control: The Rise of the Insane Asylum," *Social Problems* 24 (1977):338–51.

heavy dependence on ideas and examples that were borrowed from abroad.[6]

In what follows, I shall examine the developments that led, between 1810 and 1824, to the construction of a number of lunatic asylums on the eastern seaboard of the United States. I shall suggest that while each of these so-called corporate asylums[7] had its idiosyncrasies, they all also exhibited striking similarities. I shall also suggest that these "family resemblances" mark them as a distinct departure in the history of American responses to insanity. I shall show that, taken together, these institutions had a profound impact on the movement to "reform" the treatment of lunatics in the United States, notwithstanding their eventual fate as asylums for the rich, precursors of the dual, class-based system that is still characteristic of our approach to mental disorder. And I shall demonstrate that the early history of these corporate asylums is marked at every turn by evidence of European inspiration and influence.

The new corporate asylums were not, of course, the first institutional provision made for lunatics in the United States. From its foundation in 1751, the Pennsylvania Hospital had made some provision for the distracted, first in the basement of the original building and later in a separate structure adjacent to the rest of the hospital.[8] Prompted largely by the urgings of two successive provincial governors, the Virginia burgesses had set up a "madhouse," modeled to some extent on London's Bethlem, in 1773.[9] And when a hospital for New York was first canvassed in 1769, its projectors urged that provision be made for maniacs as well as for medical and surgical cases. After its long-delayed opening in 1791, the maniacs were assigned to the basement; by 1803 a third story had to be added to accommodate them; and in 1808 they were moved to a separate building on the hospital grounds.[10] But each of these early institutions was little more than a "place of safekeeping" where the inmates could be "disabled from injuring themselves and others."[11] At best, those in charge hoped that "the wretched maniac, sequestered from society,

6. Though I shall not do so here, a similar case could be made about the origins of the penitentiary. Cf. in this regard Michael Ignatieff, *A Just Measure of Pain: The Penitentiary in the Industrial Revolution* (New York: Pantheon, 1978); and R. Evans, "A Rational Plan for Softening the Mind" (Ph.D. dissertation, Essex University, 1974).

7. "So-called" because they were built primarily with funds raised by private appeals to the public.

8. See Nancy J. Tomes, "The Persuasive Institution: Thomas Story Kirkbride and the Art of Asylum Keeping, 1841–1883" (Ph.D. dissertation, University of Pennsylvania, 1978).

9. Norman Dain, *Disordered Minds* (Williamsburg, Va.: Colonial Williamsburg Foundation, 1971), esp. 7–9.

10. S. I. Pomerantz, *New York—An American City, 1783–1803* (New York: Columbia University Press, 1938).

11. *Bloomingdale Asylum Annual Report* (1818), 11.

might be made subject to such regimen and regulations, which if not always the means of recovery, would at least ensure safety, decency and order."[12] As this implies, these institutions were intended "to secure" rather than "cure,"[13] and the treatment that was given was dispensed haphazardly, consisting of the application of such standard medical therapies of the period as bleedings, purges, and emetics.

If these eighteenth-century institutions had looked to contemporary English developments for their models—to the growing number of voluntary hospitals of the period and to idealized accounts of the success of the regime at Bethlem—their nineteenth-century counterparts, too, looked across the Atlantic for inspiration, though with rather different results. Both England and France were by now in the throes of their own movements to reform the treatment of the insane, and it was to the work of Pinel and (to a much greater extent) of Tuke that the founders of the new corporate asylums looked for guidance. The means by which they obtained that guidance were sometimes more, sometimes less, direct, but the impact in each case was marked, and the outcome was an influential group of asylums that exemplified a radically different approach to the insane,[14] even while giving that approach some peculiarly American overtones.

The most direct lines of influence are found in the cases of the Friends' Asylum at Frankford and in the Bloomingdale Asylum in New York. The Friends' Asylum, as its name suggests, was, like its inspiration, a Quaker foundation. The prime mover in the enterprise was Thomas Scattergood, who had visited the York Retreat during an extended religious sojourn in England between 1794 and 1800. Beginning at their meeting in the spring of 1811, the Philadelphia Friends began to debate the question of making "provision for such of our members as may be deprived of the use of their reason."[15] Even from three thousand miles away, Tuke's grandson Samuel played a direct role in the process, contributing an anonymous article, "Hints on the Treatment of Insane Persons," to the October 1811 issue of the Philadelphia *Eclectic Repertory and Analytic Review*. The Philadelphia Friends subsequently sponsored an American edition of Tuke's *Description of the Retreat,* which appeared only a matter of months after the original English printing. The latter "was circulated among Friends in Philadelphia and the adjoining districts of the Yearly

12. Pennsylvania Hospital Archives, Board of Managers' Minutes, 6:390–92, quoted in Tomes, "Persuasive Institution," 42.

13. William Malin, clerk at the Pennsylvania Hospital, 1828, cited in Tomes, "Persuasive Institution," 67.

14. See chapters 2 and 4.

15. *An Account of the Rise and Progress of the [Frankford] Asylum, Proposed to Be Established near Philadelphia for the Relief of Persons Deprived of the Use of Their Reason* (Philadelphia: Kimber and Conrad, 1814), 2.

Meeting and served to stimulate the interest of Friends in collecting funds and in pushing forward the work to completion."[16] By 4 June 1813, the management committee had raised $24,092.50, having received "extensive approbation of the proposed institution" and contributions from a large number of individual subscribers as well as from more than twenty district Quaker Meetings.[17] The site selection and construction now proceeded alongside further fund-raising efforts, and in 1817 the asylum finally opened its doors to an exclusively Quaker clientele.[18]

The direct lines of communication between English and American Quakers played a similarly important role in the founding of the Bloomingdale Asylum in New York. Unlike Frankford, this was not a completely new foundation, but it resulted from a sharp change in the arrangements for dealing with the insane at an existing institution. As we have seen, the New York Hospital had begun by placing its lunatics in basement cells, but subsequently, it had moved them to a separate building on the hospital grounds, in an effort to diminish the deleterious impact on the remaining patients of the noise and confusion they created. This expedient proved to be little more than a palliative measure, as the accumulation of chronic cases, the lack of any systematic plan of treatment or management, the limited interest of the hospital's physicians in dealing with lunacy, and the absence of any unified authority over the insane department combined to create recurring difficulties for the hospital's governors.[19]

It was, therefore, with conditions ripe for change that, in April 1815,

16. "A History of Friends' Asylum," Friends' Hospital Archives, Philadelphia (typescript, n.d.), 16.

17. *Friends' Asylum Contributors' Book,* vol. 1, 4 June 1813. Both the fund-raising procedures and the organization of the Contributors' Association were borrowed directly from those used by the founders of the York Retreat.

18. These included the publication of reports, in editions of a thousand and more, designed to stimulate further interest in the project. To the 1814 version, "An abridged account of the proceedings of Friends relative to the Retreat near York, in England, is added, in order to convey correct information of the nature of the proposed establishment, the views of both institutions being nearly the same" (*Rise and Progress of the Asylum,* 18). Quaker clientele: Again, it followed here the example of the York Retreat. But unlike the English establishment, the Frankford Asylum was unable to generate sufficient inmates to fill the available space, a situation that persisted until the rule restricting admissions to Quakers was abandoned in 1834.

19. For an insightful discussion of the emergence of similar problems at another "mixed" institution, the Pennsylvania Hospital, see Tomes, "Persuasive Institution," chap. 1. Tomes astutely suggests that these administrative difficulties may have contributed to the managers' receptivity to moral treatment. But I feel she pushes her case too far when she argues that "moral treatment must be looked at as a product of institutional experience at least as much as emulation of foreign precedents" (ibid., 69). In this connection, one may note that the Pennsylvania Hospital did not adopt the new approach until 1841, long after the administrative difficulties to which she refers had become apparent.

Thomas Eddy set about converting his fellow members of the hospital board to the advantages of "a course of *moral* treatment for the lunatic patients, more extensive than had hitherto been practiced in this country, and similar to that pursued at 'The Retreat' near York, in England."[20] Highly active in many of the Quaker-inspired reforms of the period (he has been called "the American Howard" for his role in prison reform), Eddy had almost certainly learned of the new approach through the publications and appeals of his fellow Quakers who were on the asylum committee in Philadelphia. However, he also corresponded regularly with Lindley Murray, a member of the York Quaker Meeting and a close friend of the Tuke family.

Mention of his project to Murray brought forth a swift and detailed response from Samuel Tuke himself concerning the principles that should guide "the erection of an asylum for lunatics." Tuke's suggestions were published as a pamphlet in New York in 1815.[21] Eddy proposed both a new asylum on a separate site, a farm in the northern part of Manhattan Island, and an immediate attempt to apply the principles of moral treatment in the existing building[22]—proposals whose realization was made easier when the New York legislature voted an annual subvention of $10,000 to support the erection of more extensive accommodations for the insane.

The new Bloomingdale Asylum opened in 1821.[23] Like the Friends' Asylum at Frankford, it bore a pronounced physical resemblance to the York Retreat, which is perhaps not surprising in view of Tuke's emphasis on the contribution architecture could make to the patients' recovery.[24] All three institutions concurred on the primary qualification of a successful asylum superintendent: he should, in the words of the Bloomingdale

20. Quoted in Henry Hurd, *The Institutional Care of the Insane in the United States and Canada* (Baltimore: Johns Hopkins University Press, 1916), 3:137.

21. Samuel Tuke, *A Letter to Thomas Eddy of New York on Pauper Lunatic Asylums* (New York: Samuel Wood, 1815).

22. See Thomas Eddy, *Hints for Introducing an Improved Mode of Treating the Insane in Asylums* (New York: Samuel Wood, 1815).

23. Significantly, it is referred to in some early hospital sources as "the Rural Retreat." Cf. William L. Russell, *The New York Hospital: A History of the Psychiatric Service, 1771–1936* (New York: Columbia University Press, 1945), 178.

24. See Andrew Scull, "The Architecture of the Victorian Lunatic Asylum," in *Buildings and Society: Essays on the Social Development of the Built Environment*, ed. A. D. King (London and Boston: Routledge and Kegan Paul, 1980). The Friends' Asylum was particularly reminiscent of the York Retreat, incorporating only some minor modifications that had been suggested by Tuke himself, based on his experiences at the Retreat. The most important of these was building patients' rooms on only one side of the corridors in the wings, to make the structure more light and airy. In other respects, the Frankford institution's indebtedness is evident even to the untrained eye, and extended to even so fine a detail as the use of Tuke's design for iron-window sashes. The use of sashes would obviate the need for bars and thus make the building more nearly resemble an ordinary residence.

committee, be "reasonable, humane, moral and religious, possessing stability and dignity of character, mild and gentle, . . . resolute, . . . compassionate, [and] of just and sagacious observation."[25]

The omission of medical qualifications was neither accidental nor insignificant. Moral treatment, as I have pointed out elsewhere, had been developed at the York Retreat by laymen.[26] Following this precedent, both the Friends' and Bloomingdale Asylums placed this position of superintendent in lay hands.[27] At the New York Hospital, William Handy announced that medicine was "rarely given" and that "we do not believe in the specific power of any drug in curing madness." Reiterating Tuke's own conclusions in an American context, he denounced bloodletting, emetics, violent cathartics, setons, and blisters as generally useless and asserted that with the addition of warm baths, recovery "will be the most certainly accomplished by strict attention to a moral regimen."[28] The superintendent at Friends' Asylum made similar efforts to insist on the primacy of moral treatment but faced some opposition, for the resident physician continued to demand the frequent use of medicine.[29]

Boston had neglected to build a general hospital in the eighteenth century, possibly, as Leonard Eaton suggests, because the homogeneity of the elite there and the consequent lack of religious and social rivalry hampered the kind of competitive philanthropy that aided the establishment of the Pennsylvania and New York hospitals.[30] By 1810, however, some of the more ambitious young Boston physicians, perhaps resenting the provincial status quo to which the lack of such a hospital consigned them, were urging the establishment of a hospital and lunatic asylum.[31] The campaign quickly attracted the support of some of "the wealthiest and most respectable men of Boston." However, delayed somewhat by unsettled political conditions, the construction of the two institutions was

25. Bloomingdale Asylum, *Annual Report* (1818), 13.

26. See Andrew Scull, *Museums of Madness: The Social Organization of Insanity in Nineteenth-Century England* (London: Allen Lane; New York: St. Martin's Press, 1979).

27. Isaac Bonsall and his wife at Frankford; and Laban Gardner and his wife at Bloomingdale. Both institutions differed from the Retreat, however, in having from the outset a *resident* as well as a visiting physician. I shall discuss the significance of this fact further on in this essay.

28. Bloomingdale Asylum, *Annual Report* (1818), 7–10. See also Russell, *New York Hospital*, 178–79.

29. Cf. Norman Dain and Eric T. Carlson, "Milieu Therapy in the Nineteenth Century: Patient Care at the Friends' Asylum, Frankford, Pennsylvania, 1817–1861," *Journal of Nervous and Mental Disease* 131 (1960): 284–85.

30. Leonard K. Eaton, *New England Hospitals, 1790–1833* (Ann Arbor: University of Michigan Press, 1957), 11–13.

31. See the 20 August 1810 appeal from Dr. Warren and Dr. Jackson, reprinted in Nathaniel I. Bowditch, *A History of the Massachusetts General Hospital* (Boston: Privately printed, 1851), 3–6.

not completed until 1818.[32] Having learned from the experiences of
New York and Philadelphia, the trustees of the new Massachusetts General Hospital had planned from the beginning to keep the hospital and
lunatic asylum physically and administratively separate. Now they also
sought to imitate the novel and supposedly more curative system of
moral treatment. Accordingly, before taking up his appointment as the
first superintendent of the asylum, Dr. Morrill Wyman was dispatched
by the trustees to view and report back to them on conditions at the Philadelphia, New York, and Frankford asylums.[33]

At New York, he was conducted round by Thomas Eddy, who then
presented him with a copy of Tuke's *Description of the Retreat*.[34] His subsequent practice indicates that he became a convinced disciple. In his only
separately published writing, a lecture delivered in 1830, Wyman suggested a very restricted role for conventional medical therapeutics because they were "seldom useful in relieving mental disease [and were]
usually injurious and frequently fatal." The contrast with the value of
Tuke's approach was stark: obviously, "without symptoms of organic disease, a judicious moral management is more successful." However, he
went on, "moral treatment is indispensable even in cases arising from organic disease."[35]

The evidence we have about Wyman's practice at the McLean Hospital reinforces this portrait. Chains and straitjackets were absent; high
qualifications were demanded of the attendants; patients ate at the superintendent's table, rowed on the Charles River, took country rides,
and in some instances were allowed to visit the newly founded Boston
Athenaeum. In the words of an English visitor, "To gain his confidence
and imperceptibly lead him to the exercise of his disused energies and
faculties . . . is all that the physician studies in the management of his
patient."[36]

In their early years of operation, then, these three asylums tended
to play down the importance of the medical armamentarium and to
urge that moral treatment be employed widely in its place. In this respect, they differed sharply from the fourth corporate lunatic asylum
that was built in this era, the Hartford Retreat. For here, from the outset,

32. Eaton, *New England Hospitals*, 43–46.

33. Nina F. Little, *Early Years of the McLean Hospital* (Boston: Countway Library of
Medicine, 1972), 63. He made a verbal report to the trustees on 2 June 1818.

34. This copy is still in the McLean Archives.

35. Rufus Wyman, *A Discourse on Mental Philosophy as Connected with Mental Disease, Delivered Before the Massachusetts Medical Society* (Boston: Office of the Daily Advertiser,
1830), 24.

36. Edward Sturit Abdy, cited in Helen E. Marshall, *Dorothea Dix: Forgotten Samaritan*
(Chapel Hill: University of North Carolina Press, 1937), 78–79. See also Eaton, *New England Hospitals*, 136–37.

medicine was accorded primacy, an approach that came to characterize American treatment of insanity during the remainder of the nineteenth century.[37]

This inversion of emphasis is scarcely surprising in view of the central place that was occupied by medical men in creating and running the Hartford Retreat. An asylum for the state had first been proposed before the Connecticut State Medical Society in 1812. At that time, little action was taken. But the project was revived again in 1820 by a group of Hartford physicians led by Eli Todd. In a speech before the local Hartford County Medical Society in December 1820, Todd articulated his conviction that "mental disorder is as definitely a manifestation of disease as is a fever or fracture. It is our duty as civilized men to attack this disease. Let us make diligent inquiry, find out how prevalent this disease is, and then establish an institution for its treatment and cure."[38] Within a year, the state medical society supported the asylum proposal and thereafter played a major role in bringing the plan to fruition. Society funds were made available to publicize the project and to print appeals for contributions; with the aid of local clergy, committees were formed throughout the state to collect donations; the public was repeatedly informed of the benefits and advantages of asylum treatment; and a state subvention was successfully sought.

Because Connecticut lacked the concentrations of wealth that were present in New York, Pennsylvania, and Massachusetts, fund-raising proved to be far more difficult there than it had been elsewhere,[39] and one may reasonably doubt that the Hartford Retreat would have been built at this time without the sustained initiative of the medical society— the more so since the state's wealthy inhabitants could clearly avail themselves of the new asylums in New York and Boston. The society's leaders were convinced that "no-one conversant with the records of our profession, can hesitate for a moment to believe that its interest would be greatly promoted by adopting the plan which we have suggested."[40] And in setting up the new institution, the society went to great lengths to ensure the dominance of the profession's interests.[41] The state charter that

37. On this last point, see Gerald Grob, "Samuel B. Woodward and the Practice of Psychiatry in Early Nineteenth-Century America," *Bulletin of the History of Medicine* 36 (1962): 420–43.

38. Eli Todd, quoted in John Winkler and Adele Norton, "History of the Institute" (i.e., the Hartford Retreat), Institute of Living Library, Hartford (typescript, chapters paginated separately), chap. 1: 19.

39. Cf. Eaton, *New England Hospitals*, 72.

40. Connecticut State Medical Society, *Report of a Committee . . . Respecting an Asylum for the Insane, with the Constitution of a Society for Their Relief* (Hartford: Bowles and Frances, 1821), 12.

41. Particularly prominent in the asylum movement were Dr. Eli Todd, Dr. Mason Fitch Cogswell, Dr. George Sumner, and Dr. Samuel Woodward (who later, on Todd's

was passed in 1822 provided that at least a quarter of the committee of trustees were to be physicians, as were all six of the official asylum visitors. Perhaps even more significantly, the power of appointing the superintendent rested with the state medical society, thereby cementing the profession's dominance.[42]

As the very name of the institution indicates, those setting up the Hartford Retreat were heavily influenced by the recent developments in England and France. In his declining years, looking back on his role on the planning committee for the asylum, George Sumner commented, "We had no other guides than 'Pinel on Insanity' and 'Tuke's History of the Retreat,' near York, in England."[43] The English institution was the most frequently mentioned in the fund-raising literature, the public being assured that, in accordance with Tuke's approach, "the inmates of this asylum will in all cases be treated with humanity, subjected to no unnecessary rigour of discipline, and controlled by no force unless their safety requires it. The chains and the scourge, which have too often been the implements of correction, must be abolished, and every attendant dismissed from the institution who resorts to violence in the performance of his ordinary duties."[44]

Shortly after the Hartford Retreat opened its doors in 1824, its new superintendent, Eli Todd, informed the public of the principles that guided his practice:

These are to treat [the insane], in all cases, as far as possible, as rational beings. To allow them all the liberty and indulgence compatible with their own safety and that of others. To cherish in them sentiments of self-respect. To excite an ambition for the good will and esteem of others. To draw out the latent sparks of natural and social affection. To occupy their attention, to exercise their judgement and ingenuity, and to administer to their self-complacency by engaging them in useful employments, alternated with amusements. To withdraw, in most instances, their minds as much as possible from every former scene and every former companion, setting before them a new world and giving an entire change to the current of their recollections and ideas.[45]

---

recommendation, became superintendent of the new Worcester [Massachusetts] State Hospital).

42. Connecticut State Medical Society, *Report* (1821), 15. This situation contrasted markedly with that at the McLean, where in the early years the state directly appointed four of the trustees; and with that at Frankford, where lay managers were clearly the final authority in the institution's affairs.

43. George Sumner, "Sketches of Physicians in Hartford in 1820 and Reminiscences," Paper read before the Hartford Medical Society, 1 January 1848 (Hartford: Case, Lockwood, and Brainard, 1890), 8–9.

44. Connecticut State Medical Society, *Report* (1821), 10.

45. Cited in Winkler and Norton, "History of the Institute," chap. 3:6.

The techniques, even the very wording, come directly from the *Description of the Retreat*.

But the Hartford Retreat was no mere copy of its namesake. Breaking sharply with his model, and criticizing the other American corporate asylums for failing to do so, Todd placed great stress on the value of medical treatment. The York Retreat had marked a distinct advance in the treatment of insanity: "Its managers appear, however, to have placed too little reliance upon the efficacy of medicine in the treatment of insanity, and hence their success is not equal to that of other asylums in which medicines are more freely employed." [46] And the managers of the McLean, Bloomingdale, and Friends' asylums had perpetuated the error, with the result that "their treatment is feeble [as] compared to the lofty conceptions of truly combined medical and moral management." [47] "The aid of medicine" was essential, since

> the mind and body are so connected that there can scarcely be a disease of either in which the other is not involved, and in which medical and moral treatment may not be advantageously combined. When mental derangement originates entirely in a diseased state of the body—medication constitutes the paramount, and moral treatment the subsidiary, means of cure. On the other hand, when bodily disease is merely the effect of mental derangement, then there is a complete inversion of the relative importance of these curative means. In most states of insanity, therefore, a judicious combination of both promises the most successful results. [48]

Gradually, practice at the other corporate asylums began to resemble that at Hartford. Stress was placed on the traditional medical therapeutics and was soon accompanied by the growing reliance on opium and morphine that became characteristic of American asylum practice. The McLean from the outset had a medical superintendent, albeit one skeptical of the value of medical as opposed to moral treatment of insanity. [49] But at Bloomingdale and the Friends' Asylum, the administrative structure was more fragmented and confused, and here the realignment in treatment philosophies was signaled and in large part produced by changes in the asylums' internal organization.

As we have seen, the latter asylums had initially opted for lay superintendents; but they also had a resident physician, a young man who prac-

46. Connecticut State Medical Society, *Report* (1821), 10.

47. Eli Todd, speech before the Hartford County Medical Society, December 1820, cited in Winkler and Norton, "History of the Institute," chap. 1:19.

48. Todd, cited in ibid., chap. 3:6.

49. Bulfinch, the asylum architect, had tried to persuade the trustees that appointing a medical man, rather than a lay administrator, to the post of superintendent was "very objectionable." (His report is reprinted in *Isis* 41 [1950]:8–10). But the board ignored the suggestion, deciding that "it is expedient to unite in one person the offices of Physician and Superintendent of the Asylum" (quoted in Bowditch, *Massachusetts General Hospital*, 37).

ticed under the supervision of two or more visiting physicians.[50] The superintendent was "entrusted with the general control of the concerns of the Institution" and the supervision of the moral regimen; the medical men dealt with the strictly medical treatment.[51] At Bloomingdale, this system was abruptly abandoned in 1831, "the position of attending physician being dispensed with and the resident physician given immediate control of the moral and medical treatment of the patients." The lay superintendent, meanwhile, was reduced to the status of a steward.[52] At the Friends' Asylum, the changes were more gradual and subtle: perhaps the Quaker managers here were less willing to abandon Tuke's original vision.

Symptomatic of growing medical ambition, the attending physicians' contribution to the *Annual Report* for 1830 for the first time moved beyond the compilation of routine statistics to a more elaborate discussion of the medical role in patient care. Two years later, the superintendent and his wife resigned, and the appointment of their replacements was accompanied by upheavals in the medical department, with "Dr. Robert Morton and Dr. Charles Evans, appointed attending physicians to the House."[53]

Like Eli Todd, Evans and Morton were convinced that moral and medical treatment were inextricably linked:

> Where a judicious system of medical treatment is steadily pursued [they commented] it exerts a strong influence on the other departments, which would not at first sight be obvious. . . . A course of moral treatment is almost a necessary consequence of a proper sense of the value of medical remedies. They, in fact, are parts of the same system. After what have been called medical means have been successfully resorted to, to remove obvious physical disease, moral treatment will then be found very efficient in restoring and strengthening the functions of the diseased organ.—And we believe that it is only by thus uniting them that full benefit can be derived from either.[54]

Subsequently, they sought a steadily larger role than the superintendent in the dispensing of the "moral" side of the treatment, a campaign bolstered by an insistence on insanity's somatic basis. In a complaint

---

50. The relative status of the two resident officers is clearly indicated by their respective salaries: at Frankford, at its opening, these were $500 per annum for the superintendent (and $250 for his wife, who acted as matron), and only $100 for Dr. Charles Lukens, the resident physician (*Friends' Asylum Contributors' Book*, vol. 1, 19 March 1817).

51. Ibid.

52. Hurd, *Institutional Care*, 3:140–41. The steward retained some residual power via his control over materials; but clearly this was of minor importance and ultimately, in 1877, even this source of independence was lost.

53. Friends' Asylum, *Annual Report* (1832), 3; (1833), 3.

54. In ibid. (1833), 3. See also Dain and Carlson, "Milieu Therapy."

seemingly intended as much for internal as for external consumption, they commented that "instead of regarding it, as it really is, strictly a morbid state of some of the physical organs, and the deranged manifestations of the mind merely the symptoms of that state, it has been too common to look upon it as an unintelligible malady of the immaterial existence itself; and the unhappy lunatic has been left . . . a victim to the idle and ignorant belief that his disease was immedicable."[55]

The success of their efforts can be measured in a series of changes in the asylum's rules. A new codification in 1840 for the first time included the provision that "it shall be their [the attending physicians'] duty to act in concert with the Superintendent in the moral treatment of the patients and promote their restoration with all the means in their power."[56] A decade later, this uneasy joint authority came to an end. In a further revision of the rules, it was laid down that "the Superintendent shall be a well-qualified Physician, and shall be the official head of the Institution. . . . He shall . . . direct such medical, moral and dietetic treatment, as may be best adapted to [the patients'] relief or comfort."[57]

Important as they were, administrative turbulence and realignments were not confined to these changes or, indeed, to these asylums. At none of the four corporate asylums were the founders familiar with the administrative problems associated with the organization and running of large institutions. It is thus not surprising that their first efforts in this sphere usually created unwieldy administrative structures. Thus the McLean was originally seriously understaffed[58] and placed trivial administrative tasks on the superintendent's shoulders—a situation mitigated somewhat only by the appointment in 1823 of a steward who was to assume some of these burdens.[59] Even the Hartford Retreat did not entirely escape these problems. Here, the superintendent from the outset had the aid of a steward, but even during Eli Todd's tenure (1824–33),

55. In Friends' Asylum, *Annual Report* (1836), 9.

56. Friends' Asylum, *Rules for the Management of the Asylum, Adopted by the Board of Managers, First Month 20th, 1840* (Philadelphia: Rakestraw, 1840), 11–12.

57. Friends' Asylum, *Rules. . . . 1850* (Philadelphia: Rakestraw, 1850), 13–14. Again, the degree to which American developments recapitulated similar events elsewhere is quite striking. In my work on lunacy reform in England, I have demonstrated the extent to which the advent of moral treatment rendered medical control over the treatment of the insane highly problematic for a time, and I have documented the maneuvering by which medical dominance was reestablished. See Chapter 6 and Andrew Scull, "Mad-doctors and Magistrates: English Psychiatry's Struggle for Professional Autonomy in the Nineteenth Century," *European Journal of Sociology* 17 (1976): 279–305; and see also William Bynum, "Rationales for Therapy in British Psychiatry, 1780–1835," in *Madhouses, Mad-Doctors, and Madmen: The Social History of Psychiatry in the Victorian Era*, ed. Andrew Scull (Philadelphia: University of Pennsylvania Press; London: Athlone, 1981), 35–57.

58. Eaton, *New England Hospitals*, 127.

59. Little, *McLean Hospital*, 39.

there were squabbles occasioned by the absence of clear lines of authority.[60] After his death, the problem became more acute, for his successor as superintendent, Silas Fuller, gave much of his attention to outside activities that were designed to augment his income. The lay steward and matron, who had previously served for four years under Todd and who claimed (correctly) to know more than Fuller about asylum treatment, sought to exploit this situation to expand their own roles. Ultimately, the managers only succeeded in restoring the *status quo ante* by obtaining the resignations of all three in 1840. Thereafter, Brigham (Fuller's replacement) quickly destroyed all remnants of divided authority and regained undisputed medical control of the institution.[61]

Thus after a period of experiment, all four institutions converged upon a standard system of authority relationships, one that gave all-embracing hegemony to the medical superintendent. Moreover, in every institution, moral treatment came to be defined as the physicians' responsibility, and its administration was inextricably bound up with the employment of conventional medical therapeutics. Consequently, in these matters, as in so many others, these new institutions established the basic framework and ground rules within which subsequent asylums were to operate.

To an important extent, the rapid spread of the asylum idea in mid-century America rested on the well-publicized success of these early institutions. In their first fund-raising efforts, the asylums' founders had perforce to conduct an extensive campaign to convince the public of the superior merits of their chosen solution. Subsequently, in their printed annual reports and in more occasional addresses (often distributed in editions of 2,000 or more)[62] the asylum's officers initiated increasingly complex and extensive discussions of the nature of insanity and its proper treatment, all explicitly aimed at modifying public opinion on these matters.

The public was warned of the inconvenience and danger associated with leaving the mad at large. The threats to life and property, and the distress and hardship visited on families forced to cope with an insane member, meant that "the whole community is indirectly disturbed by the malady of the one."[63] There were more subtle and perhaps more serious dangers, including those of contagion: "When an individual becomes insane, unless he is removed from his family and associates, it is probable

60. Eaton, *New England Hospitals*, 66–67.
61. See Winkler and Norton, "Institute," chaps. 5 and 6.
62. E.g., Robert Waln, Jr., *An Account of the Asylum for the Insane . . . near Frankford* (Philadelphia: Kite, 1825); Wyman, *Discourse on Mental Philosophy;* Charles Evans, *An Account of the Asylum for the Relief of Persons Deprived of Their Reason near Frankford, Pennsylvania* (Philadelphia: Rakestraw, 1846).
63. Connecticut State Medical Society, *Report* (1821), 7.

that some of them will become the subjects of the same disorder."[64] Families and physicians alike should recognize that

> in private practice no disorder is more unmanageable. The patient suffers for the want of that steady course of discipline, which is equally remote from cruelty and indulgence—for the want of attendants, qualified for their task and faithful in its performance, and for want of that medical skill which is rarely possessed, by those whose attention is chiefly directed to other diseases. . . . A madman in his own house, has of all situations the worst. The same causes which produced his disorder continue to operate with their original force, and oppose every exertion which is made to mitigate its symptoms or arrest its progress.[65]

The obverse was true, of course, of the controlled environment of the asylum. The evil reputation the madhouse had long possessed in England was not unfamiliar to Americans, even if they possessed scarcely any domestic examples of the phenomenon.[66] The asylum authorities sought energetically to supplant it with the image of a humane institution that was carefully designed as a curative apparatus.[67] And they insisted repeatedly that "it is only in Lunatic Hospitals that the course of treatment indicated by an intelligent consideration of the different phases of insanity can be applied."[68]

Even before their asylums opened, committees announced confidently that, based on European experience, the new structures would markedly *"diminish the number of the insane."*[69] Subsequent experience seemed to suggest that such claims had been overly modest. As little as three years after opening its doors, the superintendent of the Hartford Retreat informed the public that "during the last year there [have] been admitted twenty-three recent cases, of which twenty-one have recovered, a number equivalent to 91 3/10 per cent. The whole number of recent cases in the Institution during the year was twenty-eight, of which twenty-five have recovered—equal to 89 2/10 per cent"[70]—a result he attributed to the judicious combination of medical and moral treatment. Following the announcements of similar successes in 1830

---

64. Ibid.

65. Ibid., 8.

66. William L. Parry-Jones, *The Trade in Lunacy* (London: Routledge and Kegan Paul, 1972).

67. E.g., *Bloomingdale Asylum Annual Report* (1818), p. 13; Connecticut State Medical Society, *Report* (1821); Friends' Asylum, *Account of the Present State of the Asylum for the Relief of Persons Deprived of the Use of Their Reason* (Philadelphia: Brown, 1816).

68. Hartford Retreat, *Twentieth Annual Report* (1844), 17.

69. Connecticut State Medical Society, *Report* (1821), 10 (italics in the original). For the actual experience in England, cf. Scull, *Museums of Madness*, esp. chap. 3; and John Walton, "The Treatment of Pauper Lunatics in Victorian England: The Case of Lancaster Asylum, 1816–1870," in *Madhouses, Mad-Doctors, and Madmen*, ed. Scull, 166–97.

70. Hartford Retreat, *Third Annual Report* (1827), 5.

and 1831,[71] he underlined the moral: "It is not an extravagant calculation that three fourths of these would have continued under the influence of mental derangement if no institution like the Retreat had been
prepared for their reception."[72] As the "attending physician" at the
Friends' Asylum, Charles Evans, had pointed out, the joint experience of
the new asylums had demonstrated that, given early treatment, "this deplorable malady is equally with other diseases of the human system
under the control of proper medical treatment, the proportion of cures
being as great."[73]

There can be little doubt that the superintendents successfully com-
municated their message to "informed" opinion; or that the optimism
they did so much to foster had much to do with the rapidity with which
the asylum solution was to spread. Captain Basil Hall was only the first of
a number of English travelers touring the United States to comment fa-
vorably on conditions in the new asylums and to extol their superintendents' extraordinary therapeutic success. That the praise was an isolated
moment in the midst of a parade of sour and scornful comments on
American manners and mores only increased the attention it received.[74]
The result, as Pliny Earle pointed out, was that "the newspapers took
it up and sent it throughout the land, and in this way, whatever a few
physicians might have learned from the report itself, the people at large
received the impression that insanity is largely curable."[75] By the mid-
1830s, the *North American Review* could inform its readers, with no little
satisfaction, that "no fact relating to insanity appears better established
than the general *certainty* of curing it in its early stage." The *Review* was
able to cite in support of this claim not just such foreign authorities as
Tuke and Dr. Francis Willis, Dr. George Man Burrows, and Dr. William
Ellis, but also the "uniform testimony" provided by the experience of
Bloomingdale and McLean asylums and the Hartford Retreat. Follow-

71. Hartford Retreat, *Sixth Annual Report* (1830), 5; *Seventh Annual Report* (1831), 5.

72. Friends' Asylum, *Seventh Annual Report* (1831), 7.

73. Friends' Asylum, *Eleventh Annual Report* (1835), 8. During Wyman's years at the
McLean, he refrained from making "the exaggerated claims put forward by most of his
fellow superintendents; the highest percentage of recoveries he ever announced was forty-
three percent" (Eaton, *New England Hospitals*, 144–45). Perhaps this accounts for the clear
preference most visitors showed for the Hartford Retreat. Under Bell, however, the
McLean contributed its voice to the chorus.

74. See Basil Hall, *Travels in North America in the Years 1827 and 1828*, 2d ed. (Edinburgh: Cadell, 1830), 2:191–97. See also E. S. Abdy, *Journal of a Residence and Tour in the
United States of North America*, 3 vols. (London: Murray, 1835); and Charles Dickens' similarly favorable response to the Hartford Retreat in his otherwise equally jaundiced *American Notes* (London: Penguin, 1972), 122–24.

75. Pliny Earle, *The Curability of Insanity: A Series of Studies* (Philadelphia: Lippincott,
1887), 21. The press had earlier given much favorable attention to the founding of the
corporate asylums, to the "humane" principles on which they were based, and to the high
cure rate they promised to achieve. Cf. Eaton, *New England Hospitals*.

ing a review of that experience, the journal sounded a theme that was
to be the leitmotiv of the American reform movement in the following
decade: "We doubt not but that every State in the Union will, within
a very few years, be supplied with at least one [asylum]. Interest will
prompt the States to this, if feelings of benevolence do not; for it requires but slight observation to see, that the expense of supporting the
insane poor will be much lessened by providing them with a good Asylum."[76] In the succinct words of the Pennsylvania Prison Discipline Society, *"The expense incurred in making a proper provision for this class of
paupers is a very profitable investment."*[77]

Again and again in her crusade across the American continent in behalf of state asylums, Dorothea Dix was to draw upon such claims, cou-
pling them with her own vivid (and sometimes imaginary) recital of the
abuses to which the insane were exposed in the community. Repeatedly
she informed state legislatures that "all experience shows that insanity
reasonably treated is as certainly curable as a cold or a fever." She drew
upon the elaborate statistics provided by her allies among the asylum superintendents (most notably Luther Bell of the McLean) to provide estimates to the penny of the money to be saved by "a combination of medical and moral treatment" in an asylum.[78] And always she succeeded in
loosening the states' purse strings.

In the early years at least, the new state asylums continued to be be-
holden in a variety of ways to the preceding generation of corporate asylums. This indebtedness was true even of new *corporate* asylums built in
the 1840s. For example, prior to his appointment in 1841 as the superintendent of the Pennsylvania Hospital's newly separate branch for the insane, Thomas Kirkbride had served a year in 1833 as resident physician
at the Friends' Asylum at Frankford; and before assuming his new duties, he supplemented that experience with a tour of the Bloomingdale
and McLean asylums and the Hartford Retreat, as well as the recently
opened Worcester State Hospital.[79] And during the construction and or-

76. "Insanity and Insane Hospitals," *North American Review* 44 (1837):99, 101, 114.

77. *Pennsylvania Journal of Prison Discipline and Philanthropy* 1 (1845):60 (italics in the
original). For similar comments and for a calculation that the potential savings of asylum
treatment on only 150 patients was $179,420 (without taking into account that those cured
would then return to work), see Connecticut Assembly, *Report of the Committee for Locating a
Site for a Hospital for the Insane Poor* (New Haven: Babcock and Wildman, 1840), 12–13.
Note the spurious precision.

78. See, among many examples, Dorothea Dix, *Memorial Soliciting a State Hospital for
. . . Pennsylvania* (Harrisburg, Pa.: Lescure, 1845), 57; idem, *Memorial Soliciting an Appropriation for the State* [of Kentucky] (Lexington: Hodges, 1846), 10; idem, *Memorial to the Senate
and House of Representatives of the State of Illinois* (Springfield: State Printer, 1847), 19,
24–25; idem, *Memorial Soliciting a State Hospital for . . . Alabama* (Montgomery: Office of
the Advertiser, 1849), 13–15.

79. Earle D. Bond, *Dr. Kirkbride and His Mental Hospital* (Philadelphia: Lippincott,
1947), 39.

ganization of the Butler Hospital for the Insane in Rhode Island, the committee utilized Luther Bell of the McLean as its consultant.[80]

The two most influential state hospitals of this period, which set the pattern for similar institutions elsewhere, were the Worcester State Hospital in Massachusetts[81] and the Utica Asylum in New York. Again, both had close links to the corporate asylums. When Horace Mann sought, in the late 1820s, to secure a state asylum for Massachusetts, he frequently sought advice and support for his project from Eli Todd of the Hartford Retreat, and often visited that asylum himself to observe the new regime at first hand. Later, when the Worcester asylum was about to open, he tried unsuccessfully to induce Todd to become its first superintendent. When Todd refused, Mann accepted his suggestion that he appoint Samuel Woodward instead. (Woodward, an old friend of Todd's, had played one of the most active parts in securing the establishment of the Hartford Retreat, and he was intimately familiar with that asylum's operation.)[82]

Even the external appearance of the Worcester asylum—widely copied by other states—was modeled on an existing corporate asylum, this time the McLean.[83] There were important differences, however, emblematic of which was the use of brick in place of stone. As a consequence, Worcester's "cheap and flimsy style of construction presented a striking contrast to the finished massive features of the other. Being intended for the poorer classes, it was the first considerable example of very cheap construction, and one, unfortunately, which building committees have been too ready to imitate."[84]

Todd was at least as influential in New York. "When the New York Assembly first began to debate the advisability of a state hospital for the insane, several of its members visited the Connecticut Asylum."[85] Subsequently, both Todd and Amariah Brigham (who became superintendent at the Hartford Retreat in 1840) were consulted on the construction of the Utica Asylum. And in 1843, Brigham resigned his post at Hartford to take over the new state institution.[86]

The spread of state hospitals was to have important consequences for the corporate asylums as a whole, strengthening and intensifying some

80. Isaac Ray, *Description of the Butler Hospital for the Insane* (reprinted from the *American Journal of Insanity* 5 [1848]: 2–3).

81. See Gerald Grob, *The State and the Mentally Ill: A History of Worcester State Hospital* (Chapel Hill: University of North Carolina Press, 1966).

82. See Winkler and Norton, "History of the Institute," chap. 3.

83. Cf. Grob, *State and the Mentally Ill*, 33–34.

84. Isaac Ray, "American Hospitals for the Insane," *North American Review* 79 (1854): 75.

85. Eaton, *New England Hospitals*, 157.

86. Winkler and Norton, "Institute," 6: 19–20. Similarly, from its opening in 1836 until 1872, the Vermont Asylum employed William Rockwell, a former assistant at the Retreat, as its superintendent.

preexisting tendencies and increasing the homogeneity of their patient populations. In their early years, as virtually the only specialized institutional provision for the insane, the private asylums (with the exception of the Friends' Asylum at Frankford)[87] had been under considerable pressure to make some space available for the poor. They responded with varying degrees of reluctance. At the McLean, in return for a contribution from the state to the initial fund-raising, the trustees had not only given the state the power to nominate four of their number, but had agreed to set aside thirty beds for the indigent insane. Two years before the asylum even opened, however, discreet lobbying had secured the repeal of this provision. In the short run, this created problems, especially since the poorer classes were, if anything, more anxious than the wealthy to obtain an asylum.[88] Accordingly, the trustees felt impelled to publish signed notices in the *Columbian Sentinel*, the *Commercial Gazette*, and the *Independent Chronicle* refuting the widespread belief that the asylum would accept only monied patients. These announcements were followed up, in 1817, with "an address to the public [devised] to obviate an impression that the Insane Hospital was designed exclusively for the wealthy."[89] Notwithstanding the repeated denials, the suspicions proved well founded. Two sizable bequests within the first few years of operation rendered the asylum independent of state support; and in response, the McLean became the first of the corporate institutions systematically to exclude the poor and thus to avoid "the odor of pauperism."[90]

At Bloomingdale and Hartford, the situation was somewhat different, and the exclusion of the poor came more slowly. With a much less generous endowment than the McLean, the Hartford Retreat perforce had to continue to rely on state subsidies. And in 1817, the governors of the New York Hospital had accepted an annual subsidy of $10,000 from the New York legislature, to remain in effect for thirty years.[91] Hence both, with some misgivings, took substantial numbers of poor patients. Bloomingdale's proportion of publicly supported patients grew from 17 percent in 1828 to 40 percent a decade later; while Hartford's share of the total jumped still more abruptly in 1842 and 1843, when the state legis-

87. As a sectarian institution, which had sought no subsidy from the state and which retained an exclusively, or almost exclusively, Quaker clientele, the Friends' Asylum was largely spared these pressures.

88. Eaton (*New England Hospitals*, 48) shows that, while the poorer wards contributed twice as much for the insane asylum as for the general hospital, the wealthier wards gave the asylum much less preference.

89. Bowditch, *Massachusetts General Hospital*, 26.

90. Massachusetts State Board of Charities, *Annual Report No. 8* (1871), xli.

91. This was by no means the first such subsidy they had accepted, and, as Grob points out, for a time it gave both branches of the hospital a "quasi-public character" (Gerald Grob, *Mental Institutions in America: Social Policy to 1875* [New York: Free Press, 1973]), 63–64.

lature granted both capital funds and an annual maintenance sum, provided that the asylum would make provision for pauper lunatics.

Eli Todd's fears that any such moves "would lower the character of the Institution" were amply borne out.[92] Complaints were quickly voiced of "filthy, noisy or dangerous pauper lunatics" filling the asylum;[93] reported cure rates declined; and the quality of the physical plant began to deteriorate. Bloomingdale experienced a similar decline. By 1847, the superintendent reported that "the House is filled with a mass of chronic and incurable cases," and the trustees conceded that most "were listless and indifferent and wholly unoccupied."[94]

There was obviously an acute danger that both asylums would lose their well-to-do clientele. Of the two, Bloomingdale was able to respond to the situation more quickly. Taking advantage of the opening of the Utica State Hospital in 1843 and the Kings County Lunatic Asylum in Flatbush in 1856, it no longer offered space for the pauper insane and ceased to accept state support in 1847.[95] Henceforth, it concentrated upon "the wealthy" and "indigent persons of superior respectability and personal refinement"—"families of clergymen, and other professional persons, . . . teachers and businessmen who have experienced reverses, . . . [and] dependent unmarried females."[96]

At Hartford, however, the managers remained hamstrung for a decade more by the failure of the Connecticut legislature to build a state facility. Their situation grew more desperate as the decline of state hospitals into warehouses for the unwanted intensified upper-class objections to any association with paupers. It was therefore with scarcely disguised relief that they greeted the legislature's decision in 1866 to build a state hospital at Middletown:

> It is evident [said John Butler, the superintendent] that different classes will require different styles of accommodation. The State should provide for its indigent insane, liberally and abundantly, all the needful means of treatment, but in a plain and rigidly economical way. Other classes of more abundant means will require, with an increased expenditure, a corresponding increase of conveniences and comforts, it may be of luxuries, that use has made essential. This common sense rule is adopted in other arrangements of our social life—our hotels, watering places, private dwellings and various personal expenditures.[97]

92. Hartford Retreat, *Sixth Annual Report* (1830), 5.

93. Hartford Retreat, *Nineteenth Annual Report* (1843), 5.

94. Cited in Rothman, *Discovery of the Asylum*, 279.

95. Hurd, *Institutional Care*, 3:141.

96. Bloomingdale Asylum, *Annual Report* (1851), 15–16; (1856), 19–20; (1862), 11; (1866), 17–25.

97. Hartford Retreat, *Forty-third Annual Report* (1867), 33.

To compete successfully for a monied clientele required a substantial immediate expenditure to upgrade the physical facilities. Renovations began within weeks of the removal of the state patients, and at a cost of about $133,500, the managers secured a "beautiful homelike structure, resembling a country residence of a private gentleman more than a public building or a hospital." [98]

Ultimately, therefore, all the corporate asylums came to adhere to Luther Bell's dictum that "to the polished and cultivated it is due as much to separate them from the coarse and degraded, as to administer to them in other respects." [99] The asylums resembled one another in still a further respect: their decline from curative to custodial institutions. For all the extravagant expenditure of money—the opulent surroundings, the provision of French lessons, drawing classes, singing classes, theaters, and the like—they faced the same decline in curability as the "plain and rigidly economical" state asylums. No matter that "its scale of expenditure is from six to eight times as costly" as the pauper institution; that "its sane population (physicians, attendants, nurses, etc.) is about half as numerous as the insane patients, while at [the state asylum] the sane are but one in thirty as compared with the insane." Inescapably, "like the State hospitals, and almost to the same extent, it has become the resort of incurable lunacy, and its noble endowments are bestowed, not so much for the cure or prevention as for the alleviation of this disease." [100]

In this study, I have shown that the influence of the corporate asylums upon American lunacy reform was pervasive. They played an important role in the conversion of the public to the merits of institutionalization as a response to the problems posed by the mentally disordered. It was through these institutions that Tuke's and Pinel's new "moral treatment of the insane" was most dramatically made known to an American audience. It was here that moral treatment was absorbed and became part of the therapeutic armamentarium of the medical profession. It was the apparent and widely publicized "success" of their programs that encouraged large-scale emulation and expansion of the asylum system. And even if they ultimately became resorts for the upper classes, distinctively different and self-consciously as remote as possible from the harsh realities of the state hospital system, this differentiation should not lead us to

98. Hartford Retreat, *Forty-fourth and Forty-fifth Annual Reports* (1870), 21. Modern observers have thought that a more appropriate comparison would be "a luxurious spa hotel" (Winkler and Norton, "Institute," 7:21).

99. McLean Asylum, *Twenty-second Annual Report* (1839), in Massachusetts General Hospital, *Annual Report* (1839), 16.

100. Massachusetts State Board of Health, Lunacy, and Charity, *First Annual Report* (1879), xxxii. The comparison may be extended, of course. The same therapeutic failures characterized the English asylums for the rich. See Scull, *Museums of Madness*, 204–8.

slight their part in creating, and to some degree shaping, that system. For the earliest state hospitals, the corporate asylums provided not only a model to be copied, but a source of professional staff and advice once they opened. Lastly, given the extent to which the corporate asylums in turn drew upon European antecedents, parochial theories about the American discovery of the asylum must surely collapse.

CHAPTER SIX

From Madness to Mental Illness: Medical Men as Moral Entrepreneurs

"From Madness to Mental Illness" was the first paper I published on matters psychiatric. (It was also, as a matter of fact—though in a somewhat different form—the first chapter I completed a couple of years earlier when writing my doctoral dissertation.) It appeared in print in early 1975, a few months after William Bynum had published "Rationales for Therapy in British Psychiatry, 1780–1835," in which he independently developed a closely related line of argument.[1] When these articles were written, serious historical research on English responses to insanity in the seventeenth and eighteenth centuries, with the important exceptions of Parry-Jones' work on English madhouses[2] and Hunter and Mac-Alpine's book on George III's madness[3] and their wide-ranging anthology of British "psychiatric" texts,[4] was still in its infancy. My discussion of the place of medicine in the treatment of the mad prior to the nineteenth-century events with which I was principally concerned was accordingly quite brief and limited, stressing only some of the special advantages that eighteenth-century doctors had in asserting jurisdiction over insanity and pointing out that by the latter part of George III's

Chapter 6 is reprinted from the *European Journal of Sociology,* Volume 16, 1975, pp. 219–61, by permission of the editors.

1. William F. Bynum, "Rationales for Therapy in British Psychiatry, 1780–1835," *Medical History* 18 (1974):317–34.

2. William L. Parry-Jones, *The Trade in Lunacy: A Study of Private Madhouses in England in the Eighteenth and Nineteenth Centuries* (London: Routledge and Kegan Paul; Toronto: University of Toronto Press, 1972).

3. Ida Macalpine and Richard A. Hunter, *George III and the Mad Business* (London: Allen Lane, 1969).

4. Richard Hunter and Ida Macalpine, *Three Hundred Years of Psychiatry, 1535 to 1860: A History Presented in Selected English Texts* (London: Oxford University Press, 1963).

reign, theirs was clearly the dominant interpretation of madness in elite and educated circles. Subsequent work by Michael MacDonald[5] and Roy Porter[6] has given us a far richer and more nuanced portrait of developments from the late Tudor period to the dawn of the industrial age, presenting some particularly provocative arguments about the sources from which the upper classes adopted a naturalistic and medical perspective on mental disorder, while emphasizing the survival of more eclectic, even magical and supernatural notions among the masses even at the very end of period examined.

A year after "From Madness to Mental Illness" appeared, Roger Cooter published an excellent two-part article exploring the impact of phrenology on early-nineteenth-century medical thinking about madness.[7] Although I would quarrel with some of the further claims he makes about phrenology's importance, Cooter's central argument is surely well taken: Phrenology served as a vital theoretical mediation in the attempt to assimilate moral treatment into the medical armamentarium. Its doctrines provided a clear physiological explanation of the operations of the brain, one that permitted a parsimonious account of abnormal as well as normal mental functioning, while advancing a coherent rationale for the application of *both* medical and moral treatment in cases of insanity. His essay constitutes an important elaboration and refinement of my argument about the ways in which medicine succeeded in incorporating moral treatment into its recognized sphere of expertise.

It should be apparent that what follows deals with only one aspect of the rise of a self-conscious profession monopolizing the treatment of the mentally disordered. For England, we still lack a careful prosopographical study of the changing bases of recruitment to the mad-business, or any sustained analysis of the development of an organized profession. Two such attempts *have* been made, drawing on American materials,[8] and it

---

5. Michael MacDonald, *Mystical Bedlam: Madness, Anxiety, and Healing in Seventeenth Century England* (Cambridge: Cambridge University Press, 1981); "Insanity and the Realities of History in Early Modern England," *Psychological Medicine* 11 (1981):11−25; and "Religion, Social Change, and Psychological Healing in England, 1600−1800," in *The Church and Healing*, ed. W. Sheils (Oxford: Basil Blackwell, 1982), 101−26.

6. Roy Porter, *Mind Forg'd Manacles: A History of Madness in England from the Restoration to the Regency* (London: Athlone, 1987); "Being Mad in Eighteenth Century England," *History Today*, December 1981, 42−48; "The Rage of Party: A Glorious Revolution in English Psychiatry?" *Medical History* 27 (1983):35−50; and "Love, Sex, and Madness in Eighteenth Century England," *Social Research* 53 (1986):211−42.

7. R. J. Cooter, "Phrenology and British Alienists, circa 1825−1845," *Medical History* 20 (1976):135−51.

8. John Pitts, "The Association of Medical Superintendents of American Institutions for the Insane, 1844−1892: A Case Study of Specialism in American Medicine" (Ph.D. dissertation, University of Pennsylvania, 1978); Constance McGovern, *Masters of Madness: Social Origins of the American Psychiatric Profession* (Hanover, N.H.: University Press of New England, 1985).

clearly would be extremely helpful to have a comparable analysis of the development of psychiatry in Victorian England. I continue to believe, however, that assumptions about the *somatic* basis of mental disturbance have played a quite crucial role in legitimizing medical claims to exclusive jurisdiction over the mad throughout the nineteenth and twentieth centuries and have proved similarly crucial in the determination of therapeutic practices during this period. Indeed, I plan to make an examination of these issues the focus of my next book.[9]

From Madness to Mental Illness:
Medical Men
as Moral Entrepreneurs

"When I use a word," Humpty Dumpty said, in a rather scornful tone, "it means just what I choose it to mean—neither more nor less."

"The question is," said Alice, "whether you can make words mean so many different things."

"The question is," said Humpty Dumpty, "which is to be master—that's all."

—LEWIS CARROLL,
Through the Looking Glass

This chapter seeks to provide a sociological account of one aspect of a highly significant redefinition of the moral boundaries of English society, a redefinition that saw the transformation of insanity from a vague, culturally defined phenomenon afflicting an unknown, but probably small, portion of the total population into a condition that could be authoritatively diagnosed, certified, and dealt with only by a group of legally recognized experts and that was now seen as one of the major forms of deviance in English society. Where in the eighteenth century only the most violent and destructive among those now labeled insane would have been segregated and confined apart from the rest of the community, by the mid-nineteenth century, with the achievement of lunacy "reform," the asylum was endorsed as the sole officially approved response to the problems posed by all forms of mental illness. In what

9. For some preliminary discussion, see Andrew Scull and Diane Favreau, "The Clitoridectomy Craze," *Social Research* 53 (1986): 243–60; idem, "'A Chance to Cut Is a Chance to Cure': Sexual Surgery for Psychosis in Three Nineteenth Century Societies," in *Research in Law, Deviance, and Social Control*, vol. 8, ed. Steven Spitzer and Andrew Scull (Greenwich, Conn.: JAI Press, 1986): 3–39; Andrew Scull, "Desperate Remedies: A Gothic Tale of Madness and Modern Medicine," *Psychological Medicine* 17 (1987): 561–77.

follows, I want to focus attention rather closely on one centrally important feature of this whole process: just how that segment of the medical profession we now call psychiatry captured control over insanity; or, to put it another way, how those known in the early nineteenth century as mad-doctors first acquired a monopolistic power to define and treat lunatics. I shall begin, though, with some general remarks on the sociological importance of the issues I shall be raising here.

In the first place, although the locus of responsibility for lunatics has shifted from the family and the local community to a group of trained professionals who, by reason of their expertise, claim to have a unique capacity for understanding and treating them, this change is by no means confined to the case of mental illness. The symbiotic relationship between psychiatry and insanity, with which I am here concerned, is merely a particularly important example (just how important I shall indicate in a moment) of a much more general trend in the social control practices of modern societies.[1] Elites in such societies over about the past century and a half have increasingly sought to rationalize and legitimize their control of all sorts of deviant and troublesome elements by consigning them to the ministrations of experts. No longer content to rely on vague cultural definitions of, and informal responses to, deviation, rational-bureaucratic Western societies have increasingly delegated this task to groups of people who claim, or are assumed to have, special competence in these areas. Within sociology, this reality is reflected in the current vogue of "labeling theory" and in the concern with the reactive effects of agents of social control on the problems they are supposed to solve.

The decisions these people take, and the kinds of activities they engage in, form one of the crucial ways in which deviance is now socially organized. Experts are the crucial filters in what Kai Erikson has called "the community screen."[2] In the process of sorting out certain kinds of behavior from the everyday flow of social existence, and assigning those held responsible for them to one or another of the socially recognized deviant statuses, it is their worldview that is the most widely accepted. Most of the time, it is their theories that are used, albeit in a bastardized, simplified form, by the other elements in what we might call the referral system, those involved in "blowing the whistle" on deviants. Moreover, the experts form the final and decisive part of the screening process. Through their power to legally label, they focus, define, and institutionally fix the deviant's status. In the last analysis, laymen generally de-

---

1. Robert A. Scott, "The Construction of Stigma by Professional Experts," in *Deviance and Respectability*, ed. J. D. Douglas (New York: Basic Books, 1970).

2. Kai Erikson, *Wayward Puritans* (New York: Wiley, 1966).

fer to the experts and regard their decisions as authoritative: "Their mandate is to define whether or not a problem exists and what the 'real' character of the problem is and how it should be managed."[3]

Among the most important of these groups of experts are psychiatrists. To a greater degree than some other experts specializing in the social control of deviance, they possess the attribute of professional autonomy.[4] They make the most vigorous claims to have an expertise resting on a scientific basis, and their ideology has proved so plausible that their view of deviance is an increasingly important one. At least since the end of World War II, we have been moving away from a punitive and toward what Kittrie has termed a "therapeutic" state; that is, one that enshrines the psychiatric worldview.[5] Just as "in the eighteenth and nineteenth centuries, a host of . . . phenomena—never before conceptualized in medical terms—were renamed or reclassified as mental illness,"[6] so over the last few decades most other forms of deviance are being assimilated into a quasi-medical model, being relabeled as illness and therefore "treated" rather than punished.[7] In such a situation, psychiatrists become perhaps the most strategically important of all experts to study, particularly since "the thrust of the expansion of the application of medical labels has been toward addressing (and controlling) the *serious* forms of deviance, leaving to the other institutions [law and religion] a residue of essentially trivial and narrowly defined technical offences."[8]

In what follows, I shall be concerned with how psychiatrists in England first gained control over that type of deviance that must be assumed to form their core area of competence, namely insanity. Given the particular questions I have in mind, I shall not here be concerned with the issue of whether mental illness really *is* illness, and all that en-

3. Eliot Freidson, *Profession of Medicine: A Study in the Applied Sociology of Knowledge* (New York: Dodd, Mead, 1970), 303.

4. Cf. ibid.; and Freidson, *Professional Dominance: The Social Structure of Medical Care* (New York: Atherton, 1970).

5. Nicholas A. Kittrie, *The Right to Be Different: Deviance and Enforced Therapy* (Baltimore: Johns Hopkins University Press, 1972).

6. Thomas Szasz, *Ideology and Insanity* (New York: Doubleday, 1970), 137.

7. See, for example, Freidson, *Profession of Medicine*, 248–55; Irving Kenneth Zola, "Medicine, Morality, and Social Problems—Some Implications of the Label Mental Illness" (Paper presented at a meeting of the American Ortho-Psychiatric Association, 20–23 March 1968); idem, "Medicine as an Institution of Social Control," *Sociological Review* 20 (1972):487–504; Thomas Szasz, *The Myth of Mental Illness: Foundations of a Theory of Personal Conduct*, rev. ed. (New York: Harper and Row, 1974); idem, *Law, Liberty and Psychiatry* (New York: Macmillan, 1963); idem, *The Manufacture of Madness* (New York: Dell, 1970); and Kittrie, *Right to Be Different*.

8. Freidson, *Profession of Medicine*, 249 (emphasis in the original).

tails. After all, "consequential human behavior stems from the meanings that actors impute to their experience, not from the meanings that an 'objective' observer may impute."[9] As sociologists, we are interested in how actions are socially defined rather than with what their intrinsic qualities are. In this case, regardless of whether it is correct in some ultimate ontological sense to describe insanity as an illness, once it has been identified as such, people's responses to it are mediated by and through that socially constructed meaning; so we can legitimately ask how it was that that particular social meaning was arrived at and what its consequences are. As Freidson has argued for illness in general, we can choose to focus, not on whether certain persons are mentally sick or not, but on how their life is reorganized because they are called mentally sick.

Just as in the case of bodily illness, where a profession is granted the authority to label one person's discomfort an illness and another's not, so too with mental distress, the psychiatrists possess the ultimate power to assign one person to the status of being mentally ill and to refuse the designation to another. And it is contact with society's official experts in this area, rather than manifestations of specific behavioral or mental disturbance, that most firmly and legitimately affixes the label in the eyes of the laymen. While the situation obviously varies with the nature and degree of one's alienation, the social acceptance (or rather rejection) of someone as crazy often depends on his or her new status being professionally legitimized.[10] Psychiatrists' labels stick in a way lay ones don't, not least because they are backed by the police power of the state. The psychiatrist can "transform his judgement into social reality."[11]

Psychiatrists, and other social control experts for that matter, negotiate reality on behalf of the rest of society. Theirs is preeminently a moral enterprise, involved with the creation and application of social meanings to particular segments of everyday life. Just like physicians, they "may be said to be engaged in the creation of illness as a social state which a human being may assume."[12] Indeed, in view of the indefinite criteria employed to identify and define "mental illness," its status as a socially constructed reality is, if anything, plainer than in the case of somatic illness, and the latitude granted the expert correspondingly wide. When we look at how medicine first "captured" insanity, we are in essence examining the growth and transformation of the moral order of society.

Most psychiatric historians have been inclined to equate the shift from religious or demonological "explanations" of insanity toward a concep-

9. Ibid., 213.

10. Derek Phillips, "Rejection: A Possible Consequence of Seeking Help for Mental Disorder," *American Sociological Review* 28 (1963):963–73.

11. Szasz, *Manufacture of Madness*, 75.

12. Freidson, *Profession of Medicine*, 205.

tion of it as illness with the progress of science.[13] As ideology, an account of the establishment of a medical monopoly over the treatment of insanity in these simplistic terms has obvious value, creating a myth with powerful protective functions for the profession of psychiatry. As explanation, however, its adequacy is distinctly more dubious, inasmuch as it completely ignores the social processes necessarily involved in any such transformation of perspectives.[14] Its utility is further diminished when one recalls that, whatever one's opinions on the extent of scientifically based knowledge of mental illness today, there would, I think, be a widespread consensus on the lack of any real knowledge base in early-nineteenth-century medicine that would have given the medical profession a rationally defensible claim to possess expertise vis-à-vis insanity. In what follows, then, I hope we can discount the naive "march of progress" school so popular among psychiatric historians and instead give our attention to the social processes involved.

For all intents and purposes, the insane in England were not really treated as a separate category or type of deviant much before the middle of the eighteenth century. They were simply part of the larger, more amorphous class of the poor and indigent, a category that also included vagrants and various minor criminal elements. They were a communal and family responsibility, and all save the most violent and unmanageable were kept in the community, rather than being segregated into separate receptacles that kept them apart from the rest of society. At this stage, medical interest in and concern with insanity were practically nonexistent. During the course of the eighteenth century, these old, informal mechanisms began to be abandoned. In their place, the response to all forms of deviance assumed an increasingly institutional form. Workhouses, almshouses, houses of industry and correction, all these institutions at first accommodated an essentially mixed, heterogeneous population of the troublesome and dependent and made little effort to classify inmates by age or sex or according to presumed differences in their underlying pathology.

The insane shared in this general trend, and there now emerged a number of institutions specifically concerned with dealing with them as a separate category, a process accelerated by the difficulty of handling them in one of the ordinary mixed institutions. Most of these early

13. See, for example, Gregory Zilboorg, *A History of Medical Psychology* (New York: Norton, 1941; paperback ed., 1967); Franz D. Alexander and Sheldon T. Selesnick, *The History of Psychiatry: An Evaluation of Psychiatric Thought and Practice from Prehistoric Times to the Present* (New York: Harper and Row, 1966).

14. In Szasz's words, we cannot proceed "as if the psychiatric historian were a socially neutral person, discovering historical 'facts'—when, in truth, he is a psychiatric propagandist, actively shaping the image of his discipline" (*Manufacture of Madness*, 111).

madhouses were private speculations run for profit. Given the difficulties others experienced managing the insane and the lack of restrictions or legal checks on the actual conduct of the business, they were generally a very lucrative investment. And it was precisely at this stage that the medical profession first began to assert an interest in lunacy. A number of doctors trying to gain a share of the lucrative new business, and possibly also to improve the treatment of the insane, began opening madhouses of their own and/or became involved in efforts to set up charity hospitals for the care of lunatics.[15]

The English medical profession at this time was composed of three separate elements—physicians, surgeons, and apothecaries—each of whom catered to a different clientele. The physicians, the elite's doctors, generally possessed a medical degree and, in London at least, were members of the Royal College of Physicians. But an M.D. was no guarantee of more than a passing acquaintance with classical authors in the fields, with no assurance of clinical experience; and membership in the college depended more on social connections than medical skill. Surgeons had only recently severed their links with the barbers' trade; entry into their ranks was usually by apprenticeship, and their status was distinctly lower than that of the physicians. Apothecaries catered largely to the middle and lower classes; they too were recruited by apprenticeship and lacked any real control over licensing and entry; so that those calling themselves apothecaries might vary from semi-illiterate quacks to highly competent practitioners by the standards of the time.[16]

15. For documentation of the societal response to insanity in England before the nineteenth century and of the emergence of medical interest in the treatment of the insane, see Andrew Scull, *Museums of Madness: The Social Organization of Insanity in Nineteenth-Century England* (London: Allen Lane; New York: St. Martin's Press, 1979), chap. 1; and William L. Parry-Jones, *The Trade in Lunacy: A Study of Private Madhouses in England in the Eighteenth and Nineteenth Centuries* (London: Routledge and Kegan Paul; Toronto: University of Toronto Press, 1972), passim.

16. An excellent example of the former was provided by William Finch. In his evidence before the Select Committee of 1815, he produced a certificate of insanity he had received from one such practitioner: "Hey Broadway A Potcarey of Gillingham Certefy that Mr. James Burt Misfortin hapened by a Plow in the Hed which is the Ocasim of his Ellness and By the Rising and Falling of the Blood and I think A Blister and Bleeding and meddeson Will be A Very Great thing. But Mr. James Burt would not A Gree to be Don at Home, Hay Broadway" (House of Commons, *Report of the Select Committee on Madhouses in England, with Minutes of Evidence and Appendices* [1815], 51). The profession as a whole did not succeed in laying down uniform standards for entry until the passage of the 1858 Medical Registration Act. The Apothecaries' Act of 1815 represented an early effort to define the legal status of that segment of the medical profession. Interestingly enough, it was George Man Burrows, one of the most well-known private madhouse keepers of the early nineteenth century and the chairman of the Association of Apothecaries and Surgeon Apothecaries, whose efforts were largely instrumental in securing its passage. See Parry-Jones, *Trade in Lunacy*, 78, 92–93.

The doctors entering the mad-business were not drawn exclusively from any one of these three classes; nor, so far as one can judge, did they differ significantly from the rest of the profession in skill or respectability. While "doctors" with little claim to the title did enter the field, so too did well-known society physicians and those trained at some of the best medical schools of the time.[17] By no means was the mad-business a refuge of only the most disreputable elements of the medical profession. To the contrary, those drawn from the most educated and literate elements of the profession were among the most vigorous and effective partisans of medicine's claims in this area and contributed most to its growing dominance of the field.

The earliest lay proprietors of madhouses had often attempted to attract clients by claiming to provide cures as well as care.[18] This idea that expert intervention could provide a means of restoring the deranged to reason naturally proved an attractive one. However, it was a much more plausible claim when asserted by the medical proprietors of madhouses. To understand why this should be so, one need only recall certain basic characteristics of eighteenth-century medicine.

Unlike its modern successor, eighteenth-century medicine did not involve identifying specific disease entities and then prescribing specialized treatments for them. Rather, it possessed an arsenal of what were regarded as useful weapons against all types of bodily dysfunction. No English doctor went quite so far as the American, Benjamin Rush, who reduced all illnesses to one underlying pathology and prescribed a single remedy, depletion.[19] Nevertheless, adherents of almost every one of the eighteenth-century medical "systems" exhibited a touching faith in a number of cure-alls—such things as purges, vomits, bleedings, and various mysterious colored powders, whose secrets were known only to their compounders. These theories and their associated remedies were read-

---

17. Both William Battie of St. Luke's and John Monro of Bethlem were well-known society physicians. Anthony Addington, one of George III's physicians, had formerly kept a private madhouse at Reading. Other established doctors who kept madhouses (with the university where they were trained) included Francis Willis (Oxford); Thomas Arnold (Edinburgh); Joseph Mason Cox (Edinburgh, Paris, and Leyden); Edward Long Fox (Edinburgh); and William Perfect (St. Andrew's). Ibid., 75–77.

18. See, for example, David Irish, *Levamen Infirmi, or, Cordial Counsel to the Sick and Diseased* (London: For the Author, 1700); Thomas Fallowes, *The Best Method for the Cure of Lunaticks, with Some Account of the Incomparable Oleum Cephalicum Used in the Same, Prepared and Administered by Tho. Fallowes, at His House in Lambeth-Marsh* (London: For the Author, 1705). (Fallowes' M.D. was awarded by himself.)

19. On Rush, see Norman Dain, *Concepts of Insanity in the United States, 1789–1865* (New Brunswick, N.J.: Rutgers University Press, 1964), 14–24; and Richard Harrison Shyrock, *The Development of Modern Medicine* (Philadelphia: University of Pennsylvania Press, 1936), 28–29.

ily adapted to incorporate the new disease of insanity; it was but a small leap to assert that these things would also cure lunatics.[20]

The doctors, then, had an advantage when it came to justifying their claims to cure insanity, because everybody "knew" that they possessed powerful remedies whose use demanded special training and expertise and whose "efficacy" against a wide range of complaints was generally acknowledged. They exploited this advantage to good effect. The appearance of a number of books on the medical treatment of insanity added weight to their claim, and such famous medical teachers as William Cullen began to incorporate materials on the subject into their lectures, so that some physicians could assert that they had specialized training in this area.[21] On this basis, therefore, doctors were gradually acquiring a dominant, though not a monopolistic, position in the mad-business by the end of the eighteenth century. Numerically, they might still be a minority, but the view of insanity as an illness was by now popular in elite circles, particularly after George III began to suffer from recurrent bouts of derangement.

As I have shown elsewhere, during the eighteenth and early nineteenth centuries, conditions in both medically and nonmedically run madhouses generally ranged from the bad to the appalling.[22] In part because of the lack of legal checks on entry into the business or on subsequent conduct of it, gross exploitation and maltreatment of patients

20. William Perfect advocated the use of bleedings, setons, and electricity, and the administration of emetics, digitalis, and antimony (W. Perfect, *Select Cases in the Different Species of Insanity, Lunacy or Madness, with the Modes or Practice as Adopted in the Treatment of Each* [Rochester: Gillman, 1787]; and idem, *A Remarkable Case of Madness, with the Diet and Medicines Used in the Cure* [Rochester: For the Author, 1791]). See also Thomas Arnold, *Observations on the Nature, Kinds, Causes, and Prevention of Insanity*, 2 vols. (Leicester: Robinson and Caddell, 1782–86); William Pargeter, *Observations on Maniacal Disorders* (Reading: For the Author, 1792); and Joseph Mason Cox, *Practical Observations on Insanity: In Which Some Suggestions Are Offered Towards an Improved Mode of Treating Diseases of the Mind . . . to Which are Subjoined, Remarks on Medical Jurisprudence as Connected with Diseased Intellect* (London: Baldwin and Murray, 1806).

21. See William Cullen, *First Lines of the Practice of Physic*, 2 vols. (Edinburgh: Bell and Bradfute, 1808). Among his students who opened madhouses were Arnold and Hallaran.

22. Cf. Scull, *Museums of Madness*, chaps. 2 and 3. In Dickens' words: "Coercion for the outward man, and rabid physicking for the inward man were then the specifics for lunacy. Chains, straw, filthy solitude, darkness, and starvation; jalap, syrup of buckthorn, tartarized antimony and ipecacuanna administered every spring and fall in fabulous doses to every patient, whether well or ill; spinning in whirligigs, corporal punishment, gagging, 'continued intoxication', nothing was too widely extravagant, nothing too monstrously cruel to be prescribed by mad-doctors" (Charles Dickens and W. H. Wills, "A Curious Dance Round a Curious Tree" [1852], reprinted in *Charles Dickens' Uncollected Writings from Household Words* [Bloomington and London: Indiana University Press, 1968], 2:382–83).

:re common.[23] And it was a particular instance of this kind of maltreatment, involving the death under mysterious circumstances of an inmate of the York Asylum, that provoked the decision to set up the York Retreat. Here there emerged an alternative approach to the mentally disturbed that for a time threatened the growing dominance of medicine in this field.

William Tuke, the founder of the Retreat, was a layman with a considerable, and not entirely unmerited, distrust of the medical profession of his day.[24] His primary concern was with providing humane care for insane Quakers, though he also hoped, if possible, to cure them. Skeptical as he was of medicine's value, he possessed a sufficiently open mind to investigate its claims to have specific remedies for mental illness. With his encouragement, both the first visiting physician, Dr. Thomas Fowler, and his successors made a trial of all of the various medicines and techniques that members of the profession had suggested.

The results must have been a disappointment, though perhaps not a surprise. In Samuel Tuke's words, "The experience of the Retreat . . . will not add much to the honour or extent of medical science. I regret . . . to relate the pharmaceutical means which have failed, rather than to record those which have succeeded."[25] Fowler found that

> the sanguine expectations, which he successively formed of the benefit to be derived from various pharmaceutical remedies, were, in great measure, as successively disappointed; and, although the proportion of cures, in the early part of the Institution, was respectable, yet the medical means were so imperfectly connected with the progress of recovery, that he could not avoid suspecting them, to be rather concomitants than causes. Further experiments and observations confirmed his suspicions, and led him

23. With mordant wit, William Belcher termed the madhouse proprietor of the period the "Smiling Hyena": "This animal is a non-descript of a mixed species. Form obtuse—body black—head gray—teeth and prowess on the decline—visage smiling, especially at the sight of shining metal of which its paws are extremely retentive—heart supposed to be of a kind of tough white leather. N.B. He doth ravish the rich when he getteth him into his den" (Belcher, 1796, cited in Parry-Jones, *Trade in Lunacy*, 226).

24. Cf. Kathleen Jones, *Lunacy, Law, and Conscience, 1744–1845: The Social History of the Care of the Insane* (London: Routledge and Kegan Paul, 1955), 58–65; and idem, *Mental Health and Social Policy, 1845–1955* (London: Routledge and Kegan Paul, 1960), 9. His grandfather's disapproval led Samuel Tuke to relinquish his medical studies and enter the family business instead (*Dictionary of National Biography*, s.v. "Tuke, Samuel"). Daniel Hack Tuke was the first of the family to qualify as a doctor. He "only overcame the family prejudice against that profession in 1852 after refusing to enter Tuke, Son and Co., giving up a legal career in its early stages and failing lamentably to become a poet" (Jones, *Lunacy, Law, and Conscience*, 60).

25. Samuel Tuke, *Description of the Retreat: An Institution near York for Insane Persons of the Society of Friends* (1813), facsimile ed., ed. Richard A. Hunter and Ida Macalpine (London: Dawsons, 1964), 110.

to the painful conclusion (painful alike to our pride and our humanity), that medicine, as yet, possesses very inadequate means to relieve the most grievous of human diseases.[26]

Fowler's death in 1801 and the swift demise of his successor meant that the Retreat had three visiting physicians within its first five years of operation. Both of the others arrived convinced of medicine's applicability and value. Both were disillusioned: "They have had recourse to various means, suggested by either their own knowledge and ingenuity, or recommended by later writers; but their success has not been such, as to rescue this branch of their profession, from the charge, unjustly exhibited by some against the art of medicine in general, of its being chiefly conjectural."[27] Numerous trials had shown that all the suggestions that had been made, with the exception of warm baths for melancholics, were either useless or positively harmful.

Henceforth, the visiting physician confined his attention to treating cases of bodily illness, and it was the lay people in charge of the day-to-day running of the institution who began to develop the alternative response to insanity that became known as moral treatment.[28] One cannot readily summarize in a phrase or two what moral treatment consisted of, nor reduce it to a few standard formulas, for it was emphatically not a specific technique. Rather, it was a general, pragmatic approach aimed at minimizing external, physical coercion; and it has, therefore, usually been interpreted as unproblematically "kind" and "humane." Instead of merely resting content with controlling those who were no longer quite human, which had been the dominant concern of traditional responses to the mad, moral treatment actively sought to transform the lunatic, to remodel him or her into something approximating the bourgeois ideal of the rational individual; and as part of this process, an effort was made to create an environment that removed the artificial obstacles standing in the way of the "natural" tendencies toward recovery. Tuke was convinced that "there is much analogy between the judicious treatment of children and that of insane persons."[29] One should seek to reeducate the patients, teach them to reassert their powers of self-control.[30] This ap-

26. Ibid., 111.

27. Ibid., 115. Pinel's experience at Bicêtre led him to the same conclusion: "My faith in pharmaceutical preparations was gradually lessened, and my skepticism went at length so far, as to induce me never to have recourse to them until moral remedies had completely failed" (Philippe Pinel, *A Treatise on Insanity*, trans. D. D. Davis [Sheffield: Cadell and Davies, 1806], 109). Here, too, moral treatment involved a rejection of the traditional medical paradigm.

28. In 1815, William Tuke reported that "very little medicine is used at the Retreat" (House of Commons, *Report of the Select Committee* [1815], 135, evidence of William Tuke).

29. Tuke, *Description of the Retreat*, 150.

30. Ibid., 139.

proach involved "treating the patient as much in the manner of a rational being, as the state of mind will possibly allow,"[31] rather than using motives of fear as a way of managing the patient. Far from harshness being necessary to avoid violent outbreaks among the inmates, it tended only to produce them.[32]

Treated less harshly and more nearly as rational human beings, the patients at the Retreat responded by acting less like the traditional stereotype of the raving maniac. Tuke's contention that "furious mania is almost unknown at the Retreat . . . and that all the patients wear clothes and are generally induced to adopt orderly habits"[33] agrees with the independent observations of visitors.[34] The refusal to use chains, the absence of physical abuse or coercion of patients, and the success in restoring them to a measure of dignity and self-respect, all contrasted sharply with the prevailing conditions in most madhouses of the period.[35] Perhaps even more spectacular were the changes thus effected: Despite a conservative outlook that classified no one as cured who had to be readmitted to an asylum, the statistics collected during the Retreat's first fifteen years of operation seemed to show that moral treatment could restore a large proportion of cases to sanity. Of recent cases (those of less than a year's standing), twenty-one out of thirty-one diagnosed as mania had recovered; nineteen out of thirty cases of melancholia were restored; and four others were sufficiently improved that they no longer required confinement. Even among long-standing and apparently hopeless cases, a respectable number were discharged as cured.[36] Andrew Duncan was so impressed by his visit to the Retreat that he commented: "The fraternity denominated Quakers have demonstrated beyond contradiction the very great advantages resulting from a mode of treatment in cases on Insanity much more mild than was before introduced into any Lunatic Asylum at home or abroad. In the management of this institution, they have set an example which claims the imitation, and deserves the thanks, of every sect and every nation."[37]

31. Ibid., 158.

32. "Furious mania is very often excited by the mode of management" (ibid., 144).

33. Ibid., 144.

34. See also G. De la Rive, *Lettre adressée aux rédacteurs de la Bibliothèque britannique sur un nouvel établissement pour la guérison des aliénés* (Geneva: For the Author, 1798); William Stark, *Remarks on the Construction of Public Asylums for the Cure of Mental Derangement* (Glasgow: Hedderwick, 1810); and Edinburgh Royal Lunatic Asylum, *A Short Account of the Rise, Progress, and Present State of the Lunatic Asylum at Edinburgh* (Edinburgh: Neill, 1812).

35. See Scull, *Museums of Madness*, chap. 3, passim.

36. Ten of sixty-one classed as maniacs, and six of twenty-one melancholics. Tuke, 202–3. All figures were for the period 1796–1811.

37. Dr. A. Duncan, Sr., reported in Edinburgh Royal Lunatic Asylum, *Short Account . . . of the Lunatic Asylum*, 15. Tuke's own comment: "The experience of the Retreat . . . has

These results were given considerable publicity through the efforts of a stream of visitors interested in lunacy reform and through Tuke's own writings.[38] However, though there were exceptions like Duncan, the initial response of most of the medical profession to the claims of moral treatment was one of hostility. In the face of the evidence, they simply tried to reassert the value of the traditional medical approach. Hill's book, perhaps the best-known work on the subject published at this time, assured its readers that "insanity is as generally curable as any of those violent Diseases most successfully treated by Medicine,"[39] and truculently asserted that "direct medical remedies can never be too early introduced or too readily applied."[40] Nisbet concurred: "The disease of insanity in all its shades and varieties, belongs, in point of treatment, to the department of the physician alone. . . . The medical treatment . . . is that part on which the whole success of the cure hangs."[41] And when the 1815 Select Committee asked Dr. John Weir, the official inspector of the conditions naval maniacs were kept under, for his opinion on the value of medical intervention, he qualified his answer only slightly: "In recent cases, and those unconnected with organic lesions of the brain, malformation of the skull, and hereditary disposition to insanity . . . medical treatment is of the utmost importance."[42] Nor should this reaction come as a surprise. After all, moral treatment challenged the traditional paradigm of what was suitable as a method of treating illness of any sort. Furthermore, the wholesale rejection of standard medical techniques naturally ran counter to the profession's deep intellectual and emotional investment in the value of its own theory and practice.

---

demonstrated, beyond all contradiction, the superior efficacy, both in respect of cure and security, of a mild system of treatment in all cases of mental disorder" (Tuke, *Description of the Retreat*, vi).

38. See Scull, *Museums of Madness,* 67–68.

39. George Nesse Hill, *An Essay on the Prevention and Cure of Insanity* (London: Longman et al., 1814), 201.

40. Ibid., 205.

41. William Nisbet, *Two Letters to the Right Honourable George Rose, M.P., on the Reports at Present Before the Honourable House of Commons on the State of Madhouses* (London: Cox, 1815), 7, 21.

42. House of Commons, *Report of the Select Committee* (1815), 32. Cf. the comments of Sir William Lawrence, who, among his other activities, served as surgeon to Bethlem from 1815 until 1867: "They who consider the mental operation as acts of an immaterial being, and thus disconnect the sound state of the mind from organization, act very consistently in disjoining insanity also from the corporeal structure, and in representing it as a disease, not of the brain, but of the mind. Thus we come to disease of an immaterial being, for which, suitably enough, moral treatment has been recommended. I firmly believe, on the contrary, that the various forms of insanity, that all the affections comprehended under the general term of mental derangement are only evidences of cerebral affections . . . symptoms of diseased brain. . . . Sometimes, indeed, the mental phenomena are dis-

Those outside the profession, of course, lacked any such prior commitments and so were readier converts. In particular, those laymen who, for a number of years, had been agitating for lunacy reform on humanitarian grounds but who had previously lacked a viable alternative model to existing asylums eagerly seized on moral treatment. Since it was these lay people, primarily magistrates and upper middle-class philanthropists, who were the prime movers in the effort to reorganize the treatment of insanity through changes in the law, their conversion was a highly significant one.

Within two years of the publication of Tuke's *Description of the Retreat,* which brought the Retreat national attention, a series of revelations about the conditions in other madhouses further undermined medicine's claims to expertise or special competence in the treatment of insanity. Separate investigations of conditions at Bethlem and the York Asylum, hitherto regarded as among the leading institutions under medical control, uncovered evidence of systematic cruelty and maltreatment of patients,[43] reflected in extremely high mortality rates. This discovery in itself provided a highly unfavorable comparison with the lay-run Retreat. Furthermore, the evidence of even the medical witnesses before the Select Committee provided support for William Tuke's contention that "in cases of mental derangement . . . very little can be done by way of medical treatment."[44]

The evidence given by Charles Best and Thomas Monro, physicians at York and Bethlem respectively, was particularly damaging. The Monro family had been physicians to Bethlem for almost a century, and prior to this Thomas Monro himself had been thought of as one of the foremost experts on the medical treatment of insanity. Like Best, though, the credibility of his testimony was colored by the committee's knowledge of conditions in his asylum, and he was treated as a hostile witness. Under close questioning by the committee, the extent of his medical treatment was now revealed to the public: "In the months of May, June, July, Au-

---

turbed, without any visible deviation from the healthy structure of the brain. . . . We find the brain, like other parts, subject to what is called functional disorder; but, although we cannot actually demonstrate the fact, we have no more doubt that the material cause of the symptoms or external signs of disease is in this organ, than we do that impaired biliary secretion has its source in the liver, or faulty digestion in the stomach. . . . *The effect of medical treatment completely corroborates these views. Indeed they, who talk of and believe in diseases of the mind, are too wise to put their trust in mental remedies. Arguments, syllogisms, discourses, sermons, have never yet restored any patient; the moral pharmacopoeia is quite inefficient, and no real benefit can be conferred without vigorous medical treatment, which is as efficacious in these affections, as in the diseases of any other organs* (Lawrence [1819], quoted in Richard Hunter and Ida Macalpine, *Three Hundred Years of Psychiatry, 1535 to 1860: A History Presented in Selected English Texts* [London: Oxford University Press, 1963], 750–51 [my emphasis]).

43. Cf. Scull, *Museums of Madness,* chap. 2.
44. House of Commons, *Report of the Select Committee,* 135, evidence of William Tuke.

gust and September, we generally administer medicines; we do not in the winter season, because the house is so excessively cold that it is not thought proper. . . . We apply generally bleeding, purging, and vomits; those are the general remedies we apply. . . . All the patients who require bleeding are generally bled on a particular day, and they are purged on a particular day."[45] Later in his testimony, Monro gave a few more details: all the patients under his care, except those manifestly too weak to survive such a heroic regime, "are ordered to be bled about the latter end of May, or the beginning of May, according to the weather; and after they have been bled they take vomits once a week for a certain number of weeks; after that we purge the patients."[46] Thereafter, of course, patients were kept chained to their beds at least four days out of every seven.

A committee convinced of the value of moral treatment's emphasis on treating every lunatic as an individual was in principle unlikely to approve of such indiscriminate mass medication. Under the even more hostile questioning he now faced, Monro was forced to make a still more damaging admission. "Do you think," he was asked, "it is within the scope of medical knowledge to discover any other efficacious means of treating Insane persons?" "With respect to the means used, I really do not depend a vast deal upon medicine; I do not think medicine is the sheet anchor; it is more by management that those patients are cured than by medicine. . . . *The disease is not cured by medicine, in my opinion. If I am obliged to make that public I must do so.*"[47] The only question that remained was why Monro continued to employ therapies he conceded were useless. He himself had already provided an answer to that: "That has been the practice invariably for years, long before my time; it was handed down to me by my father, and *I do not know any better practice.*"[48]

---

45. Ibid., 93.

46. Ibid., 95.

47. Ibid., 99 (my emphasis). Cf. Ellis' comment, "Of the abuses that have existed, the cause of a great proportion of them may be traced to the mystery with which many of those who have had the management of the insane have constantly endeavored to envelop it" (William Charles Ellis, *A Letter to Thomas Thompson, Esq., M.P., Containing Considerations on the Necessity of Proper Places Being Provided by the Legislature for the Reception of All Insane Persons and on Some of the Abuses Which Have Been Found to Exist in Madhouses, with a Plan to Remedy Them* [Hull: Topping and Dawson, 1815]). Expertise always flourishes where its techniques are somewhat mysterious; the expert, wherever possible "*minimizes the role of persuasive evidence in his interaction with his clientele*" (Freidson, *Professional Dominance*, 110 [emphasis in the original]). Being forced to justify his actions to laymen almost always weakens the professional's authority (cf. ibid., chap. 4, passim). Nowhere is this more clearly the case than when a challenge to produce rational grounds for one's procedures cannot be met.

48. House of Commons, *Report of the Select Committee* (1815), 95, (a nice example of medicine's bias toward active intervention). Cf. Thomas Scheff, *Being Mentally Ill: A Sociological Theory* (Chicago: Aldine, 1966), chap. 4; and Freidson, *Profession of Medicine*, chap. 12.

St. Luke's Hospital, London's other charity asylum, had not come in for the severe criticism directed at Bethlem. Nevertheless, when its physician, Dr. A. J. Sutherland, was called to give evidence, his answers were extremely circumspect, and he sought to be as noncontroversial as possible. While he felt that medicines for the stomach might be of some indirect benefit, he conceded that "moral treatment is of course more especially important in the treatment of mental disorder."[49] Similarly, when Dr. John Harness, a commissioner of the Transport Board, was asked "what was his opinion as to the utility of medical treatment of Insanity," he replied: "Although much may be effected by medical treatment, I have before stated that I am not sanguine in the expectation of a permanent advantage from it."[50]

Doctors at this time played another important role vis-à-vis the insane. Five commissioners selected from the members of the Royal College of Physicians were charged with annually inspecting metropolitan madhouses under the 1774 Act. Even conceding the defects of the act, as the reformers did, their record was hardly one to inspire confidence in a system of medical policing of asylums or in physicians' willingness to judge the work of their colleagues. According to Dr. Richard Powell, the secretary to the Royal College and himself a commissioner, the visits took no more than six days a year to perform. Often as many as six or eight madhouses were visited in a day. No attempt was made to check whether the numbers resident corresponded to those the commissioners had been notified of. The justification for medical visitation was primarily that no one else was competent to assess the medical treatment administered. Yet Powell conceded that, apart from cursory inquiries as to the condition of the patients, no effort was made to discover what medical treatment the patients received, let alone to find out how effective it was.

The most respectable medical figure to appear before the committee was Sir Henry Halford, who was already "indisputably at the head of London practice." A favorite of George III's, he was later physician to George IV and Victoria, and from 1820 to his death in 1844, president of the Royal College of Physicians.[51] As the official spokesman for the most prestigious branch of the medical profession and an influential figure in elite circles, he obviously presented his evidence with a view to making a strong case for the value of the medical approach and in an effort to rectify the damage done by Best's and Monro's testimony. In practice, his evidence was too rambling and confused for that. Having begun by asserting that medical intervention was valuable, at least in the early stages of the disorder, he subsequently conceded that "our knowledge of insanity has not kept pace with our knowledge of other distem-

49. House of Commons, *Report of the Select Committee* (1815), 136.
50. Ibid., 159.
51. *Dictionary of National Biography*, s.v. "Halford, (Sir) Henry."

pers," a situation he blamed on "the habit we find established, of transferring patients under this malady, as soon as it has declared itself, to the
care of persons who too frequently limit their attention to the mere personal security of their patients, without attempting to assist them by the
resources of medicine." "The profession," he acknowledged, had "much
to learn on the subject of mental derangement." By the end of his testimony, he had given the impression that medicine lacked reliable knowledge in this area and could offer little by way of effective therapy. In
mitigation, he declared that "we want facts in the history of the disease"
and coupled this asseveration with the vague hope that "if they are carefully recorded, under the observation of enlightened physicians, no
doubt, they will sooner or later be collected in sufficient number, to admit of safe and useful inductions."[52] As a performance, this was scarcely
calculated to convince the somewhat skeptical audience he faced. He had
provided neither evidence nor plausible argument to refute the contention of those who favored moral treatment that "against mere insanity,
unaccompanied by bodily derangement, [medicine] appears to be almost
powerless."[53] Nor had he succeeded in erasing the unfavorable impression created by earlier medical testimony.

If Monro did not know of any better weapons to use against insanity
than the traditional antiphlogistic system, the laymen who were acquainted at first hand with the results of moral treatment obviously
thought that *they* did. Both their testimony before official inquiries and
the pamphlets they were busily writing now took on a tone of considerable hostility to medicine's claims to jurisdiction in this area. When
Edward Wakefield was asked, "In consequence of the observations you
have made on the state and management of the Lunatic Establishments,
and the manner of inspecting them, are you of the opinion that medical
persons exclusively ought to be Inspectors and Controllers of Madhouses?" his response was:

> I think they are the most unfit of any class of persons. In the first place,
> *from every enquiry I have made, I am satisfied that medicine has little or no effect on*
> *the disease, and the only reason for their selection is the confidence which is placed in*
> *their being able to apply a remedy to the malady.* They are all persons interested
> more or less. It is extremely difficult in examining either the public Institu-
> tions or private houses, not to have strong impression upon your mind,
> that medical men derive a profit in some shape or form from those differ-
> ent establishments. . . . The rendering therefore, [of] any interested class
> of persons the Inspectors and Controllers, I hold to be mischievous in the
> greatest possible degree.[54]

52. House of Commons, *First Report of the Select Committee on Madhouses* (1816), 13–14.
53. [Sydney Smith], "An Account of the York Retreat," *Edinburgh Review* 23 (1814):
196.
54. House of Commons, *Report of the Select Committee* (1815), 24 (my emphasis).

Higgins, who had witnessed at first hand over many months the practices of one of the most famous medical "specialists" in the field, was, if anything, still more hostile. He pointed out that in the aftermath of Dr. Best's departure from the York Asylum and the establishment of an efficient system of lay visitation there, the number of deaths of patients fell from twenty a year to only four. Furthermore, thirty patients were almost at once found fit for discharge. In his caustic fashion he demanded to know "who after this will doubt the efficacy of my medicine—visitors and committees? I will warrant it superior even to Dr. Hunter's famous secret—*insane powders*—either green or grey—or his patent Brazil salts into the bargain."[55] Higgins was clearly angered by the efforts of the medical profession to explain away as legitimate medical techniques for "treating" insanity what he perceived as cruelty or to attribute to the progress of the condition itself what he saw as the consequences of neglect. In contemptuous tones, he commented:

> Amongst much medical nonsense, published by physicians interested to conceal their neglect, and the abuses of their establishments, it has been said, that persons afflicted with insanity are more liable than others to mortification of their extremities. Nothing of the kind was ever experienced at the institution of the Quakers. If the members of the royal and learned College of Physicians were chained, or shut up naked, on straw saturated with urine and excrement, with a scanty allowance of food, exposed to the indecency of a northern climate, in cells having windows unglazed, I have no doubt that they would soon exhibit as strong a tendency to mortified extremities, as any of their patients.[56]

William Ellis, though himself medically qualified,[57] by now possessed firsthand acquaintance with Tuke's work at the Retreat and had absorbed much of the latter's skepticism about the activities of his fellow professionals. His *Letter* to Thomas Thompson, M.P. (a member of the Select Committee), contained a number of critical remarks directed at them. In particular, he alleged that "the management of the insane has been in too few hands; and many of those who have been engaged in it, finding it a very lucrative concern, have wished to involve it in great mystery, and, in order to prevent institutions for their cure from becoming more general, were desirous that it should be thought that there was some secret in the way of medicine for the cure, not easily to be found

55. Godfrey Higgins, *The Evidence Taken Before a Committee of the House of Commons Respecting the Asylum at York; with Observations and Notes, and a Letter to the Committee* (Doncaster: Sheardown, 1816), 48. Dr. Alexander Hunter was, until his death (when he was succeeded by his protégé, Dr. Charles Best), the physician to the York Asylum. In addition to his lucrative trade at the asylum, which included extensive embezzlement of its funds, he energetically promoted his "powders" as a certain, if expensive, home remedy for insanity for those who could not afford his full-time ministrations.

56. Ibid., 48, footnote.

57. M.D., St. Andrew's, M.R.C.S.

out. Some medical men have gone so far as even to condescend to the greatest quackery in the treatment of insanity."[58] To the contrary, Ellis contended there were no medical specifics for the successful treatment of madness, and acceptance of the idea that care of the insane was best left to experts, medical or otherwise, was the surest guarantee of abuse. In his own proposals for reform, therefore, he advocated constant lay supervision of all asylums by local magistrates.[59]

The propagation of the notion that "very little dependence is to be placed on medicine alone for the cure of insanity"[60] posed a clear threat to the professional dominance of this field. Given that those most convinced of the truth of this proposition were also the prime movers in trying to obtain lunacy reform, the doctors interested in insanity were unable any longer to ignore or depreciate moral treatment. They had to find some way to accommodate it.

At first sight, moral treatment seemed to be an unpromising basis for any profession trying to assert special competence in the treatment of the insane. In Freidson's words, "One of the things that marks off professions from occupations is the professions' claims to schooling in knowledge of an especially esoteric, scientific, or abstract character that is markedly superior to the mere experience of suffering from the illness or having attempted pragmatically to heal a procession of sufferers from the illness."[61] Moral treatment had begun by rejecting existing "scientific" responses as worse than useless; and the remedies proposed in their place—warm baths and kindness—hardly provided much of a foundation for claims to possess the kinds of expertise and special skills that ordinarily form the basis for the grant of professional autonomy.

In practice, however, this feature of moral treatment proved an advantage to those bent on reasserting medicine's jurisdiction in this area. The very difficulty of erecting professional claims on such a flimsy basis largely precluded the emergence of an organized group of competitors—lay therapists. Moreover, Tuke had explicitly *not* sought to create or train a group of experts in moral treatment. To the contrary, he and his followers were deeply suspicious of any plan to hand the treatment of lunatics over to the experts. The essence of moral treatment was its emphasis on humanity, and humanity was not a quality monopolized by experts. Indeed, the grant of a measure of autonomy that accompanied the acceptance of someone as an expert threatened to remove the surest guarantee of humane treatment of the insane: searching inquiry and oversight by outsiders.

58. Ellis, *Letter to Thomas Thompson*, 7.
59. Ibid., 35. Still he thought asylums should be administered on a day-to-day basis by a doctor, a position restated more emphatically in his later work.
60. [Smith], "York Retreat," 196.
61. Freidson, *Professional Dominance*, 106.

Interestingly enough, the earliest recruits to moral treatment were primarily those who were interested in the cause of lunacy reform, but who were unlikely, given their social status, to undertake themselves the task of administering an asylum—magistrates and upper-class philanthropists. The major exception to this generalization, William Ellis (who from 1814 on ran the Refuge, a private madhouse at Hull), was a doctor rather than just an expert on moral treatment. In the absence of any rival helping group, medicine set about assimilating moral treatment within its own sphere of competence.

Even while specifically denying medical claims to expertise in the area of insanity, the promoters of moral treatment had continued to employ a vocabulary laden with terms borrowed from medicine—"patient," "mental illness," "moral treatment," and so on. This failure to develop an alternative jargon itself made the reassertion of medical control somewhat easier, inasmuch as one of the most important connotations of the label "illness," and its associated array of concepts, is the idea that the syndrome to which it is applied is essentially a medical one. Given the critical role of language in shaping the social construction of reality, to employ terms implying that something is a medical problem and yet to deny that doctors are those most competent to deal with it seems perverse.

The lack of a coherent, well-articulated theory as an alternative to the model of insanity had this further consequence: that the denial of the applicability of medicinal remedies implied a view of insanity as essentially irremediable ("incurable") or as remediable ("curable") only by accident or through the operation of spontaneous tendencies toward recovery. Tuke himself seems to have adhered to the latter view. Thus, in his efforts to secure the establishment of asylums for the insane poor, he urged that "though we can do but little by the aid of medicine towards the cure of insanity, it is surely not the less our duty to use every means in our power to alleviate the complaint, or at least place the poor sufferer in a situation where nature may take her own course, and not be obstructed in the relief which she herself would probably bring to him." [62] And his discussion of the Retreat's success in restoring patients to sanity concludes: "As we have not discovered any anti-maniacal specific, and profess to do little more than assist Nature, in the performance of her own cure, the term *recovered*, is adopted in preference to that of *cured*." [63] Such modesty may well have been warranted; yet it was scarcely as appealing as the claim that one could actively influence the outcome in the desired direction.

62. Samuel Tuke, "Essay on the State of the Insane Poor," *The Philanthropist* 1 (1811):357.

63. Tuke, *Description of the Retreat*, 216–17.

All this meant that the challenge moral treatment posed to the medical dominance of insanity was not as clear-cut as it might have been. Furthermore, the medical profession possessed certain initial advantages as it sought to reassert its jurisdiction, advantages that could, however, have proved purely ephemeral. After all, there were, as yet, no legal barriers to the development of an organized rival group of therapists, and language is not immutable. The interested segments of the medical profession now moved to secure what they rightly perceived to be their imperiled position.

The potential consequences of taking Tuke seriously were most clearly articulated by Browne half a century later: "If therapeutical agents are cast aside or degraded from their legitimate rank, it will become the duty of the physician to give place to the divine or moralist, whose chosen mission it is to minister to the mind diseased; and of the heads of establishments like this [lunatic asylum] to depute their authority to the well-educated man of the world, who could, I feel assured, conduct an asylum fiscally, and as an intellectual boarding-house, a great deal better than any of us."[64] Earlier he had complained that "a want of power or inclination to discriminate between the inutility of medicine from its being inapplicable, and from its being injudiciously applied, had led to the adoption of the absurd opinion that the insane ought not to be committed to the charge of medical men. A manager of a large and excellent institution, entertaining this view, has declared the exhibition of medicine in insanity was useless, and that disease was to be cured by moral treatment only."[65]

The pernicious doctrine that traditional medical remedies were useless had spread dangerously far, even among those who continued to insist that doctors were the most qualified to treat lunatics. "We must confess," said Spurzheim, "that hitherto medical art has acquired very little merit in the cure of insanity; nature alone does almost everything."[66] When the *Quarterly Review*'s correspondent argued for medical control, he simultaneously made the dangerous concession that "the powers of medicine, merely upon mental hallucination are exceedingly circumscribed and feeble. . . . we want principles on which to form any satisfactory indications of treatment. . . . Almost the whole . . . of what may be called the strict medical treatment of madness must be regarded, at present, at least, as empirical, and the most extensive experience proves

64. William Alexander Francis Browne, *The Moral Treatment of the Insane: A Lecture* (London: Adlard, 1864), 5.

65. W. A. F. Browne, *What Asylums Were, Are, and Ought to Be* (Edinburgh: Black, 1837), 178.

66. J. G. Spurzheim, *Observations on the Deranged Manifestations of the Mind, or Insanity* (London: Baldwin, Craddock, and Joy, 1817), 197.

that very little is to be done."[67] Casting about for justifications for his insistence on medicine's entitlement to preeminence, he found remarkably few. The administration of warm baths now became something that could only be done under careful professional supervision. After all, the use of such a powerful technique had to be guided by an expert assessment of the condition of the individual patient. Cathartics were somehow rescued from the oblivion into which other medical remedies had been cast, once more with the caution that "the practice of purging" was by no means "of so simple and straight-forward a nature as might be at first sight conceived."[68] Conscious that these contentions might seem less than compelling, he resorted to the argument from experience: "Were it only an account of the frequent opportunities which more strictly medical practitioners have of witnessing aberrations of the intellect, from different sources, these would appear to be the fittest persons for the treatment of lunacy."[69]

The necessity for a more strenuous and convincing defense of professional prerogatives was clear. In the aftermath of the findings of the 1815–16 Select Committee, the reformers in the Commons attempted to devise a system of strict outside supervision and control of madhouse keepers, to ensure against the repetition of previous abuses. In 1816 and 1817, bills were introduced to set up a Board of Inspection of madhouses for each county, to be chosen annually from among the county magistrates. The proposal was revived in 1819, with the addition of a permanent Board of Inspection for the whole country, which was to visit all houses "at different and uncertain times."

All three of these bills would have empowered the boards of laymen to inquire into the treatment and management of patients, to direct discontinuance of practices they considered cruel or unnecessarily harsh, and to order the discharge of any patient they considered restored to sanity. If one follows Freidson in considering autonomy (the right to deny legitimacy to outside criticism of work and its performance) as the core characteristic of any profession, such proposals to introduce lay control and evaluation of expert performance must clearly be seen as of enormous strategic importance and as likely to provoke intense opposition from those threatened by such control. And that opposition was indeed forthcoming from doctors in the mad-business.

---

67. [David Uwins], "Insanity and Madhouses," *Quarterly Review* 15 (1816):402.
68. Ibid., 402–3.
69. Ibid., 403. Ellis, in the same bind, justified medical control of asylums as necessary to ensure that the physical ailments of the insane were properly treated: "Insane patients being liable to every complaint that others are subject to, together with those brought on by the body's sympathising with the mind, it seems now generally admitted that it is necessary to have a medical man to administer such establishments" (Ellis, *Letter to Thomas Thompson*, 11).

Burrows, in particular, was scathing in his criticisms of these bills. Somewhat disingenuously, he commented: "The provision of this [1817] Bill induces me to conclude that I certainly misinterpreted the import of many of the queries of the Members of the Committee of Inquiry; for I was led to think that a conviction had arisen out of the investigation, that all houses for the reception of insane persons ought to be under the superintendence of men of character and ability, and particularly of medical men."[70] Assuming that this was so (a large assumption, of course), it was simply absurd to allow the judgment of rank amateurs to override the mature judgment of a competent expert. If the legislature was convinced of the necessity of appointing commissioners to inspect madhouses, these ought, as in the past, to be medical men. One faced a situation in which "the most experienced will acknowledge the liability of being deceived, even where frequent opportunities of judging of the sanity of the mind have occurred. How then can those who are not only casual but unprofessional visitors pretend to decide on any particular case, or prescribe any alteration, or condemn any mode of treatment?"[71] It made no sense to ask a layman to pass judgment on the curative treatment of a patient, "for if any difference of opinion were to arise upon a question relative to the management or release of a patient, it were surely most proper that the medical opinion should prevail."[72] Furthermore, allowing "country gentlemen" to visit asylums, unaccompanied by medical men, in order to check for possible abuses, threatened the welfare of the patients in the most serious possible degree. The commotion their visits would cause, and the interference their ignorance might lead them to indulge in, would set at naught the asylum doctor's most skillful efforts to cure his patients. Consequently, the reformers could proceed with their plans only at "the hazard of great injury to the patients."[73]

70. George Man Burrows, *Cursory Remarks on a Bill Now in the House of Peers for Regulating of Madhouses, . . . with Observations on the Defects of the Present System* (London: Harding, 1817), 51. This pamphlet was dedicated: "To the Royal College of Physicians in London, the Constitutional Guardians of the Public Health, and the only Public Body which, by reason of its learning and experience, is truly competent to arrange and to carry into execution an Efficient Plan for the Amelioration of the Condition of the Insane."

71. Ibid., 23.

72. Ibid., 24.

73. Ibid., 25. There is an obvious parallel here with the modern psychiatrist's emphasis that the patient can "be greatly damaged if unskilled action is taken in . . . crucial, precarious therapeutic matters, necessitating the strict control of non-medically qualified mental hospital staff lest they engage in amateur psychotherapy" (Erving Goffman, *Asylums: Essays on the Social Situation of Mental Patients and Other Inmates* [Garden City, N.Y.: Doubleday, 1961], 377–78). As Freidson has shown for the medical profession as a whole, "where dangerous consequences can follow upon improper work . . . the *claim* of emergency and of possible dangerous consequences is a potent protective device" (Freidson, *Profession of Medicine*, 45). Cf., in this connection, Burrows' stated objections to the 1817 Bill: "It may be asserted . . . that if the insane be visited in the indiscriminate and judicial manner which

In the Commons, the lunacy reformers, remaining unmoved by these arguments, managed to secure the passage of each of the bills they introduced. The House of Lords, however, proved more receptive and in each instance exercised its veto powers. Undoubtedly, in so doing they were not motivated simply by the desire to protect the prerogatives of the medical profession. A strong faction there was opposed to any effort to extend the scope of central government authority. Aristocratic families with a lunatic in the closet were determined to avoid publicity, and hence the provisions in the 1816 and 1817 bills for a central register of "single lunatics" provoked further opposition.[74] Furthermore, the High Tories in the Upper House were disposed to reject on principle all type of "liberal" reform—their principal spokesman, Lord Eldon, the Lord Chancellor, once referred to "philanthropists" as "men pretending to humanity but brimful of intolerance, and swollen with malignity, which they all are."[75]

At the very least, however, the protests of the medical profession provided the Lords with a convenient ideological cloak for their opposition,

---

this Bill invites and empowers, that neither medical nor moral remedies will be of the least avail. . . . Who can say but some meddling inconsiderate justice might from ignorance . . . interfere; and by doing so blast all prospect of future happiness even of scores of his miserable fellow creatures. . . . The humane and skillful superintendent is, perhaps, on the point of seeing the fruition of all his cares and anxieties; and is anticipating the restoration of the faculties of his charge, and the well-earned remuneration for his troubles and cares; the relatives and friends of the patient, from the depths of despondency . . . are raised to the utmost pinnacle of hope and expectation; when lo! comes a fatal visitation—the patient must not be denied—he must be examined as to the state of his mind—the fatal chord is touched on which depends harmony of his mental with his corporeal frame; a tremendous explosion follows, and in one moment, the toil of months is destroyed: the wavering reason is lost, and sometimes forever!" (Burrows, *Regulating of Madhouses*, 25, 27, 29–30). If further evidence is needed that the purpose of this protest was the protection of professional prerogatives, Burrows' own version of the type of reform acceptable to the profession provides it: "The fundamental principles of all reformation or improvement in the management of madhouses or in the medical treatment of insane persons, therefore, consist: 1. In the fitness of the qualification of those who are permitted to take charge of them; 2. In having regular members of the faculty as superintendents; 3. In leaving superintendents uncontrolled in their management; 4. In protecting *Superintendents* against the malicious allegations of patients or outsiders; 5. In employing competent (i.e. Medical) Visitors" (ibid., 79). An opponent summarized his position as follows: "Dr. Burrows contends that Parliament has no right to interfere with the internal management of private lunatic asylums, and that the visits of medical men on the part of patients or their friends, is an intrusion, and no more warranted than the surveillance of the same persons in private practice" (Anonymous, *On the Present State of Lunatic Asylums, with Suggestions for Their Improvement* [London: Drury, 1839], 14).

74. Similar concerns had played a part in restricting the scope of the 1763 House of Commons Inquiry and emasculating the 1774 Madhouse Act.

75. Brenda Parry-Jones, "A Calendar of the Eldon-Richards Correspondence c. 1809–1822," *Journal of the Merioneth Historical and Record Society* 5 (1965): 39–50, cited in W. L. Parry-Jones, *Trade in Lunacy*, 16–17.

and while votes may actually have been swayed by other considerations, they were justified on these neutral, technical grounds. The Marquis of Landsdowne, who introduced the 1819 bill into the Lords, clearly foresaw the direction the debate would take and sought to reassure his audience that, while some systems of visitation and control by outsiders "might retard the cure of persons so affected," the insane would only benefit from the specific provisions of this bill.[76] Speaking against the bill, Eldon brushed this assuagement aside and reiterated the standard professional line: "It was of the utmost importance, with a view to the proper care of these unhappy individuals, and with a view to their recovery that they should be under the superintendance [*sic*] of men who had made this branch of medicine their peculiar study, and that the superintendence of physicians should not be interfered with." Yet this was precisely what the bill before them sought to do, and in consequence, "he conscientiously believed its regulations would tend to aggravate the malady with which the unfortunate persons were afflicted, or to retard their cure." One of the most objectionable features of the bill from his (and the medical profession's) perspective was that it "gave a number of penalties, half of which were to go to the informer, and *it was evident that the informer would be found amongst the attendants and servants in receptacles for lunatics, who would thus be made the judges of the conduct of the physicians,* and it would be impossible for the latter, under such circumstances, to resort to many of these means which their experience had taught them were most effectual for the cure of their unhappy patients."[77] Eldon had the authority of the best medical opinion behind him, when he asserted that "there could not be a more false humanity than an over-humanity with regard to persons afflicted with insanity," and in the division which followed, the bill was rejected 35 to 14.[78]

Temporarily, at least, the mad-doctors had successfully resisted efforts to restrict their professional autonomy, for with the rejection of the 1819 bill, the reform movement lost its momentum. Their victory was a fragile and uncertain one, however, so long as it rested on a marriage of convenience with political forces whose power was on the wane, and so long as they remained vulnerable to charges from moral-treatment enthusiasts that their expertise had no scientific or practical foundation. If they were to overcome their vulnerability, they had to develop a more sophisticated justification of their privileged position.

As part of this process, from about 1815 onwards, a veritable spate of books and articles purporting to be medical treatises on the treatment of

76. *Hansard's Parliamentary Debates,* 1st ser., vol. 40 (1819), col. 1345.
77. Ibid. (emphasis added).
78. Ibid. Jones, *Lunacy, Law and Conscience,* 109–11, condemns this action as "illiberal," but entirely neglects the role of the medical lobbying in ensuring the defeat of these early efforts at "reform," presumably because it would be at odds with her naive Whiggish perspective, which sees the doctors as the purveyors of scientific enlightenment.

insanity began to appear.[79] Similarly, the claim that instruction in its treatment formed a part of the normal curriculum of medical training, which had been made by earlier generations of mad-doctors, was reinforced when Dr. (later Sir) Alexander Morison, a well-known society physician, began a course of lectures on the topic. These he repeated annually from 1823 to the late 1840s, while the published version simultaneously went through a number of editions. All this activity was probably

79. Among those which I have consulted are: Matthew Allen, *Cases of Insanity, with Medical, Moral and Philosophical Observations upon them* (London: Swire, 1831), and idem, *Essay on the Classification of the Insane* (London: Taylor, 1837); Samuel Glover Bakewell, *An Essay on Insanity* (Edinburgh: Neill, 1833); Nathaniel Bingham, *Observations on the Religious Delusions of Insane Persons . . . with Which Are Combined a Copious Practical Description . . . of Mental Disease, and of Its Appropriate Medical and Moral Treatment* (London: Hatchard, 1841); George Man Burrows, *An Inquiry into Certain Errors Relative to Insanity* (London: Underwood, 1820), and idem, *Commentaries on the Causes, Forms, Symptoms, and Treatment, Moral and Medical, of Insanity* (London: Underwood, 1828); Andrew Combe, *Observations on Mental Derangement: Being an Application of the Principles of Phrenology to the Elucidation of the Causes, Symptoms, Nature, and Treatment of Insanity* (Edinburgh: Anderson, 1831); John Conolly, *An Inquiry Concerning the Indications of Insanity, with Suggestions for the Better Protection and Care of the Insane* (1830), facsimile ed., ed. Richard A. Hunter and Ida Macalpine (London: Dawsons, 1964); W. C. Ellis, *A Treatise on the Nature, Symptoms, Causes, and Treatment of Insanity, with Practical Observations on Lunatic Asylums, and a Description of the Pauper Lunatic Asylum for the County of Middlesex at Hanwell, with a Detailed Account of Its Management* (London: Holdsworth, 1838); R. Fletcher, *Sketches from the Casebook to Illustrate the Influence of the Mind on the Body, with the Treatment of Some of the More Important Brain and Nervous Disturbances* (London: Longman, 1833); Thomas Forster, *Observations on the Phenomena of Insanity* (London: Underwood, 1817); William Saunders Hallaran, *Practical Observations on the Causes and Cure of Insanity* (Cork: Hodges and M'Arthur, 1818); John Haslam, *Medical Jurisprudence as It Relates to Insanity, According to the Law of England* (London: Hunter, 1817); Thomas Mayo, *An Essay on the Relation of the Theory of Morals to Insanity* (London: Fellowes, 1834); John Mayo and T. Mayo, *Remarks on Insanity* (London: Underwood, 1817); J. G. Millingen, *Aphorisms on the Treatment and Management of the Insane, with Considerations on Public and Private Lunatic Asylums, Pointing out the Errors in the Present System* (London: Churchill, 1840); Alexander Morison, *Outlines of Lectures on the Nature, Causes, and Treatment of Insanity*, ed. Thomas C. Morison (London: Longman et al., 1825; 4th ed. 1848); William B. Neville, *On Insanity: Its Nature, Causes, and Cure* (London: Longman et al., 1836); John Parkin, *On the Medical and Moral Treatment of Insanity, Including a Notice on the Establishment for the Treatment of Nervous and Mental Maladies: Manor Cottage, King's Road, Chelsea, Established in 1780* (London: Martin, [1843?]); James Cowles Prichard, *A Treatise on Insanity and Other Disorders Affecting the Mind* (London: Sherwood, Gilbert and Piper, 1835), and idem, *On the Different Forms of Insanity in Relation to Jurisprudence* (London: Bailliere, 1842); John Reid, *Essays on Insanity, Hypochondriacal and other Nervous Affections* (London: Longman et al., 1816); Edward J. Seymour, *Observations on the Medical Treatment of Insanity* (London: Longman et al., 1832); Spurzheim, *Deranged Manifestations;* John Thurnam, *Observations and Essays on the Statistics of Insanity, Including an Inquiry into the Causes Influencing the Results of Treatment in Establishments for the Insane: To Which Are Added Statistics for the Retreat near York* (London: Simpkin Marshall, 1845); David Uwins, *A Treatise on Those Disorders of the Brain and Nervous System, Which Are Usually Considered and Called Mental* (London: Renshaw and Rush, 1833); Francis Willis, *A Treatise on Mental Derangement* (London: Longman et al., 1823; 2d ed., 1843).

stimulated at least in part by the increased attention all members of the educated elite were giving to insanity, in the wake of two major parliamentary inquiries into the subject within the short space of eight years and in consequence of the revelations of the second of these about conditions in madhouses. But more importantly than that, it represented an effort to reassert the validity of the medical model of mental disturbance and to ensure a maximum of professional autonomy in the treatment of lunatics.

Dr. Francis Willis explicitly wrote his treatise to emphasize the medical nature of insanity, an endeavor rendered "the more necessary, because derangement has been considered by some to be merely and exclusively a mental disease, curable without the aid of medicine, by what are termed moral remedies; such as travelling and various kinds of amusements."[80] The language used by John and Thomas Mayo was even more revealing. Their announced purpose in publishing their *Remarks on Insanity* was "to vindicate the rights of [our] profession over Insanity, and to elucidate its medical treatment,"[81] two tasks that were obviously closely connected. For the mere existence of a large body of what purported to be technical literature passing on the fruits of scientific knowledge about the management of the insane gave impressive-seeming substance to the claim of expertise, regardless of its practical usefulness or merits. Complicated nosographies like that developed by Prichard bewildered and impressed the average layman; given such an array of diagnostic categories, recognition of the precise form of mental disease an individual lunatic was laboring under clearly became a matter for expert determination.

When medical ideas about insanity had to be presented to a lay audience, the availability of a large body of specialized knowledge was valuable in a different way. For it enabled writers who wanted to advance medicine's cause to circumvent the ordinary requirement that they produce evidence in support of their contentions. Nontechnical discussion of the medical treatment of insanity could be justified on the grounds of the general importance of making the public aware of the potential contribution medicine could make, but any pressures to move beyond vague generalities could now be resisted as being "more properly the province of journals exclusively devoted to technical science."[82] Such "purely professional" topics would "only be interesting to a comparatively small number of our readers,"[83] and would simply be above the heads of the majority of lay readers, since they lacked the requisite training.[84]

80. Willis, *Mental Derangement*, 2.
81. Mayo and Mayo, *Remarks on Insanity.*
82. David Uwins, "Inquiries Relative to Insanity," *Quarterly Review* 24 (1820–21): 169.
83. Ibid.
84. In the discussion of specific techniques, this point was emphasized over and over

Morison's lectures were the most visible sign that members of the medical profession were in fact receiving training. It scarcely mattered that Morison himself had no practical experience that would have given him justification for claiming expertise in this area; or that his lectures were an unoriginal mélange of ideas uncritically assembled from existing works in the field.[85] Instruction in "a curriculum that includes some *special* theoretical contact (whether scientifically proven or not) may represent a declaration that there is a body of special knowledge and skill necessary for the occupation,"[86] which is not otherwise obtainable. Here, the availability of special education, regardless of its specific content or scientific validity, bolstered the medical profession's claims to expertise and esoteric knowledge.

The effort to press these claims proceeded on other fronts as well. The more respectable part of the medical profession used its prestige and ready access to elite circles to promote its cause. As part of this process, medical men running asylums made strenuous and eventually successful efforts to persuade their lay audience that they possessed a more common and/or intense commitment to a service orientation than did their nonmedically qualified competitors. At a time when madhouses were acquiring considerable disrepute, Nisbet took pains to emphasize that "out of thirty-three licenses for the metropolis, only three are in the hands of medical men. The chief part is in the hands of persons unacquainted with medicine, who take up this branch of medicine as a beneficial pursuit, and whose object is to make the most of it."[87] Similarly, Conolly urged the importance "of making medical men as familiar with disorders of the mind as with other disorders; and thus of rescuing lunatics from those whose interest it is to represent such maladies as more obscure, and more difficult to manage than they are."[88] Burrows' writings[89] and his evidence before the 1828 Select Committee

---

again: "It would be altogether inconsistent with our *plan* to enter into the detail of such cases" (Unwins, "Insanity and Madhouses," 403); "We have not the leisure to enter into any detail respecting the mode of employing this remedial process, and shall therefore merely observe that its use requires always to be regulated by the circumstances and constitutional condition of the patient" (ibid., 402) (which, it goes without saying, were matters only a doctor was competent to evaluate).

85. Morison undertook these lectures primarily as an exercise in self-promotion, and with the hope that the publicity would expand his practice among the upper classes. In these respects he was successful, even though his course attracted a total of only 150 students between 1823 and 1845. Cf. Hunter and Macalpine, *Three Hundred Years of Psychiatry,* 305–9; Daniel Hack Tuke, *The Moral Management of the Insane* (London: Churchill, 1854), 78.

86. Freidson, *Professional Dominance,* 134–35.

87. Nisbet, *Two Letters,* 8–9.

88. Conolly, *Indications of Insanity,* 7.

89. See esp. Burrows, *Inquiry into Certain Errors.*

of the House of Lords likewise both reflected and promoted "the wide-spread view that lay proprietors were more likely to be corrupt and avaricious than their medically trained colleagues."[90] So that when the *Quarterly Review* informed its readers that "the superintendent of a mad-house ought to be a man of character and responsibility," it recommended in the same breath that "he should always be chosen from the medical profession."[91]

The articles that appeared in the leading journals of the period either were themselves written by a physician[92] or presented an account of insanity sympathetic to the medical viewpoint.[93] The profession did not neglect the opportunity to show itself in a favorable light. Those, for instance, who relied on the *Edinburgh Review*'s summary for an account of the findings of the 1815–16 Inquiry learned that "it is the decided opinion of *all* the most judicious and experienced witnesses examined before the Committee, that the proper employment of medicine, though neglected most deplorably in several public asylums, and in almost all the private establishments, has the best effect in cases of insanity."[94] Similarly, Burrows informed his readers that "from a perusal of the replies to the Questions put by the Committee, it is evident that insanity is greatly under the control of medicine—a fact that strictly accords with my own observations."[95]

The profession was able to use its representation in Parliament, as well as its position as one of the three ancient learned professions, to ensure that its views received due consideration. When there was a renewed inquiry into conditions in private madhouses, it could call on the services of eminently respectable society physicians like Sir Anthony Carlisle and Dr. John Bright to lend their authority to the contention that this was a medical problem. Medical certification of insanity (for private patients only) had been required by the 1774 Madhouse Act as an additional security against improper confinement of the sane, and the doctors now sought to clarify and extend their authority in this area, so as to develop an officially approved monopoly of the right to define (mental) health and illness.[96] Further efforts to get medicine's special competence vis-à-vis the insane recognized and written into the growing

90. W. L. Parry-Jones, *Trade in Lunacy*, 82.
91. Uwins, "Inquiries Relative to Insanity," 190.
92. For example, W. H. Fitton, M.D., "Lunatic Asylums," *Edinburgh Review* 28 (1817).
93. Uwins, "Insanity and Madhouses"; idem, "Inquiries Relative to Insanity," 169–94; "Esquirol on the Treatment of the Insane," *Westminster Review* 18 (1833): 123–38.
94. Fitton, "Lunatic Asylums," 454–55.
95. Burrows, *Regulating of Madhouses*, 97.
96. Freidson, *Profession of Medicine*, 5. Cf. Dr. John Bright's complaints about the ease of certification and the vagueness of the qualifications demanded of the certifiers. He could attract support for his recommendation that the signatures of two physicians, sur-

volume of lunacy legislation based on the findings of the 1827 Select Committee was pending in the House of Lords, where a special committee sat to hear the views of the medical profession on the proposed changes. The testimony of men like E. L. Fox, W. Finch and W. T. Monro is indicative of considerable resentment of supervision and inspection by magistrates, particularly when efforts were made by these laymen to meddle with decisions that were properly the prerogative of the professional, such as when a patient was ready for discharge.[97] While legislation was pending, the Royal College of Physicians appointed a committee of its own to (as Parry-Jones delicately puts it) "enquire into the expediency of the provisions of the 1828 Bill."[98] And at the same time, a rash of pamphlets written by members of the medical profession appeared, urging that further inspection was "a useless inquisition into private concerns, destructive of all that privacy that is truly desirable for the patient" and that the proposal itself "betrays a want of confidence in their [mad-doctors'] moral and medical character."[99]

Some outside regulation and inspection of asylums was made inevitable by the continuing revelation in their absence of abuses and maltreatment of patients. Hence, the doctors sought to turn this into a system of professional self-regulation by obtaining a dominant role for medical practitioners. Under the 1828 Act, in the provinces only the medical visitor, and not the magistrates who accompanied him, received payment, while among the newly created metropolitan commissioners in lunacy, five out of fifteen were physicians. This representation was not achieved and maintained without a struggle. As late as 1842, Ashley expressed considerable skepticism about any requirement that commissioners, to inspect asylums, should be medically qualified, arguing that "although so far as health was concerned the opinion of a medical man was of the greatest importance, yet it having been once established that the insanity of a patient did not arise from the state of his bodily health, a man of common sense could give as good an opinion as any medical man he knew [respecting his treatment and the question of his sanity]."[100] Thomas Wakely, M.P., the editor of the leading medical periodical, the Lancet, defended his profession's prerogatives, terming insanity "a griev-

---

geons, or apothecaries be required because of the widespread concern that some people would be incarcerated in madhouses by corrupt relatives seeking control of their property. See House of Commons, *Select Committee on Pauper Lunatics and on Lunatic Asylums* (1827), 154, evidence of Dr. John Bright.

97. See House of Lords, *Minutes of Evidence Taken Before the Select Committee of the House of Lords on the Bills Relating to Lunatics and Lunatic Asylums* (1828).

98. W. L. Parry-Jones, *Trade in Lunacy*, 19.

99. All cited in Hunter and Macalpine, *Three Hundred Years of Psychiatry*, 791.

100. *Hansard's Parliamentary Debates*, 3d ser., vol. 61 (1842), col. 806.

ous disease" and stigmatizing any proposal to have lunatic asylums inspected by lawyers alone as "an insult to the medical profession."[101] Such a proposal now formed a part of the Licensed Lunatics Asylums Bill, introduced to expand temporarily the jurisdiction of the metropolitan commissioners to allow them to inspect asylums throughout the country, in preparation for a further national reform. When the bill came up again, Wakely renewed his attack: "He objected to the clause appointing barristers to the office of commissioners of lunatic asylums. What could be more absurd than to select members of the legal profession to sit in judgement on cases of mental derangement? Was not insanity invariably associated with bodily disease? The investigations in which the commissioners would be involved would be purely of a medical character, and therefore barristers, if they were appointed, would be incompetent to perform the duties which would devolve upon them."[102] "On the contrary," observed Lord Granville Somerset, "the commissioners were solely concerned with whether [the lunatic] was treated properly and with kindness," and this could as well be discovered by a lawyer as by a doctor.[103]

Both sides had their adherents in the debate that followed, and eventually some sentiment emerged for a compromise, whereby the commissioners would operate in pairs, one with legal and one with medical training. This was the solution eventually adopted, so that the number of metropolitan commissioners was expanded to include seven doctors—John Bright, Henry Herbert Southey, and John Robert Hume were joined by Thomas Turner, Thomas Waterfield, Francis Bisset Hawkins, and James Cowles Prichard.[104] Since the 1844 Commission Report formed the basis of the 1845 reforms, this expanded medical representation was of considerable importance. When the Report discussed the nature of insanity and its medical and moral treatment, the lay members of the commission deferred to the specialized knowledge of their medical colleagues, and thus these sections of the Report faithfully reflected the orthodox medical viewpoint. In turn, this official acknowledgment of medicine's legitimate interest in insanity (and Ashley was now one of the converted) helped shape the legislation and its subsequent implementation.

---

101. Ibid., col. 804.

102. *Hansard's Parliamentary Debates,* 3d ser., 62 (1842), col. 886.

103. Ibid., col. 887.

104. This arrangement was continued when the national Lunacy Commission was set up. It permitted a useful professional division of labor. While the lawyers checked that the legal niceties had been observed with respect to admission and discharge documents, record-keeping, and so on, the doctors attended to more strictly "medical" matters such as diet and clothing.

Simultaneously, the profession was active on the local level, where the magistrates who were engaged in setting up the new system of public asylums were an obvious target for these efforts. In some counties the magistrates were already convinced that insanity was a medical province and hence needed no prompting to place their asylum in the hands of the local doctor. At Nottingham, for instance, Reverend Becher, who was the man most responsible for getting the asylum built, was convinced that the management of insanity "is an art of itself,"[105] and madness a disease having its basis in organic lesions of the body that only doctors were competent to treat.[106] In consequence, an apothecary was placed in charge of the day-to-day management of the asylum, subject to the control of a visiting physician "who shall be entrusted with the medical treatment of the patients."[107] The magistrates at Hanwell and Wakefield followed a similar plan, except that here ultimate authority rested in "the hands of the Resident Physician."[108]

Elsewhere, however, asylum committees chose to place the daily control of the institution in the hands of a lay superintendent, or even tried to run it themselves. The Staffordshire magistrates chose a layman as their chief resident officer. At the Cornwall Asylum at Bodmin after the first appointment of a surgeon, James Duck, as superintendent proved unsatisfactory, he was replaced by a lay "Governor and Contractor."[109] The magistrates at Bedford initially also chose this latter plan. Among the candidates they considered to head their asylum were a former assistant keeper at St. Luke's and a house painter, who had some experience looking after a lunatic he had come across in the course of his business.[110] The magistrates had previously decided that, since the medical care needed by the lunatics was slight, and they "will not . . . require the same species of unremitting attention during the whole of the four and twenty hours as Patients in Hospitals do," that "Mr. Leach, our House Surgeon at the Infirmary who so ably discharges his duties there might from the Contiguity of the Establishments" be induced to attend to the occasional medical needs of the Asylum patients.[111] At a subsequent

105. John Thomas Becher, *An Address to the Public on the Nature, Design, and Constitution of the General Lunatic Asylum near Nottingham* (Newark, Nottinghamshire: Ridge, 1811), iv.

106. Ibid., xi–xii.

107. Nottingham Lunatic Asylum, *The Articles of Union Entered into and Agreed upon Between the Justices of the Peace for the County of Nottingham; the Justices of the Peace for . . . the Town of Nottingham; and the Subscribers to a Voluntary Institution; for the Purpose of Providing a General Lunatic Asylum* (Newark: Ridge, 1811), 17–19.

108. Middlesex Lunatic Asylum, "Visiting Justices' Minutes" (1830), 2:324, manuscript at the London County Record Office, Middlesex Division.

109. Jones, *Lunacy, Law and Conscience*, 118–20.

110. Bedfordshire County Asylum, "Minutes Book," 15 July 1812, 1:7, manuscript at the Bedfordshire County Record Office.

111. Ibid., 4–5.

meeting held on 27 April 1812, the house painter, William Pether, and his wife were appointed "the Governor and Matron of the Lunatic Asylum with a Salary of Sixty Guineas per Annum."[112]

Within less than a year, local physicians were seeking their first foothold in the new institution. A letter was received from a Dr. G. O. Yeats offering "to undertake the office of the Medical Superintendent and Physician of this Institution gratuitously."[113] He justified the need for such assistance by pointing out that there were "a considerable number of lunatics whose diseases will require medical aid." Naturally enough, the offer was accepted.[114] A few more months went by before Yeats tried to convince the magistrates that medicine could be used not merely to cure the patients' physical ailments, but also to help restore them to sanity. In a second long letter to the managing committee, he argued that "however anxious the legislature has been strictly to confine the inmates of the house and to guard against the possibility of there being restored to the world unfit members of society, yet equal anxiety is expressed that every possible care should be taken by medical means for such restoration. . . . It is very desirable then, in order to render the Asylum, not only a place for incarceration, but one where every facility may be given for the amelioration of the condition and for the cure of the maladies of its unfortunate inmates, that the medical officer be given broader powers over the treatment of the patient."[115]

The process by which the physician invoked the privileges of his office to subordinate the lay superintendent to medical control, and eventually to squeeze him out altogether, had now begun. Three days later Pether received his new instructions: "It was ordered that the Governor in all matters relating to the Health and Distribution of the Patients with a view to their Convalescence or their Medical Treatment, do obey implicitly the instructions of the Physician."[116] In February of the following year, Yeats was obliged to submit his resignation as nonresident Medical Superintendent, as he was moving to London; but his colleague, Dr. Thackeray, offered to assume the position, once more gratuitously.[117]

During Thackeray's term in office, he and various other doctors made efforts to educate the magistrates to the fact that insanity was a disease just like any other disease physicians were called on to treat and that there ought therefore to be provision for a full-time resident medical officer to run the asylum. In 1815, he complained in a letter to the mag-

112. Ibid., 9.   113. Ibid., 2 January 1813, 39.   114. Ibid., 41.

115. Letter from Dr. G. O. Yeats to the Committee of Magistrates on the Asylum, 21 April 1813. Miscellaneous Papers Relating to the Foundation of the County Lunatic Asylum, Bedfordshire County Record Office.

116. Bedfordshire County Asylum, "Minutes Book," 24 April 1813, 46, manuscript at the Bedfordshire County Record Office.

117. Ibid., 5 February and 5 March 1814.

istrates of "the insufficiency of the present Medical Means to fulfill the benevolent designs of the Institution. Their asylum affords a solitary example in which a large and important medical establishment is conducted without the assistance of a Resident director in the character of House apothecary. The defect in its constitution by totally precluding the employment of all remedies requiring attention to their effects and by preventing the observation and accumulation of Facts for the advancement of the Science of medicine greatly limits its service as a Medical Institution."[118] Such a state of affairs was rendered the more deplorable because proper classification of the varieties of mental disease revealed that each major subtype was almost certainly the consequence of an underlying physical pathology—mania reflected a disorder of the brain, melancholia a dysfunction of the abdominal viscera, and nervousness a disturbed state of the nervous system.

Thackeray felt that "if there be any foundation for this classification of mental disease, great encouragement I think is held out in it for placing a Lunatic Asylum on the footing of a Medical Institution."[119] The magistrates clearly did not. Dr. Maclean, who had replaced Leech as House Surgeon at the Infirmary, continued to hold that post and to perform the duties of secretary and head apothecary at the infirmary, so that his attendance on the asylum patients was a distinctly part-time affair; and Thackeray still contributed his services on a voluntary, unpaid, visiting basis. On Maclean's resignation from his various posts in June 1823,[120] the governors ordered that his successor should perform these same duties, and in September a Mr. Harris accepted the appointment.[121]

Further efforts were now made to dislodge the layman, Pether, and to replace him with a resident medical officer. The large proportion of chronic derelicts among the asylum population here posed a problem for those advocating a greater role for medicine, since it was not clear what benefits, if any, the increased expenditure for a full-time medical officer would bring. Thackeray conceded the difficulty but sought to persuade the magistrates that it was a temporary state of affairs, the consequence of the failure to employ medical treatment while such cases were still curable, a mistake they should take care to avoid in the future. As he explained,

> The present state of the house in which there are but few subjects under medical treatment may perhaps have led to the idea that little occasion exists for the establishment of such a department. Were this state a *perma-*

118. Thackeray to the Magistrates' Committee, 7 August 1815, Miscellaneous Papers Relating to the Foundation of the Lunatic Asylum, Bedfordshire County Record Office.
119. Ibid.
120. Bedfordshire County Asylum, Visitors' Book A, 2 June 1823.
121. Harris was in fact a surgeon, an occupation that to this day takes the title "Mr." in Britain.

nent condition of the house the conclusion would be just; but it should be regarded [as] wholly an *accidental* one, depending on the Infancy of the Institution. The asylum is at present filled chiefly with patients whose disorder from their *long* standing, discourage every hope of benefit from medical exertion. In the progress, however, of time *recent* cases of derangement will be continually presenting themselves, when much encouragement will be offered for the active interference of Art.[122]

For a while, the magistrates still proved recalcitrant. Thackeray and Harris submitted further memoranda in support of their position and obtained testimonials reinforcing their contentions from other physicians who happened to visit the asylum. Finally, the magistrates bowed to the weight of professional opinion: "Dr. Thackeray and Mr. Harris having separately called the attention of the magistrates to the expediency of providing regular resident medical aid to the Institution and the Magistrates having noticed a similar suggestion centered in the visitors' journal by the Medical Superintendent of the Bicêtre of Paris and another foreigner and Dr. Thompson of the twenty-fifth of July last, and having taken the same into their consideration, resolved to recommend the subject to the next court of Quarter Sessions."[123] Pether's position swiftly became untenable, as he lost almost all his remaining authority. Finally, in 1828 he resigned his position as general manager, and was succeeded by Harris.[124] Paramount authority over all aspects of asylum administration now rested in medical hands.

The activities, both local and national, we have just been discussing all made use of, and owed much of their success to, the arguments developed in the medical literature of the period. For it was the contentions advanced here that convinced almost all the educated classes that insanity was indeed a disease and that its treatment ought therefore to be entrusted to doctors. Consequently, I now want to devote some time to a consideration of just what such arguments were.

Moral treatment lacked a well-developed ideological rationale for why it should work. Tuke had explicitly eschewed any desire to develop a theoretical account of the nature of mental disturbance and had refused to elaborate moral treatment into a rigid "scientific" therapy.[125] In the past, "the want of facts relative to this subject, and our disposition to

---

122. Memorandum from Dr. Thackeray, M.D., Miscellaneous Papers Relating to the Foundation of the County Lunatic Asylum, Bedfordshire County Record Office (emphasis in the original).

123. Bedfordshire County Asylum, Visitors' Book, 5 February 1827.

124. Ibid., 6 October 1828.

125. For instance, he was "far from imagining that this Asylum is a perfect model for others, either in regards to construction or management. If several improvements have been successfully introduced, it is probable that many others remain unattempted" (S. Tuke, *Description of the Retreat*, xxii).

hasty generalization, have led to many conclusions equally unfriendly to the progress of knowledge, and the comfort of patients." [126] He therefore resisted efforts to achieve a premature systematization of knowledge and encouraged a pragmatic approach: "I have happily little occasion for theory, since my province is to relate, not only what ought to be done, but also what, in most instances, is actually performed." [127] He even refused to choose between a psychological and somatic etiology of insanity, arguing that "whatever theory we maintain in regard to the remote causes of insanity, we must consider moral treatment of very high importance." [128] If its origins lay in the mind, "applications made immediately to it are the most natural, and the most likely to be attended with success"; if they lay in the body, "we shall still readily admit, from the reciprocal action of the two parts of our system upon each other, that the greatest attention is necessary to whatever is calculated to affect the mind." [129]

Undoubtedly, though, the nature of the therapy he advanced, and the manner in which advocates of moral treatment persistently and explicitly denied the value of a medical approach, could, at the very least, be more readily reconciled with a mental rather than a somatic etiology of insanity. Francis Willis was not alone in accusing those favoring moral treatment of propagating the doctrine that "mental derangement must arise from causes, and be cured by remedies, that solely and exclusively operate on the mind." [130] Physicians stigmatized this as an "absurd opinion" [131] but were obviously afraid of the threat it posed to their position.

The single most effective response to an attack along these lines would have been to demonstrate that insanity was in fact caused by biophysical variables. A somatic interpretation of insanity would place it beyond dispute within medicine's recognized sphere of competence and make plausible the assertion that it responded to medicine's conventional remedies for disease. The trouble was that the doctors could not

126. Ibid., viii.

127. Ibid., 138. This refusal to reduce moral treatment to a set of formulas and the insistence that it rested on a commonsense approach to the problem of insanity, aimed at eliminating artificial obstacles to recovery, made for a refreshing lack of dogmatism. At the same time, the adoption of these positions was a crucial factor in weakening the ability of the proponents of moral treatment to resist takeover and transformation by those espousing a less modest ideal; for by denying that schooled human knowledge and intervention were needed to cope with insanity, those advocating moral rather than medical treatment at least delayed the rise of an occupational group claiming training in their new therapy.

128. Ibid., 131.

129. Ibid., 131–32.

130. Willis, *Mental Derangement*, 2d ed., 4. This was an idea he thought could not "for a moment be rationally entertained" (ibid.). I shall show why in a moment.

131. Browne, *What Asylums Were*, 178.

show the existence of the necessary physical lesions, and this inconvenient fact was already in the public domain.[132]

Unable to produce scientific evidence in support of their personal predilection for a somatic interpretation,[133] the doctors invented an ingenious metaphysical argument that, dressed in the trappings of science, proved an equally satisfactory functional alternative. They began by postulating a Cartesian dualism between mind and body. The mind, which was an immortal, immaterial substance, identical with the Christian doc-

132. "In three fourths of the cases of insanity, where they have been subjected to, dissection after death, the knife of the anatomist has not been able, with the most scrutinizing care, to trace any organic change to which the cause of the disease could be traced" (Nisbet, *Two Letters*, 21–22). For even more pessimistic conclusions (from the medical viewpoint), see Haslam, *Medical Jurisprudence*; House of Commons, *Report . . . on Pauper Lunatics* (1927), 50–52, evidence of Sir Anthony Carlisle.

133. That insanity was a somatic disease was asserted with complete confidence and virtual unanimity in the medical literature of the time: "Madness has always been connected with disease of the brain and its membranes" (Haslam, *Medical Jurisprudence*, 238); "Insanity, always originates in a corporeal cause: derangement of the intellectual faculties is but the effect" (Burrows, *Regulating of Madhouses*, 102); "Insanity it must be contended for, is as much within the province of medical acumen, as any other disorder incidental to animal life. . . . Insanity, it will be shewn, is, in every instance, associated with organic lesion" (Hallaran, *Practical Observations*, 2); "Instead of delirium, derangement and insanity, being merely mental disorders, each of them must be, in fact, and in its origin, a bodily one" (Willis, *Mental Derangement*, 5; 2d ed., 3); "I believe that insanity is as much a bodily disease as a fever or a bunyon on any finger. . . . It is a disease of the brain just as much as dyspepsia [is] of the stomach" (House of Commons, *Report . . . on Pauper Lunatics* [1827], 65, evidence of Dr. Edward Wright, superintendent of Bethlem); "The remote causes of insanity may be . . . undefined and countless; but the proximate cause, or in fact the disease itself, will always be found to arise from the diseased state of the structure of the brain" (Andrew Halliday, *A General View of the Present State of Lunatics and Lunatic Asylums in Great Britain and Ireland, and in Some Other Kingdoms* [London: Underwood, 1828], 5); "Madness is sometimes immediately excited by mental circumstances but even when that is the case, the disorder is bodily" (Uwins, *Disorders of the Brain*, 229); "Insanity may be defined as 'disordered' function of the brain generally" (Neville, *On Insanity*, 18); "[Insanity is] strictly a bodily disease having its origins in organic lesions of the brain" (Browne, *What Asylums Were*, 4); "Insanity has been considered in all cases, to be a disease of the brain" (Ellis, *Treatise on . . . Insanity*, 146, and cf. chap. 2, 22–40); "Now it was well known, that insanity never existed without some organic affection of the human body—that the mind itself never became deranged or disordered in its functions but from some derangement in the structure of the human frame. . . . In general, there was an inflammatory attack going on, requiring to be treated and subdued and when subdued the derangement disappeared" (Thomas Wakeley in Hansard's *Parliamentary Debates*, 3d ser., vol. 66 [1844], col. 1278). See also Mayo and Mayo, *Remarks on Insanity*, which emphasizes "the physical phenomena" of insanity; Prichard, *Treatise on Insanity*, 234–49; and Morison, *Outlines of Lectures*, 4th ed., 422–23. A few doctors located the cause somewhere other than the brain: "I would say, that where a hurt or disease or disorder exists in the brain, there is at least an equal number where it exists in the stomach" (House of Commons, *Report . . . on Pauper Lunatics* [1827], 52, evidence of Sir Anthony Carlisle); Prichard (*Treatise on Insanity*, 249) concurred. But for Burnett, "both reason and science favour the idea that insanity is not and ought not in the first instance, and often to the very last, to be regarded as a disease of

trine of the soul, was forced in this world to operate through the medium of a material instrument, namely the brain.[134] This was an apparently innocuous distinction, but once it had been conceded, the doctors had no trouble "proving" their case. For to argue that the mind was subject to disease, or even, in the case of outright idiotism, death, was to contradict the very foundation of Christianity, the belief in an immortal soul. On the other hand, adoption of a somatic viewpoint provided a wholly satisfactory resolution to the dilemma: "From the admission of this principle, derangement is no longer considered a disease of the understanding, but of the centre of the nervous system, upon the unimpaired condition of which the exercise of the understanding depends. The brain is at fault and not the mind."[135] The brain, as a material organ, was liable to irritation and inflammation, and it was this which produced insanity.[136] "But let this oppression [of the brain] be relieved, this irritation be removed, and the mind rises in its native strength, clear and calm, uninjured, immutable, immortal. In all cases where disorder of the mind is detectable, from the faintest peculiarity to the widest deviation

---

the brain, but as a disease floating in the blood, having no fixed or local character" (C. M. Burnett, M.D., *Insanity Tested by Science, and Shown to Be a Disease Rarely Connected with Organic Lesion of the Brain, and on That Account Far More Susceptible of Cure than Has Hitherto Been Supposed* [London: Highley, 1848], 5). Halliday informed the public of the importance of the "discovery" that insanity had a somatic basis: the earlier, mistaken notion that insanity was a disease of the mind could not but lead to a deep therapeutic pessimism, since neither doctors nor anyone else could act on this immaterial substance. However, "truth has taken the place of fiction, and madness is found to proceed in all cases from some real tangible bodily ailment. It can now be treated according to the known rules of practice— made amenable to the ordinary discipline of the apothecary's shop—and is often more easily removed than less important diseases that have made a temporary logement in the human frame" (Halliday, *Present State of Lunatics*, 444).

134. Laymen were assured that "the connection of the faculties of the mind with the brain, or, to speak more accurately, their dependence on this organ, is a point . . . certainly demonstrated by the labours of modern physiologists and pathologists," (Neville, *On Insanity*, 18). But no one explained just how these two things were connected, or how it was that a purely psychological therapy, like moral treatment (which the doctors were in the process of claiming as their own) could affect a physical disorder. Burrows comments that "to discuss the validity of this or that hypothesis would be plunging into an inextricable labyrinth" (Burrows, *Inquiry into Certain Errors*, 7); Browne dismissed the question as unimportant: "In what manner this connection between mind and matter is effected, is not here inquired into. The link will, perhaps, ever escape human research." (Browne, *What Asylums Were*, 4); Bingham gravely informed his readers that "it is not impossible that a vomit may be the accidental cause of dislodging a foolish notion which has long stuck in the brain" (Bingham, *Religious Delusions*, xiv–xv), but left the precise mechanism through which this was accomplished to their imagination. Fortunately, this was scarcely a pressing problem, save in a purely logical sense, since the moral-treatment people themselves had not developed a clearly articulated theory of how or why their treatment worked. Consequently, the doctors were not challenged on this vulnerable point in their argument.

135. Browne, *What Asylums Were*, 4.

136. Morison, *Outlines of Lectures*, 35–37.

from health, it must and can only be traced directly or indirectly to the brain."[137]

The failure to *observe* physical lesions of the brain in most cases of insanity could now be explained in either of two ways, neither of which threatened the somatic interpretation. On the one hand, it might be that existing instruments and techniques were simply too crude to detect the very subtle changes involved.[138] On the other hand, it could be that insanity in its early stages was correlated only with functional changes in the brain, which only at a later stage, when the patient became chronic, passed over into structural ones.[139]

The intuitive appeal of this explanation to an audience of convinced Christians was enormous and suffered scarcely at all from its extrascientific character.[140] And by "proving" that insanity was a somatic complaint, it decisively reinforced medical claims to jurisdiction in this area. The obvious achievements of moral treatment could not be simply overlooked—they were too well established in the public mind for that. However, it could be, and was, just absorbed into the realm of ordinary medical techniques.

Moral treatment now became just one weapon among many (even if a

137. Browne, *What Asylums Were*, 4. For the elaborations of this entire somatic ideology that most clearly reveal that ultimately theological grounds on which the explanation was offered (and accepted), see Morison, *Outlines of Lectures*, 34–44, and Halliday, *Present State of Lunatics*, 5–8. Revealing in a rather different sense was Burrows' contention that "no impression, perhaps, has been more detrimental than the scholastic dogma, that the mind, being independent of the body, can simulate all its functions and actions; can sicken, be administered to, recover, and relapse; and that consequently all but moral remedies must be secondary, if not nearly useless, every other being incompatible with an immaterial essence like mind" (Burrows, *Inquiry into Certain Errors*, 6–7). One is led to ask, detrimental to what? And it is difficult to avoid the conclusion, detrimental to the claim that insanity is a medical problem, one that only doctors are qualified to handle.

138. Morison, *Outlines of Lectures*, 411. Morison produced a subtle and ingenious argument to show that the changes in the brain must be slight in the early stages of the disease. It was a common observation that recent cases of insanity recovered in greater numbers than those of long standing. This must mean that the changes in the structure of their brains had not proceeded very far, for serious structural changes would naturally be irreversible, and hence impossible to cure. Ibid., 422.

139. Neville, *On Insanity*, 60. The proof of *this* position was that "cases of any standing that terminate fatally are, we may venture to say, *never* investigated by the skillful pathological anatomist without obvious traces of structural disease being discovered" (ibid., 60–61 [emphasis in the original]).

140. Parenthetically, it may well be that scientific theories under some circumstances are not very effective weapons for converting laymen, since they may depart too radically from the lay world-view and/or be too complicated to lend themselves to a convincing simplistic presentation to a lay audience. For propaganda purposes, quasi-theories like this one, which don't really have a scientific status, may be a better way of persuading laymen that one has expertise, simply because they provide a closer fit with the preconceptions of the expert's audience. In this case, there is a rather delightful irony: the doctors were forced to rely on spiritual assumptions to prove a materialist case.

particularly valuable one) that the skillful physician used in his battle against mental illness. Texts like Prichard's included a chapter on moral treatment as a matter of course,[141] while those who rejected the conventional medical methods were accused of unnecessarily reducing their chances of curing their patients. In support of this position, certain mad-doctors claimed to have cured a higher percentage of their patients than had the Retreat[142] and attributed this to their willingness to use both moral *and* medical means.[143] Others claimed to provide proof of the efficacy of medical means in certain cases, proof that took the form of citing instances of insanity known to the author where the patients had recovered at some time after the administration of traditional medical remedies.[144]

A number of doctors now proposed a truce. Extremists on both sides might argue for the unique value of a moral or a medical approach. But all reasonable men could see that a judicious *combination* of these two therapies was likely to be more valuable than either taken by itself.[145] "To

141. Cf. Prichard, *Treatise on Insanity.*

142. Burrows claimed he had cured "on recent cases, 91 in 100; and on old cases, 35 in 100" (Burrows, *Inquiry into Certain Errors,* 48).

143. Burrows commented that "insanity was formerly in that asylum [the Retreat] scarcely considered to be a remediable complaint; and consequently, medical aid was resorted to only when patients were affected with other disorders" (Burrows, *Commentaries,* 558). For himself: "Having the fullest conviction of the great efficacy of medicine in the majority of cases of insanity, I have ever viewed with regret the little confidence professed by the benevolent conductors of the Retreat in its powers; and have always considered that the exercise of a more energetic remedial plan of treatment was the only thing required to render the system they pursue perfect" (Burrows, *Inquiry into Certain Errors,* 31).

144. Prichard, having defended medical treatment as "the use of remedies which act upon the body and are designed to remove the disorder of cerebral or other functions, known or believed to be the cause of derangement in the mind," cited a string of such cures following the use of bleeding, purges, vomits, opium, digitalis, and the like (Prichard, *Treatise on Insanity,* 250–56). Thurnam conceded that "perhaps we cannot produce any facts which actually prove that pharmaceutic treatment, considered separately, has in any particular institution influenced the results on any large scale; yet we cannot doubt that the proportion of recoveries is greater, and in particular, that the mean mortality will be less in a hospital for the insane, in which attention is paid to a discriminating and judicious medical treatment," (Thurnam, *Statistics of Insanity,* 100–101). After all, if insanity was a medical problem, no other conclusion made sense. The same resort to *petitio principii* was apparent in his account of the results of his own treatment of cases at the York Retreat: given a belief that insanity was a physical disease, "I cannot but attach great importance to the use of physical means in the treatment of mental disorders, for if insanity really depends on some morbid conditions of the bodily frame, it follows, as at least highly probably, that everything tending to the restoration or maintenance of bodily health must be of primary importance in its treatment" (ibid., 28).

145. Looking back on the time when the threat to medical control was greatest, Browne commented: "Benevolence and sympathy suggested and developed, and in my opinion, unfortunately enhanced the employment of moral means, either to the exclusion or to the undue disparagement of physical means, of cure and alleviation. I confess to have aided at

those acquainted with the workings of the malady and its peculiar characteristics," said Neville, "it will be easy to perceive the errors and partial
views of such as profess to apply a medicinal agent only, as a specific, or
those who advocate a course of moral treatment only for a cure. There is
no doubt that a cooperation of medicinal and moral means is requisite to
effect a thorough cure." [146] Now while from one perspective this attitude
represented a concession, particularly when compared with earlier emphases on the exclusive value of medicine, the concession was a harmless
one. For it left the physician, as the only person who could legitimately
dispense the medical side of the treatment, firmly in control. Thus, Neville thought that moral and medical treatment could be carried out only
"under the guidance of persons of sound professional education, and
mature experience of the disease," [147] while Ellis commented: "From
what has been said on the treatment of the insane in Lunatic Asylums, it

---

one time in this revolution; *which cannot be regarded in any better light than as treason to the
principles of our profession*" (Browne, *Moral Treatment of the Insane*, 5 [emphasis added]). Most
doctors who were converts to moral treatment continued to give their primary loyalty to
medicine, and so emphasized that medical skill still had a role (e.g., Browne and Ellis). Gardiner Hill did not, and his case provides us with an interesting indication of a profession's
response to a heretic from within its own ranks who challenges its competence. Hill had
every right to be recognized as one of the outstanding figures of nineteenth-century psychiatry. It was his efforts at Lincoln that showed the feasibility of the total abolition of mechanical restraint. His practical demonstration convinced Conolly, who then adopted it at
Hanwell, from which it spread to become the reigning orthodoxy in all British asylums.
Conolly achieved high place in the psychiatric historians' pantheon of heroes and widespread honor in his own time. Hill, within two years of his first success, was forced to resign
from his position at Lincoln, assailed over a period of years in the *Lancet* as a charlatan, saw
his achievement attributed to E. P. Charlesworth, his nominal superior at Lincoln, and remained a perpetually marginal figure in his chosen profession. His response was to write a
series of books vindicating his claim and attempting to gain public recognition of his accomplishment, books that, given his isolation, took on an increasingly paranoid tone
(Robert Gardiner Hill, *A Lecture on the Management of Lunatic Asylums, and the Treatment of the
Insane* [London: Simpkin Marshall, 1839]; *A Concise History of the Entire Abolition of Mechanical Restraint in the Treatment of the Insane* [London: Longman et al., 1857]; *Lunacy: Its Past
and Present* [London: Longman, Green et al., 1870]). The enmity of the medical profession
and the venom of the attacks in the leading medical periodical of the time seem puzzling at
first sight. But we must remember that, in Browne's words, Hill was a "traitor" to his profession: from the outset he had insisted that "in the treatment of the insane, medicine is of
little avail, except (of course) when they are suffering from other diseases, to which lunatics
as well as sane persons are liable. *Moral treatment with a view to induce habits of self-control, is all
and everything.* [In consequence] the use of the lancet, leeches, cupping, glasses, blisters,
drastic purgatives, and the practice of shaving the head are totally proscribed in this Asylum" (*Management of Lunatic Asylums*, 45 [emphasis in the original]). When, in the teeth of
the interests of the profession, he persisted in this opinion (it was reiterated word for word
in *Abolition of Mechanical Restraint*, 72), he was rewarded with ostracism and abuse. For further discussion of Conolly and Hill, see Chapter 7.

146. Neville, *On Insanity*, 14. Cf. Bingham, *Religious Delusions*, esp. pp. 62–63.
147. Neville, *On Insanity*, 14.

will be obvious, that, according to my notions, no-one, except a medical man, and a benevolent one, ought to be entrusted with the management of them."[148]

And indeed, that was exactly what did happen. By the 1830s almost all the public mental hospitals had a resident medical director. Moreover, the magistrates' committees, which in several instances had been heavily involved in the day-to-day administration of asylums, increasingly left everything to the experts. The metropolitan commissioners, not entirely approvingly, commented in 1844 that the pattern at Bedford was being generally emulated, with "almost the entire control of the County Asylum being delegated to the Medical and General Superintendent."[149] Similarly, in the private sector, the more reputable private institutions acquired either a medical proprietor or a full-time resident medical superintendent.[150] Symptomatic of medicine's gains in this respect was the appointment of a resident physician to run the York Retreat, where moral treatment had originated and which, for the first forty-two years of its existence, had had a succession of lay superintendents.[151]

Finally, the asylum doctor solved the problem of restricting access to his clientele and transforming his dominance of the treatment of mental illness into a virtual monopoly, in a typically professional manner, by arranging "to have himself designated as the expert in such a way as to exclude all other claimants, his designation being official and bureaucratic insofar as it is formally established by law."[152] The Madhouse Act of 1828 introduced the first legal requirements with respect to medical attendance: each asylum had to make arrangements for a doctor to visit the patients at least once a week and for him to sign a Weekly Register.

148. Ellis, *Treatise on . . . Insanity*, 314. Cf. Browne, *What Asylums Were*, 178: "But to whom, rather than the well-educated physician, is such a sacred and momentous trust to be consigned?"

149. Metropolitan Commissioners in Lunacy, *Report* (1844), 25–26. The metropolitan commissioners were concerned lest the superintendent's power was becoming unduly autocratic: "We consider that the appointment and dismissal of servants is a trust of great importance, which is vested in the Visiting Justices for the purpose of checking any undue power or influence being used by the superintendent over the servants of the Asylum" (ibid., 26). But by the time of their *Seventh Report*, in 1853, their successors, the national commissioners, had concluded that such a concentration of power *was* desirable and that lay interference in all aspects of asylum affairs ought to be kept to a minimum.

150. For example, by 1831, forty-four out of sixty-eight provincial licensed houses were described as having a proprietor with medical or surgical qualifications (W. L. Parry-Jones, *Trade in Lunacy*, 78). Numerous families in the mad-business, many of whose fathers had been laymen, now obtained medical qualifications. Among the more notable examples were the Coxes, the Bakewells, the Finches, and the Warburtons.

151. The appointment was of Dr. Thurnam, later the first superintendent of the Wiltshire County Asylum at Devizes, and took place in 1838 (Thurnam, *Statistics of Insanity*, 15).

152. Freidson, *Professional Dominance*, 161.

Where an asylum contained more than a hundred patients, it had to employ a medical superintendent. These requirements were stiffened by the 1845 Lunatics Act, which required, among other things, that all asylums keep a Medical Visitation Book and a record of the medical treatment of each patient in a Medical Case Book. And from 1846 on, the lunacy commissioners, who included a large contingent from the medical profession, manifested a steadily growing hostility to nonmedically run asylums. With the help of elite sponsorship, the asylum doctors were now able to drive competing lay people out of the same line of work and to subordinate those who stayed in the field to their authority. And their position controlling the only legitimate institutions for coping with the mentally ill gave them powerful leverage to discourage any future efforts to enter the field.[153]

153. Two final points: First, notice that the lay people the asylum doctors had to convert to the recognition of medical expertise weren't at all the same as those they had to persuade/coerce/treat. Members of the upper class shared the medical profession's universe of discourse; their "clients" did not. A crucial sociological question that therefore arises concerns the means by which the experts on insanity maintained their professional authority in the context of the asylum. (Such an analysis is presented in Scull, *Museums of Madness,* chap. 5). Second, what this account has emphasized, and what Freidson has suggested, is true for the professions in general: When this emerging profession sought to establish its dominance and authority, "the process determining the outcome was essentially political and social rather than technical in character, a process in which power and persuasive rhetoric were of greater importance than the objective character of the knowledge, training, and work" (Freidson, *Profession of Medicine,* 79).

CHAPTER SEVEN

John Conolly:
A Victorian Psychiatric Career

There is a venerable tradition of hagiography in the history of psychiatry (as in the histories of science and medicine). As psychiatric history
has become less frequently the province of well-meaning amateurs, one
consequence of their long-standing fixation on "great doctors and hu-
manitarians" has been to make biographical studies a somewhat unfash-
ionable, even disparaged form of inquiry. Prosopographical research,
since it allows a measure of quantification and resolutely avoids focusing
on the singular hero, has for the most part been spared this stigma, and
in the late 1970s it provided a vantage point from which a handful of
doctoral students began to examine the early history of psychiatry.[1] Such
studies can unquestionably teach us a great deal,[2] and it is a matter of
regret that as yet their focus has been all but exclusively on American
psychiatry.

Still, it would be foolish to think the only worthwhile form of biography is collective biography, or that a concentration on the individual precludes one from developing a greater understanding of larger themes

---

Chapter 7 is reprinted from William Bynum, Roy Porter, and Michael Shepherd, eds., *The
Anatomy of Madness*, Volume 1, 1984, by permission of the publisher, Tavistock Press.

1. For example, John Pitts, "The Association of Medical Superintendents of American
Institutions for the Insane, 1844–1892: A Case of Specialism in American Medicine"
(Ph.D. dissertation, University of Pennsylvania, 1978); and Constance McGovern's Univer-
sity of Massachusetts Ph.D. dissertation, subsequently published in book form as *Masters of
Madness: Social Origins of the American Psychiatric Profession* (Hanover, N.H.: University Press
of New England, 1985).

2. Splendid demonstrations of this, albeit focused on general medical practice rather
than psychiatry, are provided by Irvine Loudon, *Medical Care and the General Practitioner,
1750–1850* (Oxford: Clarendon Press, 1986); and M. J. Peterson, *The Medical Profession in
Mid-Victorian London* (Berkeley: University of California Press, 1978).

and issues. Over the past few years, some of the most valuable contributions to our understanding of medical responses to madness have come from those who have refused to be put off by the general prejudice against a focus on the individual practitioner: Michael MacDonald's pioneering foray into the casebooks of the astrologist-cum-magician-cum-healer-cum-physician-cum-divine, Richard Napier, to illuminate the nature of seventeenth-century English views of madness and its treatment; Nancy Tomes' examination of the treatment of well-to-do American mental patients through an examination of the life and career of Thomas Story Kirkbride, superintendent of the psychiatric branch of the Pennsylvania Hospital; and Samuel Shortt's study of the largely unremarkable, but (for that very reason) probably representative late-nineteenth-century Canadian alienist, Richard Bucke.[3]

John Conolly was anything but an unremarkable figure, and a study of him would clearly be mandatory for anyone fixated on the grand figures of nineteenth-century English psychiatry. But, paying due attention to the professional and social context of Conolly's life and career, one discovers that his biography teaches us a great deal about the larger issues associated with the emergence of a professionalized psychiatry in Victorian England. In my earliest researches for *Museums of Madness,* I necessarily devoted considerable time and attention to the surviving Hanwell records, not only because of the asylum's size and its metropolitan location, but also because of the great contemporary attention it drew as the inspiration for nonrestraint, the orthodoxy of nineteenth-century English asylumdom. My interest in Conolly was still greater, because he occupied such a paradoxical role in the whole process of lunacy reform: the most formidable proselyte for the county asylum system in the 1840s, and yet a decade or so before, the most scathing critic of the emerging professional consensus about the necessity of the asylum in the treatment of mental disorder. How was one to account for such a puzzling transformation? The question fascinated me, and yet it was obviously tangential to the main thrust of the analysis I wanted to pursue in the book. But over the next few years, I kept stumbling across additional materials that shed new light on the subject, while revealing that Conolly's career and intellectual development were even more convoluted than I had previously realized. Finally, when an extended stay in England allowed me to tie up some of the loose ends, I gave the project more sustained attention and was able to write up the following essay shortly after my return to San Diego.

3. Michael MacDonald, *Mystical Bedlam: Madness, Anxiety, and Healing in Seventeenth Century England* (Cambridge: Cambridge University Press, 1981); Nancy Tomes, *A Generous Confidence: Thomas Story Kirkbridge and the Art of Asylum Keeping, 1840–1883* (Cambridge: Cambridge University Press, 1984); S. E. D. Shortt, *Victorian Lunacy: Richard M. Bucke and the Practice of Late Nineteenth-Century Psychiatry* (Cambridge: Cambridge University Press, 1986).

John Conolly:
A Victorian Psychiatric Career

We have in this asylum, Sir,
Some doctors of renown
With a plan of non-restraint
Which they seem to think their own.
All well-meaning men, Sir,
But troubled with a complaint
Called the monomania
Of total non-restraint.

—EPISTLE TO MR. EWART, M.P.,
by a Reverend Gentleman lately a patient in the Middlesex Asylum, 1841 [1]

John Conolly's place in the pantheon of heroes of English psychiatric history seems secure. Contemporaries likened his achievement in introducing nonrestraint in the treatment of the insane paupers at Hanwell Lunatic Asylum to Howard's labors in the cause of penal reform and Clarkson's role in the abolition of slavery.[2] Lord Shaftesbury, for forty years the chairman of the English lunacy commissioners and chief spokesman for the lunacy reform movement, referred to Conolly's work as "the greatest triumph of skill and humanity" that the world had ever known.[3] And the doyens of late-nineteenth-century medicine were only marginally less hyperbolic: for Sir James Crichton-Browne, "no member of his profession—except Jenner and Lister—has done a tithe as much as he to ward off and alleviate human suffering."[4] "It is to Conolly," said Sir Benjamin Ward Richardson, "that we really owe the modern humane treatment of the insane as it exists today in all its beneficent ramifications. . . . The abolition of restraint . . . has placed us first among all the nations as physicians of medical disease."[5] These are judgments that historians have for the most part been content to echo,[6] crediting Conolly

---

1. Quite possibly, the author of this piece of doggerel was actually the chaplain at Hanwell, one of several staff members who bitterly opposed Conolly's introduction of nonrestraint.

2. *The Lancet*, 14 October 1843, 71–72, quoting the *Morning Chronicle*.

3. House of Commons, *Report from the Select Committee of the House of Commons on Lunatics, with the Minutes of Evidence* (1859), 45–49, evidence of Lord Shaftesbury.

4. Sir James Crichton-Browne, *Victorian Jottings* (London: Etchells and MacDonald, 1926).

5. Sir Benjamin Ward Richardson, "Medicine Under Queen Victoria; The First Advancement: The Treatment of the Insane," *The Asclepiad* (1877): 203–14.

6. An exception is Dennis Leigh, *The Historical Development of British Psychiatry* (London: Pergamon Press, 1961).

with completing the work begun by Pinel and Tuke, by introducing "reforms which simultaneously gave freedom to the mentally ill and psychiatry to medicine."[7]

But Conolly's medical career is too long and varied to be reduced to a simple tale of his triumph as the author of "nonrestraint." Quite apart from any other considerations, the system he is popularly assumed to have initiated[8] was, as he periodically acknowledged, not his invention at all. Moreover, he was well into middle age before he became the resident physician at Hanwell, and he occupied that post for less than four years. A more extended look at his professional life provides valuable insight into some of the vicissitudes attending the choice of a medical career in Victorian England; and the sharp transformations that mark his thinking on psychiatric matters, closely paralleling the twists and turns of his own career, point up the intimate relationship that often exists between developments in disinterested medical "knowledge" and the varying social interests of those propounding it.

John Conolly was born at his grandmother's house in the small town of Market Rasen in Lincolnshire, in 1794. His father, "a younger son of a good Irish family . . . had been brought up to no profession; had no pursuits; [and] died young," leaving his wife with three young children to raise. The three boys were soon separated, and John, at the age of five, found himself boarded out, like "an inconvenient superfluity," with an elderly widow, a distant relative of the family, in the decaying borough of Hedon. Here he spent a "barren" and "wretched" boyhood, receiving a "dull, mechanical," and, as he later confessed, grossly inadequate education at the local grammar school. The descent from even a shabby gentility "to the commoner arrangements inseparable from school, and to a society of the lower kind, where nothing was tasteful, and nothing was beautiful, and nothing was cheerful"[9] made a profound impression on Conolly. The experience may well have contributed to the insistent concern he displayed in his later years that others acknowledge his gentlemanly status; and they certainly must have intensified the pressures engendered by the uncertain course that marked his professional and financial life until the age of forty-five.

Conolly's mother had moved to Hull in 1803 and supported herself by opening a boarding school for "young ladies." Within a few years she

7. Richard Hunter and Ida Macalpine, "Introduction" to John Conolly, *An Inquiry Concerning the Indications of Insanity,* facsimile ed. (London: Dawsons, 1964), 1.

8. "[Conolly] originated a non-restraint movement which spread to all Europe and America. His follower, Robert Gardiner Hill (1811–1878), chief surgeon of the Lincoln Asylum, . . . wrote a good deal against any form of restraint" (Gregory Zilboorg, *A History of Medical Psychology* [New York: Norton, 1967], 387).

9. John Conolly, "Autobiographical sketch," reprinted in Leigh, *British Psychiatry,* 211–15.

remarried, her new husband being a Mr. Stirling, an émigré Scot from Paris who taught languages; and in 1807, she brought her son John home to live with them. Despite the further decline in social status that these domestic arrangements implied, Conolly seems to have enjoyed the next five years. With his stepfather's encouragement, he became fluent in French, dabbled in Enlightenment philosophy, and obtained a rudimentary general and literary education. In 1812, at the age of eighteen, he procured a commission as an ensign in the Cambridgeshire militia and spent the closing years of the Napoleonic Wars in Scotland and Ireland. Apparently he found military life to his taste, for Henry Maudsley reports enduring many conversations filled with "lively and pleasant recollections" of his service.[10] Napoleon's defeat and exile, however, foreclosed the possibility of a military career, and by 1816, Conolly had resigned his commission and returned to Hull.[11] With the death of his mother and stepfather he received a small inheritance, and in March of 1817, married Eliza Collins, daughter of the recently deceased Sir John Collins (himself the illegitimate son of the second Earl of Abermarle). Such an early marriage, with very little capital and no real prospects would by itself have struck most Victorians as foolhardy, and the couple quickly compounded their difficulties by the sort of financial ineptitude that Conolly was to exhibit throughout his life. After the marriage, they left immediately for France and spent an idyllic year in a cottage near Tours, on the banks of the Loire. At the end of this period, with the arrival of his first child and the rapid shrinking of his capital, it seems finally to have dawned on Conolly that he had to develop some stable source of income.

For those in early Victorian England who were without independent means but aspired to gentlemanly status, the choice of careers was meager indeed.[12] Anything connected with "trade" was out of the question, leaving only law, the Church, and perhaps medicine as ways of gaining a livelihood without irrevocable loss of caste. Medicine, in fact, was not an unambiguously acceptable choice: as Trollope observed (in the person of Miss Marable), "She would not absolutely say that a physician was not a gentleman, or even a surgeon; but she would not allow to physic the absolute privilege which, in her eyes, belonged to the law and the church."[13] Still, it was on medicine that Conolly settled (based in part on the advice of his older brother William, who was already medically qualified); and

10. Henry Maudsley, "Memoir of the Late John Conolly," *Journal of Mental Science* 12 (1866): 161.

11. Leigh, *British Psychiatry*, 216. Hunter and Macalpine, "Introduction," 4.

12. M. Jeanne Peterson, *The Medical Profession in Mid-Victorian London* (Berkeley: University of California Press, 1978).

13. Anthony Trollope, *The Vicar of Bullhampton*, quoted in Peterson, *Medical Profession*, 194.

like many an ill-connected and impecunious provincial, he elected to obtain his training in Scotland, first at Glasgow and then, for two years, at Edinburgh.

Possessed of a talent for making friends and for moving easily in society,[14] Conolly enjoyed a moderately successful student career, becoming one of the four annual presidents of the Royal Medical Society in his second year. He was strongly influenced by Dugald Stewart, the professor of moral philosophy,[15] and like a number of Edinburgh students of this period[16] he developed a special interest in the problem of insanity. Reflecting this, his M.D. dissertation of 1821 was devoted to a brief discussion of *De statu mentis in insania et melancholia.*[17]

He now had to earn his living and encountered immediately the dilemma of where to set up his practice. Lacking the means to buy into an established practice, and without any family ties he could call on to help obtain a clientele, Conolly faced an uphill battle.[18] His difficulties were further compounded by the fact that he already had a wife and child to support. And since his Scottish training left him without any institutional or personal linkages to the London hospitals and medical elites, he had perforce to begin his career in a provincial setting. Inevitably, this meant engaging in general practice in an isolated and highly competitive environment,[19] in which it generally took several years before one began to earn even a modest competence and where one was highly dependent

14. Maudsley, "Memoir," 164.

15. Leigh, *British Psychiatry,* 216.

16. Alexander Crichton, John Haslam, and Thomas Arnold are among the best-known of his predecessors.

17. Reminiscing at the end of his career, Conolly recalled: "My interest in the insane, and my observation of the phenomena of mental disturbance, began early, and became increased as years advanced . . . because the most active years of my life happened to be passed in a period signalised by an almost total change in the character of Lunatic Asylums. In the first year of my medical studies, my thoughts, which had previously and often been directed to metaphysical reading, were more consistently directed to mental phenomena, and especially to those of minds in a disordered state, by an accidental visit to the old Lunatic Asylum of Glasgow—from which visit it has happened that all my subsequent life has taken its colour. . . . The impression made in that and several other visits by the conversation of the patients, and by the several forms and degrees of eccentricity and unreason there witnessed, has never been effaced" (John Conolly, "Recollections of the Varieties of Insanity, Part I," *Medical Times and Gazette* 10 [1860]: 6–9).

18. On the importance of possessing either a family tradition of medical practice and/or the means to short-circuit the otherwise laborious and uncertain business of building a general practice by purchasing an existing one, see Peterson, *Medical Profession,* passim, especially 91–98.

19. Irvine Loudon's meticulous study of general practice from the mid-eighteenth to the mid-nineteenth century has recently demonstrated that the 1820s were an extraordinarily inhospitable period in which to try to launch a medical career, a time of unparalleled intraprofessional rivalry in a grossly overcrowded professional marketplace—an environ-

on somehow securing the approval and patronage of the well-to-do.[20] To make matters worse, medical men working in such settings were regarded with ill-concealed contempt by the professional elites of Edinburgh and London, reflecting their marginal status in the larger social world. They were, sniffed the *Edinburgh Medical and Surgical Journal*, "engaged in the trading, money-making parts of the profession, and not one in a hundred of them distinguished by anything like science or liberality of mind."[21]

Conolly's first efforts to make his way in this difficult environment met with abject failure. After a three-month stay in Lewes, he abandoned the attempt to build a practice there and removed his family to Chichester to try again. Here, however, he had to compete with another young practitioner, John Forbes.[22] Though the two were to become lifelong friends, there was insufficient work to support them both, and within a year it had become apparent that it was Conolly who would have to leave. Of the two, he was undoubtedly "the greater favourite in society, his courteous manner, his vivacity of character, and his general accomplishments, rendered him an agreeable companion."[23] But however enjoyable the local notables found his company, when they required professional medical services, they turned instead to Forbes. Conolly, as his son-in-law Henry Maudsley later remarked, was a poor "practical physician," with little talent or ability to inspire confidence in "the exact investigation of disease, or in its treatment; he had little faith in medicines, and hardly more faith in pathology, while the actual practice of his profession was not agreeable to him."[24]

Now blessed (or burdened) with a second child, his son Edward Tennyson, Conolly once more uprooted his family and moved, this time to

---

ment that fueled intense and bitter competition for patients and prosperity, with the ensuing struggle for survival proving too much for many of those entering upon it. See Irvine Loudon, *Medical Care and the General Practitioner, 1750–1850* (Oxford: Clarendon Press, 1986).

20. Peterson, *Medical Profession*, pp. 24–26. The situation had not changed much even forty years on: "The profession of a medical man in a small provincial town is not often one which gives to its owner in early life a large income. Perhaps in no career has a man to work harder for what he earns, or to do more work without earning anything. It has sometimes seemed to me as though the young doctors and the old doctors had agreed to divide between them the different results of their profession—the young doctors doing all the work and the old doctors taking all the money" (Anthony Trollope, *The Small House at Allington* [London: Oxford University Press, 1980], 209).

21. *Edinburgh Medical and Surgical Journal* 75 (1851): 255.

22. In later years Forbes was appointed physician to the queen's household. For his career, see *Lives of the Fellows of the Royal College of Physicians of London, 1826–1925* (London: For the College, 1955), 34–35 (hereafter cited as *Munk's Roll*).

23. Maudsley, "Memoir," 164.

24. Ibid., 172.

Stratford-upon-Avon, then a small town of some 4,000 inhabitants. Here he at last began to prosper, albeit in a very modest way. He was elected to the Town Council and twice served as mayor, the 80-pound salary serving as a useful supplement to his still slender professional income. He took a leading role in establishing a dispensary for the treatment of the sick poor and was active in civic affairs more generally, the well-worn path for a young practitioner trying to make his way.[25] Perhaps because of the interest he had developed in the subject while in Edinburgh, and no doubt because the honorarium attached supplemented his inadequate income, he also secured an appointment as "Inspecting Physician to the Lunatic Houses for the County of Warwick," a position that required only that he accompany two local justices of the peace on their annual inspection of the county's half-dozen madhouses.

In his best year at Stratford, though, Conolly's income is reported "not to have exceeded 400 pounds," an amount barely sufficient to maintain a suitable life-style for a professional man with a growing family.[26] Quite suddenly, however, the prospect arose of substituting the rewards of a London teaching and consulting practice for the dull routines of general practice in a provincial backwater. The founders of the new University of London had decided to include a medical school in the new foundation. Somewhat to his surprise, Conolly managed to obtain an appointment as professor of nature and treatment of diseases, helped in part by being previously known to Dr. George Birkbeck[27] and Lord Brougham,[28] two of the prime movers in the project. While the university had "sought to engage men of high standing, . . . it could offer but small emoluments and a precarious future" in its early years.[29] And accordingly, a number of the early appointments were of young or relatively unknown men.[30]

In general, however, "assured income and national visibility . . . went with status as full physician or surgeon at a hospital and as teacher at a

25. Cf. Peterson, Medical Profession.
26. On medical incomes in this period, cf. ibid., 207–24; and Loudon, Medical Care, chaps. 11 and 12.
27. George Birkbeck (1776–1841), M.D., Edinburgh, 1799, was a friend of Brougham's at Edinburgh, famous for his role as the founder of mechanics' institutes, including the London Mechanics' Institute (now Birkbeck College).
28. Lord Henry Brougham (1778–1868) was educated at Edinburgh University and was one of the founders of the Edinburgh Review. A barrister, Whig politician, and law reformer, he later served as lord chancellor in the Lord Grey and Melbourne administrations. Almost certainly, Conolly's Edinburgh connections helped secure Brougham's and Birkbeck's patronage.
29. H. H. Bellot, University College London, 1826–1926 (London: University of London Press, 1929), 37.
30. There were some famous names, however, including Charles Bell, A. T. Thomson, and D. D. Davis. For biographical details, see Munk's Roll.

medical school" in London,[31] and Conolly undoubtedly thought that he was about to cross successfully the great divide that marked off the social and financial world of elite London physicians from the humble surroundings of the rest of the profession. He instantly wrote back accepting: "Gratified, as I cannot but be, by the confidence which has been placed in me, an untried person, I know that it only remains for me to justify it by my services."[32] Though the first scheduled teaching session was not to begin until October 1828, some fourteen months hence, he at once refused offers to write and edit for London publishers on the grounds that "the attention and care required by the lectures of so inexperienced a teacher as I am . . . occupy almost every hour of my time."[33] And toward the end of 1827, he announced plans to travel to Paris for three months to obtain materials that would assist him in preparing his lectures.[34]

On 2 October, 1828, Conolly gave his inaugural lecture, the second at the new medical school.[35] It was apparently quite successful,[36] although largely given over to some rather platitudinous advice to his students. He informed them:

> I have watched with some interest, the fate and conduct of many of those who were pursuing their studies at the same time as myself. Of these, some were of course idle, and despised the secluded pursuits of the studious; I do not know *one* whose progress has been satisfactory: many of them, after trying various methods of dazzling the public, have sunk, already, into merited degradation. But I do not know one among the industrious, who has not attained a fair prospect of success; many of them have already acquired it; and some of them will doubtless be the improvers of their science in our own day, and remembered with honour when they are dead.[37]

Naturally enough, Conolly aspired to belong to the latter group. Nevertheless, his lecture's one departure from the expected was an announcement that "it is my intention to dwell somewhat more fully on Mental Disorders, or to speak more correctly, of disorders affecting the mani-

---

31. Peterson, *Medical Profession,* 161.

32. Conolly to Leonard Horner, 21 July 1827, College Collection, University College London Library (hereafter cited as UCL).

33. Conolly [to Messrs. Longman], 21 July 1827; 28 May 1828, Wellcome Institute for the History of Medicine Collection, London. See also Conolly to Thomas Coates, 3 April 1828: "I cannot at present let anything draw my attention away from my University duties" (Society for the Diffusion of Useful Knowledge Collection [hereafter cited as SDUK Coll.], UCL).

34. Conolly to Leonard Horner, 26 September 1827; 7 November 1827, UCL.

35. He had been preceded by Charles Bell.

36. *Morning Chronicle,* 3 October 1828, 3A; 4 October 1828, 2D. See also *The Life and Times of Henry Brougham by Himself* (London: Blackwood, 1871), 2:498–99.

37. John Conolly, *An Introductory Lecture Delivered in the University of London, October 2, 1828* (London: Taylor, 1828), 23.

festations of the mind than has, I believe, been usual in lectures on the practice of medicine."[38] Conolly's attempts, over the next two years, to get permission to give students clinical instruction in mental disorders at a London asylum proved unavailing. After initially encouraging him, the University Council rejected the idea.[39] Thwarted in this direction, he decided instead to publish a book on the subject, not least because "I disapprove entirely of some part of the usual management of lunatics."[40]

An Inquiry Concerning the Indications of Insanity, published in 1830, is, in many respects, a rather conventional treatise, "investigating the mind's history, from its most perfect state, through all its modifications of strength and through all its varieties of disease, until it becomes affected with confirmed madness."[41] But Conolly broke sharply with contemporary orthodoxy over the key issue of how and where the lunatic ought to be treated. His book appeared in the midst of the early-nineteenth-century campaign for "reform" in the treatment of lunatics—a movement that took some thirty years to achieve its goals, and one whose proponents were absolutely convinced that asylum care was the only appropriate form of treatment for the insane. The heightened public attention to the problems posed by the mentally disturbed stimulated a large number of medical men to produce books and pamphlets on insanity, and running through this literature, and repeated with growing emphasis and conviction, was the assertion that all forms of madness required institutional care and treatment and that the sooner those displaying signs of mental imbalance were removed from domestic to asylum care, the greater their chances of ultimate recovery.[42]

From this almost universal consensus about "the improbability (I had almost said moral impossibility) of an insane person's regaining the use of his reason, except by removing him early to some Institution for that purpose,"[43] Conolly issued a lengthy and closely argued dissent. Seeking to offer "no opinions which have not received some confirmation from observation and experience,"[44] he asserted that the emphasis on the centrality of the asylum "originated in erroneous views of mental disorders, and has been perpetuated with such views."[45] Existing authorities ar-

38. Ibid., 16. See also University of London, *Second Statement by the Council of the University of London Explanatory of the Plan of Instruction* (London: Longman, 1828), 150.

39. Maudsley, "Memoir," 165–66.

40. Conolly, *Introductory Lecture*, 16–17.

41. Review of *An Inquiry into the Indications of Insanity*, *Medicochirurgical Review* 13 (1830): 289–308.

42. On these developments, see generally Andrew Scull, *Museums of Madness: The Social Organization of Insanity in Nineteenth-Century England* (London: Allen Lane; New York: St. Martin's Press, 1979), esp. chap. 3.

43. Robert Gardiner Hill, *A Lecture on the Management of Lunatic Asylums, and the Treatment of the Insane* (London: Simpkin Marshall, 1839), 4–5.

44. Conolly, *Indications of Insanity*, 9.

45. Ibid., 31.

gued that any and all forms of mental unsoundness warranted—indeed required—confinement. If this doctrine of "indiscriminate treatment, including deprivation of property and personal liberty," were to prevail, then, said Conolly,

> no man can be sure that he may not, with a full consciousness of his sufferings and wrongs, be one day treated as if all sense and feeling were in him destroyed and lost; torn from his family, from his home, from his innocent and eccentric pursuits, and condemned, for an indefinite period, to pass his melancholy days among the idiotic and the mad."[46]

"Restraint," as he saw it, was "seldom apportioned to the individual case, but is indiscriminate and excessive and uncertain in its termination."[47] (Later in Conolly's career, restraint was to acquire a narrower meaning, referring to the use of chains, straitjackets, and the like to impose physical controls on the insane, but here, significantly, it is used in the broad sense of removal from ordinary social life and confinement in an institution.) It was precisely the expert's task, not just to distinguish the mad from the sane, but "to point out those circumstances which, even in persons decidedly insane, can alone justify various degrees of restraint."[48] And the latter was clearly the more difficult accomplishment. At present, "certificates of insanity" were heedlessly and ignorantly . . . signed,"[49] with the result that "the crowd of most of our asylums is made up of odd but harmless individuals, not much more absurd than numbers who are at large."[50] Moreover,

> once confined, the very confinement is admitted as the strongest of all proofs that a man must be mad. . . . It matters not that the certificate is probably signed by those who know very little of madness or of the necessity of confinement; or by those who have not carefully examined the patient; a visitor hesitates to avow, in the face of such a document, what may be set down as a mere want of penetration in a matter wherein nobody seems in doubt but himself; or he may be tempted to affect to perceive those signs of madness that do not exist.[51]

Hence, the central importance of clinical instruction of medical students in the recognition and treatment of insanity. As the medical curriculum was presently constructed,

> during the term allotted to medical study, the student never sees a case of insanity, except by some rare accident. . . . The first occurrence, consequently, of a case of insanity, in his own practice, alarms him: he . . . has recourse to indiscriminate and, generally, to violent or unnecessary means; or gets rid of his anxiety and his patient together, by signing a certificate, which commits the unfortunate person to a mad house.[52]

46. Ibid., 8–9.   47. Ibid., 6.   48. Ibid., 1.   49. Ibid., 28.
50. Ibid., 17.   51. Ibid., 4–5.   52. Ibid., 2.

Such an outcome might be avoided by teaching students not only how to solve the relatively simple problem of distinguishing those of unsound mind, but also how to decide *"whether or not the departure from sound mind be of such a nature to justify the confinement of the individual, and the imposition of restraint upon him, as regards the use or disposal of his property."* [53]

The task was rendered the more urgent because asylum treatment was, as he saw it, more pernicious than beneficial. Perhaps a trifle disingenuously, Conolly announced that he had "no wish to exaggerate the disadvantages of lunatic asylums." [54] There were, after all, certain classes of patients for whom public asylums were "unavoidable evils." [55] "For a hopeless lunatic, a raving madman, for a melancholy wretch who seems neither to see nor to hear, or for an utter idiot, a lunatic asylum is a place which affords all the comforts of which unfortunate persons are capable." [56] But their regrettable necessity as places of last resort must not be allowed to obscure the fact that

> it is a far different place for two-thirds of those who are confined there. . . .
> To all these patients confinement is the very reverse of beneficial. It fixes and renders permanent what might have passed away and ripens eccentricity or temporary excitement or depression, into actual insanity. [57]

The first principle of asylum treatment was the isolation of the mad from the sane. This sequestration from the world was alleged to be therapeutic, a notion Conolly scathingly attacked: "Whatever may be said, no one in his senses will believe, that a man whose mind is disordered is likely in any stage of his disorder to derive benefit from being surrounded by men whose mental faculties are obscured, whose passions and affections are perverted, and who present to him, in place of models of sound mind, in place of rational and kind associates, in place of reasonable and judicious conversation, every specimen of folly, of melancholy, and of extravagant madness." [58] People's mental and moral capacities varied markedly according to the circumstances in which they were placed, and their thoughts and actions were, in large degree, the product of an interaction between habits, situational pressures, and the influence and reactions of their associates. The capacity to control one's wayward passions and imagination and to avoid the perils of morbid introspection [59] was thus essentially dependent on social reinforcement and support. Granting these realities of our mental life,

53. Ibid., 35 (emphasis in the original). 54. Ibid., 25. 55. Ibid., 7.
56. Ibid., 17. 57. Ibid., 17–18. 58. Ibid., 30–31.
59. Michael Clark, "Victorian Psychiatry and the Concept of Morbid Introspection," (Paper, Oxford University, 1981). A published version of this paper will appear in *The Anatomy of Madness*, ed. W. F. Bynum, Roy Porter, and Michael Shepherd, vol. 3 (London: Tavistock, 1988).

who can fail to perceive that in such an unhappy situation [as asylum life provided] the most constant and vigorous assertion of his self-command would be required to resist the horrible influences of the place;—a place in which a thousand fantasies, that are swept away almost as soon as formed in the healthy atmosphere of our diversified society, would assume shapes more distinct; a place in which the intellectual operations could not but become, from mere want of exercise, more and more inert; and the domination of wayward feelings more and more powerful.[60]

Taking even "the most favourable case for the asylum," its effects were likely to be harmful.[61]

Of course, the men running such places sought to reject these charges. They claimed that the inmates of the asylums were not abandoned and subjected to a pernicious atmosphere of uncontrolled ravings and delusions, but were carefully monitored and controlled by a sane superintendent and judiciously coaxed and encouraged to resume an independent, self-governing existence. Conolly remained unconvinced:

> To say that persons in this state are not left, are not abandoned, is by no means satisfactory to those who have opportunities of knowing how little of the time of the superintendent is, or can be, commonly devoted to the professed objects of his care, and yet who, like children, demand constant watching and attention.[62]

Hence the "numerous examples" to be found "in which . . . a continued residence in the asylum was gradually ruining the body and the mind."[63]

To some extent, the antitherapeutic effects of the asylum derived from "the monotonous wretchedness of the unhappy patient's existence; debarred from home, from the sight of friends, from the society of their families; . . . shut out from even a hope of any change that *might* prove beneficial to them."[64] But criticisms of this sort suggested that a more enlightened and flexible administration, and the provision of more varied amusements and diversions, could obviate the difficulty. They could not. Superintendents, some of whom

> are men of great intelligence and humanity, . . . may point to the spaciousness of their grounds, to the variety of occupations and amusements prepared for their patients, to the excellence of their food and the convenience of their lodging; and urge that as little restraint is employed as is compatible with their safety: but the fault of the association of lunatics with each other, and the infrequency of any communication between the patient and persons of sound mind, mars the whole of the design.[65]

The defect was thus, as Conolly saw it, a structural one, and hence not removable by any conceivable reform. Confinement in an institution

---

60. Conolly, *Indications of Insanity*, 22–23.   61. Ibid., 18.   62. Ibid., 19–20.
63. Ibid., 20.   64. Ibid., 21.   65. Ibid., 31.

acted like a self-fulfilling prophecy, intensifying and even creating the very behaviors that were its alleged justification:

The effect of living constantly among mad men and women is a loss of all sensibility and self-respect or care; or not infrequently, a perverse pleasure in adding to the confusion and diversifying the eccentricity of those about them. . . . In both cases the disease grows inveterate. Paroxysms of violence alternate with fits of sullenness; both are considered further proofs of the hopelessness of the case.[66]

For whole classes of lunatics, therefore, asylum treatment was grossly inappropriate. Given that "so long as one lunatic associates with another, supposing the case is to be curable, so long must the chances of restoration to sanity be very materially diminished,"[67] recent and curable cases did not belong in an institution. This was particularly the case "during the mental weakness of their convalescence," when confinement exposed them to "the presence of a company of lunatics, their incoherent talk, their cries, their moans, their indescribable utterances of all imaginable fancies or their ungovernable frolics and tumult." These, said Conolly, "can have no salutary effect on a mind just reviving from long depression."[68] On the contrary, they were "the very circumstances most likely to confuse or destroy [even] the most rational and healthy mind."[69]

Another class of patients for whom a lunatic asylum is a most improper place consists of those who, in various periods of life become afflicted with various degrees of weakness of intellect. . . . But there is little or no extravagance of action, still less is there anything in the patient which would make his liberty dangerous, or, if he were properly attended to and watched, even inconvenient to others or himself.[70]

Such patients, along with the chronically insane, were subject to a more insidious but equally debilitating and damaging effect of confinement in an institution, the gradual atrophy of their social capacities: "After many hopeless years, such patients become so accustomed to the routine of the house, as to be mere children; and are content to remain there, as they commonly do, until they die."[71]

If social practices could be brought to reflect these realities, "the patients *out* of the asylum being the majority, and consisting of all whose circumstances would insure them proper attendance—better arrangements might be made for the smaller number of public asylums, or central houses of reception."[72] Such asylums must, first of all, be public, that is, state supported, for only by removing the distorting effects of the profit motive could one avoid the problems created by a system in which "the patients are transmitted, like stock-in-trade, from one member of a

66. Ibid., 22.   67. Ibid., 29.   68. Ibid., 26.   69. Ibid., 23.
70. Ibid., 29–30.   71. Ibid., 21.   72. Ibid., 483.

family to another, and from one generation to another": a free trade in lunacy that attracts, besides a handful of "respectable, well-educated, and humane individuals," the "ignorant and ill-educated" and those "capable of no feeling but a desire for wealth."[73] Second, each asylum should become a center in which aspiring medical men could be taught to recognize and treat mental disorder.[74] The possession of such clinically derived skills and knowledge—the fruit of the sort of arrangement he had unsuccessfully urged on the university—would give the average medical practitioner both the competence and the confidence to treat most cases of insanity on a domiciliary basis.

If Conolly hoped that the publication of *An Inquiry Concerning the Indications of Insanity* would serve to advance his reputation and enlarge his private practice, he was soon disabused. One reviewer, in the *Medical-Chirurgical Review,* did praise him for performing "a very important service to the profession, in calling their attention to the construction and properties of the mind," and for the superior "language and style" in which he expressed himself.[75] But for the most part, Conolly's suggestions were not even debated,[76] but simply ignored. For by now the overwhelming weight of opinion among both the profession itself and those laymen interested in lunacy reform was that in cases of insanity, asylum treatment was indispensable and could not be embarked upon too quickly for the patient's own good—a position Conolly himself was to embrace less than a decade later.

In the meantime, he was involved in a series of controversies at the medical school, that within six months, were to prompt his resignation. The early years of the university were stormy ones. The council, chosen from among the university's proprietors, exhibited a constant disposition to interfere with the conduct of the institution, threatening to send inspectors to check on the quality of lectures given, to exercise the power to censor the books used in teaching, and "to regulate minutely not only the number, length, and hours, but also the scope and content of the various courses."[77] In general, "it regarded the professors in the same light as any other of its employees, and all its employees with suspi-

73. Ibid., 13–14.

74. Ibid., 7, 37–38.

75. *Mediochirurgical Review* 13 (1830): 289–308.

76. The German alienist Maximilian Jacobi did object a few years later that "Doctor Conolly takes occasion . . . to recommend the treatment of such persons in their own houses in far too unconditional a manner, and without any adequate consideration of the objections against" and insisted on the value of asylum treatment (Jacobi, *On the Construction and Management of Hospitals for the Insane* [London: Churchill, 1841], 77–80 [the original German ed., 1834]). But such direct attempts to refute Conolly's claims were otherwise notable by their absence.

77. Bellot, *University College London,* 191.

cion."[78] The friction such conduct was sure to arouse was exacerbated by the activities of the warden, Leonard Horner, the salaried officer to whom the council had delegated day-to-day supervision of university affairs. For Horner, too, had an exalted view of his position, and his arrogant and autocratic manner, his constant petty interference and intrigue aroused widespread discontent among the professoriate—an antipathy strengthened by the fact that the warden, though paid four or five times as much as those he supervised, was an erstwhile linen manufacturer possessed of limited education and no scholarly qualifications.[79]

The medical faculty considered that "a Hospital is absolutely necessary for the prosperity of the Medical School,"[80] since only by providing clinical instruction could they hope to compete effectively with rival London institutions for students. For a time it appeared that a suitable arrangement could be reached with the nearby London Fever Hospital, but when the council insisted on being given complete control, its intransigence led to the collapse of the negotiations. As a temporary, if inadequate, substitute, Conolly and his colleagues proposed the establishment of a university dispensary, which they would attend "without compensation . . . as a help to a rising school"[81]—a plan to which the parsimonious council quickly agreed.[82] But the dispensary soon became a new source of friction. It was to have a resident apothecary, and Conolly and his colleague Anthony Todd Thomson immediately expressed concern that the appointee be someone who aspired "solely to being efficient in that useful but still subordinate capacity."[83] Their concern to protect their status soon proved prescient, for Horner began to use John Hogg, who had secured the position, to check on the professors' performance of their duties. Conolly viewed such "very offensive" machinations as an intolerable affront to his dignity:

> You have constituted the Apothecary, who ought to be under the orders of the physicians and surgeons, a kind of spy over those physicians and

78. Ibid.

79. Ibid., 193–96. Leonard Horner (1785–1864) was born and educated in Edinburgh. An active Whig politician with a notoriously great respect for "people of station and property," he was, like his older brother Francis, one of Brougham's intimate circle—which doubtless explains his appointment as warden. Following his resignation from that position, in March 1831, he was to achieve fame for his role as one of the chief inspectors under the Factories Act, a position he occupied until 1856. For details of his life, see Katherine M. Lyell (ed.), *Memoir of Leonard Horner, Edited by his Daughter*, 2 vols. (London: Women's Printing Society, 1890).

80. University College, London, Minute-Book of the Faculty of Medicine, Inaugural Meeting, 26 October 1987.

81. Conolly to Horner, 10 July 1830, UCL.

82. Hunter and Macalpine, "Introduction," 25–26.

83. Conolly to Horner, 18 August 1828, UCL.

surgeons, and have thereby completely subverted the discipline of the establishment. Among respectable men of my own rank in the medical profession, I find but one opinion concerning this matter; and that opinion makes it impossible for me to continue my attendance at the Dispensary. . . . The Council have no right to impose a degradation on me, and I cannot submit to it.[84]

Two months later, Horner informed him that "the Council considered it a part of the duty of the Professor of the Practice of Medicine to attend as Physician at the Dispensary."[85] But Conolly stood his ground: "No opinion of the Council, or of any body of men, can, or ever shall, induce me to act inconsistently to my character as a physician and a gentleman." Only a change in the lines of authority at the dispensary would induce him to return.[86] Eventually a meeting with the council itself led to the quarrel being patched up, though not until Conolly had incurred further slights from the warden.[87]

On other fronts, too, the relationship between the university and its professors grew strained. The proprietors wished to move to a system in which a professor's pay was directly proportional to the income he generated from his lectures. Initially, they had been forced to modify this plan in order to attract faculty to a new and untried enterprise, offering salary guarantees for the first three years of the university's existence. By the spring of 1830, however, financial difficulties were increasing as student numbers declined, and "the University was eating up its capital at a rate of 1,000 pounds a year."[88] Rumors began to circulate that the council was contemplating an early end to the system of guaranteed salaries. A number of professors, Conolly among them, responded by laying out an alternative plan to rescue the institution's finances. They insisted that "a salary should be secured for every professor in the event of his fees from pupils not attaining a certain amount," arguing that the institution was still too new for payment by results to work and that the failure to provide such a guarantee would inhibit the professors' study of their subjects, since such activities would be "unproductive of immediate pecuniary advantage."[89] Some professors' lectures fees amounted to less than 100 pounds, of which the university proposed to take a third, and yet "it is expected that the professor will subsist in the rank of a gentleman upon the balance." To balance the budget, they proposed tailoring

84. Conolly to the University Council, 5 May 1830, see also John Hogg to L. Horner, 8 May 1830, UCL.

85. Horner to Conolly, 8 July 1830, UCL.

86. Conolly to Horner, 10 July 1830, UCL.

87. Ibid., 19 July 1830.

88. Bellot, *University College London*, 177.

89. *A Letter to the Shareholders and Council of the University of London on the Present State of that Institution* (London: Taylor, 1830), 12–15.

the length of courses to the convenience of students, since the university could not expect, "for many years to come, to draw any considerable number of students from the upper ranks [of society]";[90] and *reducing* fees so as to attract additional students who would otherwise attend the cheaper courses given by such places as the Royal Institution and the London Institute. Finally, a great deal of money could be saved by abolishing the office of warden, with his salary of 1,200 pounds a year (a suggestion scarcely inclined to endear its authors to Horner). These proposals were leaked to the press and met by anonymous responses from the warden, a war of words that continued until 21 April 1830, when the *Sun* reported that with some lecture rooms all but empty, the proprietors had decided to reduce the salary guarantees to the least successful professors.[91]

This news must have been a considerable blow to Conolly, for his financial situation had been precarious since his arrival in London. On the same day that the new salary policy was announced, he wrote to Horner declining to repeat the summer session lectures he had given the year before, partly because the number of students was likely to be small, rendering the course unremunerative, and also because "I am under the necessity of employing some of the year in occupations unconnected, or not immediately connected, with my Professorship, which I could not possibly do if I were to lecture ten months out of twelve."[92] During the 1829–30 session, his university salary declined from 300 pounds to 272 pounds, 15 shillings, and before the year was out, he was forced to request an advance of "100 pounds on account" from the warden he detested,[93] a humiliation he was compelled to undergo twice more before he finally left London the following spring.[94]

Conolly could scarcely have viewed the prospect of a further decline in his guaranteed salary with equanimity, for, notwithstanding all his laborious preparation and his personal charm, his lectures "were not great successes, if they were not in truth failures, [being] somewhat vague and diffuse, wanting in exact facts and practical information."[95] Here, as elsewhere, in the judgment of one of his friends, "the aid which Dr. Conolly rendered to the diffusion of knowledge was not special or professional."[96] Unfortunately, his efforts to augment his income from private practice were likewise unsuccessful. Conolly was blessed with consider-

---

90. Ibid., 23, 28.
91. *The Sun*, 21 April 1830, 4, col. D.
92. Conolly to Horner, 21 April 1830, UCL.
93. Ibid., 16 November 1830.
94. Ibid., 1 March 1831; 28 April 1831.
95. Maudsley, "Memoir," 172.
96. Charles Knight, *Passages from a Working Life*, quoted in Leigh, *British Psychiatry*, 219. Hunter and Macalpine ("Introduction," 32) have disputed this negative verdict on

able advantages that ought to have brought him patients: Lords Russell, Auckland, and Brougham provided aristocratic sponsorship; his university affiliation ought for once to have been an advantage; and he was amply provided with the necessary social graces.

> Though by nature passionate and impetuous, he had great command over his manner which was courteous in the extreme. Indeed he never failed to produce, by the suavity of his manner and the grace and ease of his address, the impression of great amiability, kindness, and unaffected simplicity; while his cheerful and vivacious disposition and his lively conversational powers rendered him an excellent social companion."[97]

He sought to capitalize on these advantages, following the well-worn path of the aspiring London practitioner. He joined the Medical and Chirurgical Society of London, and became an active member of the Society for the Diffusion of Useful Knowledge. He took the examination of the Royal College of Physicians and became a licentiate; and he secured election to the staff of the London Fever Hospital. Notwithstanding all his efforts, however, "practice did not come sufficiently quickly."[98] On a larger stage, he experienced a repetition of his failures at Lewes and Chichester, and almost certainly for the same reasons: his own deficiencies in the investigation of disease, his evident lack of faith in the medicine he prescribed, and his dislike of the tasks medical practice imposed, coupled with his settled disposition "to shrink from the disagreeable occasions of life, if it were possible, rather than encounter them with deliberate and settled resolution."[99]

Unlike the deficiencies of some of his colleagues, at least Conolly's failures were not the focus of public attention. Granville Sharp Pattison, the professor of anatomy, was not so fortunate. Having been one of Conolly's teachers at Glasgow, he had subsequently emigrated to the United States to an appointment at the University of Maryland. Apparently his tenure there was less than an overwhelming success (he was attacked in a pamphlet published in Philadelphia as "an adventurer with a tainted

---

Conolly's capacities as a lecturer, but it must be said that the four lectures he committed to print (John Conolly, *Four Lectures on the Study and Practice of Medicine* [London: Sherwood, Gilbert and Piper, 1832]) serve only to confirm the accuracy of Maudsley's claim that they were "vague and discursive."

97. Maudsley, "Memoir", 173–74.

98. Obituary of John Conolly, *Journal of Mental Science* 12 (1867): 148.

99. Maudsley, "Memoir," 172–73. Cf. Sir George Thane's comments: "In spite of the friendship of Lord Brougham, Lord John Russell, and other very influential men, John Conolly failed to practice as a London physician, nor does it appear that his duties were performed with any distinguished ability" (Thane, *Medical Biographies*, quoted in Kathleen Jones, *Lunacy, Law, and Conscience, 1744–1845: The Social History of the Care of the Insane* [London: Routledge and Kegan Paul, 1955], 154).

reputation"),[100] but he succeeded in securing one of the first chairs at the University of London, Conolly providing a testimonial in his behalf. The appointment proved to be a mistake. He neglected his work or performed it incompetently, giving superficial and perfunctory lectures when he bothered to attend. By contrast, J. R. Bennett, who had been appointed demonstrator in anatomy and had previously taught in Paris, "was a competent and popular teacher, and came to feel a contempt for Pattison as an anatomist which he was at no pains to conceal."[101] Conflict flared in the very first session and continued intermittently for more than two years. Pattison at first secured the support of many of his colleagues by alleging that Horner, whom they detested, was plotting his removal. But by the spring of 1830, student complaints about his performance grew more insistent, and the scandal surfaced in the medical press. A student memorial published in the *London Medical and Surgical Journal* "charge[d] him with *unusual ignorance* of old notions, and *total ignorance of* and *disgusting indifference* to new anatomical views and researches. . . . He is ignorant, or, if not ignorant, indolent, careless, and slovenly, and above all, indifferent to the interest of science."[102]

Conolly remained one of Pattison's staunchest supporters. He complained to the council that "the most heartless and iniquitous persecution has been carried on against the Professor of Anatomy . . . because his ruin would be convenient to the Warden's friends."[103] And for a few months, Pattison managed to cling to his position. But when the new session opened in October 1830, student discontent grew increasingly unmanageable. Pattison's classes were periodically boycotted and routinely disorderly. By February 1831, the students had opted for open rebellion, and "for over a month it was impossible to lecture. The scenes in the anatomy theatre reminded a contemporary reporter of Covent Garden during O. P. [Old Price] riots."[104] Conolly, too, began to lose control of some of his students, and on at least one occasion, nearly half of his class failed to attend his lecture.[105] Ultimately, the tumult subsided only after Horner abruptly relinquished his post and Pattison was forced to resign.[106] By then Conolly, too, had left the university.

Pattison was not the only colleague of doubtful competence whom Conolly sought to defend. His intervention on behalf of John Gordon Smith proved similarly unavailing, perhaps not surprisingly in view of its

100. *Correspondence Between Mr Granville Sharp-Pattison and Dr Nathaniel Chapman,* 3d ed. (Philadelphia: Webster, 1821).

101. Bellot, *University College,* 198–99.

102. *London Medical and Surgical Journal* 5 (1 November 1830): 443–48.

103. Quoted in Hunter and Macalpine, "Introduction," 29.

104. Bellot, *University College London,* 207–8.

105. Conolly to Horner, 30 March 1831; 8 April 1831, UCL.

106. For a fuller version of these events, see Bellot, *University College London,* chap. 6.

maladroitness. Smith was a former army surgeon who had secured an appointment as professor of medical jurisprudence. A knowledge of forensic medicine conferred few obvious advantages on those seeking to practice medicine, and Smith's prospects of attracting a sufficient number of students to his classes were not aided by his rambling and disjointed lecture style. "Condensation . . . is not a virtue of Dr. Smith's," the *Morning Chronicle* commented on the occasion of his inaugural lecture,[107] and students voted with their feet not to listen to interminable stories of his wartime exploits. In early December 1830, while depressed and in his cups, he offered the council his resignation; then on sobering up, sought to withdraw it. Conolly's intervention can only have sealed his fate. He had been treating Smith, he informed the council, for a periodic "severe affection of the stomach" (most probably this was a side effect of Smith's heavy drinking). These episodes lasted for only a few days at a time, but

> on the decline of each attack, he is subject to a peculiar, but temporary, excitement of the nervous system which has once or twice, I believe, led to the interference of his friends. It was during one of these afflicting accessions that he lately conveyed to you his determination not to lecture in the University unless certain concessions were made to which he has ceased to attach any importance; and I know that he unfeignedly and extremely laments that he made such a communication to you.[108]

Lament he might, for the council, notwithstanding Conolly's warning that the loss of Smith's chair would be "an irretrievable, perhaps a ruinous calamity to him,"[109] gratefully accepted the opportunity to be rid of him. (Conolly, incidentally, proved a better prophet than advocate: within three years, Smith was dead, dying of alcoholism in a debtor's prison.)[110]

Conolly's manifold failures and disappointments make his resignation from the university not unexpected, but its manner and timing were nevertheless distinctly odd, lending weight to Maudsley's observation that he was "apt to do serious things in an impulsive way."[111] Only a few hours after sending a letter to the council begging it to ignore Smith's resignation, Conolly submitted his own. Bellot comments that "the reasons for Conolly's resignation are obscure,"[112] and Conolly himself, in requesting Horner "to lay my resignation before the Council," added: "I

107. *Morning Chronicle*, 23 October 1828, 3, col. B.
108. Conolly to the University Council, 4 December 1830, UCL.
109. Ibid.
110. He had previously been an unsuccessful candidate for the appointment as first superintendent at the new Hanwell Lunatic Asylum—ironically, a job Conolly was to seek and obtain some years later.
111. Maudsley, "Memoir," 161.
112. Bellot, *University College London*, 250–51.

have not troubled them with a useless detail of all my motives, but I am anxious that they should not think that I resigned from any want of interest in the university." [113] The penultimate paragraph of the same letter suggests that the council's refusal to heed his pleas on Smith's behalf may have constituted the final straw. ("I am sorry to have to trouble the Council with a second communication on the same day, but Dr. Smith is so deeply concerned in my doing so that I hope it will be excused"); and there are hints that some of his colleagues may have been glad to see him go ("I cannot doubt that Dr. Thompson and Mr. Amos will approve of what I have done in this matter"); [114] but finally, Conolly is content to express no more than a veiled hope that his successor will have "a more favourable combination of circumstances than those in which I have endeavoured to perform [my duties]." [115]

Characteristically, his valedictory address given at the end of the academic year offers little substance at great length. He acknowledges that others may be puzzled by his decision:

> Retiring as I do, from a station, none of the prospective advantages of which have altogether escaped my attention—from a station which I was, four years ago, ambitious to obtain, and to which I felt it a great honour to be appointed—retiring, too, without the excuse of years, or any consciousness of a growing incapacity for exertion—I feel that a few words of explanation may be thought necessary, addressed to those who have interested themselves in my success. [116]

Many words but no explanation then follow. He grants that "it will be believed that powerful motives must exist which induce me to resign all these expectations, and when every previous hope has been sacrificed, to retire from a scene of public activity in which I might at least have continued without discredit." He then adds, "I think I could show that circumstances exist—have for some time existed—which so limit my usefulness here as to make it no less my duty, than it is my inclination, to withdraw from this institution." But the nature of those "circumstances" he glides over in silence, not wishing "to carry with me any unpleasant recollections." [117]

Whatever the precise reasons for his departure, the blow it constituted to his pride, to say nothing of his prospects, must have been staggering. Victorian medicine was marked by an enormous "division between the prestigious and influential men at the top of the profession

113. Conolly to Horner, 4 December 1830, UCL.
114. Ibid.
115. Conolly to the University Council, 4 December 1830, UCL—his official resignation.
116. John Conolly, "Valedictory Lecture on Retiring from London University," *London Medical Gazette* 8 (1831): 161–62.
117. Ibid., 161, 167.

and the ordinary practitioners [beneath]."[118] Having once had hopes of belonging to the elite, Conolly now appeared to be thrust back, all but irretrievably, into the ranks of provincial obscurity. As one who later confessed "that he did not care for money, but that he very much liked the comfort and elegancies which money brings,"[119] the prospect was scarcely inviting.

Placing his furniture in storage (where it was to remain for eighteen months until he could afford to rent a house large enough to contain it), he gathered his wife and four children (a third daughter, Anne Caroline, had been born in 1830) and removed once more to Stratford. But the attempt to pick up the threads of his old practice was a failure, and within a few weeks he felt compelled to uproot them all again, and move to the nearby town of Warwick.[120] His one remaining tie to the metropolis was Thomas Coates, the secretary of the Society for the Diffusion of Useful Knowledge, now Horner's replacement at the university (though at a salary of 200 pounds rather than 1,200 pounds); and the correspondence between them gives us what little insight we have into Conolly's existence over the next seven years.

Conolly at first feigned optimism. While complaining that the demands of practice, being "unsettled as to house, and distracted at times with the noise of children," were interfering with his book on Ardent Spirits for the society, he boasted that "my practice [at Warwick] began at once, and the average thus far has equaled that of my best year before I left Warwickshire to be tormented 'for some sin' in the University." As for the future of "that Institution . . . , much may be hoped from the timely (or untimely) death of some of the Council and Professors."[121] Two weeks later, the attractions of the provincial backwater had begun to diminish. Conolly had begun a second book for the society, a popularization for the lower classes of medical ideas about cholera, only to discover that "this is a land when no books are to be borrowed or even stolen. The latest publication in the hands of any of my medical neighbours is a dissertation on the diseases which followed the Great Flood." Perforce he had to order three or four from London, "very unwillingly," because he could scarcely afford to purchase them. "Since these are for a piece on Cholera for the Society," he wondered whether "the publishers for the Society have the means of getting them more advantageously than I can do."[122] In the future, he assured Coates, his financial position

118. Peterson, *Medical Profession*, 25.
119. Maudsley, "Memoir," 173. As Maudsley waspishly commented, this was "an amiable sentiment, which however, when closely analyzed, might be made to resolve itself into a liking for enjoyment without a liking for paying the painful cost of it."
120. Conolly's residence here was on Theatre Street.
121. Conolly to Thomas Coates, 13 October 1831, SDUK Coll., UCL.
122. Ibid., 27 October 1831.

was bound to improve: "I really begin to think that at last I shall become a prosperous man, for I find myself getting Jewish." [123]

Such expectations were doomed to disappointment. In late December, he wrote an answer to Coates' "kind inquiry about my proceedings here. I think I am getting on so as to have a hope in time, of struggling through many difficulties." [124] But the difficulties were formidable. He finished the manuscript on cholera just before Christmas 1831,[125] but the small sum it earned him was swallowed up in the attempt to satisfy some of the creditors he had left behind in London: "After the 15th, Mr. Denies of 27 Princes Street Bank who is occasionally 'paying off' things for me will call to receive the fifty pounds—to save you any trouble." The companion volume on Ardent Spirits, first promised for December, then for January,[126] remained unwritten, though Conolly in each letter promised its imminent dispatch.[127] Meanwhile, he proposed that he write other titles for the society, only to have Coates decline them.[128]

By May of 1832, the burden of his past failures and the struggle to scratch an inadequate living from his practice began to show in his letters:

> I have been very busy lately, both in practice, and in lecturing to the Mechanics' Institution here, and in commemorating Shakespeare's birthday at Stratford. But I require constant task work to overcome a restlessness which what I suffered latterly in London has left in my brain and nervous system, which I sometimes fear will never leave me.[129]

And his protestations that, except for the Society for the Diffusion of Useful Knowledge, "I hardly regret having lost anything else that London contains" [130] sound increasingly hollow. After a long silence, he wrote plaintively to Coates, "Once upon a time there was a professor of my name, where is he now? May I flatter myself that you sometimes wonderingly ask that question?" If Coates were to visit him in Warwick, "you will find me a very rustic physician with some provincial fame, no doubt, but as my foolish friends say, buried." Revealingly, he continued, "I often wish I really were. . . . The London University has provided me for life with incurable care—but 'what's that'!—I have learned that resignation is the best philosophy." [131]

The "incurable care" was not to be vanquished so easily, however. Less than two years later, Conolly wrote to Coates again, begging for a

---

123. Ibid.   124. Ibid., 27 December 1831.
125. Ibid., 18 December 1831.   126. Ibid., 13 October 1831.
127. See, for example, ibid., 14 February 1832; 2 February 1833 ("I venture to promise to finish forthwith my part of the Book of Gin"); 13 May 1834 (it would be done in three weeks if he could but get rid of his patients); 14 January 1836 (he finally abandoned the project later that year).
128. Ibid., 17 January 1832.   129. Ibid., 7 May 1832.   130. Ibid.
131. Ibid., 13 May 1834.

commission to write a series of popular treatises for working men on diseases of the chest, stomach, brain, and so on, to appear in the *Working Man's Companion.*

> It is but candid to say that I am in some degree driven to the idea of this industry by necessity. . . . I have long been trying[?] to extricate myself from the ruin [*sic*] which London brought me. . . . I am looking out for work. I am convinced I could prepare the little volumes of the Physician *one every three months.* Please think about it, and drop me a line soon— something I must set about and nothing takes my fancy more.[132]

But nothing came of this proposal, and in 1838, still drowning in debt,[133] Conolly embarked on a desperate attempt to escape from his provincial exile. "Not much encouraged thereto by his friends, who regarded such a step as the suicide of reputation and the confession of complete failure in life,"[134] he applied for the vacant position of superintendent of the Middlesex County Lunatic Asylum, at Hanwell. At least this offered the security of a salary of 500 pounds per annum, together with free room and board for his family in the asylum; and he had, after all, a long-standing interest in the treatment of the insane, had written on insanity, and had served as inspector of the Warwickshire madhouses. To his dismay, however, his application was rejected, and in his stead the magistrates appointed J. R. Millingen, a retired army surgeon with no discernible background in the treatment of insanity.[135]

Conolly's humiliation was now complete. "The outlook into the future as black as ever, family cares increasing," he once more uprooted his household and moved to Birmingham, to see whether, in a different setting, his luck would change.[136] At forty-four, this latest failure appeared to have permanently dashed all the hopes he had once nurtured "of ob-

132. Ibid., 14 January 1836.

133. Hunter and Macalpine speculate that by this period, to make matters worse, his wife may have gone mad and required confinement in an asylum (Hunter and Macalpine, "Introduction," xxxiv). However, the evidence they present for this assertion is slender indeed.

134. Maudsley, "Memoir," 167. Cf. Granville's later comment: "It is inconceivable that a man of position and culture would allow his family to have any connection with an asylum" (J. Mortimer Granville, *The Care and Cure of the Insane*, 2 vols. [London: Harwicke and Bogue, 1877], 1 : 99).

135. A year later, Conolly discovered that it was his progressive politics and association with efforts to educate the working classes that had cost him the job: "I lost my election to Hanwell last year solely by my exceedingly moderate Northhampton lecture; and I daresay nothing would give more annoyance to the Magistrates than my setting off to inflame county towns after the old fashion." Suitably chastened, he declined Coates' invitation to lecture for the SDUK at Lewes: "[Though I continue to believe] that those who endeavour, however humbly, to advance the intellectual condition of the people are their truest benefactors, I feel my exertions in that direction are closed" (Conolly to Coates, 26 August 1839, SDUK Coll., UCL).

136. Maudsley, "Memoir," 167.

taining, through my exertions . . . , that reputation and those advantages of fortune, about which no reasonable man can, or ought to be indifferent."[137] His fixed disposition to refuse "to recognize or accept the painful necessities of life" meant that throughout his life, "troubles, shirked at the time, were gathered up in the future, so as to demand at last some convulsive act of energy, in order to disperse them."[138] But by this time, it must have seemed that even convulsive efforts would not suffice.

Ironically enough, Conolly was to be rescued from this depressing prospect by someone else's failures. The superintendency at Hanwell had originally fallen vacant when the Middlesex magistrates decided to experiment with a system of divided authority, allowing the superintendent to continue as the final arbiter of medical matters, but handing over administrative chores to a lay steward.[139] The arrangement proved unworkable, and exacerbated by Millingen's inexperience and quarrelsome disposition, conditions in the asylum degenerated until they verged upon anarchy. Finally the magistrates were forced to intervene, dismissing the steward, Mr. Hunt, and accepting Millingen's resignation.[140] This time Conolly's application was successful. Less than a year after his initial rejection, a few lines appeared in the *Times* announcing that "Dr. Conolly, late of [Warwick], is appointed to the very important office of Resident Physician at the Hanwell Lunatic Asylum, Middlesex."[141]

Quite unexpectedly, the stern critic of asylum treatment, a man apparently incapable of managing his own affairs with even a modest degree of success, turned out to be an able and effective administrator of what was already the largest and—because of its metropolitan location—the most visible English asylum. Within a few weeks, the magistrates cheerfully announced that a remarkable change for the better had already taken place in the discipline and order of the establishment.[142] Conolly had at last found something he could do well, and to his final days was to insist "that if his life were to come over again, he should like nothing better than to be at the head of a large public asylum, in order to superintend its administration."[143] All the doubts he had once expressed about the appropriateness of the asylum solution, all questions about the deleterious effects of institutional existence, were at once suppressed in his enthusiasm for his new task.

Thomas Bakewell, not many years before, had commented that "the

137. Conolly, "Valedictory Lecture," 161.

138. Maudsley, "Memoir," 173.

139. *Hanwell County Lunatic Asylum Visitors' Reports*, no. 45 (1838): 187–88. The existing superintendent, Sir William Ellis, resigned rather than submit to the change.

140. Ibid., no. 49, 1839, 12–13.

141. *The Times*, 15 May 1839, 3, col. F.

142. *Hanwell County Lunatic Asylum Visitors' Reports*, no. 50 (1839): 26.

143. Maudsley, "Memoir," 172.

regular [medical] practitioner has little advantage either of reputation or [of] profit to expect from the treatment of [insanity]."[144] But whatever the general merits of this proposition, in Conolly's case it was emphatically disconfirmed. His achievements at Hanwell brought him, in rapid succession, national attention, royal notice and favor, election to a fellowship of the Royal College of Physicians, and ultimately recognition as "the most valuable consulting physician in mental disorders in Great Britain, and I suppose, in the world."[145] In Maudsley's words, "On the crest of the wave which he raised and rode he was carried to great fame and moderate prosperity."[146]

The first half of the nineteenth century witnessed a long struggle to "reform" the treatment of the mentally ill.[147] Indeed, Hanwell, like all other "County Asylums," was one product of this movement. It was the proud boast of the reformers that the adoption of their program, based on the new system of moral treatment pioneered by the Tukes at the York Retreat, did away with the cruelties previously visited upon the insane, and replaced them with a regime based on kindness and forbearance. Whips and chains, those traditional accoutrements of the madhouse, were, like the straw and stench that were their inevitable accompaniment, to be banished from the modern asylum. The most sanguine hopes of the reformers had their limits, though. In Samuel Tuke's own words,

> With regard to . . . the necessity of coercion, I have no hesitation in saying, that it will diminish or increase, as the moral treatment of the patient is more or less judicious. We cannot, however, anticipate that the most enlightened and ingenious humanity, will ever be able entirely to supercede the necessity of personal restraint.[148]

Yet it was precisely this extraordinary feat that Conolly claimed to have accomplished. Beginning with his very first report of Hanwell, he boldly asserted "that the management of a large asylum is not only practicable without the application of bodily coercion to the patient, but that, after the total disuse of such a method of control, the whole character of

144. Thomas Bakewell, *The Domestic Guide in Cases of Insanity* (Stafford: For the Author, 1805), ix. Bakewell was perhaps the best-known nonmedical asylum proprietor of the early nineteenth century.

145. Edward Jarvis to Almira Jarvis, 31 May 1860; 5 June 1860, Jarvis Papers, Concord Free Public Library, Concord, Massachusetts. I am grateful to Gerald Grob for this reference.

146. Maudsley, "Memoir," 169. A Southern Californian is irresistibly drawn to a picture of Conolly surfing his way to success.

147. Cf. Scull, *Museums of Madness;* Jones, *Lunacy, Law, and Conscience.*

148. Samuel Tuke, *Description of the Retreat: An Institution near York for Insane Persons of the Society of Friends* (1813), facsimile ed., ed. Richard A. Hunter and Ida Macalpine (London: Dawsons, 1964), 163.

the asylum undergoes a gradual and beneficial change."[149] So far from being a regrettable necessity, or even a means of cure, restraint "was in fact creative of many of the outrages and disorders to repress which its application was commonly deemed indispensable;"[150] and to that extent "restraints and neglect, may be considered as synonymous."[151] In their place,

> we rely wholly upon constant superintendence, constant kindness, and firmness when required. . . . Insanity, thus treated, undergoes great, if not unexpected modifications; and the wards of lunatic asylums no longer illustrate the harrowing description of their former state. Mania, not exasperated by severity, and melancholia, not deepened by the want of all ordinary consolations, lose the exaggerated character in which they were formerly beheld.[152]

These were large and astonishing claims, and they were greeted in many quarters with skepticism, if not outright hostility. They were, sniffed "Medicus" in the correspondence columns of the *Times,* "a piece of contemptible quackery and a mere bait for the public ear."[153] Millingen seized the opportunity to denounce his successor: "Nothing can be more absurd, speculative, or peculative than the attempts of theoretic visionaries, or candidates for popular praise, to do away with all restraint. Desirable as such a management might be, it can never prevail without much danger to personal security, and a useless waste and dilapidation of property."[154] Others went further still and reiterated the traditional medical claim that restraint was a form of therapy. Dr. Samuel Hadwin, former house surgeon at the Lincoln Lunatic Asylum, wrote:

> Restraint forms the very basis and principle on which the sound treatment of lunatics is founded. The judicious and appropriate adaptation of the various modifications of this powerful means to the peculiarities of each case of insanity, comprises a large portion of the curative regimen of the scientific and rational practitioner; in his hands is a remedial agent of the first importance, and it appears to me that it is about as likely to be dispensed with, in the cure of mental diseases, as that the various articles of the materia medica will altogether be dispensed with in the cure of the bodily.[155]

149. Conolly, quoted in Maudsley, "Memoir," 169.

150. Conolly, quoted in Granville, *Care and Cure,* 1 : 111.

151. Conolly, *Treatment of the Insane,* 323.

152. Conolly, quoted in Sir James Clark's *A Memoir of John Conolly, M.D., D.C.L.* (London: Murray, 1869), 22, 28.

153. *The Times,* 10 December 1840, 6, col. A; see also ibid., 5 January 1841, 7, col. B.

154. J. G. Millingen, *Aphorisms on the Treatment and Management of the Insane* (London: Churchill, 1840), 106.

155. *The Times,* 5 January 1841, 7, col. B. This was perhaps an unfortunate comparison, given the subsequent fate of the bulk of the nineteenth-century pharmacopoeia. For

But while many medical men viewed nonrestraint with extreme suspicion, the new system quickly attracted powerful support in other quarters. During the first month of 1840, the correspondence columns of the *Lancet* were opened impartially to both proponents and opponents of the new system, in an effort "to contribute, in any way, to the solution of a question of so much importance."[156] However, the strain of such uncharacteristic even-handedness eventually told on its editor, Thomas Wakley. Never one to abide by his own admonition to the disputants that "angry recrimination can do no good, and may do much evil,"[157] he soon switched to a fervent advocacy of the cause of reform, couched in his inimitable mixture of panegyric and vituperation.[158] More respectable opinion also rallied to Conolly's support. The venerable Samuel Tuke visited and bestowed his benediction ("Who can visit or contemplate the establishment of Hanwell, containing 800 insane persons, governed without any personal restraint, without gratitude or surprise?").[159] Lord Anthony Ashley Cooper, by now leader of the parliamentary forces seeking "lunacy reform," saw nonrestraint as the vindication and epitome of reform: He "could not speak too highly either of the system itself, or of the manner in which it was carried out by the talented Superintendent, Dr. Conolly."[160] Meanwhile, the *Illustrated London News* brought Conolly's achievements to the notice of a still wider audience, extolling still another British contribution to the triumph of humanity.[161]

Perhaps the most important force in transforming Conolly into a national celebrity was, however, the *Times*. Beginning in late 1840, it devoted close and sympathetic attention to the progress of his experiment

---

earlier versions of Hadwen's position, see William Cullen, *First Lines of the Practice of Physic* (Edinburgh: Bell and Bradfute, 1784), 4:151–55; John Haslam, *Observations on Madness and Melancholy*, 2d ed. (London: Callow, 1809), 280–91; and George Man Burrows, *Commentaries on the Causes, Forms, Symptoms and Treatment of Insanity* (London: Underwood, 1828), 686. Alexander Morison sought to rally opposition to nonrestraint in the early 1840s by forming the Society for the Improvement of the Condition of the Insane.

156. "Editorial," *The Lancet*, 4 April 1840, 58. There were some fifty contributions of one sort or another to this debate during the first six months of 1840.

157. Ibid.

158. See *The Lancet*, 22 November 1842, 326. See also *Hansard's Parliamentary Debates*, 3d series, vol. 76, 23 July 1844, cols. 1275–81. Compare Wakley's characteristic description of the elites who controlled the Royal Colleges of Physicians and of Surgery as "crafty, intriguing, corrupt, avaricious, cowardly, plundering, rapacious, soul-betraying, dirty-minded BATS" (*The Lancet* 1 October 1831, 2). On Wakley and his "crusades," see S. S. Sprigge, *The Life and Times of Thomas Wakley* (London: Longman, Green, 1899); and Charles W. Brook, *Battling Surgeon* (Glasgow: Strickland, 1945).

159. Samuel Tuke, "Introduction" to Jacobi, *Construction and Management of Hospitals*, xxxv.

160. *Hansard's Parliamentary Debates*, 3d ser., vol. 65 (16 July 1842), col. 223.

161. *Illustrated London News*, 21 May 1843; see also 15 January 1848.

for a period of some four years.[162] Commenting on the "very considerable opposition . . . the attempt to obtain so desirable an object" had stirred up, it noted that such resistance had also surfaced within the institution, "not simply on the part of several of the county magistrates, but even from many of the servants and officers of the asylum." Fortunately, "that humane gentleman," Dr. Conolly, had, with the staunch support of another faction among the magistrates, vanquished the peculiar notion that there was "more actual cruelty hidden under the show of humanity in the system of non-coercion than was openly displayed in muffs, strait-waistcoats, leg-locks, and coercion chairs," and had successfully brought to fruition "one of the greatest works that the dictates of the humane mind could suggest."[163] Three weeks later, a report on the celebration of "Old Year's Night" at Hanwell demonstrated for the paper's readers the happy effects of the salutary system of nonrestraint. The furies of madness were thoroughly domesticated, and "the utmost tranquility prevailed." Indeed, when the 400 patients assembled for the commencement of the merriment, "scarcely a word was to be heard and the effect produced was most striking and pleasing."[164] Soon afterwards, nonrestraint received the royal imprimatur: The Duke of Cambridge arrived and spent two and a half hours at "this admirable institution," lunched with Conolly (presumably not on ordinary asylum fare), and left proclaiming himself "highly delighted" with all he had seen.[165]

Basking in this unexpected praise of and attention to one of their pauper institutions, the Middlesex magistrates at once issued Conolly's first four annual reports bound together in a single new edition. Professional recognition of his achievement also grew apace. At the third annual meeting of the new Association of Medical Officers of Asylums and Hospitals for the Insane, Conolly was asked to take the chair.[166] In 1844,

162. See, for example, *The Times*, 18 November 1840, 6, col. E; 10 December 1840, 6, col. E; 30 December 1840, 3, col. B; 8 December 1841, 3, col. A; 14 December 1841, 3, col. D; 5 January 1842, 5, col. F.

163. Ibid., 8 December 1841, 3, col. A; 14 December 1841, 3, col. D.

164. Ibid., 5 January 1842, 5, col. F. The praise may strike modern readers as misplaced, even itself bizarre, but the Victorians exhibited an unalloyed delight in the reduction of the vicious, the depraved, and the unruly to at least a simulacrum of order and decorum. Such practical demonstrations of the power of "reason and morality" evidently possessed great symbolic power, and those who successfully staged them could count on widespread approval and acclaim. I shall discuss the sources of this praise in a moment. On the changing meaning (and methods) of domesticating the mad, from the early eighteenth to the mid-nineteenth century, see Chapter 3.

165. *The Times*, 8 March 1842, 13, col. E.

166. The association was founded in 1841, mainly through the efforts of Dr. Samuel Hitch of the Gloucester Asylum. Intended to draw together the nascent specialty and to protect the professional interests of its members, it drew its membership from the chief medical officers of both public and private asylums. In 1865, it was renamed the Medico-Psychological Association, and it is now the Royal College of Psychiatry.

he was elected a fellow of the Royal College of Physicians.[167] The 1844 Report of the Metropolitan Commissioners in Lunacy, it is true, exhibited rather more ambivalence about the value of nonrestraint,[168] but two years later, the new national Lunacy Commission had thrown aside such doubts, and nonrestraint became the ruling orthodoxy of British asylumdom.

Conolly had thus become, in the eyes of his admirers, "one of the most distinguished men of the age, and one whose name will pass down to posterity with those of the Howards, the Clarksons, the Father Mathews, and other great redressers of the wrongs, crimes, and miseries of mankind." [169] Oxford University awarded him an honorary D.C.L.; and his marble bust was executed by Benzoni.[170] In 1850, the Provincial Medical and Surgical Association feted Conolly at their annual meeting at Hull.[171] And two years later, with Lord Shaftesbury presiding,[172] Conolly's achievements were again celebrated, and he was presented with a gift of a three-quarter-length portrait by Sir John Watson Gordon, R.A., and an allegorical piece of silver plate standing two feet high and valued at 500 pounds, which illustrated mental patients with and without restraint, all surmounted by the god of healing.[173]

Such extraordinary praise and recognition suggest that Conolly's achievement had a symbolic significance for the Victorian bourgeoisie that extended far beyond its contribution to the welfare of the mad. Confronted by the threats of Chartism and a militant working class; surrounded by the all-but-inescapable evidence of the devastating impact of industrial capitalism on the social and physical landscape; and themselves the authors of a New Poor Law assailed by its critics (most memorably in Dickens' *Oliver Twist*) as the very embodiment of inhumanity and meanness of spirit, the Victorian governing classes could at least find a source of pride in the generous and kindly treatment now accorded to the mad. In a wholly practical way, the work of the lunacy reformers constituted a proof of their society's progressive and humane character. (Hence the curious claim made by Sir George Paget, that the

---

167. See *Munk's Roll*, 4:33.

168. "Report of the Metropolitan Commissioners in Lunacy, 1844," *Sessional Papers of the House of Lords*, vol. 26 (1844).

169. *Morning Chronicle*, 5 October 1843.

170. Leigh, *British Psychiatry*, 227.

171. See *The Lancet*, 10 August 1850, 181–82; 17 August 1850, 224.

172. Ashley, who had now succeeded to his father's title, remained one of Conolly's staunchest admirers, referring to his achievement before the 1859 Select Committee of the House of Commons as "the greatest triumph of skill and humanity the world ever knew" (House of Commons, *Select Committee on the Care and Treatment of Lunatics, 1859–1860*, 45–49).

173. *The Lancet*, 3 April 1852, p. 339; Clark, *Memoir*, 44–51.

Victorian asylum was "the most blessed manifestation of true civilization the world can present.")[174]

As the man who epitomized and had brought the new approach to perfection, John Conolly had thus richly earned his audience's applause. The paternal order he had established demonstrated that even the irrational and raving could be reduced to docility, and by moral suasion and self-sacrifice rather than force. Here, as he put it in the concluding lines of his panegyric on the new asylum,

> calmness will come; hope will revive; satisfaction will prevail. Some unmanageable tempers, some violent or sullen patients, there must always be; but much of the violence, much of the ill-humour, almost all the disposition to meditate mischievous or fatal revenge, or self-destruction will disappear. . . . Cleanliness and decency will be maintained or restored; and despair itself will sometimes be found to give place to cheerfulness or secure tranquility. [The asylum is the place] where humanity, if anywhere on earth, shall reign supreme.[175]

A Potemkin village characterized by an absence of conflict and strife, it constituted a veritable utopia wherein the lower orders of society could coexist in harmony and tranquility with their betters (personified by the figure of a superintendent devoted to their welfare and content to "sacrifice . . . the ordinary comforts and conventionalities of life" for their sake.[176]

In celebrating Conolly's accomplishment, Victorians were thus simultaneously affirming the moral validity of their social order itself; and his powerful friends, while acknowledging that he "no doubt received important assistance from fellow-labourers in the same field," now closed ranks around the proposition that "Dr. Conolly himself put an end to the use of all forms of mechanical restraint in our asylums."[177]

But such claims were, as Conolly himself periodically acknowledged,[178] at best a serious distortion. Nonrestraint was introduced, not by him, but by Robert Gardiner Hill, then a twenty-four-year-old house surgeon at

---

174. George E. Paget, *The Harveian Oration* (Cambridge: Deighton, Bell, 1866), 34–35.

175. John Conolly, *On the Construction and Government of Lunatic Asylums* (London: Churchill, 1847), 143.

176. Ibid. For another contemporary version of this vision, see W. A. F. Browne, *What Asylums Were, Are, and Ought to Be* (Edinburgh: Black, 1837), esp. 229–31. David Rothman has likewise argued that American alienists and others saw the asylum as a model for the proper functioning of the larger society, though he fails to make explicit the ideological resonance of these claims. See David Rothman, *The Discovery of the Asylum* (Boston: Little, Brown, 1971).

177. Clark, *Memoir*, vii–viii.

178. For example, Hanwell Lunatic Asylum, *Annual Report* (1840), 52; Conolly, *Treatment of the Insane*, 177–78; idem, "President's Address," *Journal of Mental Science* 5 (1859), 74; Clark, *Memoir*, 49.

the provincial subscription asylum at Lincoln. Hill had announced the system in a public lecture to the Lincoln Mechanics Institute in 1838: "I wish to complete that which Pinel began. I assert then in plain and distinct terms, that in a properly constructed building, with a sufficient number of suitable attendants, restraint is never necessary, never justifiable, and always injurious, in all cases of lunacy whatever." [179] For almost two years before Conolly assumed his duties at Hanwell, Hill had demonstrated in practice the feasibility of such an approach. And it was, in fact, a visit to Lincoln that prompted Conolly to try the new system. [180]

Yet Hill's obvious claims as the originator of nonrestraint brought him little honor and scant reward of any other sort. Though bearing the brunt of the early assaults on the system as speculative and wildly misguided, [181] he was granted none of the subsequent recognition and social lionization so readily accorded to Conolly. On the contrary, machinations among the staff and governors at the Lincoln Asylum forced his resignation there, [182] and he found himself unable to obtain another asylum post. Ironically,—and this failure must have been especially galling—he was even rejected when he sought the position of medical officer under Conolly at Hanwell, [183] and so was forced by default to enter general practice. [184] Though a decade later he became the proprietor of a private licensed house, he never managed to obtain an appointment at another public asylum.

One can readily imagine the effects of this on someone as sensitive to questioning of his own merits as Hill was. Apparently the last straw was

179. Hill, *Management of Lunatic Asylums*, 147.

180. He arrived in May 1839, with his brother William, proprietor of a licensed asylum at Cheltenham, and noted in the Visitors' Book, "Having read Mr. Hill's lecture . . . we visited this asylum with feelings of unusual curiosity and interest; we have been deeply impressed" (quoted in Hunter and Macalpine, "Introduction" to Conolly, *Treatment of the Insane*, x).

181. See, for example, *The Lancet*, 28 November 1840, 337–41; 9 January 1841, 532–40; 30 January 1841, 659; 15 January 1842, 544–46.

182. Robert Gardiner Hill, *A Concise History of the Entire Abolition of Mechanical Restraint in the Treatment of the Insane* (London: Longman, 1857), 13–14.

183. Alexander Walk, "Lincoln and Non-restraint," *British Journal of Psychiatry* 117 (1970), 481.

184. I have suggested elsewhere (see Chapter 6) that the professional ostracism and abuse may in part have derived from Hill's heretical insistence that "in the treatment of the insane, medicine is of little avail. . . . *Moral treatment with a view to induce habits of self-control, is all and everything*" (Hill, *Management of Lunatic Asylums*, 45 [emphasis in the original]; also quoted in *The Lancet*, 6 July 1839, 554, and in Hill, *Entire Abolition*, 72). Walk, by contrast, blames Hill's acerbic temperament and unimpressive personality (Walk, "Lincoln and Non-restraint," 488). Certainly, one must concede that Conolly's gentlemanly attributes and demeanor, to say nothing of his powerful friends, must have made him a far more suitable candidate for canonization than his unpolished, ill-educated, and obscure provincial rival. A more extended discussion of this issue appears later.

when, in his presence, he heard Conolly praised as the author of his system at the 1850 meeting of the Provincial Medical and Surgical Association. Though Conolly graciously indicated that the merit was not his alone, but was shared with Dr. Charlesworth (the visiting physician at Lincoln), and though Charlesworth then indicated that "the real honour belonged to Mr. Hill,"[185] he was not satisfied, not least, perhaps, because it was forcibly brought home to him how soon his claim to priority had been forgotten.[186]

Hill promptly sought to reassert his claims by writing to the medical press, only to be met by an attempt by his former enemies at Lincoln to claim the merit for Charlesworth.[187] And when Hill's supporters took up a collection for a testimonial to rival Conolly's, his opponents promptly erected a statue of Charlesworth, with a plaque on the base describing him as the originator of nonrestraint, on the Lincoln Asylum grounds.[188] More seriously, Hill fell afoul of Thomas Wakley's pen, and found himself traduced in the *Lancet*'s columns in the latter's typically unscrupulous fashion.[189]

Conolly's role in all of this was hardly innocent. With whatever motives, he consistently declined to give Hill his due. That he had borrowed

185. *The Lancet*, 24 August 1850, 247–48.

186. Ibid. For example, Dr. Archibald Robertson, vice president of the Provincial Medical and Surgical Association and physician to the Northampton Infirmary, wrote of Charlesworth's concession:

> The information made the greater impression on me, as it was perfectly new to *me;* so vague and imperfect was my knowledge as to the first discovery and practice of the "non-restraint system" prior to the Hull meeting, that I had thought the merit of it belonged to Dr. Conolly of Hanwell. Acting on this thought, I had . . . contributed my mite towards a testimonial to Dr. Conolly; which had been suggested at a meeting in London resided over by Lord Ashley (quoted in Hill, *Entire Abolition*, 225).

187. Charlesworth, who had been the most active of the three visiting physicians at Lincoln (see Walk, "Lincoln and Non-restraint"), but who had nevertheless freely acknowledged till now that the credit for the discovery belonged to Hill alone, henceforth maintained a studied silence on the issue.

188. Charlesworth had died before this occurred.

189. Cf. Brook, *Battling Surgeon*, 149. Hill's claims were dismissed as "the audacious assaults of envy," and his sanity was subsequently called into question (*The Lancet*, 10 October 1857, 365). Wakley's venom may in part have reflected his friendship with Conolly. It certainly also derived from the fact that Hill had the misfortune to have his cause adopted by the rival *Medical Circular*, a journal that attacked Wakley as a liar given to "senile ranting," "as insensible to evidence as he is to shame," a "licensed reviler" who was "an offense to professional nostrils" (*Medical Circular*, 11 August 1852, 304). Wakley was only too ready to respond in kind. On Wakley's generally strained relations with the rest of the medical press, see Sprigge, *Thomas Wakley*, 156–66. Cf., for example, his comment on the first issue of the *Medical Times and Gazette:* "The *Medical Gazette*, whose special mission it was to crush ourselves, died of dullness and debility; the *Medical Times* of stupidity and infamy. A hybrid spectral illusion, commemorating the joint names of these two departed journals, and putting on, as its only hope, our outward form and semblance, is all that remains" (*The Lancet* 4 March 1854, 286).

the idea of nonrestraint from Lincoln he could not deny; that the discovery was Hill's he sought constantly to obscure.[190] And when Hill in exasperation at length lashed out at his now deceased rival,[191] he succeeded only in alienating his audience and in further tarnishing his own reputation. His shrill and strident claims of priority, his wearisome marshaling of minutiae to prove his own originality,[192] were "not only boring, but repellent."[193] As he proved chronically unable to grasp, one who exhibited such boorish and ungentlemanly qualities could never hope to be accorded a place of honor in a profession desperate to dissociate itself from all that smacked of lower-class, tradesmanlike behavior.

The elegant and socially graceful Conolly inflicted no such handicaps on himself, displaying "a certain humility of manner, a degree of self-deprecation . . . which failed not to attract men; it was nonetheless captivating because it might seem the form in which a considerable dash of self-consciousness declared itself."[194] On the public stage that he had secured for himself at Hanwell, he took delight in the opportunity to display the liberal and paternalist instincts of the gentleman:

> His interest in the patients never seemed to flag. Even cases beyond all hope of recovery were still objects of his attention. He was always pleased to see them happy, and had a kind word for each. Simple things which vainer men with less wisdom would have disregarded or looked upon as too insignificant for their notice, arrested Dr. Conolly's attention, and supplied matter for remark and commendation—e.g., a face cleaner than usual, hair more carefully arranged, a neater cap, a new riband, clothes put on with greater neatness, and numerous little things of a like kind, enabled him to address his poor illiterate patients in gentle and loving accents, and thus woke up their feeble minds, caused sad faces to gleam with

190. Conolly's friends continued the process even after his death. See, for example, Clark, *Memoir*, 39. Andrew Wynter, otherwise as given to eulogizing Conolly as were most Victorians, was sharply critical of his behavior on this point: Conolly's attempt to give a share of the credit to Charlesworth "must be ascribed to a too partial friendship. Dr. Gardiner Hill is certainly not persuasive in his style, and for that reason has raised up many enemies to his assertions." But Wynter felt that Hill's rightful claims should not thereby be rejected. Modern observers have not always been so kind about Conolly's motives. Frank, for example, while acknowledging that Conolly and Charlesworth were "very friendly," places more emphasis on the fact that "Hill discredited entirely Conolly's role as a pioneer, at the same time reminding one and all that Conolly was older than he and was never influential until after Hill had made his notable Mechanics Institute speech" (Justin A. Frank, "Non-restraint and Robert Gardiner Hill," *Bulletin of the History of Medicine* 41 [1967]: 157).

191. Robert Gardiner Hill, *Lunacy: Its Past and Present* (London: Longman, Green, 1870), 53.

192. Ibid.; idem, *Entire Abolition*.

193. Walk, "Lincoln and Non-restraint," 494.

194. Maudsley, "Memoir," 174. Conolly, said the American alienist Edward Jarvis, was "one of the most polished gentlemen I have met in England" (Edward Jarvis to Almira Jarvis, 8 July 1860, Jarvis Papers, Concord Free Public Library, Concord, Massachusetts).

a smile, even though transient, and made his visits to the wards to be longed for and appreciated. Dr. Conolly rejoiced in acts of beneficence. To be poor and to be insane were conditions which at once endeared the sufferers to him; and when the insanity was removed, and when the patient left the asylum, he generally strove to obtain some pecuniary aid for her from the 'Adelaide Fund' (a fund originated for the relief of discharged patients), and supplemented this very often indeed with liberal donations from his own purse.[195]

Despite a patient population nearing a thousand, a "monstrous multitude of diseased humanity"[196] crammed into buildings originally designed for half that number, and notwithstanding a dismally low cure rate, Conolly's Hanwell was widely regarded as a splendid advertisement for the merits of reform and nonrestraint.[197] From time to time, he protested mildly that the asylum was too big[198] and objected to the Middlesex magistrate's propensity to seek cheeseparing economies. But for the most part, he sought to exploit Hanwell's fame to persuade others of the advantages, indeed the necessity, of expanding the numbers of county asylums. Such endeavors acquired a new urgency in the wake of the passage of the 1845 Lunatic Asylums Act, for although public provision for the pauper insane was now made compulsory, magistrates in many parts of the country sought to delay or evade building asylums of their own. Accordingly, Conolly wrote a series of articles for the *Lancet* (republished the following year as a monograph)[199] extolling the humanity and economy of asylums devoted to the cure of the lunatic and urging their rapid construction. Ironically enough, his own role at Hanwell was by this time much diminished and soon to end. His disengagement was not provoked by any disenchantment with administering an everlarger warehouse for the unwanted; or did it constitute a protest at the deficiencies of an overcrowded establishment later described as "a vast and straggling building, in which the characteristics of a prison, a self-advertising charitable institution, and some ambitious piece of Poor Law architecture struggle for prominence."[200] Instead, it derived from administrative changes that threatened his own authority and status.

195. John Hitchman, quoted in Clark, *Memoir,* 40–43. Hitchman, later superintendent of the Derby County Asylum, had begun his career under Conolly at Hanwell. See also [Andrew Wynter], "Non-restraint in the Treatment of the Insane," *Edinburgh Review* 131 (1870): 83.

196. Edward Jarvis to Almira Jarvis, 22 June 1860, Jarvis Papers, Concord Free Public Library, Concord, Massachusetts.

197. In 1842, he even managed to gain permission to introduce in the asylum the clinical teaching of medical students that he had originally proposed while at the University of London.

198. Conolly, *Construction and Government,* 10.

199. See ibid.

200. Granville, *Care and Cure,* 1:154. See also Edward Jarvis to Almira Jarvis, 31 May 1860, Concord Free Public Library, Concord, Massachusetts. Only in his declining years

The Middlesex magistrates had long exhibited a much greater disposition to interfere in the daily running of "their" asylum then was to be found elsewhere. Their evident belief that nonmedical administration could affect significant economies had already led them to a proposed reorganization of Hanwell that had provoked their first superintendent, Sir William Ellis, to resign. And they were apparently not dissuaded by the fact that their subsequent experiment with a system of divided authority had dismally failed, forcing the resignation of the physician and the dismissal of the steward, and thus indirectly bringing about Conolly's appointment. For when the metropolitan commissioners in lunacy insisted that Hanwell's "extreme magnitude" required more extensive supervision, the justices once more developed a scheme to place daily administration in lay hands. Conolly did not wait for the plan's implementation—in later years, he spoke of "the absurdity—I could almost say the criminality,—of committing one of the most serious of human maladies to the charge of anyone uninstructed in medicine"[201]—but promptly offered his resignation.[202]

This time, as had not been the case with Ellis, a compromise was arranged. Anxious to retain the connection with Conolly that had brought them so much favorable publicity, the magistrates offered him the post of "visiting and consulting physician" at a reduced salary of 350 pounds, and he accepted. His duties now became "to give his attendance for two days a week, and for six hours at every attendance." At other times, medical matters were to be dealt with by the house surgeons who had formerly acted as his assistants.[203] Convinced that it was imperative to have a single resident officer exercising ultimate control over the asylum and its staff, and equally certain that medical men were fit neither by temperament nor by training to assume such a role, the magistrates announced the appointment of John Godwin, a retired army officer, to fill the position.[204]

---

did Conolly vigorously protest the tendency of county asylums to be little more than "museums for the collection of insanity" (Francis Scott, "English County Asylums," *Fortnightly Review* 26 [1879]: 114–43). See Conolly, "President's Address," esp. 75; and idem, *A Letter to Benjamin Rotch, Esquire, Chairman of the Committee of Visitors, on the Plan and Government of the Additional Lunatic Asylum . . . About to Be Erected at Colney Hatch* (London: Churchill, 1847), 18.

201. Conolly, *Letter to Benjamin Rotch*, 18.

202. Shaftesbury, who had a lifelong skepticism about some aspects of the medical profession's involvement in the treatment of insanity, secretly supported the Middlesex magistrates' plan. See "Diaries of the Seventh Earl of Shaftesbury," 15 November 1844, National Register of Archives.

203. Hanwell Lunatic Asylum, *Sixty-ninth Visitors' Report*, 16 January 1844, 4.

204. Hanwell Lunatic Asylum, *Seventieth Report*, 3–7. The appointment of a lay "governor" and the choice of Godwin for the position were both secretly endorsed by Shaftesbury. See his "Diaries," 15 November 1844.

Under the terms of the appointment, it was specified that "the Governor has the power of suspending not only the servants but even the Medical Officers and Matron of the Asylum. He has, also, the entire control over the classification, employment, amusements, instruction, and general management of the patients . . . subject only to the general control of the Visiting Justices."[205] His superiority was reflected in the higher salary paid him: while the two resident medical officers received 200 pounds each, the governor was paid 350 pounds a year. In view of the range and scope of affairs in which his lay judgment was supposedly given precedence, there was a disingenuousness about the claim that "in regulating his particular duties . . . the Visiting Justices have endeavoured to reconcile his position as their officer whom they will vest with paramount authority to enforce all their orders and regulations, with the distinct responsibility of the Medical Officers in all that concern the moral management as well as the strictly medical treatment of the Patients."[206] For, in practice, to concede the doctors' right to direct the moral treatment of the patients would involve taking away from the governor the very areas of supervision where his authority was supposed to be paramount; while to refuse to concede it was to reduce the asylum physicians to mere decorative appendages. Conflict was thus unavoidable, though the ensuing struggle reached a swift conclusion.

In August of 1844, just four months after his initial appointment, the justices cryptically announced, in two lines buried at the end of their report, that Godwin's resignation had been tendered and accepted.[207] In their next report, they indicated that "after the retirement of the late Governor, the Visiting Justices resolved to defer filling up the vacancy for awhile, and to entrust the management of the Asylum to the ability and experience of the principal [i.e., medical] officers until they could determine what course for its future government it would be most advisable to adopt."[208] Already, however, they were noting "the progressive improvement in the order and discipline of the Establishment" since Godwin's departure.[209] Six months later, they conceded that under medical supervision, "good management and order prevail [and] that they have every reason to be satisfied with the way in which the Asylum continues to be conducted."[210]

The idea of employing a lay administrator to direct the asylum's affairs was now quietly buried; but the attempt to implement it had already served to all but sever Conolly's connection with Hanwell, after

205. *Metropolitan Commissioners in Lunacy Report*, 1844, 28 (emphasis added).
206. Hanwell County Asylum, *Sixty-ninth Visitors' Report*, 1844, 5.
207. Hanwell County Asylum, *Seventy-second Report*, 1844, 13.
208. Hanwell County Asylum, *Seventy-third Visitors' Report*, 1845, 1.
209. Ibid.
210. Hanwell County Asylum, *Seventy-fifth Report*, 1845, 3.

less than four years on the job. "Mutual trust between himself and the Justices was lost. He felt that they preferred the opinion of others and that his authority and system were eroded."[211] He hung on to his visiting appointment until 1852, when he finally resigned, to the relief of the magistrates, to whom his departure now meant little more than saving the ratepayers some money.

Even before this final rupture, Conolly's situation was such that he was forced to seek some alternative means of earning his livelihood. At 500 pounds per annum, his salary as resident officer at Hanwell had scarcely been munificent, but at least he was also provided with room and board, a not inconsiderable benefit. His visiting appointment, however, entailed not just a reduced salary, but also the loss of this hidden subsidy. His new-found eminence ought presumably to have allowed him to escape the penury he had endured until middle age. But the difficulty was to know how to earn a living, given that there were no defined alternative careers for alienists, outside the burgeoning asylum system.

Almost fifty, Conolly had never possessed the qualities to succeed in single-handedly defining and developing a new form of specialist practice. Not until much later in the century, with the careers of men like his son-in-law, Henry Maudsley,[212] or Sir George Savage,[213] did the alternative of a practice based almost exclusively on the consulting room become possible. Conolly's fame did lead to his being called in as a consultant in difficult cases,[214] and he was also a frequently called expert witness in criminal cases where the insanity defense was raised.[215] But as in his ear-

211. Hunter and Macalpine, "Introduction," xxxii.

212. Henry Maudsley (1835–1918), editor of the *Journal of Mental Science* (1862–78) and professor of medical jurisprudence at University College London, was the leading alienist of his generation. On his life, see Aubrey Lewis, "Henry Maudsley: His Works and Influence," *Journal of Mental Science* 97 (1951): 259–77; and Elaine Showalter, *The Female Malady* (New York: Pantheon, 1985), chap. 4.

213. Sir George Savage (1842–1921), formerly physician superintendent of the Royal Bethlem Hospital, editor of the *Journal of Mental Science*, and president of the Medico-Psychological Association and the Neurological Association, was one of the most fashionable consultants on mental diseases in late-nineteenth-century London. For Savage's role in treating Virginia Woolf, see Stephen Trombley, *"All That Summer She Was Mad": Virginia Woolf and Her Doctors* (London: Junction Books, 1981).

214. For example, when the confinement of Lady Rosina Bulwer Lytton in a private asylum threatened to become a scandal of major proportions, her husband sought advice from "the most experienced and able physicians" specializing in psychological medicine, choosing Conolly and Forbes Winslow. By a curious coincidence, Lady Lytton, whose sanity they confirmed, was an inmate in Robert Gardiner Hill's asylum, Wyke House (*The Times*, 19 July, 1858, 12, col. E.). Conolly also testified at such well-publicized commissions in lunacy as those involving the cases of W. F. Windham, Sir Henry Meux, and Mrs. Catherine Cummings.

215. For example, Robert Tate, Edward Oxford, and Luigi Buranelli. On this aspect of Victorian psychiatric practice, see Roger Smith, *Trial by Medicine* (Edinburgh: Edinburgh University Press, 1981).

lier efforts at private practice, he scarcely distinguished himself in these spheres. His forensic testimony in the Pate case, for example, prompted the *Morning Chronicle* to complain that "Dr. Conolly appears to have devoted his attention so exclusively to . . . mental disease that . . . he can apparently no longer distinguish where absolute madness begins and moral and legal responsibility ceases. There are very few of our fellow subjects, we suspect, who could get from Dr. Conolly a certificate of perfect sanity."[216]

Both lunacy inquisitions and criminal trials in which the insanity defense was invoked were highly charged occasions. While the latter were widely seen as a ruse to escape just punishment, a threat to the concept of responsibility and, thus, to the very foundation of criminal justice,[217] the former raised the specter of wrongful confinement of the sane in asylums, "a living death" that inspired periodic moral panics throughout the nineteenth century.[218] Large segments of the Victorian public seem to have questioned both the motives and the competence of alienists who claimed expertise in assessing madness, and Conolly's published opinions and his actions both helped feed these suspicions. Before entering upon a career as an asylum doctor, he had insisted that not every case of unsound mind required incarceration in an asylum. Rather, there was a need for a careful assessment of each case to determine *"whether or not the departure from sound mind be of a nature to justify the confinement of the individual,"*[219] and such inquiries were likely to disclose that "complete restraint is very rarely required."[220] A less discriminating approach posed a serious threat to individual freedom and peace of mind.[221]

Two decades later, these were almost precisely the fears his clear repudiation of his earlier views seemed calculated to arouse. In 1849, in the case of *Nottidge v. Ripley,* the lord chief baron of the Court of the Exchequer, Sir Frederick Pollock, declared that in his opinion, "no lunatic should be confined in an asylum unless dangerous to himself or oth-

216. The *Morning Post,* quoted in Hunter and Macalpine, "Introduction," xxxvii. Robert Pate, a former cavalry officer, had struck Queen Victoria on the head with his walking stick. His defense, for which Conolly appeared as an expert witness, was that his conduct stemmed from an irresistible impulse, itself caused by underlying mental derangement. This explanation provoked a memorable response from the judge, Mr. Baron Alderson: "*A man might say that he picked a pocket from some uncontrollable impulse, and in that case the law would have an uncontrollable impulse to punish him for it*" (reported in the *Medical Times* 1 [1850], 66 [emphasis in the original]).

217. Cf. Smith, *Trial by Medicine.*

218. Peter McCandless, "Liberty and Lunacy: The Victorians and Wrongful Confinement," in *Madhouses, Mad-Doctors, and Madmen: The Social History of Psychiatry in the Victorian Era,* ed. Andrew Scull (Philadelphia: University of Pennsylvania Press; London: Athlone Press, 1981), 339–62.

219. Conolly, *Inquiry,* 35 (emphasis in the original).

220. Ibid., 386.

221. Ibid., 8–9.

ers."[222] Notwithstanding the fact that Conolly's own earlier opinions were the expressed authority for this decision,[223] he at once issued a lengthy remonstrance declaring Pollock's dictum "both mistaken and mischievous."[224] It transpired that he now believed that an extraordinary range of behaviors qualified one for the madhouse: "excessive eccentricity," "utter disregard of cleanliness and decency," "perversions of the moral feelings and passions," a disposition "to give away sums of money which they cannot afford to lose," indeed all cases where people's "being at large is inconsistent with the comfort of society and their own welfare."[225] Particularly in the young, incipient madness took on protean forms, and its cure required active and early intervention. Suitable cases for treatment included

> young men, whose grossness of habits, immoderate love of drink, disregard of honesty, or general irregularity of conduct, bring disgrace and wretchedness on their relatives; and whose unsound state of mind, unless met by prompt and proper treatment, precedes the utter subversion of reason;—young women of ungovernable temper, subject, in fact, to paroxysms of real insanity; and at other times sullen, wayward, malicious, defying all domestic control; or who want that restraint over the passions without which the female character is lost. For these also such protection, seclusion, and order, and systematic treatment as can only be afforded in an asylum, are often indispensable. Without early attention and more careful superintendence than can be exercised at home, or in any private family, [many] will become ungovernably mad, and remain so for life.[226]

Conolly's eagerness to consign the morally perverse and socially inadequate to the asylum was widely shared by his colleagues,[227] but seen in other quarters as a dangerous blurring of immorality and insanity.[228] In addition, many of the public were inclined to believe that alienists' willingness to define others as mad on such slender pretext reflected their financial interests in expanding their pool of patients. Conolly's actions in the Ruck case served only to reinforce these suspicions. Ruck was an alcoholic whose wife had secured his commitment to a private asylum on

222. John Conolly, *A Remonstrance with the Lord Chief Baron Touching the Case Nottidge versus Ripley*, 3d ed. (London: Churchill, 1849), 3. See the further discussion of the Nottidge case in Chapter 12 below.

223. T. T. Wingett, *The Law of Lunacy* (Dundee: Chalmers, 1849).

224. Conolly, *Remonstrance*, 3.

225. Ibid., 4–5.

226. Ibid., 6–7. "Seclusion and systematic superintendence," were, he continued, "strictly part of the medical treatment in such cases; and to censure those who resort to it is as utterly foolish as it would be to reprove a physician for checking an inflammation by bleeding and blistering before life was endangered, or a surgeon for preventing the progress of a disease of a joint before incurable disorganization rendered amputation unnecessary."

227. McCandless, "Liberty and Lunacy."

228. *Daily Telegraph*, 7 January 1862; *The Times*, 7, 21, and 31 January 1862; *British Medical Journal*, 11 January; 8 February 1862.

certificates issued by Conolly and Dr. Richard Barnett. Enforced absti-
nence brought about a rapid recovery, but several months passed before
Ruck, at a cost of 1,100 pounds, secured an inquisition in lunacy, at
which a jury found him sane by majority vote. He then sued Conolly and
others for false imprisonment. At the trial that followed, Conolly was
forced to make a series of damaging admissions. He had issued his certificate of Ruck's lunacy after a joint examination with Barnett, a clear
violation of the law; and, more seriously, he had received a fee from
Moorcroft House, where he was the consulting physician, for referring
Ruck. The jury was obviously not impressed with Conolly's disingenuous
defense: "I know the act says that a certificate should not be signed by
any medical man connected with the establishment. I do not consider
myself connected with the establishment, as I only send male patients to
it"! [229] As a result, he faced a swingeing judgment against him for 500
pounds' damages.

Subsequently, too, his transparent rationalizations and the convenient
congruence between his beliefs and his self-interest were savagely bur-
lesqued in Charles Reade's scandalous best-seller, *Hard Cash*, where Conolly appears in thinly disguised form as the bumbling Dr. Wycherly. [230]
Wycherly, in the sardonic words of Reade's hero, Alfred Hardie, "is the
very soul of humanity," in whose asylum there are "no tortures, no hand-
cuffs, nor leg-locks, no brutality." [231] But his "vast benevolence of manner" [232] and the "oleaginous periphrasis" of his conversation concealed a
second-rate mind "blinded by self interest" and apt to perceive insanity
wherever he looked. [233] In Reade's savage caricature, Conolly/Wycherly's
pretensions to gentlemanly status are mocked, and his vaunted psychological acumen exposed as a pious fraud. "Bland and bald," this psycho-
cerebral expert was "a voluminous writer on certain medical subjects . . .
a man of large reading and the tact to make it subserve his interests," [234] a
task in which he was greatly aided by his settled disposition "to found
facts on theories instead of theories on facts." [235] As "a collector of mad
people . . . whose turn of mind, cooperating with his instincts, led him to
put down any man a lunatic, whose intellect was manifestly superior to
his own," [236] he is easily duped into diagnosing a sane man as lunatic, and
thereafter persists stubbornly in his opinion till the unfortunate inmate
is willing to grant that "Hamlet was mad." [237] In the climactic courtroom

229. "Report on the Ruck Case," *Journal of Mental Science* 4 (1858): 131.
230. Charles Reade, *Hard Cash: A Matter-of-Fact Romance* (London: Ward, Lock, 1864).
231. Ibid., 335. The reference to nonrestraint makes transparent who the target is, but
Conolly's identity becomes still more blatantly obvious in later passages.
232. Ibid., 211.   233. Ibid., 208.   234. Ibid., 203, 212.
235. Ibid., 335.   236. Ibid., 339.
237. Here, the reference to Conolly was unmistakable, for Conolly's *Study of Hamlet*,
addressed to precisely this issue, had appeared but a few months earlier. Reade mali-
ciously takes his vendetta a step further: Wycherly readily debates the sanity of Alfred
Hardie, the young man he has wrongly incarcerated, "with a philosophical coolness, the

scene that brings the melodrama to a close, Reade puts Wycherly on the witness stand and gives him for his lines Conolly's most damaging admissions in the Ruck case. Wycherly, like his alter ego, tries to bluster his way through by protesting that counsel's questions are an affront to his professional dignity—but to no avail. Question:

> "Is it consistent with your dignity to tell us whether the keepers of private asylums pay you a commission for all the patients you consign to durance vile by your certificates?" Dr. Wycherly fenced with the question, but the remorseless Colt only kept him longer under torture, and dragged out of him that he received fifteen per cent from the asylum keepers for every patient he wrote insane; and that he had an income of eight hundred pounds a year from that source alone.[238]

Along with his sometimes embarrassing forays into the courtroom, and his moderately rewarding practice as a consultant,[239] Conolly was forced to turn to the private "trade in lunacy" as an additional source of income. His private residence, Lawn House, only a stone's throw from Hanwell,[240] was adapted to take a handful of female patients.[241] Subse-

---

young man admired, and found it hard to emulate; but this philosophical calmness deserted him the moment Hamlet's insanity was disputed, and the harder he was pressed, the angrier, the louder, the more confused the Psychological physician became; and presently he got furious, burst out of the anti-spasmodic or round-about style and called Alfred a d——d ungrateful, insolent puppy, and went stamping about the room; and, finally, to the young man's horror, fell down in a fit of an epileptic character, grinding his teeth and foaming at the mouth." Alfred, by now well acquainted with the face of lunacy, has discovered Wycherly's secret: he was himself a monomaniac! (ibid., 340).

238. Ibid. 453. For someone with a powerful animus against the pretensions of Victorian alienists, Conolly was a tempting target, both because of his eminence and because of his general reputation as a great humanitarian; and in attacking him, Reade was at once ruthless, unscrupulous, and resourceful, not shrinking from quoting Conolly out of context and putting his behavior in the worst possible light. Not surprisingly, Conolly, his family, and friends (who included Charles Dickens, in whose *Household Words* Reade's novel had first appeared in serial form) were deeply distressed. On this last point, see Richard A. Hunter and Ida Macalpine, "Dickens and Conolly: An Embarrassed Editor's Disclaimer," *Times Literary Supplement*, 11 August 1961, 534–35.

239. For instance, papers at the Warwickshire County Record Office reveal that Conolly, together with Samuel Gaskell, the superintendent of the Lancaster County Asylum (and subsequently a commissioner in lunacy), was paid fifty pounds to give advice on the setting up of the new county lunatic asylum.

240. Apparently he could not bear to leave the site/sight of his earlier triumphs: "No longer residing in Hanwell Asylum, and no longer superintending it, or even visiting it, I continue to live within view of the building and its familiar trees and grounds. The sound of the bell that announces the hours of the patients' dinner still gives me pleasure, because I know that it summons the poorest creature there to a comfortable, well-prepared and sufficient meal; and the tone of the chapel bell, coming across the narrow valley of the Brent still reminds me, morning and evening, of the well-remembered and mingled congregation of the afflicted, and who were then assembling, humble, yet hopeful and not forgotten, and not spiritually deserted" (Conolly, *Treatment of the Insane*, 341–42).

241. The annual reports of the commissioners in lunacy reveal an average of five or six present at any one time.

quently, he acquired an interest in another small asylum at Wood End and opened a third house, Hayes Park, in partnership with his brother, William;[242] and in 1853 he became consulting physician to Moorcroft House Asylum from which he received both a salary and a percentage of the patients' fees.[243]

"A man," said Conolly a few years later, "must live by his profession, and a physician who devotes himself to mental disorders has to deal with a very small portion of the population, and he generally adds to his consulting practice, the plan of having a place where the treatment of patients can be conducted entirely under his own observation."[244] There can be no doubt, however, that trading in lunacy was at first distasteful to him. He had long argued that "every lunatic asylum should be the property of the State, and should be controlled by public officers,"[245] and during his time at Hanwell had become the leading spokesman for the new county asylums. Moreover, with its obvious overtones of "trade" and its long-established unsavory reputation (to which the writings of reformers like himself had in no small measure contributed), the business of running a private asylum was widely regarded as one of the most *déclassé* forms of medical practice; potentially lucrative, to be sure, but abhorrent to those of gentlemanly sensibilities.

But however repugnant, it was unavoidable. Conolly's income at Hanwell had been "barely sufficient to maintain his family," even with accommodation and food provided. Thrown back entirely on his own resources, he compounded his difficulties by being once more "very liberal-minded in practice and otherwise, and gave little attention to financial matters."[246] More seriously, however, his household remained a large, even a growing burden. His eldest daughter soon married a missionary stationed in China; but Sophia Jane did not marry until 1852, at the age of twenty-six,[247] and Anne Caroline not until 1866, at the age of thirty-five.[248]

Much the greatest source of concern, though, was his son, Edward Tennyson, who far exceeded even his father's youthful fecklessness and displayed a remarkable inability to find any settled pursuit. When he was eighteen, his father's connections had secured him a position as part-time secretary to the Society for the Diffusion of Useful Knowledge. But in 1846, with the disbanding of the society, this came to an end, and the elder Conolly's appeal to Lord Brougham for another patronage ap-

242. In 1859, he had to rescue this enterprise from bankruptcy.

243. Hunter and Macalpine, "Introduction," xxxv–xxxvi.

244. House of Commons, *Select Committee on the Care and Treatment of Lunatics,* 1859–60, 185.

245. Conolly, *Indications of Insanity,* 481.

246. Maudsley, "Memoir," 172.

247. To Thomas Harrington Tuke, one of Conolly's former pupils and the proprietor of Chiswick House private asylum.

248. To Henry Maudsley, another alienist and former pupil.

pointment for his son met with no response.[249] Five months later, Edward himself renewed the petition, asking specifically for an appointment with the new Railways Commission.[250] Spurned, he was not discouraged. Three years later, he sought Brougham's assistance to obtain a position as "a Poor Law Inspector," urging his experience as "one of the Guardians of the Poor for Brentford Union, [undertaken] in the absence of any more remunerative employment," as a qualification for the job.[251] He was no more successful on this occasion, and since he had now reached his late twenties, it seems at last to have occurred to him that further efforts of his own were required. An attempt to practice as a barrister brought no improvement: "Prospects of . . . business are anything but encouraging, and I am every year more desirous of doing something profitable in the world." The upshot was still another appeal to Brougham: "I venture to apply to your lordship to know whether there is likely to be any appointment connected with new Charities Commission which I have any chance of obtaining."[252] There was not.

Now married, Edward still remained almost entirely dependent on his father's largesse, a burden that was further augmented with the arrival of the first of a series of children. At thirty-three, he had "been four years at the bar; . . . had hardly any practice," and decided to renew his entreaties: "My Lord, I have been so often troublesome with applications that I am ashamed to make another." Nevertheless, he did not let a little embarrassment stand in his way, this time seeking the vacant post of secretary to the Lunacy Commission.[253] But even the Conolly name could not secure this appointment or a similar post with the Scottish Lunacy Commission, for which he applied some two years later.[254] As late as 1864, his father still did not know what was to become of him: "Past forty—seven or eight children [sic]—no present means of educating them, nor of emigration where they might prosper, no friends whom he has continued to see—no prospects at the Bar, etc., etc."[255] (In 1865, however, a year before his father's death, he finally adopted the favorite strategy for failed scions of the Victorian middle classes, and emigrated to New Zealand, where he became a Supreme Court judge.)[256]

Faced with these demands on his income, it is not surprising that John Conolly had to swallow his pride and seek financial reward where he

249. John Conolly to Lord Brougham, 19 June 1846, Brougham Collection, UCL.

250. Edward Conolly to Lord Brougham, 10 November 1846 (a request he reiterated on 27 November 1846), Brougham Collection, UCL.

251. Ibid., 3 February 1851.

252. Ibid., 27 December 1853.

253. Ibid., 6 December 1855.

254. Ibid., 8 August 1857. "I do not know if I am asking too much." He was.

255. John Conolly to Thomas Harrington Tuke, quoted in Hunter and Macalpine, "Introduction," xxxvi.

256. Leigh, British Psychiatry, 227.

could find it. But just as he had earlier turned from a skeptic about asylum treatment into an advocate of a greatly expanded asylum system, so he now publicly defended the private institutions he once anathematized. Repudiating his prior stance on domestic treatment, he contended that "the management essential to recovery is impracticable in [the lunatic's] own house, or in any private family." [257] Yet out of the strong desire to conceal the presence of insanity, the wealthy attempted to resort to these expedients, with the result that "the whole house becomes a kind of asylum, but without the advantages of an asylum." [258] The consequences were necessarily antitherapeutic: "The alarm and even the affection of surrounding friends lead to hurtful concessions and indulgences, and to the withdrawal of all wholesome control; until the bodily disorder present in the first stages is increased, and the mind is much more irritated, thus making eventual recovery more difficult, and often altogether doubtful or impossible." [259] Still less enviable was the situation of those placed "in detached residences, where no other patient is received." Gloom, solitude, and neglect, both physical and moral, were their lot, "such, indeed, as to make the position of lunatics of wealthy families inferior to that of the lunatic pauper." [260] Private asylums had once been notorious for similar abuse and neglect. But their current proprietors were, with few exceptions, men "of high character and education"; and the institutions themselves "are now so well conducted as to present every advantage adapted to the richer patients, and to secure all the care and comfort which the poorer patient enjoys in our admirable county asylums"; with the result that the patient's reception into the asylum "is usually followed by an immediate alleviation of his malady, and

257. John Conolly, "On Residences for the Insane," *Journal of Mental Science* 5 (1859): 412–13.

258. Ibid., 413.

259. Ibid., 412.

260. Ibid., 415–17. It is instructive to compare these opinions with those voiced only a few years later by Charles Lockhart Robertson and John Charles Bucknill. They had also relinquished the superintendencies of county asylums (Sussex and Devon), but both had subsequently become chancery visitors in lunacy, in that capacity visiting rich lunatics in both asylum and domestic settings. Robertson confessed, "I could not have believed that patients who were such confirmed lunatics could be treated in private families the way Chancery lunatics are, if I had not personally watched these cases" (House of Commons, *Report of the Select Committee on the Operation of the Lunacy Law* [1877], 53–55). And Bucknill went further still: "The author's fullest and latest experience has convinced him that the curative influences of asylums have been vastly overrated, and that of isolated treatment in domestic care have been greatly undervalued. . . . It has long been the accepted doctrine [among alienists] that insanity can only be treated curatively in asylums. . . . A wider knowledge of insanity . . . would have taught them that a very considerable number of cases of insanity run a short course and recover in domestic life with no great amount of treatment, and that perhaps not of a very scientific kind" (J. C. Bucknill, *The Care of the Insane and Their Legal Control* [London: Macmillan, 1880], 114).

he becomes at once surrounded by every circumstance and means favourable to cure."[261]

This Panglossian portrait was far from universally admired. Sir John Charles Bucknill dismissed private asylums as "institutions for private imprisonment";[262] and the success of Charles Reade's *Hard Cash*, a story centering upon the improper confinement of its hero in a series of private madhouses, suggests that Bucknill's opinion reflected a widespread public suspicion.[263] But Conolly's views certainly corresponded closely with the official mythology of the Victorian asylum system and were fitting for one who now ranked as the doyen of his profession.

The publication of his defense of private asylums represented Conolly's last significant public activity. By 1860, he lived "in an elegant retirement" at Lawn House,[264] consulting occasionally in difficult cases, but for the most part concentrating upon *A Study of Hamlet*, an essay designed to show that the prince was indeed mad.[265] His health steadily worsened until, on 4 March 1866, he suffered a massive stroke. By the following day, he was dead. "His name," as the *Journal of Mental Science* puts it, "liveth forevermore."[266]

Not only did John Conolly play a central role in the success of the Victorian lunacy reform movement, but the vicissitudes of his individual biography nicely illustrate some of the general sociological features that attended the constitution of Victorian alienism as a specialism.[267] His widely publicized work at Hanwell contributed significantly to the crea-

261. Conolly, "On Residences for the Insane," 417–18.

262. Bucknill, *Care of the Insane*, 128.

263. As Reade put it (*Hard Cash*, 330): "The tenacity of a private lunatic asylum is unique. A little push behind your back and you slide into one; but to get out again is to scale a precipice with crumbling sides."

264. Edward Jarvis to Almira Jarvis, 31 May 1860, Jarvis papers, Concord Free Public Library, Concord, Massachusetts. "Dr. Conolly is apparently seventy or more [*sic*], yet hale and vigorous; very kind, bland, affectionate in his manners. Having ever cultivated the higher moral and intellectual [*sic*], he manifests a beautiful spirit. He is retired from active practice and devotes himself to study, writing, social enjoyment, and some consultation practice."

265. Cf. John Conolly, *A Study of Hamlet* (London: Moxon, 1863). See also W. F. Bynum and M. Neve, "Hamlet on the Couch," in *The Anatomy of Madness*, vol. 1, ed. W. F. Bynum, Roy Porter, and Michael Shepherd (London: Tavistock, 1985), chap. 12.

266. "Obituary of John Conolly," *Journal of Mental Science* 12 (1866): 146.

267. On the constitution of Victorian alienism, see Chapter 6; and Andrew Scull, "Mad-Doctors and Magistrates: English Psychiatry's Struggle for Professional Autonomy in the Nineteenth Century," *European Journal of Sociology* 17 (1976): 279–305. It would be useful to compare Conolly's career patterns with those of others within the emergent profession of alienism, and I would like briefly and tentatively to address that issue here. The uncertain and halting progress of Conolly's career bears some interesting similarities to that of his contemporary, James Cowles Prichard (see Leigh, *British Psychiatry*); and it is equally apparent that by the time of Conolly's death, careers in alienism were developing

tion of a marketplace for the alienists' services and helped legitimize medical monopolization of the treatment of lunacy. Both ideologically and practically, his activities consolidated the Victorian commitment to institutional "solutions" to the problems posed by the deviant and the dependent. Furthermore, notwithstanding his skepticism about the value of most medical remedies for madness, and his own overt reliance on and preference for moral suasion and management in the treatment of his charges, he was most insistent on the crucial importance of medical control over the treatment of the insane. Any alternative to this professional monopoly he stigmatized as fatally misguided, almost "criminal." In this judgment he echoed and lent the considerable weight of his prestige to the opinions of his colleagues.[268]

As was generally true of Victorian alienists, it was his prerogatives as a professional that Conolly defended most fiercely against outside threats. Thus it was a proposal to limit the authority of the medical superintendent, not such critical issues as the unwieldy size and organized monotony of the Victorian asylum, that provoked his resignation from Hanwell—though size and routine undoubtedly contributed the more powerfully to the transformation of the ideal of curative institutions into the reality of museums for the collection of the unwanted.[269] So far from acquiescing in the dilution of his authority, Conolly was among the first to insist that, for the alienist, everything that occurred within the institution was relevant to cure, and in consequence nothing could be safely delegated into lay hands. This claim, as I have pointed out elsewhere,[270] was widely shared in the profession at this time, reflecting the importance of monopolistic control of asylum administration as support for an otherwise shaky professional authority. Hence the urgency with which alienists sought to persuade their employers that they alone should have

---

on a wholly different and much more systematic basis. Instead of the haphazard patterns of recruitment and disparate background experiences that appear to characterize the first generation of nineteenth-century alienists, the growing size and number of public asylums created a substantial and growing number of entry-level positions for assistant physicians. Increasingly, superintendents were recruited from the ranks of these experienced apprentices, in one sense signaling the maturation of the profession of alienism and perhaps contributing to the growing conservatism and bureaucratic inertia that marked late-nineteenth-century asylumdom. Unfortunately, however, it is difficult to go beyond these generalities, since we lack any study of English alienism to compare with John Pitts' interesting study of their American counterparts, "The Association of Medical Superintendents of American Institutions for the Insane, 1844–1892: A Case Study of Specialism in American Medicine" (Ph.D. dissertation, University of Pennsylvania, 1978). A detailed prosopographical study of the English profession over the course of the nineteenth century would unquestionably be most welcome.

268. Scull, "Mad-Doctors and Magistrates."
269. Scull, *Museums of Madness,* esp. chaps. 3 and 6.
270. Scull, "Mad-Doctors and Magistrates," 300–302.

authority over the most minute details of day-to-day activity in this "special apparatus for the cure of lunacy."[271]

As we have seen, Conolly's major concern, in the course of his writings on insanity, was with the administrative aspects of the treatment of insanity, and over the course of his career he evinced a declining interest in contributing to the scientific understanding of the condition itself. Almost certainly, this hierarchy of concerns accounts for a good measure of the hostility that lurked just beneath the surface of Henry Maudsley's strikingly ambivalent "Memoir" of his late father-in-law.[272] The markedly different—almost diametrically opposed—priorities of these two men (probably the leading figures of their respective generations of British alienists), in turn, mirror the sharp alteration of the context within which the profession operated in the two periods: the movement from what came to be seen as the naive optimism of the first half of the century, that medicine possessed the means to diagnose and successfully treat insanity, to the deepening pessimism of late Victorian psychiatry, with its sense that insanity was all but incurable, the product of defective heredity and Morelian degeneration. For those adhering to the latter orthodoxy, the issue of improving the treatment of the insane naturally lost some of its urgency, to be replaced by the need to explain (or explain away) the profession's apparent therapeutic impotence.

But even Conolly's own position underwent dramatic internal evolution in the course of his career. In his earliest writings on insanity, the product of a period in which he was very much the outside critic of existing practices, he assailed the indiscriminate confinement of the insane, urged the elimination of the private, profit-making "madhouses," and touted the merits of domiciliary care. A decade later, on his appointment as superintendent of one of the largest of the existing county asylums, he became one of the most important and effective proselytes of the expansion of the asylum system, and before long was railing against those who wanted to confine asylum admissions to lunatics dangerous to themselves or others. Toward the close of his career, during a period in which he had become one of the leading private specialists in the treatment of insanity, he exhibited yet another volte-face, using the occasion of his second presidential address to the Medico-Psychological Association to issue a lengthy defense of the social utility—indeed indispensability—of the private asylum system.

It is possible, if one is charitably inclined, to view the evolution of his views as the product of greater experience and maturity. The inex-

271. Granville, *Care and Cure*, 1 : 15.

272. "As a writer on insanity, he painted eloquently and pathetically the external features of the disease, but the philosophical depths of mental phenomena he never cared to sound, and the exact scientific investigation of mental disease he never devoted himself to" (Maudsley, "Memoir," 172).

perienced observer of his earlier years was disposed to promote imprac-
tical, if superficially attractive, visionary schemes of nonasylum treatment. Later acquaintance with the realities of treating insanity and the
therapeutic possibilities of asylum treatment forced him to revise his
ideas, as did his subsequent experience of running a private asylum.
Equally, of course, one may opt for a cynical interpretation of his intellectual "progress." As Conolly himself remarked, early in his career,
"When men's interests depend upon an opinion, it is too much to expect
that opinion always to be cautiously formed, or even in all cases honestly
given."[273] The close correspondence between the evolution of his ideas
and the unfolding of his career is too marked to escape comment. And
even in the nineteenth century, there were those who saw the parallels as
more than coincidental. Sir John Charles Bucknill, whose own intellectual development was in precisely the opposite direction to Conolly's—
from an enthusiastic advocate to a scathing critic of the asylum system, both public and private[274]—was convinced that Conolly's judgment
had been subverted by self-interest. Praising the positions Conolly had
adopted in *An Inquiry Concerning the Indications of Insanity* ("Nothing
which Dr. Conolly ever wrote does more credit to his head and heart
than these opinions"), he noted with sorrow his later repudiation of
them. One could only regret that "advancing years and personal interests had made him indulgent to the evils he had denounced."[275]

The less moralistically inclined may prefer to adopt a rather different
perspective on the internal evolution of Conolly's ideas. It is instructive
to note how difficult it is for modern readers to portray his intellectual
journey as "progress." For our generation has learned to view the asylum
as an almost unmitigated disaster, a fatally mistaken approach to the
problems of managing the mad, and one that cannot be too swiftly consigned to the dustbin of history. Viewed from this perspective, Conolly's
changing views appear to mark an almost perverse shift from enlightenment to error. It is to his earliest work that our contemporaries turn,
when they count him the author "of principles of treatment that have
scarcely been improved in all the succeeding epochs of vanguard practice."[276] But for the Victorians, it was precisely this early critique of the
asylum and advocacy of domiciliary care that was anomalous; and the

273. Conolly, *Indications of Insanity*, 3.

274. Matching the development of his own career, from superintendent of the Devon
County Asylum to an extraasylum career as chancellor's visitor in lunacy and as private
consultant.

275. Bucknill, *Care of the Insane*, 60.

276. Peter Sedgwick, *Psychopolitics* (London: Pluto Press; New York: Harper and Row,
1982), 141. For a critique of modern "community care," see Andrew Scull, *Decarceration:
Community Treatment and the Deviant—A Radical View*, 2d ed. (Oxford: Polity Press; New
Brunswick, N.J.: Rutgers University Press, 1984).

abandonment of such aberrant opinions in favor of an elaborate defense of asylum treatment required no special explanation: it simply represented an acknowledgment of the findings of modern medical science. Here, as elsewhere, we observe how slippery the concept of "scientific knowledge" is in the human sciences, and how profoundly dependent the content of that "knowledge" is on the nature of the larger social order.

CHAPTER EIGHT

Moral Architecture: The Victorian Lunatic Asylum

The following paper was originally commissioned by Anthony King for a collection of interdisciplinary essays on the social development of the built environment. Sociologists, anthropologists, historians, even architects themselves, have begun to place "much greater emphasis on an historical understanding of the economic, functional, and cultural aspects of built form and the social conditions within which particular types of built form have evolved."[1] Drawing in part on this scholarship, the aim of King's volume was to explore what buildings and the social organization of space could teach us about the society that produced them and to trace the reverse connections, in an attempt to decipher how changes in society at large were reflected in the physical configuration of buildings and spatial environments.

The asylum lends itself particularly well to analysis of this sort. As the example of Bethlem makes clear, the segregation and confinement of a small number of lunatics had long historical roots in England (even though "the Great Confinement" of which Foucault makes so much was scarcely part of the English historical experience). But Bethlem was the exception, not the rule: not until the eighteenth century was there any noticeable increase in the number of private establishments in the business of confining the mad;[2] and the development of a large and elabo-

Chapter 8 is reprinted from Anthony King, ed., *Buildings and Society: Essays on the Social Development of the Built Environment*, 1980, pp. 37–60, by permission of Routledge and Kegan Paul.

1. *Journal of Architectural Research* 5 (1976), quoted in Anthony D. King, "Introduction" to *Buildings and Society: Essays on the Social Development of the Built Environment* (London: Routledge and Kegan Paul, 1980), 8.
2. See William L. Parry-Jones, *The Trade in Lunacy: A Study of Private Madhouses in England in the Eighteenth and Nineteenth Centuries* (London: Routledge and Kegan Paul; To-

rate network of state-run asylums and the routine consignment of the lunatic to the tender mercies of asylum administrators were very much a creation of the Victorian age.

One must realize, too, that these buildings directly embodied a particular and peculiar set of cultural assumptions about madness; radically transformed what it meant to be labeled mad (even affecting who was susceptible to being so labeled); and acquired a transhistorical symbolic resonance of very substantial proportions. For the nineteenth-century asylum was, in a historically unprecedented and very distinctive sense, a purpose-built structure—an example of the new era's passion for a new form of "moral architecture." In the rehabilitation of the insane, as in the reform of the criminal classes,[3] spatial arrangements were seen as quite central to any serious effort to remoralize the dangerous and defective. And the looming presence of the mammoth structures built in response to the reformers' utopian visions remained, even after asylums and penitentiaries had degenerated into mere holding pens, grotesque parodies of the regenerative vision they had originally claimed to embody.

Moral Architecture:
The Victorian Lunatic Asylum

Were we to draw our opinions on the treatment of insanity from the construction of the buildings destined to the reception of patients, we should conclude that the great principle adopted in recovering the faculties of the mind was to immure the demented in gloomy and iron-bound fastnesses; that these were the means best adapted for restoring the wandering intellect, correcting its illusions, or quickening its torpidity: that the depraved or lost social affections were to be corrected or removed by coldness or monotony.[1]

Scattered widely across the English landscape, sometimes surrounded now by urban and suburban sprawl, sometimes still incongruously in-

---

ronto: University of Toronto Press, 1972); and Roy Porter's recent study of English responses to madness, *Mind Forg'd Manacles: A History of Madness In England from the Restoration to the Regency* (London: Athlone Press, 1987).

3. The best discussion of the application of the principles of "moral architecture" to the criminal classes is to be found in Robin Evans, *The Fabrication of Virtue: English Prison Architecture, 1750–1842* (Cambridge: Cambridge University Press, 1982). Michel Foucault, of course, places one example of this fascination with built form, Jeremy Bentham's Panopticon, at the very center of his discussion of penality. See *Discipline and Punish: The Birth of the Prison* (New York: Pantheon; London: Allen Lane, 1978), esp. pts. 3 and 4.

1. "Lunatic Asylums," *Westminster Review* 43 (1845): 167.

stalled in the midst of sylvan countryside, are to be found one of the
most notable architectural curiosities inherited from the nineteenth century, the Victorian "loony bins." Huge, ramshackle, decaying structures,
once hailed as "the most blessed manifestation of true civilization the
world can present,"[2] they now apparently exist on borrowed time—a
collection of "doomed institutions" merely awaiting the setting of "the
torch to the funeral pyre."[3] Not that they go unused in the meanwhile:
on the contrary, mental hospital admission rates have seldom been
higher. But the number of patients under treatment on any given day
falls remorselessly, as the mentally disturbed are processed and discharged at an ever more rapid rate. And as the targets of a mounting
attack on their therapeutic failings and harmful effects on those they
treat, the asylums steadily lose ground to newer, "community-based"
alternatives.

Still, the association between mental disorder and these grim relics of
Victorian humanitarianism remains indelibly fixed in our minds. For almost two centuries, madness and the built form within which it has been
contained have been virtually synonymous. The link will not easily be
obliterated. Nor, I suspect, will the buildings themselves. In this chapter,
I shall examine the social forces that lay behind the emergence of asylums as the dominant response to madness, and I shall explore some of
the factors that led to the transformation of these institutions into museums for the collection of the unwanted.

CAPITALISM AND THE TRANSFORMATION OF SOCIETY

The rise of the asylum forms part of a much larger transformation in
social control styles and practices that took place in England roughly between the mid-eighteenth and mid-nineteenth centuries. Prior to this,
the control of deviants of all sorts had been an essentially communal and
family affair. The amorphous class of the morally disreputable, the indigent, and the helpless—including such elements as vagrants, minor
criminals, the insane, and the physically handicapped—was managed in
essentially similar ways. Characteristically, little effort was made to segre-
gate such "problem populations" into separate receptacles designed to
keep them apart from the rest of society. Instead, they were dealt with in
a variety of ways that left them at large in the community. Most of the
time, families were held liable to provide for their own, if necessary with
the aid of temporary assistance or a more permanent subsidy from the
community. Lunatics were generally treated no differently from other

2. George E. Paget, *The Harveian Oration* (Cambridge: Deighton, Bell, 1866), 34–35.
3. The words are Enoch Powell's, spoken when he was minister of health in the
1959–64 Macmillan government.

deviants:[4] only a few of the most violent or troublesome cases might find themselves confined in a specially constructed cell or as part of the heterogeneous population of the local gaol.

By the mid-nineteenth century, however, virtually no aspect of this traditional response remained intact. In the course of a century or so, a remarkable change in social practices and a highly significant redefinition of the moral boundaries of English society had taken place. Insanity had been transformed from a vague, culturally defined phenomenon affecting an unknown, but probably small, proportion of the population into a condition that could be authoritatively diagnosed, certified, and dealt with only by a group of legally recognized experts and that was now seen as one of the major forms of deviance in English society. Finally, and of critical importance for my present concerns, whereas in the eighteenth century only the most violent and destructive among those now labeled insane would have been segregated and confined apart from the rest of the community, with the achievement of what is conventionally called "lunacy reform," the asylum was endorsed as the sole officially approved response to the problems posed by mental illness. Throughout the length and breadth of the country, huge specialized buildings had been built or were in the process of being built to accommodate the legions of the mad.

What had happened to bring about these profound changes? It is frequently suggested that the shift toward institutional modes of handling deviance represents no more than a quasi-automatic response to the realities of life in an urban-industrial society. Supposedly, the sheer scale of the problems associated with the advent of the Industrial Revolution proved beyond the adaptive capacity of a community and household-based relief system, prompting the resort to the asylum and the workhouse. In practice, however, not only is this account excessively mechanistic, but, in addition, no clear-cut connection exists between the rise of asylums and the growth of large cities. The drive to institutionalize the lunatic begins too soon to be simply a response to the problems created by urbanization; and at a very early stage in the process rural areas exhibit a marked enthusiasm for the asylum solution.

Instead, as I have argued at greater length elsewhere,[5] the main driving force behind the rise of a segregative response to madness (and to other forms of deviance, come to that) can much more plausibly be asserted to lie in the direct and indirect effects of the advent of a mature capitalist market economy and the associated ever more thoroughgoing commercialization of existence. While the urban conditions created by

4. A. Fessler, "The Management of Lunacy in Seventeenth Century England," *Proceedings of the Royal Society of Medicine, Historical Section* 49 (1956): 901–7.

5. See Andrew Scull, *Musuems of Madness: The Social Organization of Insanity in Nineteenth-Century England* (London: Allen Lane; New York: St. Martin's Press, 1979), on which I have drawn at various points throughout this chapter.

industrialization initially had an impact that was quite limited in geographical scope, the market obeyed few such restrictions. Rather, it had increasingly subversive effects on the whole traditional rural and urban social structure—changes that, as I shall suggest later, in turn prompted the abandonment of long-established techniques for coping with the poor and troublesome.

Quite obviously, of course, the origins of capitalism in England lie much further back in time than the end of the eighteenth century. One may trace commercialized production back at least as far as the fifteenth century, and by 1750 England was already by some definitions a single national market economy.[6] But for all the importance of these earlier developments, it remains incontrovertible that, until the latter part of the eighteenth century, the market continued to exercise "only a weak pull on the economy" and had only a limited impact on English social structure.[7] This situation, in turn, allowed the persistence, until well into the eighteenth century, of a relatively unchanging agriculture and a social order that exhibited substantial continuities with the past. The mass of workers were not yet fully proletarianized; and notions of the just price and the just wage coexisted with and at times inhibited market determination of wages and prices.[8] Put another way, though the rationalizing impact of capitalism was present, it operated only within strict limits.[9]

Beginning in the late eighteenth century, however, capitalism broke the social bonds that had formerly held it in check. There occurred a massive reorganization of society as a whole along market principles—a development Karl Polanyi has termed "the running of society as an adjunct to the market."[10] The old social order was undermined and then destroyed, and profound shifts took place in the relationships between superordinate and subordinate classes: changes we may sum up as the movement from a paternalistic social order dominated by rank, order, and degree to a society based on class.[11] The sources of this transformation are too many and complex to go into here,[12] particularly since my

6. E. J. Hobsbawm, *Industry and Empire* (Harmondsworth: Penguin, 1969), 27–28.

7. L. A. Clarkson, *The Pre-industrial Economy in England, 1500–1750* (London: Batsford, 1971), 22 and passim.

8. E. P. Thompson, "The Moral Economy of the English Crowd in the Eighteenth Century," *Past and Present* 50 (1971): 76–136.

9. Karl Polanyi, *The Great Transformation* (Boston: Beacon, 1957), passim, esp. 70; Clarkson, *Pre-industrial Economy*.

10. Polanyi, *Great Transformation*, 57.

11. A. Briggs, "The Language of 'Class' in Early Nineteenth Century England," in *Essays in Labour History*, ed. Asa Briggs and John Saville (London: Macmillan, 1960), 43–73; idem, *The Making of Modern England* (New York: Harper and Row, 1965); Harold Perkin, *The Origins of Modern English Society 1780–1880* (London: Routledge and Kegan Paul, 1969).

12. Among the most important were improvements in transport and the widening of internal markets; the rise in domestic population and the associated expansion of demand, further fueled by the growing industrial sector of the economy; and the additional stimu-

present concern is rather with the social impact of the process than with its origins. Turning to these consequences, in the first place, the rationalization of production increasingly forced the closing off of all alternatives except wage work as a means of providing for subsistence. And wage earners, whether agricultural laborers or industrial workers, shared a similar incapacity to make adequate provision for periods of economic depression. Yet employers increasingly convinced themselves that they owed the workers only wages, and that once these had been paid, the employees had no further claim on them.[13] To make matters worse, one of the most notable features of the economy in this period was its tendency to oscillate wildly between conditions of boom and slump. Thus, for the lower classes, family members unable to contribute to their own subsistence became a serious drain on resources. Such dependent groups as the aged and children became a much greater burden—as, of course, did the insane.

These changes in structures, perceptions, and outlook provided a direct source of bourgeois dissatisfaction with the traditional, noninstitutional response to the indigent. There were others, however. Most notably, the dislocations of the social structure associated with the transition to an industrial economy led to a sizable rise in the proportion of the population in receipt of poor relief—at precisely the time when the growing power of the bourgeoisie and their increasing dominance of intellectual and cultural life was reducing the inclination to tolerate this. In the circumstances, the upper classes readily convinced themselves that laxly administered household relief *promoted* poverty rather than relieved it (a position for which they found ample ideological support in the writings of Malthus and others).[14] In its place, they were increasingly attracted toward an institutionally based system. For, in theory at least, workhouses and the like enabled a close and continuing watch to be kept on who was admitted. They could be used to punish idleness. Moreover, their quasi-military authority structure seemed ideally suited to instill "proper" work habits among those resisting the monotony, routine, and regularity of industrialized labor. In Bentham's caustic phrase, they would function as "a mill to grind rogues honest and idle men industrious":[15] and in this way the whole system would be rendered efficient and economical.

---

lus to domestic food production resulting from the Napoleonic Wars. For further discussion, see Eric J. Hobsbawm and George Rude, *Captain Swing: A Social History of the Great English Agricultural Uprising of 1830* (Harmondsworth: Penguin, 1969; New York: Norton, 1975), chaps. 1 and 2; Hobsbawm, *Industry and Empire;* Briggs, *Making of Modern England.*

13. Paul Mantoux, *The Industrial Revolution in the Eighteenth Century* (London: Jonathan Cape, 1928), 428.

14. Thomas R. Malthus, *An Essay on the Principle of Population* (London: Johnson, 1798), esp. chap. 5.

15. Bentham to J. P. Brissot, in Jeremy Bentham, *Works,* vol. 10, ed. J. Bowring (Edinburgh: Tait, 1843), 226.

If the general receptivity of the English ruling class to institutional responses to indigence can be traced to these underlying structural transformations of the society, what in turn accounts for the tendency not merely to institutionalize, but to divide up and categorize the previously amorphous class of the indigent, the troublesome, and the morally disreputable? More specifically for our present concerns, how and why was insanity differentiated in this way? The establishment of a market economy, and, more especially, a market in labor, provided the initial incentive to distinguish far more carefully than hitherto between different categories of deviance. If nothing else, under these conditions, stress had to be laid for the first time on the importance of distinguishing between the able-bodied and non-able-bodied poor. For a labor market was a basic prerequisite of capitalism,[16] and to provide aid to the able-bodied threatened to undermine that market in a radical fashion and on many different levels. As Adam Smith pointed out,[17] relief to the able-bodied interfered with labor mobility; it created cost differentials between one town and region and another; and it had a wholly pernicious effect on labor discipline and productivity. Instead, it was felt that want ought to be the stimulus to the capable, who must therefore be distinguished from the helpless. The significance of this distinction thus increases in direct relationship to the rise of the wage labor system.

One can see the primitive beginnings of this process even in the Elizabethan Poor Law of 1601, which distinguishes between the able but workless, the aged and impotent, and children. But until much later than this, the boundaries between what today would be termed the unemployed, the unemployable, and the employed remained much more fluid than the modern reader is apt to realize.[18] Moreover, while the Tudors and Stuarts did not scruple to invoke harsh legal penalties to force the poor to work, their efforts were inspired at least as much by the need to defuse the political threat posed by a landless "army" of vagrants as by more directly economic considerations.[19]

As economic considerations grow in importance, so does the pressure to separate the able-bodied and to force them to work. At first the compulsion to work came through threats of judicial punishment, but gradually this approach was abandoned in favor of one best summed up by the Quaker pamphleteer, John Bellers: "The Sluggard shall be cloathed in Raggs. He that will not work shall not eat."[20] The superiority of the whip-

16. Karl Marx, *Capital*, vol. 1 (New York: International Publishers, 1967), 578, 717–33; Max Weber, *The Protestant Ethic and the Spirit of Capitalism* (London: Allen and Unwin, 1930), 22.

17. Adam Smith, *The Wealth of Nations* (New York: Modern Library, 1937), 135–40.

18. Polanyi, *Great Transformation*, 86.

19. Dorothy Marshall, *The English Poor in the Eighteenth Century* (London: Routledge, 1926), 17.

20. J. Bellers, *Proposals for Raising a College of Industry* (London: T. Sowle, 1696), 1.

lash of hunger over legal compulsion was clear. Not least, it appeared as a purely economic and "objective" form of compulsion, a suprahuman law of nature. As that well-known humanitarian Thomas Robert Malthus put it: "When Nature will govern and punish for us, it is a very miserable ambition to wish to snatch the rod from her hands and draw upon ourselves the odium of the executioner."[21]

In this way, then, the functional requirements of a market system promoted a relatively simple, if crucial, distinction between two broad classes of the indigent. Workhouses and the like were to be an important practical means of making this vital theoretical separation, and thereby of rendering the whole system efficient and economical. Notwithstanding the intentions of their founders, however, workhouses quickly became filled with the decaying, the decrepit, and the unemployable; and an unintended consequence of this concentration of the deviant in an institutional environment was to exacerbate the problems of handling at least some of them—most notably those who could not or would not abide by the rules of the house.

Among the most important of these were the acutely disturbed and refractory insane. The problems presented by the mad gathered together in an institution were quite different from those they had posed when scattered through the community. The order and discipline of the whole establishment were jeopardized by the presence of people who, even by threats of discipline and punishment, could not be persuaded or induced to conform. Hence the adoption of an institutional response to all sorts of problem populations greatly increased the pressures and incentives to differentiate among them. Under the impact of multiplying complaints from both administrators and inmates of workhouses, gaols, and hospitals, efforts were made to exclude the insane.

Initially, this situation provided simply an opportunity for speculation and profit for those willing to traffic in this species of human misery. Those involved with "the disposal of lunatics" increasingly placed them with individual entrepreneurs "in private dwelling houses which gradually acquired the description of 'mad' houses."[22] Large as some madhouses became, and lucrative as the "trade in lunacy" often was, few of these places were purpose-built. The resulting structural deficiencies of the buildings, together with the lack of restraints on entry into or conduct of the business, undoubtedly had some connection with the widespread reliance on chains, manacles, and physical coercion to manage patients. Their importance in this respect should not be exaggerated, however. Alongside the profit-making madhouses, and in addition to

21. Thomas R. Malthus, *Principle of Population*, 6th ed. (London: Murray, 1826), bk. 2, 339.

22. William L. Parry-Jones, *The Trade in Lunacy: A Study of Private Madhouses in England in the Eighteenth and Nineteenth Centuries* (London: Routledge and Kegan Paul; Toronto: Toronto University Press, 1972), 7.

the ancient establishment of Bethlem (which had been rebuilt in 1676),[23] the eighteenth century also saw the foundation of a number of charity asylums supported by public subscription. And though these institutions were housed in buildings *built* to contain lunatics, here, too, madness was considered "a display of fury and violence to be subdued and conquered by stripes, chains, and lowering treatments."[24]

"LUNACY REFORM"

Beginning in the early years of the new century, however, a movement began to replace the private madhouses and to accommodate in state-supported asylums those lunatics still housed in gaols, in poor-law institutions, or hidden in attics and closets. Particularly in its early stages, lunacy reform formed part of a much broader movement of "philanthropic" social reform characteristic of the late eighteenth and early nineteenth centuries. Borrowing both personnel[25] and ideas from these related movements, it was at first a somewhat confused and ill-defined enterprise. Those involved in it shared in varying degrees a concern to protect society from the disorder threatened by the raving; a desire to simplify life for those charged with administering the local poorhouses and gaols; and an equally unfocused and unsystematic feeling that the insane themselves deserved to be treated in a more "humane" fashion. But they possessed no clear ideological vision of what could or should replace existing arrangements. This lack of clarity was evident both in

23. Bethlem was a medieval foundation that for centuries had been the only specialized institution for the insane, albeit a small one. In 1632 it contained only twenty-seven inmates, and in 1642, forty-four. The new building, for about 150 inmates, opened in 1676 and was further enlarged in the 1720s.

24. Richard A. Hunter and Ida Macalpine, *Three Hundred Years of Psychiatry, 1535 to 1860: A History Presented in Selected English Texts* (London, Oxford University Press, 1963), 475. One should note, however, that it scarcely makes sense to describe even these charity asylums as "purpose-built" in the sense in which this term becomes applicable in the nineteenth century. Little connection was seen at this time between architecture and "cure"— the latter being held to depend primarily upon physical treatments of various sorts. Apart from its uses for decorative purposes or for show (the exterior of Bethlem, for example, was modeled on the Tuileries), the architecture of these places was designed primarily to secure "the safe confinement and imprisonment of lunatics" (House of Commons, *Report of the Select Committee on Madhouses* [1815], 76) an aim that led later generations to comment on "the prison-mindedness of eighteenth-century insane asylum designers." (The words are J. D. Thompson and G. Goldin's, taken from their study of hospital design, *The Hospital: A Social and Architectural History* [New Haven: Yale University Press, 1975]; but such sentiments were a commonplace in nineteenth-century reform circles.) It is perhaps of interest to recall, therefore, that the architect of St. Luke's Hospital—perhaps the most influential of the eighteenth-century charity asylums—was George Dance the Younger, who was also responsible for the design of the new Newgate Prison.

25. For example, Sir Samuel Romilly, Samuel Whitbread, and William Wilberforce at the parliamentary level; and Sir George O. Paul and the Rev. John Thomas Becher at the local level.

the first parliamentary inquiry the reformers instituted into the treatment of the insane, which simultaneously found little but insufficient institutional provision to complain about and bestowed considerable praise on precisely the existing madhouses and asylums the reformers were shortly to criticize so vehemently;[26] and in the vague, weak permissive legislation of 1808 that the reformers then secured. Counties were henceforth allowed (although not required) to provide asylum accommodation at public expense; but even the reformers appeared to have little conception at this point of why the asylum was desirable or what kind of institution it should be.[27]

Within less than a decade, they possessed answers to both questions. A hitherto obscure provincial Quaker institution, the York Retreat, attracted national attention and provided the reformers with both a model to be copied and an account of the superiority of properly run asylums as a treatment setting.[28] Sharply departing from traditional practices, the staff at the Retreat insisted upon "the superior efficacy . . . of a mild system of treatment." External, physical coercion was minimized and, in its most blatant forms—"gyves, chains, and manacles"—done away with entirely. In its place came an emphasis on "treating the patient as much in the manner of a rational being as the state of mind will possibly allow" and on carefully designed measures to induce the inmates to collaborate in their own recapture by the forces of reason[29] (see Figure 8).

26. House of Commons, *Report of the Select Committee on Criminal and Pauper Lunatics* (1807).

27. Magistrates were provided with scarcely any guidance concerning the construction or administration of the new asylums, other than the advice that they should be placed "in an airy and healthy situation, with a good supply of water, and which may afford the probability of the vicinity of constant medical assistance" (Preamble to 48 Geo III c96)—simply an adaptation of John Howard's prescription of the proper site for a reform prison: "It should not be cramped among other buildings, but should be in open country—perhaps on a rise of a hill to get the full force of the wind, and it should be close to a running stream" (quoted in Robin Evans, "'A Rational Plan for Softening the Mind': Prison Design, 1750–1842: A Study of the Relationship Between Functional Architecture and Penal Ideology" [Ph.D. dissertation, Essex University, 1975], 107).

28. Particularly important in drawing attention to the Retreat, which had been opened in 1796, were the book by the founder's grandson, Samuel Tuke (*Description of the Retreat: An Institution near York for Insane Persons of the Society of Friends* [1813], facsimile ed., ed. Richard A. Hunter and Ida Macalpine [London: Dawsons, 1964]), and its review in the *Edinburgh Review* (1814) by Sydney Smith. One should note that, though it was the Retreat's experience that became the reformers' model, the approach adopted here was not unique. A number of other madhouse proprietors were independently experimenting along similar lines in this period: cf. E. L. Fox, *Brislington House: An Asylum for Lunatics* (Bristol: For the Author, 1806); John Ferriar, *Medical Histories and Reflections*, vol. 2 (London: Cadell and Davies, 1795).

29. Tuke, *Description of the Retreat*, vi, 158. For a critical reexamination of this decisive shift in our characteristic ways of responding to and coping with the mentally disturbed, and an exploration of its links to larger social movements and processes, see Chapter 4 above.

Figure 8. The original building of the York Retreat, opened in 1796. The
domestic architecture of this establishment reminded one early visitor of "une
grande ferme rustique." In the early nineteenth century, the institution (at
first, with only thirty patients) acted as a model for lunacy reformers. From:
D. H. Tuke, *Reform in the Treatment of the Insane* (London: Churchill, 1892), 18.
(Courtesy of the Wellcome Trustees.)

From most perspectives, the Retreat was an outstandingly successful
experiment. It had demonstrated, to the reformers' satisfaction at least,
that the supposedly continuous danger and frenzy to be anticipated
from maniacs were the *consequence* of rather than the occasion for harsh
and misguided methods of management and restraint; indeed, that this
reputation was in great measure the self-serving creation of the madhouse keepers. It apparently showed that the asylum could provide a
comfortable and forgiving environment that not only spared the insane
the neglect that would otherwise have been their lot, but played a vital
role in restoring a substantial proportion of them to sanity.

Now that the reformers had before them a practical realization of
their own half-formulated ideals, their reaction to conditions in most
existing madhouses became one of fierce moral outrage. Since the free
trade in lunacy simply multiplied the opportunities and incentives for
keepers to maltreat the mad (or so they now concluded), only a system of
state-supported, rigorously inspected asylums would allow the extension
of the benefits of moral treatment to all the insane. As early as 1815,
therefore, the reformers were seeking legislation to secure these ends.

Any such measures, however, threatened a transformation in political relationships whose importance extended far beyond the narrow sphere of lunacy reform. If enacted, it would have set the precedent for a notable expansion of the central coercive machinery at the disposal of the state. Opposition to such a concentration of power at the national level remained extraordinarily widespread and well entrenched at both the structural and the ideological levels,[30] so that it took some thirty years for the lunacy reformers to secure legislative enactment of their plans. (Indeed, they succeeded only after the obstacles to central administration had been confronted and dealt a decisive defeat, not over the marginal issue of the treatment of lunatics, but over the critically important issue of Poor Law reform.) In the interim, the reformers devoted themselves to winning over public opinion, through the periodic exposure of the evils necessarily attendant upon the continued operation of the private madhouse system and through the development of a steadily more elaborate ideological account of the virtues of properly constructed and run asylums.

Though it was further developed and refined by the newly emerging class of professional "alienists," the new institutional ideology drew heavily on the York Retreat for inspiration.[31] It was insistently proclaimed that in the successful treatment of insanity, the requisite "means and advantages can rarely, if ever, be united in the private habitations even of the opulent."[32] In part, this superiority simply reflected the much greater experience of asylum personnel with the shapes and forms of mental disturbance, which allowed them to handle the insane more easily and skillfully, in situations where the well-meaning but clumsy and misdirected interventions of relatives only aggravated the condition. But, beyond this, the public must recognize that "a private dwelling is ill-adapted to the wants and requirements of such an unfortunate being." Experience had convinced the experts charged with curing lunatics of "the improbability (I had almost said moral impossibility) of an insane

30. Edward P. Thompson, *The Making of the English Working Class* (New York: Vintage Books, 1963), 82 and passim.

31. The emerging institutions provided, on the one hand, a guaranteed market for an emerging profession and, on the other, the opportunity for an occupational group to develop empirically based skills in coping with madmen. The asylums thus formed the breeding ground for a new group of "experts" in the management of the mad, first known as "mad-doctors," later as "alienists," and only in the latter part of the nineteenth century referred to as "psychiatrists." For discussions of the growth and consolidation of the English psychiatric profession in this period, see W. F. Bynum, "Rationales for Therapy in British Psychiatry: 1780–1835," *Medical History* 18 (1974): 317–34; Chapter 6 above; and Andrew Scull, "Mad-Doctors and Magistrates: English Psychiatry's Struggle for Professional Autonomy in the Nineteenth Century," *European Journal of Sociology* 17 (1976): 279–305.

32. William Charles Ellis, *A Letter to Thomas Thompson Esq., M. P., . . .* (Hull: Topping and Dawson, 1815), 8.

person's regaining the use of his reason, except by . . . a mode of treatment . . . which can be fully adopted only in a Building constructed for
the purpose."[33] The very physical structure, as this implied, was "a special apparatus for the cure of lunacy"[34] quite as important as any drugs
or other remedies in the alienist's armamentarium. In the words of
Luther Bell, a leading American member of the fraternity,

> An Asylum or more properly a Hospital for the insane, may justly be con-
> sidered an architectural contrivance as peculiar and characteristic to carry
> out its designs, as is any edifice for manufacturing purposes to meet its spe-
> cific end. It is emphatically an instrument of treatment.[35]

DESIGNING THE PURPOSE-BUILT ASYLUM

Many aspects of the asylum's physical structure and siting contributed to
its value as a therapeutic tool. In the first place, Tuke and his followers
placed a wholly new emphasis on the importance of classification as a
means of control and resocialization.[36] Segregation of inmates by other
than social class was largely ignored in the eighteenth century. When
John Howard visited Bethlem in 1788, for example, he discovered that
"the patients communicate with one another from the top to the bottom
of the house, so that there is no separation of the calm and the quiet
from the noisy and turbulent, except those who are chained in their
cells."[37]

By contrast, in the reform institutions, separation was a key management device, the technique that made possible the discarding of cruder,
more obvious ways of inducing a measure of conformity from the asylum's inmates. Once "the patients are arranged into classes, as much as
may be, according to the degree in which they approach to rational or
orderly conduct,"[38] the asylum authorities had a powerful weapon at
their disposal with which to prevail upon the patients to exercise self-

---

33. R. G. Hill, *A Lecture on the Management of Lunatic Asylums* (London: Simpkin, Marshall, 1839), 4–6.

34. Cited in J. Mortimer Granville, *The Care and Cure of the Insane*, 2 vols. (London:
Hardwicke and Bogue, 1877), 1:15.

35. Cited in D. Dix, *Memorial Soliciting Adequate Appropriations for the Construction of a
State Hospital for the Insane in the State of Mississippi* (Jackson: Fall and Marshall, 1850), 20.

36. Wholly new as applied to lunatics, that is: for criminals, classification was the key
disciplinary tool to be used in the new penitentiaries from the time of John Howard onwards. Here too, therefore, "the programme of reformatory discipline outlined by the philanthropists . . . could only be implemented in a building designed for the purpose. Because reformation relied so much on demarcation and division, to isolate prisoner from
prisoner, architecture was acknowledged to be the crucial factor in setting the whole process in motion" (Evans, "Rational Plan," 179).

37. Cited in Thompson and Goldin, *Hospital*, 69.

38. Tuke, *Description of the Retreat*, 141.

restraint: "[The insane] quickly perceive, or if not, they are informed on the first occasion, that their treatment depends in great measure on their conduct."[39] If a patient misbehaved, he was simply demoted to a level where "this conduct is routinely dealt with and to a degree allowed," but where the available social amenities were sharply curtailed. Only by exhibiting a suitable willingness to control his disagreeable propensities was he allowed to obtain his former privileges, always with the implied threat that their grant was purely conditional and subject to revocation. As Goffman has pointed out, "What we find here (and do not on the outside) is a very model of what psychologists might call a learning situation—all hinged on the process of an admitted giving in."[40] The importance of this approach as a mechanism for controlling the uncontrollable is perhaps indicated by the persistent employment of architecture to permit classification, long after its use for the other purposes the reformers had in mind had been abandoned. (See Figure 9.)

For beyond the utility of physical barriers to enforce moral divisions in the patient population, the building's design was important for the reformers in countless other ways. Their ideal institution was to be a home, where the patients were known and treated as individuals, where the mind was constantly stimulated and encouraged to return to its "natural" state. Such a nicely calibrated treatment could be administered only in an institution of manageable size. The Retreat itself had begun with only thirty patients, though later expansion almost doubled that number. For the new pauper asylums to be built at public expense, it was felt that these standards could be relaxed, though not by much. "It is evident," said Sir William Ellis,

> that for the patients to have all the care they require, there should never be more than can, with comfort, be attended to: from 100 to 120, are as many as ought to be in any one house; where they are beyond that the individual cases cease to excite the attention they ought; and if once that is the case, not one half the good can be expected to result.[41]

Others thought that the number might be raised to 200, or even 250, but all the major authorities agreed that it should not rise beyond this point.[42]

39. Ibid. For further discussions of the importance of classification, see, for instance, Maximilian Jacobi, *On the Construction and Management of Hospitals for the Insane* (London: Churchill, 1841); and W. A. F. Browne, *What Asylums Were, Are, and Ought to Be* (Edinburgh, Black, 1837).

40. Erving Goffman, *Asylums: Essays on the Social Situation of Mental Patients and Other Inmates* (Garden City, New York: Doubleday, 1961), 361–62.

41. W. C. Ellis, *A Treatise on the Nature, Symptoms, Causes, and Treatment of Insanity* . . . (London: Holdsworth, 1838), 17.

42. See, for example, Jacobi, *Construction and Management*, 23; "Report of the Metropolitan Commissioners in Lunacy, 1844," *Sessional Papers of the House of Lords*, vol. 26 (1844), 23.

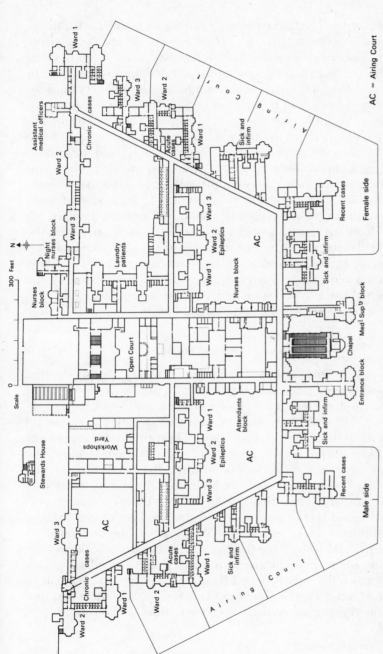

Figure 9. Ground floor plan of the Claybury County Asylum at Woodford, Essex, begun in 1887. The asylum was designed for 2,000 patients. In addition to its four "curative" asylums (of which this was one), Middlesex also made use of two asylums for incurables at Caterham and Leavesden (see Figures 13 and 14), each taking approximately 2,500 patients. As with the hospital and prison, the architecture of the asylum developed in association with the system of classifying and organizing the inmates. Based on drawings from *The Builder*, 23 November 1889, and from H. C. Burdett, *Hospitals and Asylums of the World* (London: Churchill, 1893), 158.

The building itself should emphasize as little as possible the idea of imprisonment or confinement. It should be sited where the patients could enjoy the benefits of fresh, bracing country air, and where there was an extensive and pleasing view of the surrounding countryside to divert the mind from its morbid fantasies. The insane were very sensitive to their surroundings, and though "some have been disposed to contemn as superfluous the attention paid to the lesser feelings of the patients, there is great reason to believe it has been of considerable advantage."[43] It was thus not an extravagance to design and build institutions that emphasized cheerfulness by being aesthetically pleasing. The architect could help secure these ends even through small and apparently insignificant details: for example, by substituting iron for wooden frames in the sash windows, security could be maintained without the need for iron bars.[44] Similarly, patients ought to be able to change rooms in the course of the day to get a change of scenery, and provision ought always to be made for extensive grounds to be attached to an asylum. These features would allow scope for recreation and harmless diversions, the kinds of mental and physical stimulation that would counteract the tendency of insanity to degenerate into outright fatuity.

"MONASTERIES OF THE MAD"

Such utopian reveries bore little relationship to reality. During the first twenty years after the passage of the permissive County Asylums Act of 1808, the ten asylums built were all of moderate size, averaging 115 inmates each. (Cheshire County Asylum, built for 110 patients [Figure 10] is typical of the asylums built in this period.) Thereafter, however, county asylums rapidly and inexorably grew ever larger. By the mid-1840s, the average size was in the region of 300 inmates; the Lancashire Asylum contained over 600 inmates; and the Middlesex Asylum at Hanwell as many as a thousand.[45] Thus, almost from the outset, local magistrates exhibited a profound skepticism about the reformers' arguments in favor of small institutions. Faced with the problem of providing for a horde of derelict paupers, they opted for the concrete economies of scale over the hypothetical savings small curative institutions would allegedly produce.

Subsequent events only stiffened their resolve. Over the last half of the nineteenth century, the number of certified lunatics increased dramatically, multiplying more than five times, from 20,809 in 1844 to

43. Tuke, *Description of the Retreat,* 102.

44. At the Retreat itself, the use of this device "and the garden in front being defended from the road only by a neat common hedge, prevent, entirely, the appearance of a place of confinement" (ibid., 94).

45. "Report of the Metropolitan Commissioners," 23–24, 209.

Figure 10. Cheshire County Asylum, built in 1828. Accommodating 110 patients, the asylum already looks more "institutional" than its supposed inspiration, the York Retreat. Within a generation, such small-scale asylums had vanished. Engraving by Dean. (Courtesy of the Wellcome Trustees.)

117,200 in 1904, while the population merely doubled. In part this massive increase reflected the failure of the asylum doctors to cure more than a fraction of those they treated, with the consequent accumulation of chronic cases. But beyond this, the very existence and expansion of the asylum system created an increased demand for its own services. The availability of the "humanitarian" and "scientific" alternative of treatment in a specialized institution operated steadily to reduce family and community tolerance, encouraging the abandonment of the struggle to cope with the troublesome, and thereby inducing both the experts and their public to take a more expansive view of what constituted madness. In Andrew Wynter's words,

> The very imposing appearance of these establishments acts as an advertisement to draw patients towards them. If we make a convenient lumber room, we all know how speedily it becomes filled up with lumber. The county asylum is the mental lumber room of the surrounding district; friends are only too willing, in their poverty, to place away the human encumbrance of the family in a palatial building at county expense.[46]

Even the experts in the magistrates' employ, the asylum superintendents, conceded that a steadily dwindling proportion of this enormous mass of lunatics—drawn overwhelmingly from the lower classes—was susceptible of cure. By 1875, they were estimating that fewer than eight in a hundred of their charges would recover,[47] a prophecy that proved remarkably accurate.[48] The doctors were disposed to blame this low cure rate not on the bankruptcy of their own therapeutic techniques,[49] but on the failure of their patients to seek treatment soon enough following the onset of insanity, coupled with the deleterious effects of their employers' parsimony. But such complaints, while useful for bolstering the alienists' sagging morale, had no discernible impact on the authorities' actions.

If magistrates were unwilling to spend "extravagant" sums of money on pauper lunatics, they were still less inclined to do so for *incurable* pauper lunatics. Propelled by the overriding desire to economize, local justices almost everywhere adopted the practice of tacking wing after wing, story upon story, building next to building, in a haphazard and fortuitous fashion, as they strove to keep pace with the demand for accommodation for more and more lunatics. In the weary words of one

46. [Andrew Wynter], "Non-restraint in the Treatment of the Insane," *Edinburgh Review* 131 (1870): 221. For a more extended discussion of this point, see Chapter 9 below.

47. House of Commons, *Report of the Select Committee on the Operation of the Lunacy Law* (1877), 386.

48. Commissioners in Lunacy, *Annual Report* (1891), 96–99.

49. In fact, however, even in private asylums geared to the upper classes, with no shortage of money, staff, or facilities, reported cure-rates declined to abysmally low levels. Between 1880 and 1890 they fluctuated between 6 and 7 1/2 percent per year of those under treatment.

asylum administrator, "Once christen the disease insanity, and the cost of treatment shrinks in the public estimation, to less than that of living in health."[50] Remorselessly, the size of the average asylum grew, climbing to 542 beds by 1870 and to 961 beds by 1900. By the last quarter of the nineteenth century, asylums such as the one at Claybury in Essex (Figure 9), the fourth county asylum for Middlesex, were almost commonplace. Accommodating upwards of 2,000 patients and several hundred staff, these places were "more like towns than houses" and partook "rather of the nature of industrial than medical establishments,"[51] but they sufficed to "herd lunatics together . . . where they can be more easily visited and accounted for by the authorities."[52]

Despite their failure to live up to their original promise, asylums remained a convenient place to get rid of inconvenient people. The community was used by now to disposing of the derelict and troublesome in an institution, where, as one doctor put it, "they are for the most part harmless because they are kept out of harm's way."[53] In other respects, too, confinement provided its own rationale. Why else were lunatics locked up in the first place, unless it was unsafe for them to be at large? Since the public was convinced (not without supporting "evidence" supplied by the asylum doctors) that "these establishments are the necessary places of detention of troops of violent madness, too dangerous to be allowed outside the walls,"[54] asylums were now seen as an essential guarantor of the social order, as well as an important symbolic reminder of the awful consequences of nonconformity. Reflecting these related demands for "economy, . . . safe custody, and physical repression," the asylum designers produced a "bald and monotonous architecture, which has scarcely recognized more than physical necessities."[55]

Homogeneous in these respects, asylum design did vary in others. In particular, it is possible to distinguish three basic architectural types, though some institutions took on intermediate forms. In the first place, some asylums were what has been termed "irregular or conglomerate" in construction—that is, they were largely a hodgepodge of miscellaneous structures, exhibiting little or no unity of style and often composed of

50. P. J. Bancroft, "The Bearing of Hospital Adjustments upon the Efficiency of Remedial and Meliorating Treatment in Mental Diseases," Appendix to H. C. Burdett, *Hospitals and Asylums of the World*, 2 vols. (London: Churchill, 1891), 2:271.

51. House of Commons, *Select Committee on the Care and Treatment of Lunatics* (1859), 99, evidence of Lord Shaftesbury; J. T. Arlidge, *On the State of Lunacy and the Legal Provision for the Insane* (London: Churchill, 1859), 36.

52. J. C. Bucknill, *The Care of the Insane and Their Legal Control* (London: Macmillan, 1880), 122.

53. Hanwell County Asylum, *Twenty-fifth Annual Report* (1870), 36.

54. [Wynter], "Non-restraint," 224.

55. Bancroft, "Hospital Adjustments," 271.

buildings of widely varying age. A number of asylums of this sort were housed in buildings converted from other uses. Such was the case at the Suffolk County Asylum, for example. Originally a conversion of an existing workhouse, it opened in 1827; with additions and further remodeling, it was still being used to house over 500 patients at the end of the nineteenth century. Other asylums were originally purpose-built to a more or less symmetrical design and only gradually acquired this higgledy-piggledy appearance. Typical of these last was the Gloucester County Asylum, which by 1890 had grown from its original 120 to some 780 inmates. As its superintendent confessed, "In order to defer as long as possible the evil day of building a second asylum, all sorts of queer, fantastic additions have been made to the original building, until it now resembles nothing so much as a rabbit warren." [56]

Certainly the most frequently used asylum design, in England at least, was the corridor type. As its name suggests, these asylums consisted of a series of corridors with wards and other rooms opening off them, connected together in wings at right angles to one another, or in echelon. Usually, as at Hanwell (Figure 11), these corridors doubled as the day rooms, to which the patients were consigned on being expelled from their sleeping quarters. While some asylums had rooms on only one side of the corridors, others had rooms on both, adding to the problems of securing sufficient ventilation and light. At Colney Hatch (Figure 12), built on the latter plan, "the wards were tunnel-like and dark at the centre, ill-heated, sparsely furnished, and unpainted, with lavatories opening directly into the gallery, and deficient wash and bath facilities." [57] Here, as in other institutions built on this plan, the central portion of the building contained the main entrance and administrative department, as well as a large center hall for exercise in wet weather. [58] Regarded on its completion as the most modern asylum in Europe, it was from the outset designed for more than 1,000 patients. In consequence, its wards and passages taken together were more than six miles long. Subsequently, it grew still more enormous: within a decade and a half it had expanded to contain over 2,000 inmates. [59] Contemporaries remarked that the exterior was "almost palatial" in character.

> Its facade, of nearly one third of a mile, is broken at intervals by Italian campaniles and cupolas, and the whole aspect of the exterior leads the visitor to expect an interior of commensurable pretensions. He no sooner

56. Cited in Burdett, *Hospitals and Asylums*, 2:61.

57. Richard A. Hunter and Ida Macalpine, *Psychiatry for the Poor* (London: Dawsons, 1973), 30–31.

58. In the standard plan, the central structure also contained reception rooms, a dining hall, kitchens, and perhaps the superintendent's accommodation.

59. Commissioners in Lunacy, *Annual Report* (1867), 62.

Figure 11. Twelfth Night entertainments at Hanwell Lunatic Asylum. The illustration was designed to display the achievements of lunacy reform to the public at large. The group in the right foreground is the Asylum Committee and its guests. Behind them stretches the cavernous corridor that, save on this festive occasion (a Christmas party), served as a day room for male patients. (From the *Illustrated London News* 12 [1848]: 27.)

crosses the threshold, however, than the scene changes. As he passes along the corridor, which runs from end to end of the building, he is oppressed with the gloom; the little light admitted by the loopholed windows is absorbed by the inky ashphalte paving, and coupled with the low vaulting of the ceiling gives a stifling feeling and a sense of detention as in a prison. The staircases scarcely equal those of a workhouse; plaster there is none, and a coat of paint, or whitewash, does not even conceal the rugged surface of the brickwork. In the wards a similar state of affairs exists: . . . of human interest they possess nothing.[60]

"Long, narrow, gloomy and comfortless," each room contained as many as eight inmates. And from their dormitories and dayrooms the inmates escaped only for brief periods into "airing courts [which], although in some instances carefully planted, are uninviting and prison-like."[61] The consequences of this situation were recorded even in the reports of the official supervisors of the whole asylum enterprise, the lunacy commissioners. Such structures were characterized by

60. "Lunatic Asylums," *Quarterly Review* 101 (1857): 353.
61. Granville, *Care and Cure*, 1 : 154; Edward Pierce, "Report on a Visit to Some European Asylums," in Massachusetts State Board of Charities, *Tenth Report* (1873), 114–15.

Figure 12. Colney Hatch Lunatic Asylum, opened in 1851. The original building, with its facade of a third of a mile, accommodated over 1,000 patients on the corridor plan, the second main type of asylum design and the most frequently used in mid-nineteenth-century England. According to one report, its interior was characterized by "long cold corridors, huge wards, and a general aspect of cheerlessness." Wood engraving by Laing. (Courtesy of the Wellcome Trustees.)

the utter absence of any means for engaging the attention of the Patients, interesting them in any occupations or amusements, or affording them a sufficient variety of exercise outdoors. Besides a large number crouching on the floors, many were in or upon their beds, some for very trivial causes, and some as if they had merely sought relief there from the noise and monotony of the galleries.[62]

Finally, in the late 1860s, a third basic building type made its appearance—the so-called pavilion asylum (see Figure 13). This was characterized by the replication of uniform blocks in two parallel rows, each housing between 150 and 200 patients, one row for male patients and the other for females. Between the buildings assigned to each sex was a third row of buildings, containing the administration, accommodation for the superintendent and staff, and that critical part of every well-wrought Victorian asylum, the chapel, in which the inmates could be brought the consolations of organized religion. The first asylums of this type, those at Caterham and Leavesden, were identical institutions explicitly designed to siphon off the most hopeless and decrepit cases from the existing metropolitan asylums. Scarcely any of these "patients" were expected to recover, and few did (less than 1 percent in an average year). Here, then, the drive for economy reached its apotheosis, in institutions housing more than 2,000 inmates accommodated in huge, barnlike dormitories, two to a building, of eighty beds apiece. As the floor plan reveals (Figure 14), even at the outset each dormitory was partitioned once only, into two groups of forty beds, with scarcely room for passage between them; and subsequently, they were to be "adapted" to cram in still more patients. Apart from this barren, featureless room, the inmates' only change of scene was to be removed *en masse* to the building's single day room, 105 feet long by 36 feet wide and 14 feet high—"home" for some 160 human beings.[63]

Everything was now "well arranged for the storage (we use the word advisedly) of imbeciles."[64] The rapid collapse of the asylum's pretensions to provide cure in the post-1845 era had been matched by the decay and disappearance of all the crucial features of moral treatment—those elements that were supposed to distinguish the asylum from the prison. Nowhere was this more apparent than in the physical appearance of these institutions. The cheerful and pleasing architecture, which in the initial formulations of moral treatment was to have played such a vital role in creating and sustaining the optimistic and familylike atmosphere so essential to success, had come to be considered an "unnecessary cost," so that the buildings themselves now offered mute testimony that the

62. Commissioners in Lunacy, *Annual Report* (1862), 138.
63. *The Builder* 26 (1868): 541–42.
64. Burdett, *Hospitals and Asylums*, 1:8.

Figure 13. Design for asylums at Leavesden Woodside, near Watford, and at Caterham, near Croydon, 1868. This drawing shows a typical example of the pavilion asylum, the third basic type developed in the late nineteenth century to provide efficient storage for pauper lunatics. The emphasis on a healthy environment in a "country setting," as well as social distance from the town, is well illustrated in this drawing. From: *The Builder*, 25 July 1868, 551.

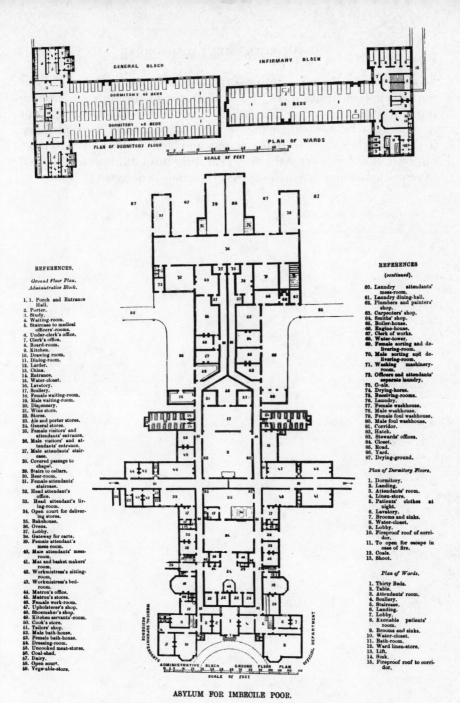

ASYLUM FOR IMBECILE POOR.

Figure 14. Floor plan of the general, infirmary, and administrative blocks of the asylums for the chronic insane at Caterham and Leavesden, 1868. Note the spacing of the beds in the dormitories. For lack of room, the patients' clothes were stored outside each dormitory at night.
From: *The Builder*, 25 July 1868, 550.

asylum was now "a mere refuge or house of detention for a mass of hopeless and incurable cases."[65] The distressing truth thus confronting those who looked back on the work of the reformers in the early part of the century was "how closely the complaints and aims of the reformers, in the days when there were few county and borough asylums, resemble our own. It is in respect to the very evils these institutions were designed to remedy that they are themselves conspicuously defective."[66]

65. Granville, *Care and Cure*, 1 : 8.
66. Ibid, 1 : 86.

CHAPTER NINE

Was Insanity Increasing?

In a Maudsley lecture delivered to the Royal College of Psychiatrists in late 1982, Edward Hare contended that the incidence of serious mental disorder had increased sharply over the course of the nineteenth century. He argued that this rise in the number of mad folk accounted for the abrupt development of medical interest in lunacy at the beginning of the century and for the rapid publication of a series of early-nineteenth-century medical treatises on insanity. Moreover, in a wholly "straightforward" way, and without resort to the complications introduced by sociologists, the existence of this "epidemic" provided "a medical explanation of the asylum era." In his view, one could take the argument a step further: the madness that fueled all these changes was what the psychiatric profession now calls schizophrenia; and the transformation of "schizophrenia" in this era from a rare to an all-too-common disorder reflects its probable etiology, as a virulent viral infection laying waste the susceptible members of society.

Dr. Hare's contention is not the first attempt at psychiatric reductionism, nor is it likely to be the last. An earlier flirtation with an infectious etiology for the major psychoses (this time of a bacteriological rather than a viral sort) was attended with some rather bizarre and untoward consequences for those deemed victims of toxicity.[1] One trusts that its latest incarnation will not be greeted so ingenuously and uncritically.

Portions of Chapter 9 appeared in the *British Journal of Psychiatry*, Volume 144, 1984, pp. 432–36, and are reprinted by permission.

1. See Andrew Scull, "Desperate Remedies: A Gothic Tale of Madness and Modern Medicine," *Psychological Medicine* 17 (1987): 561–77.

I cannot pretend to possess Dr. Hare's talent for diagnosis at a distance (indeed, for diagnosis *tout court*); and I concede that the ingenuity of his explanation, its ability to reduce surface complexities to the simplicity of a single underlying somatic cause, would do credit to a professor at the Grand Academy of Lagado.[2] But I confess that in the last analysis I find his account a trifle speculative, requiring perhaps too large a leap of faith for one of my agnostic disposition. Accordingly, in what follows, I offer the sketch of a rather different version of events, one that leaves but a minute place for the microbes, even though it insists (with Dr. Hare) that insanity was indeed increasing over the course of the nineteenth century.

Was Insanity Increasing?

Upon reflection, one quickly comes to recognize that Society must protect not only the life, but also the property and honor of individuals, as well as public order. Hence the number of the insane that can, on various counts, be prejudicial to public safety is singularly increased.

—J. FALRET,
Des aliénés dangereux et des asiles spéciaux pour aliénés

One of the central paradoxes of the Victorian reforms in the treatment of the mentally ill was the curious fact that the "scientific" discovery of mental illness and the adoption of a more rational approach based on this discovery—an approach that aimed at treating and curing lunatics, rather than neglecting them or incarcerating them in a gaol or workhouse—were associated with an explosive growth in the number of insane people. Edward Hare's recent Maudsley Lecture raises again the interesting question of whether or not this surge reflects a true increase in the incidence of mental illness in nineteenth-century England. As he correctly notes, the aggregate data collected at the time do not allow a "decisive answer," but I am pleased that his reassessment of the probabilities led him to endorse my prior conclusion that its incidence was indeed increasing.[1]

Hare does dispute, however, the explanation I offered of this increase, which attributed much of it to the development of a more expansive view of madness. Instead of an expansion of the boundaries of what constituted mental illness, he argues that the growth in numbers reflects

2. See Jonathan Swift, *Gulliver's Travels* (New York: Modern Library, 1958), 142–54.

1. Andrew Scull, *Museums of Madness: The Social Organization of Insanity in Nineteenth-Century England* (London: Allen Lane; New York: St. Martin's Press, 1979).

a real rise in the most serious forms of mental disorder, more specifically, "a slow epidemic of schizophrenia."[2] The dispute between us is not purely an academic debate (in the bad sense of that term) since Hare argues that the adoption of his explanation provides some "speculative" support for "a medical explanation of the asylum era" and for a viral etiology of schizophrenia.[3] I should therefore like to point to some of the evidence that seems instead to favor my own hypothesis, recognizing (as does Hare) that in this matter we can at best obtain an approximation of the truth, given the data with which we have to work.

At least prior to the adoption of the third edition of the *Diagnostic and Statistical Manual* of the American Psychiatric Association in 1980, the research evidence demonstrates that even twentieth-century psychiatric diagnoses lacked reliability and validity. Diagnosis remained dependent on clinical supposition and consensus, with the consequence that "the reliability of diagnoses of mental disorders, including those considered most severe, measured by independent rater agreement, often failed to rise over 50 per cent."[4] Everything we know of the practice of nineteenth-century psychiatrists suggests an even stronger reliance on clinical experience to legitimize and certify the authenticity of the individual practitioners' decisions. Certainly, many of the leading men in the field devoted a good deal of their energies to the elaboration of complex nosologies, encompassing a plethora of subtypes and varieties of insanity, but as Henry Monro noted, those who tried to rely on these categories in their practice were soon obliged to abandon the attempt in despair:

> All who have charge of asylums must well know how very different the clear and distinct classification of books is from that medley of symptoms which is presented by real cases. . . . It is useless to attempt to paint pictures with more vivid colours than nature presents, and worse than useless if practical men (or rather, I would say, men obliged to practice) receive these pictures as true representatives.[5]

2. E. Hare, "Was Insanity on the Increase?" *British Journal of Psychiatry* 142 (1983): 451.

3. Ibid.

4. S. J. Morse, "A Preference for Liberty: The Case Against Involuntary Commitment of the Mentally Disordered," in *The Court of Last Resort: Mental Illness and the Law,* by Carol A. B. Warren, with contributions by Stephen J. Morse and Jack Zusman (Chicago: University of Chicago Press, 1982), 82. See also R. L. Spitzer and J. Fleiss, "A Re-analysis of the Reliability of Psychiatric Diagnosis," *British Journal of Psychiatry* 125 (1974): 341–47; A. T. Beck, "The Reliability of Psychiatric Diagnosis: 1. A Critique of Systematic Studies," *American Journal of Psychiatry* 119 (1962): 210–16; L. J. Chapman and J. P. Chapman, "Illusory Correlations as an Obstacle to the Use of Valid Psycho-diagnosis Signs," *Journal of Abnormal Psychology* 74 (1969): 271–80.

5. Henry Monro, *Remarks on Insanity: Its Nature and Treatment* (London: Churchill, 1850), 1–2.

Notwithstanding all efforts to alleviate the situation, and with the exception of extreme cases of violent mania or complete dementia, alienists were forced to confess that "the task of declaring this to be reason and that insanity is exceedingly embarrassing and, to a great degree, arbitrary. . . . No palpable distinction exists, no line of demarcation can be traced between the sane and the insane."[6] Thus, "the practitioner's own mind must be the criterion by which he infers the insanity of any other person."[7]

"Such emphasis," as Freidson has noted, "is directly contrary to the emphasis of science on shared knowledge, collected and tested on the basis of methods meant to overcome the deficiencies of the individual experience. And its efficacy and reliability are suspect."[8] In this instance, beyond the initial hard core of easily recognizable behavioral and/or mental disturbance, the boundary between the pathological and the normal was left extraordinarily vague and indeterminate. Hence the frequent and embarrassing disputes between alienists over individual cases in the courts.[9] In the circumstances, the assumption that identifying who is and who is not mentally ill was an activity governed by some uniform, objective, and unchanging standard will not survive critical scrutiny.

As Hare notes, I have suggested that asylum doctors' professional self-interest provided one set of motives for the adoption of an expansionary view of madness.[10] But other forces also prompted them to behave in this fashion. On humanitarian grounds, for example, since doctors were convinced that asylums were benevolent and therapeutic institutions and that laymen were incompetent to cope with, and liable to maltreat, the mentally ill, they were impelled to seek out still more cases rather than reject any that were proffered. Moreover, professional "imperialism" provides only one—and to my mind by no means that most important—reason to suspect an ever-wider practical application of the term "mental illness." The asylum provided a convenient and culturally legitimate alternative to coping with "intolerable" individuals within the family, offering, if its proponents were to be believed, a level of care and possibilities of cure far beyond what even the most dedicated family could hope to provide in its midst. So far from being blamed, families were encouraged to place their mentally unbalanced relatives where they could receive professional care and treatment at the earliest pos-

6. W. A. F. Browne, *What Asylums Were, Are, and Ought to Be* (Edinburgh: Black, 1837), 8.

7. J. Haslam, *Observations on Madness and Melancholy*, 2d ed. (London: Callow, 1809), 37. See also T. Mayo, *Medical Testimony and Evidence in Cases of Lunacy* (London: Parker, 1854).

8. Eliot Freidson, *Profession of Medicine: A Study in the Sociology of Applied Knowledge* (New York: Dodd, Mead, 1970), 347.

9. Roger Smith, *Trial by Medicine: Insanity and Responsibility in Victorian Trials* (Edinburgh: Edinburgh University Press, 1981).

10. Hare, "Was Insanity on the Increase?," 453.

sible moment. The attraction was obviously greatest for those with fewer resources for coping with the dependent and economically unproductive. Significantly, the statistics demonstrate that by far the largest portion of the increase in insanity occurred among those drawn from the lowest socioeconomic classes.

Contemporary observers frequently commented on the dynamics of this process: the superintendent of the Northampton General Lunatic Asylum noted in his 1858 report that "persons in humble life soon become wearied of the presence of their insane relatives and regardless of their age desire relief. Persons above this class more readily tolerate infirmity and command time and attention. The occasion may never occur in the one case, which is urgent in the other. Hence an Asylum to the poor and needy is the only refuge. To a man of many friends it is the last resort." [11] In the words of another asylum superintendent, "Poverty, truly, is the great evil: it has no friends able to help. Persons in middle society do not put away their aged relatives because of their infirmities, and I think it was not always the custom for worn out paupers to be sent to the asylum. . . . It is one more of the ways in which, at this day, the apparent increase of insanity is sustained. It is not a real increase, since the aged have ever been subject to this sort of unsoundness." [12]

Moreover, the level of disordered behavior or dependency that a family could not or would not put up with was not fixed and immutable, but likely to vary over time, with individual circumstances and with the gradual growth of the perception that there existed alternatives to the retention of the disturbed and troublesome within a domestic setting. (Such a pattern is, however, much more difficult to reconcile to the hypothesis of a viral-induced epidemic of schizophrenia.) Finally, as Maudsley himself suggested, the central government contributed significantly to the process by enacting legislation "whereby the government said in effect, to parish officials, 'We will pay you a premium of four shillings a head on every pauper whom you can by hook or crook make out to be a lunatic and send into an asylum' [thus putting] a direct premium on the manufacture of lunacy." [13]

Hare makes much of the fact that recovery rates declined over time in Victorian asylums, arguing that "milder" cases should have been more

11. Northampton General Lunatic Asylum, *Annual Report* (1858), 11.

12. James Edmund Huxley, quoted in John T. Arlidge, *On the State of Lunacy and the Legal Provision for the Insane* (London: Churchill, 1859), 95. For further discussion of Huxley's views on this subject, see Nicholas Hervey, "The Lunacy Commission 1845–60, with Special Reference to the Implementation of Policy in Kent and Surrey" (Ph.D. dissertation, Bristol University, 1987), chap. 6. (Huxley was superintendent of the Kent County Asylum.) John Charles Bucknill, superintendent of the Devon County Asylum and founding editor of the *[Asylum] Journal of Mental Science*, was equally convinced that it was poverty, not illness, that prompted many asylum admissions.

13. Henry Maudsley, "The Alleged Increase of Insanity," *Journal of Mental Science* 23 (1877): 45.

likely to recover. It is, however, not at all clear why we should accept this argument. First, there is no obvious warrant for the claim that Victorian psychiatry was more successful in treating milder cases (unless one tautologically assumes an identity between "milder" and "more treatable"). Indeed, "mild" mental symptoms often coexisted with chronic and incurable underlying disease states. Bucknill, for example, while superintendent at the Devon County Asylum, found that

> patients have been admitted suffering from heart disease, aneurism, and cancer, with scarcely a greater amount of melancholy than might be expected to take place in many sane persons at the near and certain prospect of death. Some have been received in the last stages of consumption, with that amount of cerebral excitement so common in this disorder; others have been received in the delirium or stupor of typhus; while in several cases the mental condition was totally unknown after admission and must have been unknown before, since an advanced condition of bodily disease prevented speech, and the expression of intelligence or emotion, either normal or morbid.[14]

Such catalogues of decrepit and all but moribund admissions were anything but exceptional;[15] and in the light of evidence of this sort, Hare's contention that the admission of milder cases "should have decreased" the asylum death rate[16] does not seem particularly plausible.

Second, there are other, at least equally plausible ways of accounting for the decline in cure rates. Many Victorian critics of the asylum system, including Maudsley himself, thought that there was a clear connection between increasing size and decreasing therapeutic efficacy. As John Arlidge put it,

> In a colossal refuge for the insane, a person may be said to lose his individuality and to become a member of a machine so put together, as to move with precise regularity and invariable routine; a triumph of skill adapted to show how such unpromising materials as crazy men and women may be drilled into order and guided by rule, but not an apparatus calculated to restore their pristine condition and their independent self-governing existence. In all cases admitting of recovery, or of material amelioration, a gigantic asylum is a gigantic evil, and figuratively speaking, a manufactory of chronic insanity.[17]

Modern research on "institutionalism"[18] surely lends considerable credence to this hypothesis. And we know that the average size of English

14. Quoted in Arlidge, *State of Lunacy*, 96.

15. See, for example, Caterham Lunatic Asylum, *Annual Report* (1873); Hanwell Asylum, *Annual Report* (1875, 1880); Commissioners in Lunacy, *Annual Report* (1881).

16. Hare, "Was Insanity on the Increase?," 449.

17. Arlidge, *State of Lunacy*, 102. See also J. C. Bucknill, *The Care of the Insane and their Legal Control* (London: Macmillan, 1880).

18. J. K. Wing, "Institutionalism in Mental Hospitals," *British Journal of Social and Clinical Psychiatry* 1 (1962): 38; J. K. Wing and G. W. Brown, *Institutionalism and Schizo-*

county asylums rose remorselessly through the course of the nineteenth century, from just over a hundred patients in 1827 to almost a thousand by the end of the century, paralleling the development of a steadily more hopeless and "institutional" environment. Increasingly, within such mammoth institutions, "the classification generally made is for the purpose of shelving cases; that is to say, practically it has that effect. . . . In consequence of the treatment not being personal, but simply a treatment in classes, there is a tendency to make whole classes sink down into a sort of chronic state. . . . I think they come under a sort of routine discipline which ends in their passing into a state of dementia."[19]

Almost certainly, then, increasing size and the associated changes in the treatment of the inmate population had negative effects on cure rates. In turn, this situation provoked a steadily more pessimistic assessment of the prognosis for insanity among alienists themselves, forced to account for the falling rate of cures despite the advances of medical science. As explanations of mental illness were ever more frequently couched in terms of structural brain disease, defective heredity, and Morelian degeneration, so there emerged an entrenched expectation that most cases of mental illness would prove to be incurable. Expectations of this sort, through their effects on staff morale and the quality of care provided (to say nothing of the negative placebo effect), became a relentlessly self-fulfilling prophecy, further diminishing the underlying recovery rate while providing tautological "proof" of their essential accuracy. I suggest it is this combination of factors, rather than "the admission of less favourable cases,"[20] that accounts for the dismal therapeutic results of asylum care in the late nineteenth century—though for obvious reasons this was a conclusion that both the psychiatric profession and the lunacy commissioners were reluctant even to consider.

Beyond this, a good deal of contemporary testimony supports my suggestion that the boundaries of what constituted committable madness expanded during the 1800s. A wide range of nineteenth-century observers commented on how much laxer the standards were for judging a poor person to be insane, and how much readier both local poor-law authorities and lower-class families were to commit decrepit and troublesome people to the asylum, individuals who, had they come from the middle and upper classes, would never have been diagnosed as insane.

phrenia (Cambridge: Cambridge University Press, 1970); R. Barton, *Institutional Neurosis*, 2d ed. (Bristol: Wright, 1965); Ivan Belknap, *Human Problems of a State Mental Hospital* (New York: McGraw-Hill, 1956); A. H. Stanton and M. S. Schwartz, *The Mental Hospital: A Study of Institutional Participation in Psychiatric Illness and Treatment* (New York: Basic Books, 1954).

19. J. Mortimer Granville, in House of Commons, *Report of the Select Committee on the Operation of the Lunacy Law* (1877): 396–97.

20. Commissioners in Lunacy, 1899, quoted in Hare, "Was Insanity on the Increase?," 449.

In the words of William Ley, superintendent of the Littlemore Asylum, "Orders for the admission of Paupers into the County Asylum are given more freely than would be thought right as regards the imputation of Lunacy, towards persons equally debilitated in body and mind who have the means of providing their own care."[21] Over time, this tendency grew more marked. Just over twenty years later, John Joseph Henley, the general inspector of the Local Government Board, informed a Select Committee of the House of Commons that in his inspectors' experience, "there is a disposition among all classes now not to bear with the troubles that may arise in their own houses. If a person is troublesome from senile dementia, dirty in his habits, they will not bear it now. Persons are more easily removed to an asylum than they were a few years ago."[22] Workhouse authorities, too, according to the medical inspector of the London workhouses, routinely used asylums to "relieve their wards of many old people who are suffering from nothing else than the natural failing of old age" as well as to rid themselves of troublesome people in general.[23]

As a result, Mortimer Granville noted, "it is impossible not to recognise the presence of a considerable number of 'patients' in these asylums who are not lunatic. They may be weak, dirty, troublesome, but they are certainly no[t] . . . affected with mental disease."[24] Those who had been acquainted with the county asylum system from its very earliest years could not help but notice the change in the implicit definition of mental illness, the enormous and striking difference "between the inmates of the old madhouses and the modern asylum—the former containing only obvious and dangerous cases of lunacy, the latter containing great numbers of quiet and harmless patients whose insanity is often difficult to determine."[25] At least for these well-placed observers, there could be no question but that

> the law providing that madmen, dangerous to themselves and others, shall be secluded in madhouses for absolutely needful care and protection, has been extended in its application to large classes of persons who would never have been considered lunatics when this legislation was entered upon. Since 1845, medical science has discovered whole new realms of lunacy, and the nicer touch of a finikin civilization has shrunk from the contact of imperfect fellow creatures, and thus the manifold receptacles of lunacy are filled to overflow with a population more nearly resembling that which is still at large.[26]

21. Littlemore Asylum, *Annual Report* (Oxfordshire, 1855), 5.
22. House of Commons, *Report of the Select Committee*, 166.
23. Ibid., 152. See also Commissioners in Lunacy, *Annual Report* (1861): 15.
24. J. Mortimer Granville, *The Care and Cure of the Insane*, 2 vols. (London: Hardwicke and Bogue, 1877), 1:264.
25. Bucknill, *Care of the Insane*, xxvii.
26. Ibid., 4.

Hare argues that mild cases could not have provided the reservoir from which the increased asylum population was drawn, because such cases would not have seemed sufficiently urgent to warrant the construction of so many beds. But the definition of "urgent" in this case is obviously a matter of complex social construction, not something engraved in stone. I see no reason to doubt that those committing patients in 1880 were convinced that their reasons for doing so were urgent and compelling—though one may reasonably question whether the same justifications would have seemed equally compelling some thirty or forty years earlier.[27] Nor should it surprise us that what constituted adequate grounds for commitment should shift over time in this fashion. After all, the past quarter of a century has witnessed a move in just the reverse direction, toward a much more restricted view of the appropriate criteria for involuntary commitment.[28]

CONCLUSION

Ultimately, of course, the most satisfactory way of deciding between the rival hypotheses offered by Hare and myself would be to look at a random sampling of admissions over time, to see whether the increase occurs among mild or severe cases. Unfortunately, there must be serious doubt about whether the quality of the surviving records is adequate for this purpose. Case records for upper-class asylums were extensive, as in

27. Comparative cross-sectional data provide substantial presumptive evidence in support of my argument that the supply of asylum beds itself altered the apparent incidence of insanity, and thus the demand for institutional provision for the insane. As Nicholas Hervey points out, for example ("Lunacy Commission," 379, n. 82), the boroughs of Maidstone and Canterbury were of equal size and located in the same county. The former, which provided an asylum for its insane, rapidly acquired double the number of pauper lunatics to be found in the latter, which did not. The lunacy commissioners noted this phenomenon in their 1861 *Report,* but entirely missed its significance. By contrast, Edward Jarvis had concluded, using statistics from Massachusetts, that the rate of committal to mental hospitals was always greatest in the immediately adjacent areas and decreased as the distance from the asylum increased. See "The Influence of Distance from and Proximity to an Insane Hospital, on Its Use by Any People," *Boston Medical and Surgical Journal* 42 (17 April 1850): 209–22. In a subsequent article, Jarvis discussed how the asylum created an expanded demand for its services: "The opening of these establishments for the cure or protection of lunatics, the spread of their reports, the extension of the knowledge of their character, power, and usefulness, by means of the patients they protect and cure, have created, and continue to create, more and more interest in the study of insanity, and more confidence in its curability. Consequently, more and more persons and families, who, or such as who, formerly kept their insane friends and relations at home, or allowed them to stroll about the streets or country, now believe, that they can be restored, or improved, or, at least made more comfortable in these public institutions, and, therefore, they send their patients to these asylums, and thus swell the lists of their inmates" (Jarvis, "On the Supposed Increase of Insanity," *American Journal of Insanity* 8 [1852]: 344.

28. See Chapter 12.

the Ticehurst Asylum casebooks now at the Wellcome Institute. But, as Hare notes, almost none of the increase in the incidence of mental illness occurred among private patients, so that for our present purposes, these materials are unlikely to be very helpful. On the other hand, precisely because the county asylums were so overcrowded, and were filled with paupers, their individual case records are generally too skimpy to be useful for answering this question.

I would suggest, however, that the class-specific pattern of the increase in insanity does pose certain difficulties (though I grant these are not necessarily of an insuperable sort) for Hare's argument. Somehow, the slow epidemic of schizophrenia was a *class-specific* epidemic, so that on top of the highly speculative claim that it had a viral origin, one must add the further hypothesis that the upper classes—whether for constitutional or environmental reasons—were mysteriously immune to its ravages.

It may well be that we shall have to be satisfied with an assessment of the general plausibility of each argument and with the extent to which it makes sense of the wide variety of data and observations that *have* survived. However, since Hare felt free to draw on comparative data to buttress his case, perhaps I may be allowed to do the same. Examining the growth of French psychiatry in the nineteenth century, Robert Castel argues that theoretical developments made possible a similar expansion of the boundaries of madness there. Particularly as alienists began to ground their decisions in predictions about patients' likely behavior in the future, they created a substantial area of indeterminacy. As he puts it, "By abandoning reference to real behavior in favor of surmises concerning future behavior, psychiatry begins to arrogate to itself a margin of interpretation (and thus of intervention) whose bounds are no longer discernible."[29] Ian Dowbiggin has demonstrated that this theoretical possibility proceeded to have a substantial practical effect: "By citing heredity and degeneracy, alienists were able to extend the boundaries of mental pathology to encompass marginally deviant affective symptoms and make a plausible case for the reality of partial insanity. Hereditarianism had the 'halo' effect . . . of convincing juries, magistrates, and the public that psychiatry was authorized to expand conventional medical taxa into areas of behavior previously managed by religion and law."[30]

Samuel Shortt's monograph on Richard Bucke and the London Provincial Asylum in Ontario suggests that a similar broadening of the basis for committing people as mad was characteristic of late-nineteenth-

29. Robert Castel, *The Regulation of Madness: Origins of Incarceration in France* (Oxford: Polity Press; Berkeley: University of California Press, 1988), chap. 4.

30. Ian Dowbiggin, "The Professional, Sociopolitical, and Cultural Dimensions of Psychiatric Theory in France 1840–1900" (Ph.D. dissertation, University of Rochester, 1987), 386.

century Canada. Reviewing the data on Ontario admissions in the last quarter of the century, he documents, for example, the disproportionate admission of the elderly, generally suffering from "'senile decay,' a term signifying not threatening behavior but confusion and forgetfulness of varying severity."[31] And overall, he concludes that "a major reason for admission was the inability or unwillingness of friends, family, or community to cope in alternative fashion with harmless but chronically disorderly and unproductive behavior."[32]

Of still more direct relevance, the one careful study we possess of the composition of asylum populations at the turn of the century is Richard Fox's examination of legal commitments in California between 1906 and 1929. Using a random sample of commitments from San Francisco in this period, Fox demonstrates that

> two thirds of those committed were odd, peculiar, or simply immoral individuals who displayed no symptoms indicating serious disability, or violent or destructive tendencies. The reported behavior of this 66 per cent included primarily nervous and depressive symptoms and a wide variety of fears, beliefs, perceptions and delusions. In these cases the examiners noted that behaviors which they and various witnesses deemed inappropriate, but failed to indicate any reason why the individual, for his own protection or that of the community, had to be detained.[33]

It goes almost without saying that this finding accords very well with my hypothesis and provides little or no support for Hare's.

31. S. E. D. Shortt, *Victorian Lunacy: Richard M. Bucke and the Practice of Late Nineteenth-Century Psychiatry* (Cambridge: Cambridge University Press, 1986), 51.

32. Ibid., 52.

33. Richard W. Fox, *So Far Disordered in Mind: Insanity in California* (Berkeley: University of California Press, 1978), 148.

CHAPTER TEN

Progressive Dreams, Progressive Nightmares: Social Control in Twentieth-Century America

At the Rice University conference mentioned in the introduction to Chapter 2, David Rothman and I spent a good deal of time outside the formal conference session discussing his new book, *Conscience and Convenience: The Asylum and Its Alternatives in Progressive America*, which was then just a few weeks from publication. Not long after my return to southern California, the *Stanford University Law Review* invited me to write a review essay dealing with the issues raised in Rothman's book. Delighted to have an excuse to write something on developments in the early twentieth century, and eager to continue the debate Professor Rothman and I had begun in Houston, I agreed to do so. Coincidentally, when I had nearly completed work on the essay, David Brion Davis, who had spoken at the same conference, published his own assessment of the book in the *New York Review of Books*.[1] Readers may care to compare our respective commentaries.

By the time *Conscience and Convenience* appeared, Rothman had almost completed his evolution from being simply a historian to being a historian *and* a public activist. His subsequent analysis of the horrors of institutional provision for the mentally retarded in contemporary New York, *The Willowbrook Wars*, was at once a piece of social *reportage* and a polemic against segregative and institutionally based responses to mental disorder and deficiency.[2] As such, it provided further ammunition for

Chapter 10 is reprinted from the *Stanford University Law Review*, Volume 33, 1981, pp. 575–90 by permission of the editor, copyright 1981 by the Board of Trustees of the Leland Stanford Junior University.

1. David Brion Davis, "The Crime of Reform," *New York Review of Books*, 26 June 1980.
2. David J. Rothman and Sheila M. Rothman, *The Willowbrook Wars* (New York: Harper and Row, 1984).

those critics who charged that Rothman's historical analysis had from the outset been dictated by a commitment to a particular political agenda. Rothman's own account of the intellectual origins of *The Discovery of the Asylum* casts considerable doubt on these claims, contending that his acquaintance with the advocates of deinstitutionalization, and adoption of their cause, came only after the writing of his book and its adoption by activists as an ideological weapon in their campaign against state hospitals.[3] If true (and I suspect that it is), this version of events suggests that, ironically enough, some of his critics are guilty of the same sin they so vociferously accuse him of: deducing original intentions from subsequent events.

Gerald Grob has been perhaps the sternest of these critics. The first volume of Grob's examination of post-colonial American mental health policy appeared just two years after *The Discovery of the Asylum* and is discussed in Chapter 2. The second of a planned trilogy appeared in 1983.[4]

Like its precursor, whose strengths and weaknesses it largely shares, Grob's *Mental Illness and American Society* is based on prodigious research into a wide variety of both printed and manuscript sources and provides a far more thorough and wide-ranging account of the period it covers than his rival's. The period surveyed was a bleak one for American psychiatry, and the thrust of Grob's narrative constitutes a damning critique of mental health policy and mental health professionals in the period. In his portrait, the behavior of the psychiatric profession is largely dictated by its desire to preserve its monopoly and autonomy. It offered no therapies that were demonstrably effective, and its concept of mental disease rested for the most part on little more than a vague faith in future progress. Moreover, seeking new, extra-institutional markets for its wares, the profession began an implicit abandonment of the chronically crazy, the bulk of those nominally in need of its services. Within state systems increasingly preoccupied with cost containment, the existing monasteries of the mad grew ever larger, a development that reflected the silting up of the "hospitals" with the senile and decrepit.

Grob successfully demonstrates that the profession's status concerns prompted a persistent attempt to rationalize caretaking behavior in medical terms; an ambivalent and eventually hostile relationship with potential competitors (social workers, psychologists); an insistence by many on the biological bases of mental disorder, coupled with a penchant to make use of ill-tested, often dangerous, and generally worthless somatic treatments; and a cavalier dismissal of all criticism by outsiders (in the words of one eminent psychiatrist, "'laymanization' was synon-

3. See David Rothman, "An Interview with David Rothman," *Canadian Criminology Forum* 4 (1982): 152–62.

4. Gerald Grob, *Mental Illness and American Society, 1875–1940* (Princeton: Princeton University Press, 1983).

ymous with 'ignorization'"). The impact of his analysis is weakened, however, by its embedment in a mass of dreary administrative-cum-institutional history and by Grob's wearisome insistence (familiar to readers of his earlier book) that those in charge always acted with the best of motives, making untoward consequences at worst the result of inadvertence. Such a Panglossian view of the world has, in my judgment, a profoundly distorting impact on his vision. Rather than lamenting the "agonizing dilemma" facing psychiatrists who claimed expertise but were unable to cure, one ought surely to sympathize with the patients, subjected to agonizing treatments by those concerned overwhelmingly with protecting their shaky scientific legitimacy and privileged social status.[5] Still, for those interested in the twentieth-century history of American psychiatry, both Grob and Rothman are required, if not always very lively, reading.

Progressive Dreams, Progressive Nightmares: Social Control in Twentieth Century America

One of the most notable features of recent historical literature about society's responses to its misfits—the criminal, the delinquent, and the mentally disturbed—has been the emerging sign of its break with the biases and distortions of Whig historiography. A new generation of historians, abandoning the prejudice that crime and craziness are somehow unworthy of serious scholarly attention, has begun to cast a more critical and jaundiced gaze upon the traditional portrait of society's ever more rational and benevolent response to the mad and the bad. If one leaves aside the idiosyncratic intellectual pyrotechnics of Michel Foucault[1]— who attempts a peculiar marriage of history and French structuralism in a style evocative of James Joyce at his most obscure—the most widely

5. Recently, a number of scholars have begun to look seriously, rather than sensationally, at this fascination with somatic treatments. Of particular importance in this regard are Elliot Valenstein, *Great and Desperate Cures* (New York: Basic Books, 1986); and Jack David Pressman, "Uncertain Promise: Psychosurgery and Development of Scientific Psychiatry in America, 1935–1955" (Ph.D. dissertation, University of Pennsylvania, 1986). I am presently at work on a more wide-ranging history of somatic therapies in psychiatry, which will appear as *Desperate Remedies*. See also Andrew Scull, "Desperate Remedies: A Gothic Tale of Madness and Modern Medicine," *Psychological Medicine* 17 (1987): 561–77.

1. Michel Foucault, *Discipline and Punish: The Birth of the Prison* (New York: Pantheon; London: Allen Lane, 1977); idem, *Madness and Civilization* (New York: Pantheon, 1965).

read and influential revisionist has certainly been Columbia historian David J. Rothman.

Rothman's controversial *The Discovery of the Asylum*[2] pioneered the new approach nearly a decade ago. His bold and sweeping interpretation of the origins and achievements of America's first penitentiaries, juvenile reformatories, and mental hospitals during the Jacksonian era attracted widespread attention,[3] sparking a fierce debate that prompted others to undertake research on the history of social control. Most of this work has shared with *The Discovery of the Asylum* a concern with the origins and impact of major transformations in social control structures rather than focusing on the more mundane aspects of institutionalized repression.[4]

In reentering the fray, Rothman maintains this tradition. His new book, *Conscience and Convenience: The Asylum and Its Alternatives in Progressive America*,[5] is a sequel to his earlier study that deliberately leaves unexamined the years from the Civil War to the end of the nineteenth century: For Rothman, the Progressive era—1900–1920—marks the second "major divide" in American society "in attitudes and practices toward the deviant, creating new ideas and procedures to combat crime, delinquency, and mental illness."[6] The changes, in their way as revolutionary as those of the Jacksonian era, mark a distinct shift in approach that survived, largely intact, into the mid-1960s, only then to falter in the face of the "post-Progressive—indeed, anti-Progressive"[7]—upheaval. Later in this essay, I shall argue that Rothman's approach is in certain important respects mistaken and shall examine his cautious endorsement of the current anti-Progressive revolution. I shall begin, however, by discussing the value as well as the limitations of his more concrete analysis.

That analysis begins with a brief sketch of the parlous state to which prisons and asylums had degenerated by the last decades of the nineteenth century. Even within a small compass, the recital is vivid and convincing enough. Prisons were at once lax and brutal, relying heavily on intimidation and torture to secure a measure of order. Those who ran afoul of the authorities might find themselves suspended from a cord

2. David Rothman, *The Discovery of the Asylum: Social Order and Disorder in the New Republic* (Boston: Little, Brown, 1971).

3. See Chapter 2.

4. See, for example, Michael Ignatieff, *A Just Measure of Pain: The Penitentiary in the Industrial Revolution, 1750–1850* (New York: Pantheon, 1978); and Andrew Scull, *Museums of Madness: The Social Organization of Insanity in Nineteenth-Century England* (London: Allen Lane; New York: St. Martin's Press, 1979).

5. David Rothman, *Conscience and Convenience: The Asylum and Its Alternatives in Progressive America* (Boston: Little, Brown, 1980).

6. Ibid., 43.

7. Ibid., 12.

bound round their thumbs, left to dangle till the blood ran from their mouths and the physician supervising the business ordered them cut down. Or they might be strapped into a coffinlike box with holes drilled in the lid, which, when slowly filled with water, produced the impression (and sometimes the reality) of slow drowning. Asylums were mere storage bins for human refuse, filled with chronic "patients" who seldom returned to the outside world. Here, the insane, if not the victims of violent assault by attendants or fellow inmates, passively rotted away, often spending their days restrained by camisoles and straitjackets and their nights locked into covered cribs.

During the last third of the nineteenth century, knowledge of such conditions produced a measure of criticism. The strongest complaints came from members of the newly emerging profession of neurology, who urged that the asylum's inherent deficiencies were so far-reaching as to require that it be used only as a last resort. But neither this nor any other proposal for fundamental change received serious consideration. Remarkably, society as a whole remained confident of the basic appropriateness of institutional control.[8]

In some quarters, the modest cost of incarceration was sufficient motive for perpetuating places that conveniently got rid of the inconvenient. But even those of more tender conscience could rationalize continued support of the existing system out of fear that the alternative to institutions was a still worse catalogue of horrors, or, more positively, out of a desperate collective illusion that prisons and asylums might still somehow rehabilitate and cure, a willed suspension of disbelief when confronted with claims like those of the Elmira Reformatory to reform "more than 80 percent of those who are sent there."[9]

All at once, however, such justifications lost their persuasiveness. With quite "incredible speed,"[10] there developed a crisis of institutional legitimacy that the Progressives "solved" by an equally rapid spasm of reform. They introduced strikingly similar "open-ended, informal, and highly flexible policies" and programs based on a heightened ideological concern to break with the "rigid, inflexible, and machine-like" qualities of inherited approaches.[11] Within Progressive social thought, a variety of explanations for what causes deviance competed for attention: environmental, psychological, and genetic. Yet underlying each is an almost uni-

8. See Andrew Scull, *Decarceration: Community Treatment and the Deviant—A Radical View* 2d ed. (Oxford: Polity Press; New Brunswick, N.J.: Rutgers University Press, 1984), 95–133; Bonnie Blustein, "A Hollow Square of Psychological Science: American Neurologists and Psychiatrists in Conflict," in *Madhouses, Mad-Doctors, and Madmen: The Social History of Psychiatry in the Victorian Era,* ed. Andrew Scull (Philadelphia: University of Pennsylvania Press; London: Athlone Press, 1981), 241–70.

9. Rothman, *Conscience and Convenience,* 35.

10. Ibid., 44.

11. Ibid., 43.

versal convergence on the need for a discretionary response to the individual case, coupled with blithe self-confidence in the Progressives' own capacity to design effective forms of treatment. Central, too, is a naive and dangerous faith in the benevolence of the state and its agents—a faith that prompted the new generation of reformers to promote program after program widening the scope of state action.

To individualize the response to the criminal, Progressives sought to widen the range of treatments while granting the authorities greater freedom to match diagnosis to therapy. (Use of the medical metaphor grew apace, for it legitimized official discretion and the emphasis on individual variability.) They started by making probation a more and more popular courtroom disposition.[12] For more serious offenders came parole and the indeterminate sentence, innovations by means of which "the prisoner becomes the arbiter of his own fate. He carries the key to the prison in his own pocket."[13] In addition, the prison's internal routines were adapted to permit a more flexible response to the individual offender. By the early 1920s, almost half the state prison population were serving indeterminate sentences, and more than half the prisoners released were on parole.[14]

In the sphere of juvenile justice, change came with similar speed. The juvenile court emerged in Chicago at the turn of the century, quickly spread nationwide, and "revolutionized social policy toward the delinquent"[15] by abandoning punishment for rehabilitation to help the individual child and thereby contribute to the welfare of society. Redirecting the wayward required not a response to a single delinquent act, but a global reformation of character, using techniques expertly tailored to the requirements of the individual case. And if this meant abandoning procedural safeguards and granting extraordinary latitude to intervene, Progressive reformers were willing, indeed eager, to do so.

They were likewise eager to break away from overreliance on a single solution to the problems posed by mental disorder. Instead of a monolithic asylum system, they proposed a network of psychopathic hospitals providing expert diagnosis and intensive treatment for recent curable cases; a massive effort to provide outpatient clinics and aftercare services for those discharged from the hospitals; financial aid, augmented by psychological support and counseling; and a new emphasis on *preventing* the outbreak of mental disorder through public education in mental hygiene. Central to most of these services was a new group of professionals, the social workers.

12. In 1900, only six states provided for probation. In 1915 alone, thirty-three states created or extended the procedure, and by 1920 every state permitted juvenile probation and thirty-three states adult probation. Ibid., 44.

13. Ibid., 69.   14. Ibid., 44.   15. Ibid., 205.

By far the best and most convincing part of Rothman's book is his analysis of the unholy alliance between reformist conscience and administrative convenience that supported Progressive innovations. He argues that the symbiotic relationship of these two elements accounts for both the rapid shift in public policy and the persistence of the new programs even when, measured by the reformers' own criteria, they proved to be abject failures.

On one side stood a rather shadowy and ill-defined assortment of benevolent and philanthropic men and women, disinterested "moral entrepreneurs"[16] whose impulse to do good was matched by an entirely misplaced confidence that they had discovered the "civic medicine"[17] with which to cure crime, delinquency, and insanity. These altruistic crusaders "marched under a very appealing banner, asking citizens not to do less for fear of harm, but to do more, confident of favorable results."[18] Theirs were the ideological formulations so essential to promoting change, along with the rhetoric that provided a veneer of legitimacy for the Progressive reforms. But their proselytizing succeeded only because some curious allies stood on the other side: The administrators of the very programs being attacked were eager for quite different reasons to embrace the reformers' proposals.

In welcoming this conversion of the heathen, the reformers "were never deeply disturbed by the fact that administrative convenience had become so well served in their programs."[19] This passivity was, as Rothman sees it, an error with appalling consequences: The professionals who oversaw the implementation of the reforms proceeded to make sure that the new programs served primarily their bureaucratic self-interests. If the reformers were blind to the uses to which their stress on "discretionary responses to each case"[20] were put, the administrators clearly were not. Thus, the introduction of probation and the indeterminate sentence multiplied the inducements to "cop a plea," and plea bargaining enabled judges and prosecutors to shorten trials, ease crowded court calendars, and raise the conviction rate, as well as insulate both their own and police conduct from further judicial scrutiny and review. Prison wardens welcomed the combination of parole and the indeterminate sentence with open arms, for with it the "reformers had delivered into their hands a disciplinary mechanism far more potent than the lash, and not insignificantly, far more legitimate."[21] The reformers might be con-

16. See Howard S. Becker, *Outsiders: Studies in the Sociology of Deviance* (Glencoe, Ill.: Free Press, 1963), 147–63.

17. The term was first used by the leading early twentieth-century American psychiatrist, Adolf Meyer. See his "Case Work in Social Service and Medical and Social Cooperation in Nervous and Mental Diseases," in *The Collected Papers of Adolf Meyer*, ed. Eunice E. Winters (Baltimore: Johns Hopkins University Press, 1952), 4:225, 227.

18. Rothman, *Conscience and Convenience*, 5.   19. Ibid., 10.

20. Ibid., 6 (emphasis omitted).   21. Ibid., 74.

vinced that they had placed the inmate's "destiny . . . largely in his own hands,"[22] but the wardens (and their prisoners) knew better. And although these changes apparently diminished judicial authority by transferring sentencing power to an executive and administrative body, judges gained, too. The indeterminate sentence gave them "added freedom to dispense justice as they saw fit."[23] And with the parole board as a buffer and whipping boy, judges could escape political criticism for prisoner recidivism.

Elsewhere, whether one looks to programs for the delinquent or for the mentally ill, Progressive innovations fared no better. In every setting, the reveries of reformist conscience were transmuted under the pressures of administrative convenience into harsh caricatures of themselves. They served merely to advance the self-interest of the caretaker-professionals, or, as with social work, virtually to create the profession that perpetuated them.

Progressive reformers, though not unaware of the bastardization of their programs, resisted acknowledging how far the process had gone. Recognizing that their achievements were only partial and flawed, they sought consolation in the belief that they had prevented the perpetuation of barbarism—to them, the stark and singular alternative to a leap aboard their bandwagon. Their very commitment to the idea of progress and their own self-appointed role as its agents effectively blocked any alternative perception, and left them convinced that present horrors were at least less awful than those of the past. Finally, if all else failed, such horrors could always be attributed to improper implementation of Progressive programs, reflecting "not faulty conceptualization but inadequate funding."[24]

But Rothman is determined to deny the progressives and their present-day apologists even this limited miserable measure of consolation. For him, their whole enterprise was unworkable from the outset, resting as it did on the fatally mistaken assumption that institutions "could coexist with, and even sponsor, non-institutional programs."[25] This was a lesson the reformers simply would not learn, remaining heedless of their limitations and of the need to reconsider the premises of their programs in the wake of failure. "One searches in vain," as Rothman puts it, "for any thorough reappraisal of the Progressive ideology or any coherent effort to review reform postulates in the light of their marginal relationship to actual practices."[26] In one of those cruel ironies with which the history of social control abounds, the consequence was that their ever-so-benevolently intended "reforms" only gave a further twist to the vicious logic of the existing system. Because they blithely substituted good inten-

22. Ibid., 69.   23. Ibid., 77.   24. Ibid., 289.
25. Ibid., 12.   26. Ibid., 288.

tions for knowledge and continued to give a cloak of humanity and legitimacy to the Frankensteinian monster that emerged from their blueprints, the Progressives must bear a large measure of responsibility for the nightmares they created.

Historians of social reform have traditionally taken ideology very seriously. Indeed, they have been all too prone simply to reproduce it. Their work presents an elaborate morality play that, couched in the reformers' own rhetoric, attends earnestly to expressed intentions and scarcely at all to results. By forcing a sustained examination of the neglected gaps between rhetoric and reality, Rothman has done as much as anyone to debunk these pious myths and to invalidate the general approach on which they rest. Yet, despite the very different conclusions he reaches about the nature and outcome of reform, he ultimately shares earlier historians' convictions about the centrality of ideology in historical explanation.

The account he offers of the Jacksonian discovery of the asylum in his earlier book [27] is an essentially intentionalist one, in which the new institutions emerge out of the reformers' fears for the stability of the social order and their sense that asylums to "control abnormal behavior promised to be the first step in establishing a new system for stabilizing the community, for binding citizens together." [28] When he turns to examine the invention of probation, parole, outpatient care, and the juvenile court in the Progressive era, again his primary emphasis is on "the rhetoric of the reformers—for it is here that one will find the strongest clues to the origins of the changes and sources of their success, their legitimation if you will." [29] Rothman is remarkably adept at capturing the hopes and fears of the reformers and at revealing nuances in their thought that have escaped earlier observers. At least in *Conscience and Convenience*, his examination of the fit between reformist conscience and administrative convenience moves beyond a fixation with ideas and goes some distance toward explaining why these ideas found a wider audience and were enacted so swiftly. To a significant extent, however, he remains trapped within the limitations of a fundamentally idealist worldview, and to that degree his explanations are necessarily flawed and incomplete.

The Discovery of the Asylum begins with the admonition that "institutions, whether social, political, or economic, cannot be understood apart from the society in which they flourished. The sturdy walls of the asylum were intended to isolate the inmates, not the historian." [30] But both here and in *Conscience and Convenience*, Rothman's admirable methodological

27. Rothman, *Discovery of the Asylum*.
28. Ibid., 58–59.
29. David Rothman, "Social Control: The Uses and Abuses of the Concept in the History of Incarceration," in *Social Control and the State: Historical and Comparative Essays*, ed. Stanley Cohen and Andrew Scull (Oxford: Basil Blackwell; New York: St. Martin's Press, 1981), 106–17.
30. Rothman, *Discovery of the Asylum*, xx.

prescription has a scarcely discernible impact on his own analysis. In neither book does the larger social environment that both spawned and shaped reform receive the attention it warrants. Ideas remain free-floating, and change remains the product of "the power of the rhetoric"[31] the reformers invent; both remain stubbornly unanchored in underlying transformations of social structures and practices. Beyond the occasional feeble gesture—a quasi-magical invocation of economic and demographic change or passing reference to immigration, the ghetto, and the settlement house (but scarcely a mention of class or race)—little dispels the illusion that the entire outcome rests on the rhetorical skills of a collection of moral entrepreneurs, allied with the bureaucratic self-interest of institutional administrators.

The crucial causal variable in *The Discovery of the Asylum* is allegedly a peculiarly American anxiety about the stability of the social order.[32] In the book's sequel, the reform program centers on the virtues of flexibility, discretion, and the expertly tailored response to the individual case. In neither instance are matters pursued much further. It is as though such items as anxiety and optimism constituted primitive logical terms not susceptible of further examination or investigation; as though, in this instance at least, analysis must stop at the level of the reformers' presentation of self. But of course they are not and it cannot. One wants to know, for example, which segments of Jacksonian society felt anxious, about what, and why. One wonders to what extent all the talk of looming disorder and the promotion of the institutions' reformatory functions can be understood as the rhetoric of a particular social group, who employed it for particular polemical purposes. Similarly with the Progressives' positivism: their naive sense that the facts would speak for themselves; their belief that everything was adjustable, that there were no irreconcilable conflicts of interest; and their abandonment of laissez-faire for a new ideology of expertly guided state intervention to correct the imbalances and imperfections of the social system. These should mark the starting point of the search for understanding, not its culmination.

The two books share a further defect, an odd and perverse ethnocentrism. Rothman's insistence on viewing the invention of the penitentiary and the asylum as a uniquely American phenomenon was one of the bolder features of his earlier work. It is also an idea that has been subjected to withering criticism and must now be recognized as simply untenable.[33] Yet, in David Brion Davis' words, the analysis in *Conscience and*

31. Rothman, *Conscience and Convenience*, 215.

32. See Rothman, *Discovery of the Asylum*, xviii–xx.

33. See, for example, Richard Fox, "Beyond Social Control: Institutions and Disorder in Bourgeois Society," *History of Education Quarterly* 16 (1976): 203–7; Jacques Quen, "David Rothman's Discovery of the Asylum," *Journal of Psychiatry and the Law* 2 (1974): 105; Scull, *Museums of Madness*, passim; and Chapter 5 above.

Convenience continues to exhibit an "almost defiant indifference to European influences and parallels"[34] and to proceed as though American developments can be examined in a vacuum. Other than the dearth of research on the European materials, it is difficult to understand why Rothman persists in this stance. But certainly the lapse is unfortunate, for a comparative perspective often points up the shallowness and inadequacy of solipsistic cultural "explanations" and may help uncover some of the underlying structural sources of social change.

By choosing to emphasize ideology so heavily, Rothman is led to misconstrue, and to overestimate, the significance of Progressive reforms. As we have seen,[35] he presents the changes introduced in this period as if they were of revolutionary importance—a major shift that ranks, along with the discovery of the asylum and its contemporary demise, as one of the three major watersheds in the history of social control in America. At the level of rhetoric, such a judgment is perhaps defensible. Semantically, the transformations made in the Progressive era mark a sharp break with the past. Their emphasis on procedural informality and discretion and on a highly differentiated response to the individual case is combined with savage criticism of the very different practices inherited from the nineteenth century. But even at the outset, doubts arise. For although the distinctions between Progressive *rhetoric* and Jacksonian *practice* seem clear enough, the differences are not well marked when one's point of comparison is what the early-nineteenth-century reformers *claimed* to be doing. For example, their program for rescuing the mad from maltreatment leaned heavily upon a set of principles largely borrowed from abroad, known collectively as "moral treatment," that broke with a prior emphasis on indiscriminate mass medication and insisted on a flexible, noncoercive approach to curing the mad, carefully tailored to the individual case and dispensed by an asylum administrator armed with wide discretionary powers.[36]

If the Progressives were not quite as distinctive ideologically as Rothman implies, their practice was even less so. Though he resolutely avoids confronting the implications of his findings, Rothman himself presents a remarkable array of evidence that demonstrates that most of the Progressive reformers' sound and fury in reality signified nothing: "therapeutic innovations had little effect on prison routines" and "change never moved beyond the superficial."[37]

34. David Brion Davis, "The Crime of Reform," *New York Review of Books*, 26 June 1980, 16.

35. See p. 253.

36. See, generally, Norman Dain, *Concepts of Insanity in the United States, 1789–1865* (New Brunswick, N.J.: Rutgers University Press, 1964); Gerald Grob, *Mental Institutions in America* (New York: Free Press, 1973); and Chapter 5 above.

37. Rothman, *Conscience and Convenience,* 133–34.

Reform on occasion did not even penetrate skin deep, as with the changeover from striped convict uniforms to more ordinary dress. Even when some new amenities were allowed—more exercise, more frequent visitors—the fundamental realities of prison life remained unaltered. The Progressive reformers' dream, "that they could transform a nightmarish prison, dedicated to punishment, into a community that would at once prepare the inmate for release and serve as a testing ground for society,"[38] echoed the reveries of their Jacksonian counterparts. Reality once again proved brutally recalcitrant.

Nor did alternative, noninstitutional programs fare much better. Probation was scarcely more than a sham in all but densely populated areas.[39] And even there, "the actual results were pitiful."[40] Conditions in the system "not only made the fulfillment of case work principles well nigh impossible, [they] also prevented probation from carrying out a meaningful police function."[41]

Examination of the juvenile justice system also reveals a litany of failure. Again and again, Rothman returns to the token quality of the Progressive emphasis on individualization, psychiatric guidance, and intervention, and to the persistence within institutions' walls of quasi-military routines not essentially different from those that characterized the Jacksonian asylum system. All of the reformers' brave words about breaking with the ugliness and failures of the past had little practical effect.[42] At best, "the rhetoric of treatment provided only the external trappings. Inside, incapacitation and deterrence ruled, as befit a holding operation."[43]

Finally, the gap between the Progressives' ambitions and prosaic reality was nowhere greater than in the sphere of mental health.[44] Only a handful of the network of psychopathic hospitals the reformers had envisaged were actually built. And, rather than serving as the core of intensive treatment and mental hygiene programs, they became little more than handmaidens to the traditional asylum system—"diagnostic centers" that were but "a first stop on the road to the state hospital,"[45] for they made no sustained effort to treat or cure, but simply smoothed away

38. Ibid., 127.

39. "The translation bore very little resemblance to the original text. [It was] implemented in a most superficial, routine, and careless fashion [and] never did take root in rural areas or small towns. . . . In fact only densely populated areas established probation departments" (ibid., 83).

40. Ibid., 84.

41. Ibid., 91.

42. "The ideals that justified incarceration had little relevance to actual circumstances. No matter how frequently juvenile court judges insisted that their sentences of confinement were for treatment and not punishment, no matter how vehemently superintendents declared that their institutions were rehabilitative and not correctional, conditions at training schools belied these claims" (ibid., 268).

43. Ibid., 283.   44. Ibid., 324.   45. Ibid., 326.

obstacles to easy commitment. "The effort to extend the reach of treatment and the principles of prevention into the community"[46] was likewise a dismal failure. Forced to compete for the same funds as the long-established state hospitals, while threatening to deprive them of the very patients whose labor contributed most to their low operating costs, such programs never had much chance of success. They were all but killed off by opposition from patients' families and from the community at large. Asylums endured, "and [their] needs shaped the outcome of all reform ventures."[47]

From many perspectives, then, the transformations of the Progressive era were little more than another episode in the saga of reform by word magic. Houses of refuge now became training schools or industrial schools; prisons were renamed reformatories or correctional institutes; asylums turned into mental hospitals. Euphemisms abounded, papering over the degree to which "reform" left the underlying nineteenth-century structures largely untouched.

In developing his critique of the reformers' failures, Rothman unwittingly undermines his own claims for the revolutionary significance of Progressive reform. Not that the ideological changes he analyzes are without significance; the greater emphasis placed on medical and therapeutic rhetoric did indeed help legitimize a policy of ever greater intervention. And probation and parole were important innovations, however far they departed from the reformers' intentions, and however halfhearted their implementation. Probation in particular "expanded the scope of state action and state surveillance," and though its potential for coercion "was never realized" fully, probation "did have serious consequences for civil liberties."[48] Such innovations widened the net and subjected new segments of the population to the risks of arbitrary state action; but they supplemented, rather than revolutionized, existing arrangements.

Rothman believes that one can learn from history; his work is self-consciously intended to speak to an audience far beyond those specializing in the social history of Jacksonian and Progressive America. It is "the enterprise of reform"[49] as a whole that he seeks to illuminate, and his goal "is to inform both history and social policy, to analyze a revolution in practice that has an immediate relevance to present concerns."[50] Judging by the extraordinary attention his work has attracted, he has certainly succeeded in reaching that wider audience. But what of the lessons he seeks to teach?

On one point Rothman is adamant: Notwithstanding the failures and disappointments of past attempts at reform, he will have no truck with pessimism, with those who argue that the whole enterprise is "at best

---

46. Ibid., 360.   47. Ibid., 325.   48. Ibid., 112.   49. Ibid., 5.

foolhardy, at worst deceptive."[51] He is particularly eager to distinguish his position from that of Foucault, with whom he has often been lumped as a "revisionist" or "social control" historian. Unlike Foucault, he cannot accept the portrait of an inevitable and progressive intensification of discipline in an ever more rationalized capitalist society. On the contrary, to Rothman, the history of reform is of a process in which "choices were made, decisions reached; and to appreciate the dynamic is to be able to recognize the opportunity to affect it. . . . There is much more room for maneuver than a Foucault could ever imagine or allow."[52]

The insistence that "men make their own history"[53] is a welcome and necessary corrective to the narrow structural determinism now in vogue in certain historical circles,[54] but only so long as one remembers the other half of Marx's famous aphorism: that "they do not make it just as they please; they do not make it under circumstances chosen by themselves" but as conditioned by and in the context of a particular historical inheritance and set of structural possibilities.[55] As I have already suggested, Rothman is all too inclined to neglect structural factors. Precisely because he accords such a critical role to ideology, he readily assumes that had the reformers' zeal about eliminating the horrors of the Jacksonian asylum been more thoroughgoing, instead of falling into the egregious error of strengthening the segregative institutions he finds so loathsome, they would have destroyed them.

I think he is mistaken in this assumption. Institutional structures are far less malleable than the conceptual edifices constructed by intellectuals, even though the latter can prove resistant enough to modification and change. Notwithstanding Rothman's criticism of the Progressives for remaining wedded to the foolish notion that "the appropriate task was to reform incarceration, not to launch a fundamental attack upon it,"[56] it is not at all clear how they could have done otherwise.[57] And it is even less clear that, had they concluded that more radical change was essential, they could possibly have secured the enactment of their program. Rothman's reproaches here rest on arguments that are not properly spelled out, let alone explored through systematic empirical analysis.

51. Ibid., 11.
52. Ibid.
53. Karl Marx, "The Eighteenth Brumaire of Louis Napoleon," reprinted in *Karl Marx: Selected Writings*, ed. David McLellan (London: Oxford University Press, 1977), 300.
54. See, generally, E. P. Thompson, *The Poverty of Theory and Other Essays* (New York: Monthly Review Press, 1978).
55. Marx, "Eighteenth Brumaire," 300. In his own words, "The tradition of all the dead generations weighs like a nightmare on the brains of the living."
56. Rothman, *Conscience and Convenience*, 29.
57. Certainly the claim that they should have taken "inspiration from the fact that incarceration was a relatively recent invention and therefore properly approached with skepticism" (ibid.) will not suffice to demonstrate the point.

Mutatis mutandis, the same can be said of his somewhat cautious endorsement of the anti-Progressive reforms advanced by contemporary men of conscience. Despite his insistence on learning from the past, Rothman is remarkably coy about suggesting a "platform for reform."[58] Or perhaps it is rather that any program he could suggest would be a negative one, whose central theme would be the need to avoid the hubris that bedevils reformers. Like sociologists before him,[59] Rothman has perceived that punishment and therapy are ultimately irreconcilable, and that in any attempt to combine them, the winner is predestined: "When treatment and coercion [meet], coercion [wins]."[60] He has also grasped, though the point is not as novel as he implies, that institutional control systems necessarily rest on hierarchical levels of coercion.[61] Still, he elegantly demonstrates that the problem is "not that we cannot here or there run one decent institution; [but] rather, that the decency of any one place rests ultimately . . . upon the presence of a still more coercive back-up."[62]

What distinguishes us from the Progressives, apparently, is not our greater knowledge of how to do good. Rather, it is our recognition that we *lack* such knowledge, and our realization of the harm that can result should we attempt to substitute good intentions for it. Anti-Progressives have learned—partly from Rothman's prior work—the "limits of benevolence"[63] and the dangers of expanding the boundaries of discretionary state action.

Thus, on Rothman's account, the current wave of reform—the attempt to decarcerate prisoners and patients[64]—is again to be explained by changes at the level of ideas: our recognition that institutions for the deviant are irredeemably nasty, counterproductive places; our willingness to abandon the chimera of combining reformation and punishment; our sense of the need to restrict the scope of state power. Unlike the case of the Progressives, our quarrel with the principle of incarceration is a fundamental one, and our programs of community corrections and community-based treatment of the mentally ill are replacements for, not supplements of, old institutions.

58. Ibid., 11.

59. See, for example, American Friends Service Committee, *Struggle for Justice* (New York: Hill and Wang, 1971); Jessica Mitford, *Kind and Usual Punishment: The Prison Business* (New York: Knopf, 1973).

60. Rothman, *Conscience and Convenience,* 10.

61. See, for instance, Erving Goffman, *Asylums: Essays on the Social Situation of Mental Patients and Other Inmates* (Garden City, N.Y.: Doubleday, 1961); S. Messinger, "Strategies of Control" (Ph.D. dissertation, University of California, Berkeley, 1968).

62. Rothman, *Conscience and Convenience,* 420.

63. W. Gaylin et al., *Doing Good: The Limits of Benevolence* (New York: Pantheon, 1978).

64. David Rothman, "Decarcerating Prisoners and Patients," *Civil Liberties Review* 1 (1973): 8–30.

This is not the place to argue in detail that Rothman's explanation of the genesis of contemporary reforms is fundamentally mistaken.[65] It is curious, however, that Rothman should be so willing to take contemporary reform movements at their own estimation and, like the Progressives before him, be so convinced of the horrors of past practices as to be certain beyond doubt that change *must* be for the better. Nor does he seriously appear to entertain the possibility that new forms of administrative convenience may play a crucial role in the success of contemporary men of conscience.

Yet, calls for retrenchment and cutbacks have an obvious attraction for state managers in periods of acute fiscal crisis, the more so if reductions in expenditures can simultaneously be portrayed as a splendid humanitarian gesture. Who can be surprised, therefore, that the new generation of reformers has met with such a friendly reception? For the mentally ill, at least, states have been only too willing to grant the negative right to be left alone, to be free from the obvious coercion that involuntary hospitalization represents. Neglect, after all, is cheaper than care, even at the minimal level traditionally provided by our state hospitals. Unfortunately, though, "there is no primal Arcady into which the mental patient can slip away from modern institutions of care and intervention. If he slips anywhere away from it at all, it will be into the gutter or the graveyard" or, perhaps worse, into the hands of the burgeoning class of entrepreneurs and professionals speculating in this form of human misery.[66] Benevolence here is limited indeed![67]

65. For a full discussion, see Scull, *Decarceration*.

66. The quotation is from Peter Sedgwick's stimulating *Psychopolitics* (New York: Harper and Row; London: Pluto Press, 1982), 146. On the new use of the mad as a source of profit, see, for example, Senate Special Committee on Aging, Subcommittee on Long-Term Care, 94th Cong., 2d sess. 1976, *Nursing Home Care in the United States: Failure in Public Policy*, Support Paper no. 7, *The Role of Nursing Homes in Caring for Discharged Mental Patients*, Committee Print; Comptroller General of the United States, *Returning the Mentally Disabled to the Community: Government Needs to Do More* (Washington, D.C.: Government Printing Office, 1977); A. Davis, S. Dinitz, and B. Pasamanick, *Schizophrenia in the New Custodial Community* (Columbus: Ohio State University Press, 1974); F. Arnhoff, "Social Consequences of Policy Toward Mental Illness," *Science* 188 (1975): 1277–81; E. Bassuk and S. Gerson, "De-institutionalization and Mental Health Services," *Scientific American* 238 (1978): 46–53; J. Chase, "Where Have All the Patients Gone?" *Human Behavior* (1973): 14–21; S. Kirk and M. Thierren, "Community Mental Health Myths and the Fate of Former Hospitalized Patients," *Psychiatry* 38 (1975): 209–17; H. R. Lamb and V. Goertzel, "Discharged Mental Patients—Are They Really in the Community?" *Archives of General Psychiatry* 24 (1971): 29–34; John Monahan, "Three Lingering Issues," in *Patient Rights and Patient Advocacy: Issues and Evidence*, ed. Bernard L. Bloom and Shirley J. Asher (New York: Plenum, 1981); Andrew Scull, "Deinstitutionalization and the Rights of the Deviant," *Journal of Social Issues* 37 (1981): 6–20; J. Wolpert and E. Wolpert, "The Relocation of Released Mental Patients into Residential Communities," *Policy Sciences* 7 (1976): 31–51.

67. See generally Gaylin et al., *Doing Good*.

Since nonintervention in the penal context would clearly raise serious social and political problems,[68] it is scarcely surprising that, for criminals and delinquents, community disapproval of *alternatives* to incarceration has proven as solid as it was in the Progressive era. In this setting, the reformers' conscience has once again been no match for the occupational interests of correctional and prison employees and administrators, or for public demands, partly instrumental and partly symbolic, for sterner measures to stop increasing crime. Despite rhetorical claims to the contrary, "the major results of the new movement towards 'community' and 'diversion' have been to increase the *amount* of intervention directed at many groups of deviants in the system and, probably, to increase rather than decrease the total *number* who get into the system in the first place. In other words: 'alternatives' become not alternatives at all, but new programs that supplement the existing system or else expand it by attracting new populations."[69]

In the very first pages of *Conscience and Convenience*, Rothman confronts the question of whether Progressive innovations were better than the procedures that they replaced. To his credit, he provides a forthright answer: no, they were not. "Progressive innovations may well have done less to upgrade dismal conditions than they did to create nightmares of their own."[70]

Plus ça change, plus c'est la même chose?

68. Cf. Edwin Schur, *Radical Non-intervention* (Englewood Cliffs, N.J.: Prentice-Hall, 1975).

69. Stanley Cohen, "The Punitive City: Notes on the Dispersal of Social Control," *Contemporary Crises* 3 (1979): 337, 347. See, generally, Paul Lerman, *Community Treatment and Social Control* (Chicago: University of Chicago Press, 1975); Norval Morris, *The Future of Imprisonment* (Chicago: University of Chicago Press, 1974); Thomas Blomberg, "Diversion and Accelerated Social Control," *Journal of Criminal Law and Criminology* 68 (1977): 274–82; Andrew Scull, "Community Corrections: Panacea, Progress, or Pretence?" in *The Politics of Legal Informalism*, ed. Richard Abel, vol. 1 (New York: Academic Press, 1981); 99–118; Sheldon Messinger, "Confinement in the Community," *Journal of Research in Crime and Delinquency* 13 (1976): 82–92.

70. Rothman, *Conscience and Convenience*, 9.

CHAPTER ELEVEN

Dazeland

The forces of sex and madness have historically been linked together in a multitude of ways. Notoriously, psychodynamic theories of mental disturbance, particularly those of a Freudian provenance, have accorded pride of place to sexuality in accounting for the etiology of mental disturbance. The more organically inclined, not to be outdone, have provided their own accounts of the linkage, ranging from neurological portraits of females as possessed of nervous systems of greater refinement and delicacy (and hence more susceptible to breakdown) to gynecological theorizing about peculiarly intimate ties between a woman's brain and her reproductive organs.[1] Correspondingly, one encounters insistent claims that there exist differential diagnostic practices and criteria for men and women, along with evidence that treatment itself may vary sharply by gender.[2] *Social Research* recently devoted an entire issue to a

---

An earlier version of Chapter 11 appeared in the *London Review of Books*, October 29, 1987, and portions of that essay are reprinted here with the editor's permission.

1. See Carroll Smith-Rosenberg and Charles Rosenberg, "The Female Animal: Medical and Biological Views of Woman and Her Role in Nineteenth Century America," *Journal of American History* 60 (1973): 332–56; and Andrew Scull and Diane Favreau, "The Clitoridectomy Craze," *Social Research* 53 (1986): 243–60.

2. On surgery directed at the female reproductive organs in an attempt to cure madness, see Andrew Scull and Diane Favreau, "'A Chance to Cut is a Chance to Cure': Sexual Surgery for Psychosis in Three Nineteenth Century Societies," in *Research in Law, Deviance, and Social Control*, vol. 8, ed. Steven Spitzer and Andrew Scull (Greenwich, Conn.: JAI Press, 1986), 3–39. For some discussion of the differential susceptibility of women to certain other forms of therapeutic intervention, see Carol Warren, "Electroconvulsive Therapy: 'New' Treatment of the 1980s," in the same volume, 41–55; Jack David Pressman, "Uncertain Promise: Psychosurgery and the Development of Scientific Psychiatry in America, 1935 to 1955" (Ph.D. dissertation, University of Pennsylvania, 1986), 157; and Andrew Scull, "Desperate Remedies: A Gothic Tale of Madness and Modern Medicine," *Psychological Medicine* 17 (1987): 561–77.

series of essays examining some of these interrelationships in historical and comparative perspective.[3] And Elaine Showalter has given more sustained and systematic attention to this whole range of issues, through an examination of English psychiatric practices over the past two centuries.[4]

The London Review of Books asked that I write an essay-review of Professor Showalter's book, and what follows is an expanded version of that piece. As I hope my discussion makes clear, no one should harbor any illusions that either folk beliefs about madness or psychiatric theorizing and practice are somehow gender-neutral. To the contrary, both our stereotypical images of madness and professional explanations and treatments for mental disorder are clearly saturated with overt and subliminal sexual references and assumptions.

It follows that there is an obvious temptation to place the psychiatric enterprise in a critical double-bind over this issue. I have in mind here the simultaneous assertion that women are disproportionately victimized by a male-defined double standard of mental health, which unwarrantably assigns them to the highly stigmatizing status of the psychiatric patient (most especially if they behave in ways that challenge masculine stereotypes of female propriety); and that the oppressions, constrictions, and limitations of the female role in a patriarchical society are so damaging and stressful as to drive a disproportionate share of women mad. For feminists, embracing a pair of such ideologically attractive positions makes it easy to view the psychiatric arena as simply another and particularly lurid set of illustrations of the baneful effects of the patriarchical oppression of women.

But, as always, there is a price to be paid for the polemical pleasure of "having one's cake in the form of stress theory as well as eating it in the substance of labelling or antipsychiatry theory."[5] It obviously would make little sense to claim that the same people are *driven* mad by intolerable social pressures and also are inappropriately and improperly *labelled* mad by those bent on repressing rebellion and nonconformity. One can rescue both assertions by claiming that they apply to different subgroups within the overall population of the mentally disordered, and anecdotal evidence can certainly be found to demonstrate that neither category is empirically empty. But anecdote does not suffice to establish significance. Indeed, it is necessarily silent on the crucial issue of the degree to which women's presence among the ranks of the mentally disturbed can be attributed to each of these processes, as opposed to whatever it is that accounts for the alienation of men. In the absence of firm

3. *Social Research* 53 (Summer 1986).

4. Elaine Showalter, *The Female Malady: Women, Madness, and English Culture, 1830–1980* (New York: Pantheon, 1985; London: Virago, 1987).

5. Peter Sedgwick, *Psychopolitics* (London: Pluto Press; New York: Harper and Row, 1982), 237.

evidence on this point, and given the broadly equal representation of men and women among the ranks of the mentally disordered, one must be circumspect about claims that "women, by definition . . . are viewed as psychiatrically impaired"[6] and that mental illness is "the female malady."

Dazeland

In the first place, an insane woman is no more a member of the body-politic than a criminal; second, her death is always a relief to her dearest friends; third, even in the case of her recovery from her mental disease, she is liable to transmit the taint of insanity to her children's children for many generations.
—WILLIAM GOODELL,
"Clinical Notes on the Extirpation of the Ovaries for Insanity," *Transactions of the Medical Society of the State of Pennsylvania* 13 (1881)

Most recent work on the history of psychiatry has tended to focus on the history of institutions, of ideas, and of the psychiatric profession itself, and to ignore those for whom this vast infrastructure has (at least ostensibly) been erected. It is a historiography, as David Ingleby wittily puts it, "like the histories of colonial wars[: it tells] us more about the relations between the imperial powers than about the 'third world' of the mental patients themselves."[1] Elaine Showalter's *The Female Malady*[2] is thus doubly valuable, as an exploration of popular and professional discourse about the relationships between women and madness and as an analysis of how the profession of psychiatry has treated somewhat more than half of those who fall within its territory.

On examination, in the psychiatric domain, as in the more conventionally defined Third World, the position and treatment of women consistently turn out to be even less enviable than those endured by men. Can this justify, though, a move to label madness the female malady?[3] Not in any straightforward statistical fashion, contrary to what Showalter sometimes implies. One may plausibly contend that, for much of the past two or three centuries, women have outnumbered men in the ranks of the mentally disturbed. Still, for the most part, this imbalance has not been in such gross disproportion that one could sensibly call the disorder

---

6. Phyllis Chesler, *Women and Madness* (Garden City, N.Y.: Doubleday, 1972), 108.

1. David Ingleby, "Mental Health and Social Order," in *Social Control and the State: Historical and Comparative Essays*, ed. Stanley Cohen and Andrew Scull (Oxford: Basil Blackwell; New York: St. Martin's Press, 1981), 142.

2. Elaine Showalter, *The Female Malady: Women, Madness, and English Culture, 1830–1980* (New York: Pantheon, 1985; London: Virago, 1987).

3. Ibid.

a preeminently feminine one; and there have even been occasions when men have constituted a substantial majority of those officially identified as mad.

For example, against the fact that nearly two-thirds of those who consulted the seventeenth-century astrological physician Richard Napier for treatment of their mopish or melancholic moods were women,[4] one must set the observation that, as best one can judge from the admittedly defective data, men greatly outnumbered women among the inmates of eighteenth and early-nineteenth-century madhouses.[5] It was only after the middle of the nineteenth century, when the madhouses of the Gothic novelists had supposedly been transformed into the domestic retreats favored by the Victorian lunacy reformers, that women began gradually to outnumber men among those legally designated as mad—first among the pauper residuum who contributed the bulk of the rapid rise in the ranks of mad folk, and not till the end of the century among their genteel and affluent cousins. Nor, among the institutionalized insane, did the imbalance ever amount to more than a few percent, itself quite possibly attributable to the greater longevity of the "weaker" sex and to the disposition of the asylum authorities to keep female lunatics institutionalized longer than their male counterparts. And from the late 1960s to the present, men have formed the clear majority of mental hospital populations in the United States,[6] while the best modern research can find no consistent differences by sex in the prevalence of psychotic symptoms or in rates of schizophrenic breakdown.[7]

Taking a more expansive view of what constitutes mental illness, the idea that women are more frequently troubled in mind is perhaps more supportable. If women were only marginally overrepresented among the "Bedlam mad," the rise of a nonasylum psychiatry, ministering to the neurotic, the neurasthenic, and the hysteric, quickly found itself catering to a more heavily female clientele. On the late-nineteenth-century borderlands of insanity,[8] women were disproportionately represented among the clientele of rest homes, water cure establishments, mesmeric salons, and the mind cures of the Christian Scientists. And in the pres-

4. See Michael MacDonald, *Mystical Bedlam: Madness, Anxiety, and Healing in Seventeenth Century England* (Cambridge: Cambridge University Press, 1981), 36–40.

5. John Thurnam, *Observations and Essays on the Statistics of Insanity* (London: Simpkin Marshall, 1845).

6. National Institute of Mental Health, "Changes in the Age, Sex, and Diagnostic Composition of the Resident Population of State and County Mental Hospitals, United States 1965–1975," *Mental Health Statistical Note*, no. 146 (Washington, D.C.: Department of Health, Education, and Welfare, 1978).

7. Bruce P. Dohrenwend and Barbara S. Dohrenwend, "Sex Differences and Psychiatric Disorders," *American Journal of Sociology* 81 (1976): 1447–54.

8. Andrew Wynter, *The Borderlands of Insanity* (London: Hardwicke, 1875).

ent, women are consistently found to be more prone to neurosis and manic-depressive symptoms and are much more likely to be taking psychoactive drugs.

Yet these figures, too, demand to be treated with some caution. For alongside the greater reported frequency of symptoms of mental illness among women and their more extensive utilization of psychiatric facilities, one must note that an identical pattern holds for physical illness and the use of nonpsychiatric physicians and hospital services. Puzzlingly, women consistently exhibit higher rates of morbidity and lower rates of mortality than men of comparable age and social circumstances.[9]

Still, if the statistical evidence is at best rather ambiguous, the assertion that our culture somehow equates madness and the female of the species is not without foundation; and our organized responses to these maladies repeatedly turn out to be influenced, in ways both gross and subtle, by questions of sexuality and gender. One welcomes, then, an attempt to explore what is distinctive about the female experience of madness. Drawing on an extraordinary array of sources (literary and pictorial representations of the mad, in painting, photography, and film; asylum records; the recollections of ex-patients; the words and practices of their physicians; and the private papers of eminent women who did *not* become psychiatric casualties—materials that provide eloquent testimony about the tensions and tribulations faced even by exceptionally talented, privileged, and apparently successful women trapped within the confines of a patriarchal social order), Showalter's book constructs a compelling (if at times overdrawn) portrait of the contributions of psychiatry to the wrongs of women.

Our images of madness, she argues, are overwhelmingly female: "Women, within our dualistic systems of language and representation, are typically situated on the side of irrationality, silence, nature, and body, while men are situated on the side of reason, discourse, culture, and mind."[10] Romantic portraits of Crazy Jane, a poor servant girl seduced and abandoned by her lover;[11] *Lucia di Lammermoor* and a picture

9. Constance A. Nathanson, "Illness and the Feminine Role: A Theoretical Review," *Social Science and Medicine* 9 (1975): 57–62.

10. Ibid., 3–4. Cf. a late Victorian medical version of these notions: A woman's "mental characteristics . . . offer a marked contrast with [those] of a male. Her physical organization is not fully developed, and . . . she is . . . more like a child in disposition and also anatomically . . . in a general way . . . women are less intellectual than men, less original in thought, less capable of continuity and logic of thought, and hence they have been called more childlike in their mental characteristics, and in this respect resemble rather the primitive races" (Alexander Skene, *Medical Gynecology* [New York, Appleton, 1895], 80).

11. The mythical "Crazy Jane" or "Crazy Kate" was the subject of numerous ballads, melodramas, and portraits by artists as diverse as George Shepheard and Richard Dadd, and constituted one of the most popular romantic images of madness.

of female sexuality as insane violence against men; [12] Bertha Mason and Gothic madness, violent and hideous animality kept caged in Mr. Rochester's attic lest a "clothed hyena" be let loose upon the world: [13] in novels, in drama, in poetry, in painting, in popular ballads, in opera, it is women who stand as emblems and exemplars of irrationality.

Moreover, there has been much traffic between these cultural images and psychiatric ideologies. Notwithstanding the nearly equal propensity of the two sexes to go mad, Victorian alienists developed different explanations of why men and women became deranged, elaborate accounts of women's greater vulnerability to insanity, and even speculations about their tendency to experience madness in peculiarly feminine ways. In keeping with their professional preference for somatic accounts of the etiology of mental imbalance, [14] mad-doctors increasingly emphasized the biological and ignored or were indifferent to the social and the psychological sources of their patients' distress. Indeed, in reductionist fashion, woman's "natural" place in society—her capacities, her roles, her behavior—was held to be ineluctably derived from and controlled by the existence and functioning of her reproductive organs. [15] As an organism dominated by her uterus and ovaries, and hence by crisis and periodicity, a woman necessarily possessed greater capacities for affection and aptitude for child rearing, a preference for the domestic hearth, and a "natural" purity and moral sensibility; but she was also inescapably a creature in whom the emotional predominated over the rational, someone whose physiological equipment was of surpassing delicacy and fragility, at any moment liable to give way under the strains of modern life or the unavoidably perilous passage through puberty, pregnancy, par-

12. The frenzied madness of Sir Walter Scott's heroine, Lucy Ashton, the reluctant bride of Lammermoor, who celebrated her wedding night by stabbing her spouse, was regularly reproduced on stage in the most popular of Donizetti's operas.

13. Jane Eyre, her prospective marriage to Mr. Rochester halted at the last possible moment, is taken to see the dark secret lurking in his attic: "In the deep shade, at the further end of the room, a figure ran backwards and forwards. What it was, whether beast or human being, one could not, at first sight, tell: it grovelled, seemingly, on all fours; it snatched and growled like some strange wild animal: but it was covered with clothing; and a quantity of dark, grizzled hair, wild as a mane, hid its head and face" (Charlotte Brontë, *Jane Eyre* [Garden City, N.Y.: Doubleday, 1950], 300).

14. See Chapter 6. See also Michael Clark, "The Data of Alienism: Evolutionary Neurology, Physiological Psychiatry, and the Reconstruction of British Psychiatric Theory, c. 1850–c. 1900" (Ph.D. dissertation, Oxford University, 1982); idem, "The Rejection of Psychological Approaches to Mental Disorder in Late-Nineteenth-Century British Psychiatry," in *Madhouses, Mad-Doctors, and Madmen: The Social History of Psychiatry in the Victorian Era*, ed. Andrew Scull (Philadelphia: University of Pennsylvania Press; London: Athlone Press, 1981), 271–312; Steven Jacyna, "Somatic Theories of Mind and the Interests of Medicine in Britain, 1850–1879," *Medical History* 26 (1982): 233–58.

15. For a comparative view, see Carroll Smith-Rosenberg and Charles Rosenberg, "The Female Animal: Medical and Biological Views of Woman and Her Role in Nineteenth Century America," *Journal of American History* 60 (1973): 332–56.

turition, lactation, menstruation, and the menopause. The constriction of women's lives, their legal powerlessness, and their economic marginality, which were the central features of existing social relations between the sexes, thus received the sanction of science. And confronting such weak and fragile vessels, "Victorian psychiatry defined its task with respect to women as the preservation of brain stability in the face of almost overwhelming physical odds." [16]

Theories of a differential, gender-based etiology for mental disturbance corresponded, in some important respects, to differential expectations and treatments for men and women. The early Victorian period saw the creation of a whole new network of public asylums, coupled with a system of national inspection of receptacles for the mad by the lunacy commissioners. [17] Such changes reflected a revulsion against earlier methods of managing the mad and an astonishing (and in the event sadly misplaced) optimism about the therapeutic effects of the new system of moral management. In institutions containing several hundred, even a thousand or more, inmates, alienists struggled to produce a simulacrum of the domestic scene, in the process revealing and reproducing "structures of class and gender that were 'moral,' that is, 'normal,' by their own standards." [18] Classification was quite central to the production of a docile and harmonious community (essential, in the words of the Scottish alienist, W. A. F. Browne, if one were "to inspire that respect for order and tranquility which is the basis of all sanity and serenity of mind"); [19] and rigid segregation of the sexes was quite central to their classificatory schemes. [20] The lunacy commissioners even objected to the mingling of male and female corpses in the deadhouse at the Cambridgeshire County Asylum! [21]

Kept constantly separated from their male counterparts, save at the carefully stage-managed asylum balls that were a weekly demonstration of the powers of moral management over the sexual passions, women endured an even more passive and circumscribed existence than could

16. Showalter, *Female Malady*, 74.

17. See Andrew Scull, *Museums of Madness: The Social Organization of Insanity in Nineteenth-Century England* (London: Allen Lane; New York: St. Martin's Press, 1979); Kathleen Jones, *Lunacy, Law, and Conscience, 1744–1845* (London: Routledge and Kegan Paul, 1955).

18. Showalter, *Female Malady*, 34.

19. William Alexander Francis Browne, quoted in *Journal of Mental Science* 5 (1859): 203.

20. "It would appear as though it were an offense in asylum life for men and women to meet together. . . . How can we wonder that the female patients we pass in the long galleries are eaten up by utter vacuity and dreariness; or that the men a stone's throw off herd hopelessly together?" ("Non-restraint in the Treatment of the Insane," *Edinburgh Review* 131 [1870]: 222).

21. Commissioners in Lunacy, *Twenty-fifth Annual Report* (1871), 131.

be found on the men's wards. The idle monotony of their daily round was relieved only by work at quintessentially feminine tasks: the cleaning, laundry, and sewing that were vital to the upkeep of these ever-larger museums of madness. And their improvement was measured, as often as not, by their ability to manage their dress and their appearance. In a striking analysis of the work of Hugh Diamond, the pioneer of psychiatric photography in England,[22] Showalter points out how it allows us to *see* the moral management of female insanity; how the supposedly objective lens of the photographer instead reveals, in the choice, the posing, the staging of its subjects, the imposition of cultural stereotypes of femininity and female insanity, a capturing of the madwoman in the straitjacket of her keeper's gaze. In image after image, "women were given props that symbolized, often with pathetic futility, the asylum superintendent's hope of making them conform to Victorian ideals of feminine decorum."[23] Humanitarianism had, as its hidden face, new forms of paternalistic domination.

As the hopes of the asylums' founders dimmed, and their institutions silted up with the chronically crazy, "the waifs and strays, the weak and wayward of our race,"[24] so cracks began to appear in the facade they presented to the world, providing glimpses of a moribund system, overcrowded, inefficient, ever more demoralized. Showalter adopts Veida Skultans' term, "psychiatric Darwinism,"[25] to describe the parallel evolution of medical theories of insanity, towards a grim determinism that emphasized madness as the product of a process of mental and physical degeneration. In the words of Henry Maudsley, the dominant figure of *fin-de-siècle* English psychiatry, the madman "is the necessary organic consequent of certain organic antecedents: and it is impossible he should escape the tyranny of his organization."[26] The physical signs of physiological decay were written particularly plainly on the bodies of women, and given the hopelessness of curative efforts and the vital significance of healthy offspring for the future of the race, prospective husbands were urged to inspect the merchandise carefully, searching for "physical signs . . . which betray degeneracy of stock . . . any malformations of the head, face, mouth, teeth and ears. Outward defects and deformities are the visible signs of inward and invisible faults which will have their influence in breeding."[27]

22. Sander Gilman, ed., *The Face of Madness: Hugh W. Diamond and the Origins of Psychiatric Photography* (New York: Brunner-Mazel, 1976).

23. Showalter, *Female Malady*, 87.

24. W. A. F. Browne, *Annual Report of the Crichton Royal Asylum*, (1857), quoted in *Journal of Mental Science* 4 (1858): 201.

25. Veida Skultans, *English Madness: Ideas on Insanity, 1580–1890* (London: Routledge and Kegan Paul, 1978).

26. Henry Maudsley, *The Pathology of Mind* (London: Macmillan, 1879), 88.

27. Ibid. (1895 ed.), 536, quoted in Showalter, *Female Malady*, 107.

Such rigid somaticism coincided with a barely disguised contempt for the mad and appeared to leave but little scope for expert intervention. In response, the leading alienists sought to widen the scope of their authority, to move outside the asylum walls, and to obtain a mandate to patrol the mental frontiers of society on the lookout for "incipient lunatics" whose disorders, hidden from less trained eyes, threatened future trouble and a further dangerous dilution of the quality of the breeding population. It was these shadowy inhabitants of what Mortimer Granville dubbed Mazeland, Dazeland, and Driftland [28] who now drew the attention of the most eminent mental specialists of the day—provided, of course, that their families possessed sufficient resources to pay for such expert attention. And in most instances, these mental cripples and invalids turned out to be women. Some were diagnosed as neurasthenics or anorexic (a condition recognized for the first time in 1873); but the most common diagnosis was unquestionably hysteria.

In two central chapters, Showalter examines the relationship between hysteria and women's lives and the nature of the psychiatric response to this protean, puzzling, infuriating, recalcitrant condition—a syndrome the prominent American neurologist Silas Weir Mitchell preferred to call "mysteria." [29] With its associations with capricious physical symptoms and emotional lability, here was a disorder that epitomized feminine fickleness. Its very name associated it with female sexuality, and English alienists characteristically attributed it to some combination of sexual inhibition, enforced passivity, and thwarted maternal drives, allied to faulty heredity and the biological crises of the female reproductive system and exacerbated by any attempt to transgress the "natural" limits on women's participation in society. [30] Too much education was a particularly dangerous thing. [31] Adolescent girls needed all their mental and physical energies to negotiate the treacherous shoals of puberty. Add mental strain, and one could expect, warned Maudsley, "the degeneration of the reproductive capacity, beginning with the atrophy of the breasts and ending with a total loss of 'pelvic power'"—not to mention the prospect of epilepsy, chorea, or mental breakdown. [32]

Showalter rightly notes the persistent blindness of even the most sym-

28. J. Mortimer Granville, in Andrew Wynter, *The Borderlands of Insanity*, 2d ed. (London: Renshaw, 1877).

29. Silas Weir Mitchell, quoted in Barbara Sicherman, "The Uses of a Diagnosis: Doctors, Patients, and Neurasthenia," *Journal of the History of Medicine* 32 (1977): 41.

30. See the useful discussion of late-nineteenth-century British views on the etiology and treatment of hysteria in Michael Clark, "The Rejection of Psychological Approaches to Mental Disorder in Late Nineteenth Century British Psychiatry," in *Madhouses, Mad-Doctors, and Madmen*, ed. Scull, esp. 293–300.

31. See, in particular, Henry Maudsley, "Sex in Mind and in Education," *Fortnightly Review* 15 (1874): 466–83.

32. Ibid., quoted in Showalter, *Female Malady*, 125.

pathetic male physicians to the connections between psychosomatic disorders and constricted and powerless lives, "women's intellectual frustration, lack of mobility, or needs for autonomy and control."[33] In the impassioned words of Florence Nightingale:

> To have no food for our heads, no food for our hearts, no food for our activity, is that nothing? If we have no food for the body, how we do cry out, how all the world hears of it, how all the newspapers talk of it, with a paragraph headed in great capital letters, DEATH FROM STARVATION! But suppose one were to put a paragraph in the "Times," *Death of Thought from Starvation,* or *Death of Moral Activity from Starvation,* how people would stare, how they would laugh and wonder! One would think we had no heads or hearts, by the indifference of the public towards them. Our bodies are the only things of consequence.[34]

But if hysteria was hidden protest, a rebellion against the stifling demands of a patriarchal social order, it was a feeble and ineffectual form of resistance. The secondary gains—"the sympathy of the family, the attention of the physician"—were quite incommensurate with the far more extensive primary losses, "the costs in powerlessness and silence."[35] In the words of the French feminist theorist Helene Cixous, "Silence: silence is the mark of hysteria. The great hysterics have lost speech . . . their tongues are cut off and what talks isn't heard because it's the body that talks and man doesn't hear the body."[36]

Nor was this the only price paid by the female hysteric. For English psychiatrists "found their hysterical patients personally and morally repulsive,"[37] and their treatment of them was suitably ruthless, uncompromising, even brutal. Viewing their patients as a cowardly, histrionic, deceitful, and morally wretched lot, many responded in kind, advising "observant neglect" or even active intimidation, blackmail, and threats. "Ridicule," noted F. C. Skey, "is a powerful weapon . . . but there is no emotion equal to fear and the threat of personal chastisement."[38] And for some, threats might give way to action: stopping the patient's breathing, pouring water on her head, slapping her with wet towels, exercising pressure "on some tender area." All too frequently to no avail. In the understanding and treatment of hysteria, as with psychosis, English psychiatry found itself at an impasse.

Elsewhere, first through Charcot's work, and then in Freud and

33. Showalter, *Female Malady*, 132.

34. Florence Nightingale, *Cassandra* (Old Westbury, N.Y.: Feminist Press, 1979), 41–42, quoted in Showalter, *Female Malady*, 128.

35. Showalter, *Female Malady*, 161.

36. Quoted in ibid., 160–61.

37. Ibid., 133.

38. F. C. Skey, *Hysteria*, 2d ed. (London: Longmans et al., 1867), 60, quoted in ibid., 138.

Breuer's *Studies on Hysteria,* there were experiments with a more psychologically oriented approach. In picturing hysterical symptoms as the product of unconscious conflicts beyond the individual's control, in beginning to take "women's words and women's lives seriously,"[39] Showalter sees psychoanalysis as potentially a major advance, but one whose promise soon dissolved as Freud's increasing theoretical rigidity and obsessive "insistence on the sexual origins of hysteria blinded him to the social factors contributing to it."[40] In any event, Freud's ideas met with a particularly hostile response from many English psychiatrists, notwithstanding, in Leonard Woolf's words, the "desperately meagre . . . primitive and chaotic" state of English medical knowledge of insanity on the eve of the Great War.[41]

The final, and in some ways the least successful section of *The English Malady,* deals with developments from World War I through the demise of Laingian antipsychiatry in the late 1970s, a period Showalter labels the era of psychiatric modernism. Her analysis opens promisingly enough, with a harrowing comparison of the treatment of shellshock by Lewis Yealland and by W. H. R. Rivers. The epidemic of war neurosis among the British troops was a wholly unexpected development. First interpreted as quite literally the product of the physical or chemical effects of a shell bursting at close range and assumed to have a physical cause,[42] it gradually came to be seen as the product of emotional disturbance, a male form of hysterical conversion. In effect, as Showalter puts it, "when all signs of physical fear were judged as weakness and where alternatives to combat—pacifism, conscientious objection, desertion, even suicide—were viewed as unmanly, men were silenced and immobilized and forced, like women, to express their conflicts through the body."[43]

Men's unconscious resistance provoked some of the same negative reactions as greeted their hysterical sisters—made harsher by the "unmanliness" of those who failed to fight. Many took a harshly moralistic view of the emotionally incapacitated, suggesting that shell-shock cases should be court-martialed and shot for malingering or cowardice. Yealland's "disciplinary therapy" gave barely disguised expression to these feelings, stressing "quick cures, shaming, and physical re-education,

39. Showalter, *Female Malady,* 158.

40. Ibid., 160.

41. Leonard Woolf, *Beginning Again: An Autobiography of the Years 1911–1918* (New York: Harcourt, Brace, Jovanovich, 1972), 76, quoted in ibid., 164.

42. Charles S. Myers, *Shellshock in France* (Cambridge: Cambridge University Press, 1940). See also the discussion in Martin Stone, "Shellshock and the Psychiatrists," in *The Anatomy of Madness,* vol. 2, ed. W. F. Bynum, Roy Porter, and Michael Shepherd (London: Tavistock, 1985), 242–71; and idem, "The Military and Industrial Roots of Clinical Psychology in Britain, 1900–1945" (Ph.D. dissertation, London School of Economics, 1985).

43. Showalter, *Female Malady,* 171.

which often involved the infliction of pain,"[44] and extending to the use of cigarette burns, "hot plates" thrust into the mouth, and the application of painful electrical shocks to the neck and throat. But war neurosis was four times more common among officers than among enlisted men, and for the most part, there was reluctance to treat gentlemen in such overtly harsh and brutal ways. Instead, the treatment of officers brought the first breach in English psychiatry's commitment to organicism. Siegfried Sassoon's "Soldier's Declaration," for example, a forthright denunciation of the war, could have brought him a court-martial and imprisonment. Instead, he was diagnosed as neurasthenic and shipped off to be "treated" by W. H. R. Rivers at Craiglockhart Military Hospital. Here, as Showalter points out, the treatment was kindly and gentle, and the surroundings luxurious (though in the outcome, Sassoon's political protest was invalidated by redefining it as a nervous breakdown, and he was manipulated into resuming his role at the front as "an officer and a gentleman").

The world fit for heroes now saw a bifurcated psychiatry: psychotherapy (usually some variant of psychoanalysis) for well-to-do outpatients; and a renewed commitment to organicism for the multitudes who continued to be packed off to the asylum. Psychoanalysis, notwithstanding its sizable cohort of female therapists, "hardened into a discourse that devalued women."[45] Meanwhile, in a veritable paroxysm of inventiveness, asylum psychiatry experimented with malarial therapy, metrazol-induced seizures, insulin comas, electroshock treatment, lobotomies, and finally ataraxic drugs, most notably Largactil, the "mighty drug" that was to be our culture's magic potion against the ravages of schizophrenia.[46] A number of these therapies, Showalter argues, reduced patients treated with them to a state of passivity and dependence that constitute extremes of typical female experiences; and incomplete evidence suggests that women were disproportionately the beneficiaries of lobotomies and shock treatments.

Both here and in the parallel discussion of literary representations of female madness, much of what Showalter has to say is apt and insightful. But there are also passages that strike me as too glib and simplistic, passages that violate her insistence earlier in the book that one must not romanticize madness. It may be that women's autobiographical novels "transform the experiences of shock, psychosurgery, and chemotherapy into symbolic episodes of punishment for intellectual ambition, domestic

44. Ibid., 176.
45. Ibid., 197.
46. The history of the use of somatic treatments for mental illness is the focus of my current research, to be published by the University of California Press and by Polity Press as *Desperate Remedies*. See also my paper "Desperate Remedies: A Gothic Tale of Madness and Modern Medicine," *Psychological Medicine* 17 (1987): 561–77.

defiance, and sexual autonomy," [47] but this is surely too crude and self-serving a portrait to accept at face value. Or to take another example, to assert that "during the postwar period, the female malady, no longer linked to hysteria, assumed a new clinical form: schizophrenia" [48] is to damage one's own case by engaging in polemical excess. Though Showalter briefly acknowledges that the incidence of schizophrenia is "about equal in women and men," [49] the whole thrust of the discussion that follows is to emphasize the "parallels" between "schizophrenic symptoms of passivity, depersonalization, disembodiment, and fragmentation" and "the social situation of women;" [50] to present, apparently approvingly, accounts of "schizophrenia as a protest against the feminine mystique" and portraits of "mental institutions as environments in which deviants from conventional feminine roles were forced to conform." [51]

By now, the antipsychiatric follies of R. D. Laing and his epigones are rather thoroughly discredited. The intellectual vapidity of Laing's later work, the transparent hucksterism and political opportunism he paraded as his star began to set, and the disastrous track record of Laingian therapy have all combined to make him a yesterday's man. But it is with Laing that Showalter brings her story to a conclusion. As she points out, feminists had once seen in his notion of "ontological insecurity" and in his analysis of the effects of the double bind on female adolescents "important new ways of conceptualizing the relationship between madness and femininity." [52] But having reviewed the whole sorry episode, down to the dotty view of schizophrenia as religious vision and spiritual quest, and the pathetic story of Mary Barnes, she concedes that "in retrospect, it seems clear that despite vivid representations of women's suffering, antipsychiatry had no coherent analysis to offer women" [53]—or, one might add, members of the opposite sex either. (Unless, of course, one sees David Cooper's advocacy of "bed therapy," that is, sex with David Cooper, as a contribution to the cure of schizophrenia in women.) [54]

In a brief epilogue, Showalter suggests, with considerable rhetorical flourish but without sustained argument or elaboration, that hopes for the future must now be invested in the new feminist therapy movement. Perhaps—though for those of us who are skeptical, it would help if she had spelled out just who these therapists are, what their therapeutic innovations have been, and why one should accept that their activities have radically transformed the prospects for coping with, even curing, the deranged. For my part, I fear that the miseries of madness (female *and* male), and the horrors that have been perpetrated in the name of its treatment, will not be so readily or rapidly vanquished.

47. Showalter, *Female Malady*, 210.   48. Ibid., 203.   49. Ibid., 204.
50. Ibid., 213.   51. Ibid., 216 and 215.   52. Ibid., 222.   53. Ibid., 246.
54. See David Cooper, *The Grammar of Living* (Harmondsworth: Penguin, 1974).

CHAPTER TWELVE

The Theory and Practice
of Civil Commitment

The past two decades have witnessed a significant extension of the involvement of lawyers and the legal system in matters psychiatric. Much of this activity has had a sharply adversarial edge, with mental health lawyers (many of them public-interest attorneys schooled in the civil rights movement) attacking the procedures and practices of organized psychiatry and on occasion impugning psychiatrists' claims to expert status and authority.[1] Efforts have been made to bestow both the "right to treatment" and "the right to refuse treatment" on the psychiatrically unfortunate, prompting fierce objections from psychiatrists that their clinical authority is being improperly infringed upon, to their patients' (not to mention their profession's) detriment.

Whatever the validity of these protests, it should now be apparent that the judicial system is not the most promising arena of action for those committed to psychiatric reform. In the late Peter Sedgwick's words, "If the resources of court action really did represent the high road of hope for the average institutionalised psychiatric patient, one might imagine

Chapter 12 is reprinted from the *Michigan Law Review*, Volume 82, 1984, pp. 793–809, with the permission of the editor.

1. An ACLU attorney, Bruce Ennis, has been a particularly prominent part of this movement. The title of his book (*Prisoners of Psychiatry* [New York: Harcourt, Brace, Jovanovich, 1972]) and of a subsequent law review article ("Psychiatry and the Presumption of Expertise: Flipping Coins in the Courtroom," *California Law Review* 62 [1974]: 693–753) provide a not-so-subtle index of the stance adopted by at least some mental health lawyers. In response, psychiatrists complain of "the right to rot" and of patients "dying with their rights on," rhetoric that has attracted an increasingly sympathetic audience as the expansion of deinstitutionalization, combined with the contraction of social welfare services, has made the homeless mentally ill an ever more visible affront to middle-class sensibilities.

that the United States would by now possess the finest mental-health system that legal and libertarian reason could invent."[2] To the contrary, the manifest deficiencies of contemporary American mental health policies, particularly with regard to the chronically mentally disordered, are now a staple item in the popular media, both printed and electronic. This situation is unsurprising, since civil libertarian interventions are necessarily reactive, and the law at best a crude instrument for formulating social policy, particularly when the courts attempt to intrude on quintessentially political decision-making about the allocation of funds among competing programs and priorities.

One of the major contemporary arenas of conflict between law and psychiatry has been over civil-commitment laws and procedures. From the late 1960s onwards, states generally began to circumscribe the formal criteria that justified the involuntary commitment of the mentally disordered, many of the states following the model provided by California's Lanterman-Petris-Short Act of 1967.[3] More recently, one can find evidence of a backlash against such changes. Increasingly, it seems, we are being urged to reconsider our new-found reluctance to countenance the involuntary confinement of the mentally disordered—a stance reflecting "disillusionment and frustration with commitment statutes that have made it increasingly difficult to provide treatment to psychotic patients who are not imminently dangerous, and . . . increasing demands [by an aroused public] for more extensive involuntary hospitalization."[4]

Carol Warren's *The Court of Last Resort* contains the most extended and systematic attempt we have to examine *empirically* the impact of the Lanterman-Petris-Short Act. When the *University of Michigan Law Review* asked me to write an essay on the issues raised by her study, I welcomed the opportunity to do so, not least because it seemed to me that the contemporary debates uncannily echoed arguments first rehearsed at a much earlier stage in the evolution of the psychiatric profession. To highlight the value of a historical perspective on our contemporary dilemmas, I elected to frame the discussion that follows around a mid-nineteenth century lawsuit brought by an obscure middle-aged lady enraptured by the teachings of a now-forgotten sectarian preacher—a decision that I hope gives some substance to the old saw concerning the value of historical inquiry in understanding the roots of our contemporary dilemmas.

2. Peter Sedgwick, *Psychopolitics* (London: Pluto Press; New York: Harper and Row, 1982), 216.

3. On the passage of the Lanterman-Petris-Short legislation, see Eugene Bardach, *The Skill Factor in Politics* (Berkeley: University of California Press, 1972).

4. David Mechanic, "Recent Developments in Mental Health Perspectives and Services" (Paper presented at the Conference on Mental Health Services for the Seriously Mentally Ill, University of California at Los Angeles, 12 February 1988), 14.

The Theory and Practice
of Civil Commitment

On a sweltering day in London, towards the end of June 1849, a curious throng of spectators jammed into a special sitting of the Court of the Exchequer to hear the lord chief baron, Sir Frederick Pollock, and a special jury decide the case of *Nottidge v. Ripley and another.*[1] For three days, the court remained "crowded to suffocation," while a still larger audience followed the proceedings at a distance, devouring successive installments of the real-life soap opera at breakfast, in the blow-by-blow account provided in the legal columns of the *Times*. At the conclusion of the trial, after a brief retirement, the jury found for the plaintiff, awarding her fifty pounds and costs.

The object of this unwonted celebrity, Miss Louisa Nottidge, was a quiet and retiring "maiden lady . . . at the meridian of life," and her suit was an action for damages against her brother and brother-in-law for wrongful confinement in a madhouse.[2] As the trial testimony revealed, shortly after her father's death, in May 1844, Louisa and three of her unmarried sisters (all rather advanced in years) had become enamored of the doctrines of an obscure and tiny religious cult, the Lampeter Brethren, and of the preaching of the sect's leader, a defrocked Anglican curate named Prince. Within a matter of months, they had left their maternal home to follow Prince, taking with them their private fortunes—amounting to some 6,000 pounds each. Three of the ladies promptly married, in the same ceremony, much younger (and penniless) members of the religious commune, not troubling to take the usual Victorian precaution of protecting their property through prenuptial settlements. Louisa, apparently unable to find even so unsatisfactory a suitor, nevertheless joined her sisters in Agapemone, or the Abode of Love, the country house the sect now occupied in Somerset.

Here she lived for six weeks with the other fifty or sixty members of the commune, "dazzled by its luxury, charmed with its games and pastimes, and sustained by glorious assurances of judgment being past, and heaven to come;" till at length her mother learned of her whereabouts.

1. Unless otherwise noted, my account of the trial is drawn from the daily law reports in *The Times* (London), 25 June 1849, 7, col. 4; 26 June 1849, 7, col. 2; and 27 June 1849, 7, col. 4.

2. The meagerness of the damages she received was sharply criticized in some quarters. See, for instance, *The Times* (London), 30 June 1849, 5, col. 1. Apparently the jury was reluctant to impose heavier damages because it believed that the defendants were not actuated by mercenary or other improper motives.

Convinced that her daughter "was not a free agent," that her mind was deranged, and that her continued presence in this den of sin and iniquity was "endangering her happiness in this and her welfare in a future life," Mrs. Nottidge determined to rescue her from such "a low, degrading, and disgusting association." Accordingly, she dispatched her son and son-in-law to Somerset. Gaining access to the house by stealth, they first tried to persuade Louisa to come with them to visit her sick mother. When she declined, however, they seized her, "dragged her out of the house, notwithstanding her struggles and screams, and forced her into a carriage without either bonnet, or shawl, or shoes . . . and then off they drove as fast as the horses could put their feet to the ground."[3] Two medical men were readily found to certify that her reckless disregard of her reputation and property, and her peculiar religious beliefs—or delusions, as they were now held to be—constituted clear evidence of insanity, and she was promptly carted off to Dr. Stillwell's madhouse, Moorcroft House.

The spectators at the trial listened to this gothic tale with rapt attention, occasionally mixed with gales of laughter when revelations of the goings-on at the Abode of Love provided a measure of comic relief. Miss Nottidge had remained under confinement for some fourteen months, still insisting that Prince was "God manifest in the flesh," that the day of judgment had come, and that she had been rendered immortal and should shortly "be taken up to heaven in the twinkling of an eye"—and still diagnosed by the asylum superintendent and by the lunacy commissioners, the official inspectors of all asylums, as a religious monomaniac. Then she managed to escape. She was rapidly recaptured and brought back to the asylum, but not before she had succeeded in alerting her coreligionists to her whereabouts. After a protracted struggle, they secured her release (at which point, she promptly returned to Agapemone and handed over all her assets to Prince).

The medical witnesses at the trial were uniformly convinced that Louisa Nottidge had been and still was deranged, and thus in need of protection and treatment in an institution. The lay audience was not persuaded. As the *Times* put it in its editorial on the case: "We must not stretch a harmless hallucination into legal insanity. . . . The shades and gradations of error and folly are so insensibly blended that we could not incarcerate and coerce such an [*sic*] one without danger to others."[4] And in summing up the evidence for the jury, the Lord Chief Baron all but directed a verdict for the plaintiff: "It is my opinion that you ought to

3. J. Conolly, *A Remonstrance with the Lord Chief Baron, Touching the Case of Nottidge v. Ripley* (London: Churchill, 1849), 16. *The Times* (London), 25 June 1849, 7, col. 4; 26 June 1849, 7, col. 7.

4. *The Times* (London), 30 June 1849, 5, col. 1.

liberate every person who is not dangerous to himself or others . . . and I desire to impress that opinion with as much force as I can."[5]

Periodic moral panics over the issue of the improper commitment of the sane to asylums were endemic in the nineteenth century in both England and the United States, and attempts like Pollock's to limit the criteria justifying involuntary commitment to the narrowest possible compass reflect one possible response to these spasms of anxiety.[6] But alienists fiercely resisted attempts to constrict the definition of madness within such narrow confines, and for the most part they succeeded. In the *Nottidge* case, the Lord Chief Baron's dictum drew forth an impassioned critique from John Conolly, the leading authority of his generation in matters psychiatric.[7]

Notwithstanding its "apparent conformity . . . to the liberty of the subject, and to the dictates of humanity,"[8] argued Conolly, the attempt to restrict the asylum population to lunatics who were a danger to themselves or others was thoroughly mistaken and mischievous:

> If the liberty of an insane person is inconsistent with the safety of his property or the property of others; or with his preservation from disgraceful scenes and exposures; or with the tranquility of his family, or his neighbours, or society;—if his sensuality, his disregard of cleanliness and decency, make him offensive in private and public, dishonouring and injuring his children and his name;—if his excessive eccentricity or extreme feebleness of mind subject him to continual imposition, and to ridicule, abuse, and persecution in the streets, and to frequent accidents at home and abroad;—his protection and that of society demands that he should be kept in a quiet and secluded residence, guarded by watchful attendants and not exposed to the public.[9]

Similar are the cases of young women "of ungovernable temper, . . . sullen, wayward, malicious, defying all domestic control; or who want that restraint over the passions without which the female character is lost";[10] and young men "whose grossness of habits, immoderate love of drink, disregard of honesty, or general irregularity of conduct, bring disgrace and wretchedness on their relatives. . . . People of this kind may not endanger their lives or those of others, but their being at large is inconsistent with the comfort of society, and their own welfare."[11] "To forbid the placing of such persons in asylums because they are not dan-

5. Ibid., 27 June 1849, 7, col. 5.

6. On the issue of improper confinement in the nineteenth century, see, generally, Peter McCandless, "Liberty and Lunacy: The Victorians and Wrongful Confinement," in *Madhouses, Mad-Doctors and Madmen: The Social History of Psychiatry in the Victorian Era*, ed. Andrew Scull (Philadelphia: University of Pennsylvania Press; London: Athlone Press, 1981), 339–62.

7. On Conolly, see Chapter 7.   8. Conolly, *Remonstrance*, 5.   9. Ibid., 7.

10. Ibid., 9–10.   11. Ibid., 9.

gerous . . . would be to forbid their being protected and cured,"[12] and furthermore would "bring affliction on a thousand families, and even throw society into confusion."[13] The case of Louise Nottidge was of exactly this sort: "It belonged to a class in which the patient is unequal, from feebleness and unsoundness of mind, to take care of herself or her property."[14] Confinement preserved "her money . . . from legalized robbery, and her person from the possibility of legalized prostitution."[15] Consequently, "those who exult in her liberation from the salutary control of an asylum are exulting over her ruin."[16]

It is clear that over the next century and more, while perhaps shrinking from endorsing the full measure of Conolly's attempt to equate insanity with any deviation from conventional social and moral standards, the civil commitment codes of all Anglo-American jurisdictions by and large embraced the claims made by psychiatrists to be the arbiters of the boundary between sanity and insanity. These laws accepted the need for a broad standard for commitability, based on the state's paternalistic interest in securing protection and treatment for the loosely defined class of the mentally unbalanced. Sir Frederick Pollock's attempt to narrow the criteria for individual commitment, although symptomatic of a widespread distrust of psychiatrists' character and competence,[17] had only a limited impact on the development of mental health law.

Beginning in the late 1960s, however, in the context of a virtual explosion of law and litigation in the United States relating to the mental health system, there has been a marked trend away from traditional commitment codes, with their typically loose standards and protections and broad grants of discretionary authority.[18] One of the earliest and most influential manifestations of this trend was the passage of a new commitment law in California, widely known as the Lanterman-Petris-Short Act (LPS).[19] Under LPS, the emphasis in involuntary commitment decisions shifted away from a *parens patriae* concern with "protecting" those unable to care for themselves, toward a much greater stress on the issue of danger to others and on procedural rights. Commitment for anything more than an emergency seventy-two-hour period could be achieved in only two ways: (1) through a conservatorship subject to mandatory yearly judicial review and jury trial for those persons found to be

12. Ibid., 12.   13. Ibid., 9.   14. Ibid., 12.
15. Ibid., 18.   16. Ibid., 13.
17. See, for example, McCandless, "Liberty and Lunacy," passim.
18. See, generally, Alexander D. Brooks, *Law, Psychiatry, and the Mental Health System* (Boston: Little, Brown, 1974); David B. Wexler, *Mental Health Law: Major Issues* (New York: Plenum, 1981); and idem, "Mental Health Law and the Movement Toward Voluntary Treatment," *California Law Review* 62 (1974): 671–92.
19. California Welfare and Institutional Code 5000-5464 (West 1972). On the passage of Lanterman-Petris-Short, see Eugene Bardach, *The Skill Factor in Politics* (Berkeley: University of California Press, 1972).

"gravely disabled"—that is, on the basis of clear and convincing evidence, mentally unable to provide for their "basic personal needs for food, clothing, or shelter"; or (2) through commitments lasting no more than ninety days for persons who are mentally ill and who, as evidenced by recent overt acts, attempts, or threats of violence, are found to be "imminently dangerous." Such ninety-day commitments can be renewed only if it is shown that the patient, while confined, again acted violently. Under either standard of commitment, the person alleged to be mentally ill has the right to be notified of all proceedings against him or her and to be present at all hearings; and the right to be represented by an attorney during all judicial review proceedings.[20] Thus, the California commitment law in a number of crucial respects now corresponds quite closely to the standard articulated in *Nottidge v. Ripley;* indeed, from some points of view, it is even stricter.

Carol Warren's book, *The Court of Last Resort,*[21] presents a wide-ranging analysis of court administration of this new mental health law. The book's particular focus is an empirical examination of judicial decision-making about whether to release or retain those involuntarily committed under LPS, based on extensive firsthand research and observation in "Metropolitan Court" (a pseudonym for a Los Angeles mental health court). Though she attempts to place her findings in a broader sociological context, to see courtroom decisions as to some degree conditioned by large-scale economic, political, and historical forces, the results of this effort are rather thin and insubstantial.[22] The book's real strength lies in its documentation of the gap between the formal wording of the statute and the practical application of the law and in its contribution to the current debate about the appropriate standards for involuntary commitment.

THE METROPOLITAN COURT ROUTINE

Theoretically, LPS sets up an adversarial system in the courtroom, designed (on an analogy with an idealized portrait of the criminal justice system) to protect the patient's rights. Lawyers seeking commitment confront other lawyers representing those alleged to be in need of confine-

20. For a review of commitment law in California, including some subsequent modifications of LPS, see Estate of Hofferber, 28 Cal. 3d 161, 616 P.2d 836, 167 Cal. Rptr. 854 (1980).

21. Carol A. B. Warren, *The Court of Last Resort: Mental Illness and the Law,* with contributions by Stephen J. Morse and Jack Zusman (Chicago: University of Chicago Press, 1982).

22. For example, her discussion (ibid., chap. 7) of decision-making by the court on habeas corpus writs is hampered rather than helped by a clumsy and heavy-handed attempt to structure the analysis around an examination of certain abstract "theories" of the decision-making process (conflict, legal, organizational, and individual decision-maker) and their supposed implications.

ment, and psychiatric personnel face questioning and cross-examination about the grounds for their conclusions. In practice, however, as Warren demonstrates in a variety of contexts, the norm is rather one of cooperation and mutual accommodation among a group of actors who routinely play out the same roles day after day, and who have all developed a working consensus around a "commonsense" model of madness.[23] The practical effect of a common culture and a set of shared organizational imperatives is a recognition that "we all work together here"[24] and a conviction that such a state of affairs is both natural and desirable. Thus, though courtroom procedures are dominated by elaborate rituals designed "to demonstrate compliance with procedural rules as well as with substantive law,"[25] public defenders "generally refrained from vigorous advocacy of their clients' legal rights under LPS."[26] Instead, they chose to work "together with the other participants in the hearing to come to what all could agree was the 'right decision' for the individual and for society."[27]

Notwithstanding an apparent conflict between "the medical and legal frames of reference," the practical convergence on "an underlying commonsense and a taken-for-granted perspective on mental illness" smoothed the way for an easy and tension-free collaboration. Just as "attorneys view their clients as crazy and therefore refrain from standing firmly in the way of their involuntary incarceration,"[28] so too the psychiatrists—mostly state hospital personnel who appear regularly in the same courtroom—adapt readily to "legal practices" and to the existence of "a stable release rate."[29] The judge, meanwhile, justifies "the smooth, rapid, and routine method of processing" in the courtroom, and

> the lack of an adversary approach to justice in mental health law on the grounds that the role of the defense attorney [is] to be 'a reflection of the client's personality' rather than a vigorous advocate. If the client [is] crazy, then this should not be concealed by the defense attorney.[30]

As Warren notes, this emphasis on assembly line justice closely corresponds with the pattern that obtains in the criminal courts—on whose allegedly "adversarial" procedures the reformers who wrote LPS modeled the new law.[31]

Where outside intervention in the system threatens this pattern of mutual accommodation, the main actors in the carefully staged drama move quickly to minimize its impact. Thus, in the face of the challenge

23. Ibid., 38.   24. Ibid., 140.   25. Ibid., 147.   26. Ibid., 165.
27. Ibid., 172.   28. Ibid., 140.   29. Ibid., 191.   30. Ibid., 191.
31. See, generally, David Sudnow, "Normal Crimes: Sociological Features of the Penal Code in a Public Defender Office," *Social Problems* 12 (1965): 255–76; Roberta Rovner-Pieczenik, "Labeling in an Organizational Context: Adjudicating Felonies in an Urban Court," in *The Research Experience*, ed. M. P. Golden (Itasca, Ill.: Peacock, 1976), 447–64.

posed by potentially disruptive higher court rulings, the judge, district attorneys, public defenders, and mental health counselors—"members of the organization cooperating as a whole—embarked on a search for a legal way to evade the problems attendant upon [implementation]"—as one participant put it, "'tinkering with' the new precedent until it 'came out right.'"[32] A more frequent source of disturbance was the arrival of a "new, aggressive, advocate defense attorney," full of idealism, intent on implementing the letter of the law and defending the "rights" of his clientele.[33] Such callow youths were quickly disabused, and most "would learn the ropes, and would become socialized to the way things are done."[34] The occasional nonconformist aroused anger and then protective action: Mr. William Simmons, for example, refused to "settle down." Instead,

> he persuaded a number of his conservatee clients to ask for jury trials, thus tying up Department 2 for days on end. He also spent hours studying and arguing on habeas corpus hearings, committing what was probably the most egregious organizational faux pas, talking at length to clientele. Unlike his predecessors, Mr. Simmons did not modify this behavior over time, let alone cease and desist. After a few weeks, the judge became angry. . . . Bill Simmons was fired from his job after about three months; when I asked another public defender why, he replied, "Oh, that guy—because he was stupid."[35]

As this example suggests, while the formal requirements of the law do, to a limited extent, constrain decision-making, they are far from determining outcomes. For instance, "long-term commitment based on the need for care and treatment, the standard overturned by LPS, has been restored through the use of conservatorships."[36] Patients admitted on an emergency seventy-two-hour hold as "dangerous" are subsequently relabeled as "gravely disabled,"[37] in part because of the difficulty of demonstrating dangerousness. Indeed, the LPS provision allowing a ninety-day commitment on grounds of danger to others "is almost never used in California."[38] Moreover,

> grave disability standards dealt less with food, clothing, shelter, and finances—functioning within the community—than with functioning inside the family and the mental health system. This suggests that considerations of individual rights and the protection of society are displaced in this court by considerations of the relief of family tensions and the smooth functioning of the mental health system.[39]

Perhaps even more ironic, conservatorship hearings under LPS take even less time than the five-minute average prior to the act, "the statistic

32. Warren, *Court of Last Resort* 189.   33. Ibid., 195.   34. Ibid.
35. Ibid., 195–96.   36. Ibid., 43.   37. Ibid., 40.
38. Ibid., 27.   39. Ibid., 175.

which had prompted legislative interest in involuntary civil commitment in the first place."[40]

In the courtrooms Warren studied, therefore, "decision making is particularistic, situational, and arbitrary rather than universal and fair; medical theories posture as proven facts, and organizational needs take precedence over legal and psychiatric requirements."[41] And there is every reason to believe that this is not an atypical pattern. At the very least, this situation should caution us to be wary of becoming caught up in abstract debates on the issue of civil commitment and to be skeptical about the practical impact of any given set of "reform" proposals. Still, of course, it scarcely renders irrelevant the question of what in principle constitutes appropriate grounds for involuntary commitment, and Warren's book devotes considerable space to precisely this issue.

THE DEBATE OVER ABOLITION

At one extreme, in recent years a small but vocal minority has urged that compulsory commitment is never justified, so that "the goal [of mental health policy] should be nothing less than the abolition of involuntary hospitalization."[42] Such proposals have attracted a considerable following among the legal community, though their most visible and tireless proponent has been the renegade psychiatrist, Thomas Szasz, for whom "involuntary mental hospitalization is like slavery. Refining the standards for commitment is like prettifying the slave plantations. The problem is not how to improve commitment, but how to abolish it."[43] The antithesis to this position, from one perspective, is the extraordinary array of behaviors and conditions John Conolly urged us to accept as justifications for involuntary commitment in his *Remonstrance* over the *Nottidge v. Ripley* case[44]—except that few would now defend such a stance, at least in public. Realistically speaking, therefore, the alternative to abolitionism turns out to be a much more limited, eclectic, and qualified defense of compulsory commitment, which presses for involuntary hospitalization as preferable, on balance, to the likely alternatives.

In *The Court of Last Resort*, these two competing positions are defended with considerable zeal by Stephen Morse,[45] a lawyer and psychol-

40. Ibid., 42.

41. Ibid., 211.

42. Bruce Ennis, *Prisoners of Psychiatry* (New York: Harcourt, Brace, Jovanovich, 1972), 232.

43. Thomas Szasz, *The Second Sin* (Garden City, N.Y.: Doubleday, 1972), 89.

44. Conolly, *Remonstrance;* see pages 284–85.

45. Stephen J. Morse, "A Preference for Liberty: The Case Against the Involuntary Commitment of the Mentally Disordered," in Warren's *Court of Last Resort,* 69–109. A fuller version of this argument appears in an article with the same title in *California Law Review* 70 (1982): 54–106. (Only the former version is cited in this chapter.)

ogist, and Jack Zusman,[46] a psychiatrist, with Warren joining in to argue
for the retention of certain forms of involuntary commitment. Morse's
arguments for the abolitionist position closely resemble those previously
developed by Szasz,[47] and rest upon a shared commitment to the overriding importance of what they both term "liberty"[48]—though it should
be noted at the outset that Morse's brief is less overtly polemical and consciously eschews the vituperative tone, name-calling, and attribution of
base motives to one's opponents in which Szasz seems to revel. As one
would expect from a skilled attorney, the abolitionist position is persuasively made, with logic and force that threaten to demolish the opposition's more cautious eclecticism. By contrast, Zusman and Warren's
uneasy compromises among competing values, and rueful confessions of
both the psychiatrists' limitations and the dangers inherent in the exercise of *parens patriae* powers, give their arguments a necessarily more vulnerable and compromised appearance.[49] And yet, I shall suggest that in
the final analysis, it is precisely the moral absolutism of Morse's position
that is its decisive weakness, rendering "it impotent to calculate the complex relations between means and ends, risks and benefits which hold in
real life."[50]

Morse notes that "the deprivation of liberty authorized by involuntary
commitment laws is among the most serious restrictions on individual
freedom the state may impose," and that, unlike incarceration for criminal acts, "it may be imposed on the basis of predictions, without the prior
occurrence of legally relevant behavior such as dangerous acts."[51] He begins his assault on this practice by denying the validity of the widespread
belief in our culture that the irrational behavior of the mentally ill is
compelled, while the behavior of "normal" people is freely chosen. Recent social scientific research has indeed cast some doubt on this belief,
as a blanket contention, demonstrating that in some contexts, in certain
restricted ways, psychotics can exercise a measure of control over their

46. Jack Zusman, "The Need for Intervention: The Reasons for State Control of the
Mentally Disordered," in Warren's *Court of Last Resort*, 110–33.

47. See Thomas Szasz, *Law, Liberty, and Psychiatry* (New York: Macmillan, 1963); idem,
"Involuntary Psychiatry," *University of Cincinnati Law Review* 44 (1976): 347–65.

48. For analysis and critiques of this term as used by Szasz, see Peter Sedgwick, *Psychopolitics* (London: Pluto Press; New York: Harper and Row, 1982), 149–84; and Michael
Goldstein, "The Politics of Thomas Szasz: A Sociological View," *Social Problems* 27 (1980):
570–83.

49. The plausibility of Zusman's contribution is further undermined by his reliance on
the highly dubious claim that the commitment process is now sufficiently adversarial to
"ensure" that the weaknesses underlying psychiatric opinion will be adequately considered
(Warren, *Court of Last Resort*, 116), a contention that, as we have seen, flies in the face of the
evidence presented elsewhere in Warren's book.

50. Sedgwick, *Psychopolitics*, 154.

51. Morse, "Preference for Liberty," 72.

behavior.[52] Indeed, from the early nineteenth century to the present, control of inmate behavior within the mental hospital has perforce rested on precisely this presumption "that it made some sort of sense to hold the lunatic responsible for his actions, and that by doing so his behaviour could be manipulated."[53] Morse seizes on this evidence. The mentally ill, he contends, "often . . . have as much control over their behavior as normal persons do"; and "we cannot be sure that the person was incapable, as opposed to *unwilling*, to behave rationally or to control him or herself."[54] Moreover, "the assertion that the irrationality or other behavior of mentally disordered persons is compelled . . . is a belief that rests on commonsense intuitions and not on scientific evidence."[55]

But these are disingenuous arguments. "Often" is a very long way from always, and few observers would dispute that much psychotic behavior remains uninterpretable in any ordinary sense as intentional behavior. Indeed, we cannot be *sure* that a madman's actions were uncontrollable, but it may well be more sensible (i.e., in accordance with the preponderance of the evidence) to act on that presumption than to assume that he *was* capable of control and treat him accordingly. And of course the claim that action is either free or determined ultimately rests on commonsense intuitions and not on science: How could it be otherwise when (as Morse himself concedes but a few moments later) "empirical evidence cannot definitely prove or disprove that *anyone* has or lacks free will"?[56] But what Morse neglects to note is that we may have very good grounds indeed for this commonsense presumption.[57]

Moreover, were we to adopt Morse's position, we would be committed to holding "nearly all persons, including crazy persons, responsible for their behavior."[58] Necessarily, then, we would have no grounds for objecting if substantial numbers of discharged mental patients were to end up in prison. To his credit, Morse does not try to duck this issue: instead, he meets it head on, asserting that this result is "more respectful of the dignity and autonomy of crazy persons" than the alternative of confining them in a mental hospital.[59] One cannot help admiring his audacity, even as one is dismayed by the Orwellian use of language. Fortunately, despite

52. See, for instance, B. Braginsky, D. Braginsky, and K. Ring, *Methods of Madness: The Mental Hospital as a Last Resort* (New York: Holt Rinehart, and Winston, 1969).

53. Andrew Scull, *Museums of Madness: The Social Organization of Insanity in Nineteenth-Century England* (London: Allen Lane; New York: St. Martin's Press, 1979), 202; see also Erving Goffman, *Asylums: Essays on the Social Situation of Mental Patients and Other Inmates* (Garden City, N.Y.: Doubleday, 1961), 361–62.

54. Morse, "Preference for Liberty." 75 (emphasis in the original).

55. Ibid.

56. Ibid. (emphasis added).

57. See, generally, Jeff Coulter, *Approaches to Insanity* (Oxford: Martin Robertson, 1973).

58. Morse, "Preference for Liberty," 100.

59. Ibid., 101.

the advent of 1984, we do not all (yet) inhabit a Humpty-Dumpty world in which "a word . . . means just what I choose it to mean—neither more nor less."[60] And until we do, it is unlikely that many of us will view consigning someone to jail as anything but a singularly odd way of respecting his dignity and autonomy.[61] Of equal importance, while Morse may not balk at the prospect of sending the mentally ill to prison, a common-law system of justice built around the concept of criminal responsibility almost certainly will.[62] Zusman is thus assuredly correct when he points out that "to eliminate state control as a preventive measure and allow the mentally ill to be accountable for any law-breaking and mistakes, is completely unacceptable without a massive shift in law and public opinion." On the other hand, it is equally plain that "complete disregard of rule breaking by the mentally disordered—that is, freedom to do whatever they please without any consequences—is a politically unacceptable alternative."[63]

Morse's second argument against involuntary commitment is that the mental health system "is unlikely to identify accurately those persons who should arguably be committed."[64] He is on much stronger ground here. The tendency of psychiatrists to overpredict dangerousness is pervasive and (given the structural pressures operating on them) both unsurprising and unlikely to change.[65] Thus, legitimizing commitment on the basis of dangerousness necessarily involves accepting that a high proportion of those preventively detained would not in fact have behaved violently: the most authoritative review suggests that inaccurate predictions will range as high as 60 or 70 percent.[66] Unquestionably, such statistics should give anyone pause. Whether they should also lead us entirely to abandon "dangerousness" as a ground for involuntary commitment is, however, more debatable. There is the obvious objection about the political possibility (or rather impossibility) of such a move.[67] But quite apart from these purely practical concerns, the question remains as to whether we *ought* to wait until the predicted harm occurs (if indeed it does) before we attempt to intervene. For those who share, with Morse, an absolute and overriding commitment to "liberty"—conceived of as a

60. Lewis Carroll, *Through the Looking Glass, and What Alice Found There* (New York: Peter Pauper Press, 1941), 123.

61. See James Jacobs, *Stateville: The Penitentiary in Mass Society* (Chicago: University of Chicago Press, 1977).

62. Compare the discussion in Wexler, *Mental Health Law,* 11–14.

63. Zusman, "Need for Intervention," 132.

64. Morse, "Preference for Liberty," 73.

65. On these pressures, see, generally, Thomas J. Scheff, *Being Mentally Ill: A Sociological Theory* (Chicago: Aldine, 1966); S. A. Shah, "Dangerousness: A Paradigm for Exploring Some Issues in Law and Psychology," *American Psychologist* 33 (1978): 224–39.

66. See John Monahan, *The Clinical Prediction of Violent Behavior* (Washington, D.C.: Government Printing Office, 1981).

67. Zusman, "Need for Intervention," 127.

presocial attribute of atomized individuals—no dilemma exists.[68] By contrast, if liberty is seen as a vital, but not always controlling value, and as an inextricably social phenomenon,[69] decision-making becomes much more complex, with no ready-made and all-embracing solution. One is forced to recognize, for example, that the social costs (including the costs to the liberty of a sizable number of other people)[70] imposed by the continued presence in society of a seriously disruptive and potentially violent crazy person (to use Morse's terminology) may be so great as to justify commitment, even if more than half the time the threat of violence remains merely a threat. The choices here are obviously very difficult; but I suspect that the best pragmatic resolution is to follow Monahan and Wexler's[71] suggestion and require an inverse relation between the probability and the seriousness of the harm, so that the greater the harm predicted, the lower the probability of its occurrence needs to be to justify involuntary commitment.

What of those "who are mentally unable to fend for themselves"[72] and who need to be confined for their own good? Morse denies that such cases exist:

> Of course, there are cases of disordered persons that *seem* to cry out for intervention: the delusional person who seems on the verge of a violent outburst or who appears to be destroying the fabric of his or her family; or the terribly disorganized person whose life is apparently in jeopardy because the person seems unable to cope with minimal food, shelter, clothing, or medical needs; or the person in the throes of a manic episode who appears to be jeopardizing a career or reputation; or, perhaps most compellingly, the person on the verge of suicide who appears clearly to be making a mistake in judgment about his or her own helplessness and the hopelessness of his or her life situation.[73]

Not to worry, they only *seem* that way: Morse has "an intuitive hunch" that "even the craziest person has substantial control over his or her be-

---

68. Note Morse's confession that "even if a commitment system could be devised that accurately identified very crazy and clearly dangerous people and limited commitments to those who could be successfully treated only in a hospital . . . I would still oppose involuntary commitment" (Morse, "Preference for Liberty," 96).

69. "Freedom is an achieved, not an inherent condition: it is to be measured by the development of the individual's powers in self-determination, not assumed to exist as an all-or-nothing quality whatever one does" (Sedgwick, *Psychopolitics*, 176).

70. See Peter Sainsbury and Jacquelyn Grad de Alarcon, "Evaluating a Service in Sussex," in *Roots of Evaluation*, ed. J. K. Wing and H. Hafner (London: Oxford University Press, 1973), 239–41; M. Yarrow, C. S. Schwartz, H. S. Murphy and L. C. Deasy, "The Psychological Meaning of Mental Illness in the Family," *Journal of Social Issues* 11 (1955): 12–24.

71. John Monahan and David Wexler, "A Definite Maybe: Proof and Probability in Civil Commitment," *Law and Human Behavior* 2 (1978): 37–42.

72. Zusman, "Need for Intervention," 111.

73. Morse, "Preference for Liberty," 97 (emphasis added).

havior"; and if that does not seem sufficiently persuasive, he reminds us that crazy persons, like the rest of us, possess "an inalienable right to liberty."[74]

Doubtless, the inalienable right to liberty must have been a great comfort to the severely impaired 89-year-old woman whom Warren observed, slowly starving to death in her home, wandering around a room with "barely a sign of habitation . . . bumping into things and alternately mumbling softly and shouting phrases from fragments of a past life."[75] Or to a Mrs. Simmons, of whom counsel testified:

> She was found on the floor of her apartment, where she had not gotten up for three months. She was malnourished. Maggots had eaten away part of her leg. She cannot be moved from the hospital until her leg is healed and she gains some weight. A neighbor had fed her on the floor for three months. She was lying in her own feces for three months.[76]

In the future, if such persons "really" disliked their situations, why then, they could always exercise the "autonomy" Professor Morse had so sedulously and kindly preserved for them when he blocked their involuntary commitment.

On the whole, I think we ought to prefer the commonsense view that one of the things people like this *lack* is autonomy, even if, as Morse is quick to remind us, such perceptions rest on "little more than an intuitive hunch."[77] Indeed, since the contrary view seems more than a trifle perverse, one wonders what can have led intelligent and thoughtful persons to adopt it. In part, the answer seems to lie in a continuing attachment to the Szaszian position that mental illness is simply a "myth."[78] As Warren points out, sociology made its own distinctive contribution to this belief that "mental illness was merely a matter of labeling of undesired behaviors and persons,"[79] and Morse, like others skeptical of psychiatry's pretentions, seems to have adopted substantial portions of this analysis. Hence his preference for "crazy" rather than "mentally ill," "because it is more descriptive and carries fewer connotations about disease processes that beg important questions about self-control";[80] and his penchant for minimizing the distinctiveness of the psychotic and the claims to expertise of their custodians, the psychiatrists.

For almost a quarter of a century, an intense and often acrimonious debate has raged about the medical model and the appropriate concep-

74. Ibid.
75. Warren, *Court of Last Resort,* 28–29.
76. Quoted in ibid., 29.
77. Morse, "Preference for Liberty," 97.
78. Thomas Szasz, *The Myth of Mental Illness,* rev. ed. (New York: Harper and Row, 1974).
79. Warren, *Court of Last Resort,* 5.
80. Morse, "Preference for Liberty," 73 n.3.

tualization of mental disorder, with no agreement yet in sight.[81] But whatever the final outcome of the controversy, it surely cannot alter the social reality that there exist a substantial number of people—be they victims of endogenous disease processes or of "problems in living"— who lack basic social capacities and who manifest extreme helplessness and dependency. Moreover, while I share the assessment that on balance the data at our disposal "suggest that expert psychiatric knowledge is a well-managed 'appearance of objectivity' rather than a set of 'objective facts,'"[82] I would suggest that this provides an argument for lessening the role of doubtfully "expert" testimony in the commitment process, not for abolishing commitment altogether.[83] Nor do I think that the evidence supports Morse's attempts to play down the damage associated with psychosis, an essential prop for his contention that commitment is "a simple, although unfair, answer to interpersonal, family, and comparatively *mild* social problems."[84] In this connection, it is surely significant (though of course in no sense conclusive) that Carol Warren, who began her observations in "Metropolitan Court" sharing this assumption "as an article of faith (although I saw it then as sober scientific reasoning, not belief),"[85] found herself compelled by what she experienced to recognize the existential reality of "mental disorder . . . independent of labeling"[86] and the necessity for compulsory hospitalization.

CARE, TREATMENT, AND LIBERTY

Morse is certainly correct, however, to worry about the potentially repressive consequences of allowing people to be confined "for their own good." As Conolly's remarks on the *Nottidge* case demonstrate,[87] the range of behaviors that might render one subject to such intervention (in the eyes of at least some psychiatrists) has in the past been extraor-

---

81. For a defense of medicine's claims, see, generally, John Wing, *Reasoning About Madness* (London: Oxford University Press, 1978); for alternative views, see David Ingleby, "Mental Health and Social Order," in *Social Control and the State: Historical and Comparative Essays,* ed. Stanley Cohen and Andrew Scull (Oxford: Basil Blackwell; New York: St. Martin's Press, 1981), 141–88; David Morgan, "Explaining Mental Illness," *European Journal of Sociology* 15 (1975): 262–80; and Peter Sedgwick, "Mental Illness *Is* Illness," *Salmagundi* 20 (1972): 196–222.

82. S. Pfohl, *Predicting Dangerousness* (Lexington, Mass.: Heath, 1978), 230.

83. This, incidentally, is also the conclusion Pfohl reaches (ibid., 228–30), and Morse himself agrees that involuntary commitment decisions could be taken on grounds independent of "the vagaries, unreliability, and internecine disputes of mental health science" (Morse, "Preference for Liberty," 84 n.12).

84. Morse, "Preference for Liberty," 81 (emphasis added).

85. Warren, *Court of Last Resort,* 5.

86. Ibid., 202.

87. See pages 284–85.

dinarily wide: adolescent rebelliousness, harmless eccentricity, violation of conventional standards of morality or of sexual propriety, extreme carelessness with one's money or property.[88] It is this extravagance, I suspect, that has prompted the claim that "psychiatric opinions are essentially political judgments."[89] Yet the fact that "benevolent" concern for the welfare of others has served to legitimize egregious violations of some people's freedom does not invalidate the claim that there are occasions when we may indeed be justified in intervening in others' lives "for their own good."

It may be objected, however, that mental hospitals "rarely cure, nor do they decrease the stigma."[90] Worse, "even in 'advanced' states that supposedly maintain the best services" all too often one encounters "revelations of . . . inadequate and sometimes inhumane care and treatment."[91] Again, there is a good deal of truth to both claims, though once more I shall suggest that this does not compel us to embrace Morse's chosen alternative of abolishing involuntary confinement.

The critique of the mental hospital's structural deficiencies has a very long history.[92] In the late nineteenth century, for example, neurologists—then in the process of constituting themselves as a medical specialty—provoked a bitter internecine conflict with institutional psychiatry by urging the asylum's total unsuitability for the treatment of mental disorders.[93] A long series of exposés by muckraking journalists provided further ammunition for the mental hospital's critics.[94] And, most notably of all, a mass of social scientific research in the 1950s and 1960s was devoted to the elaborate documentation of the irredeemable deficiencies of what Erving Goffman dubbed "total institutions."[95]

88. For recent examples, see Ronald Leifer, *In the Name of Mental Health: Social Functions of Psychiatry* (New York: Aronson, 1969); Bruce Ennis and Eugene Litwack, "Psychiatry and the Presumption of Expertise," *California Law Review* 62 (1974): 693–753.

89. Pfohl, *Predicting Dangerousness*, 229.

90. Morse, "Preference for Liberty," 89.

91. Ibid., 92.

92. See Andrew Scull, *Decarceration: Community Treatment and the Deviant—A Radical View*, 2d ed. (Oxford: Polity Press; New Brunswick, N.J.: Rutgers University Press, 1984), 105–33.

93. See Bonnie Blustein, "A 'Hollow Square of Psychological Science': American Neurologists and Psychiatrists in Conflict," in *Madhouses, Mad-Doctors and Madmen*, ed. Scull, 241–70; Andrew Scull, "The Social History of Psychiatry in the Victorian Era," in ibid., 17–20.

94. The most famous of this genre is Albert Deutsch's *The Shame of the States* (1948; New York: Arno, 1973); for a more up-to-date example, see Wendell Rawls, *Cold Storage* (New York: Simon and Schuster, 1980).

95. Goffman, *Asylums*, 4. See also R. Barton, *Institutional Neurosis*, 2d ed. (Bristol: Wright, 1965); Ivan Belknap, *Human Problems of a State Mental Hospital* (New York: McGraw-Hill, 1956); A. H. Stanton and M. S. Schwartz, *The Mental Hospital: A Study of Institutional Participation in Psychiatric Illness and Treatment* (New York: Basic Books, 1954); Robert Perrucci, *Circle of Madness: On Being Insane and Institutionalized in America* (Englewood Cliffs, N.J.: Prentice-Hall, 1974).

Such apparently objective findings have been widely disseminated, serving as one of the major ideological supports for the movement to deinstitutionalize the mental hospital population.[96] In the process, mental hospitals have been stigmatized as inevitably providing a disabling, counterproductive environment, one that exacerbates any preexisting pathology through an "organizational tyranny [calculated to produce] the thwarting of human possibilities."[97] Unquestionably, the historical record demonstrates that most mental hospitals have more closely resembled warehouses for the storage of the unwanted than institutions providing treatment and cures.[98] But this is a far cry from the more extravagant claims made by Goffman and his epigones. It is these more extreme "findings" that Morse and others rely on when they urge us to abolish involuntary hospitalization altogether; and yet the research purporting to document these effects is so methodologically flawed and empirically inadequate[99] that one must seriously question the wisdom of depending on it.

Of at least equal significance in the present context, those social scientists who have criticized the mental hospital have almost entirely neglected to consider what the alternatives to it are, preferring to make the bland (and untested) assumption that "the worst home is better than the best mental hospital."[100] In practice, this has proved to be a tragically mistaken belief. A growing volume of research[101] has demonstrated that community "care" for the chronically crazy is in fact community neglect

96. See Andrew Scull, "The Decarceration of the Mentally Ill: A Critical View," *Politics and Society* 6 (1976): 173–212; see also Stephen Rose, "Deciphering Deinstitutionalization: Complexities in Policy and Program Analysis," *Milbank Memorial Fund Quarterly* 57 (1979): 429–60.

97. Nicholas Perry, "The Two Cultures and the Total Institution," *British Journal of Sociology* 25 (1974): 353.

98. Gerald Grob, *Mental Illness and American Society, 1875–1940* (Princeton: Princeton University Press, 1983); David Rothman, *The Discovery of the Asylum: Social Order and Disorder in the New Republic* (Boston: Little, Brown, 1971); idem, *Conscience and Convenience: The Asylum and Its Alternatives in Progressive America* (Boston: Little, Brown, 1980); Gerald Grob, *Mental Institutions in America: Social Policy to 1875* (New York: Free Press, 1973); John Walton, "The Treatment of Pauper Lunatics in Victorian England: The Case of Lancaster Asylum, 1816–1870," in *Madhouses, Mad-Doctors and Madmen,* ed. Scull, 166–97; Nancy Tomes, "A Generous Confidence: Thomas Story Kirkbride's Philosophy of Asylum Construction and Management," in ibid., 121–43.

99. See Craig McEwen, "Continuities in the Study of Total and Non-Total Institutions," *Annual Review of Sociology* 6 (1980): 147–48; and Chapter 13 below.

100. Elaine Cumming and John Cumming, *Closed Ranks: An Experiment in Mental Health Education* (Cambridge: Harvard University Press, 1957).

101. A. Davis, S. Dinitz, and B. Pasamanick, *Schizophrenics in the New Custodial Community* (Columbus: Ohio State University Press, 1974); General Accounting Office, *The Mentally Ill in the Community: Government Needs to Do More* (Washington, D.C.: Government Printing Office, 1977); Senate Special Committee on Aging, Subcommittee on Long-Term Care, 94th Cong., 2d sess., 1976, *Nursing Home Care in the United States: Failure in Public Policy,* Support Paper no. 7, *The Role of Nursing Homes in Caring for Discharged Mental Pa-*

and that "the effective meaning of liberty for the involuntarily committed is social marginality, deprivation, and despair." [102] So far from being the grand reform of mental health care its ideologues have proclaimed, the practical implementation of community treatment has created "a system which, daily and quietly, harms and kills the sick." [103]

At least Morse recognizes that the problem exists: "The condition of many 'deinstitutionalized' ex-patients in the community is a national disgrace." [104] But he immediately seeks to evade its implications:

> One should not compare the all-too-questionable benefits of hospitalization to complete or near-complete neglect in the community. The only fair comparison is to community living and treatment where society meets its moral obligations rather than cynically avoiding them. [105]

I find this an astonishing claim. Such a comparison is "fair" only in the sense that it supports the argument Morse is advancing—but at the unacceptable price of leaving behind the social realities we must confront. Discharged mental patients do not live in a society that "meets its moral obligations." The alternatives they (and we) must face are inadequate and underfunded mental hospitals or a grossly underdeveloped and often nonexistent system of community care. Here the choices are tougher and the answers less clear-cut than those Morse provides us with; but they have the distinct merit of being the real ones. And when we confront them, I think we must conclude, as Warren does, that for a substantial proportion of the chronically crazy,

---

tients, 1976, Committee Print; Robert Emerson, E. B. Rochford, and Linda Shaw, "Economics and Enterprise in Board and Care Homes for the Mentally Ill," *American Behavioral Scientist* 24 (1981): 771–85; S. Kirk and M. Thierren, "Community Mental Health Myths and the Fate of Former Hospitalized Patients," *Psychiatry* 38 (1975): 209–17; Rose, "Deciphering Deinstitutionalization"; Scull, *Decarceration;* idem, "A New Trade in Lunacy: The Recommodification of the Mental Patient," *American Behavioral Scientist* 24 (1981): 741–54; idem, "Deinstitutionalization and the Rights of the Deviant," *Journal of Social Issues* 37 (1981): 6–20; Julian Wolpert and Eileen Wolpert, "The Relocation of Released Mental Patients into Residential Communities," *Policy Sciences* 7 (1976): 31–51.

102. Warren, *Court of Last Resort,* 203.

103. Sedgwick, *Psychopolitics,* 229–30.

104. Morse, "Preference for Liberty," 95.

105. Ibid., 100. In parallel fashion, Morse insists on comparing the reality of a psychiatric commitment process (focusing especially on the most egregious misuses of "expertise") with a wholly idealized portrait of the law as a routinely adversarial system offering clear-cut and uncompromising protections of individual rights. That our legal system bears only the most superficial resemblance to his picture of it seems to discomfort him not one whit. But those who come before the courts populate the real world, and not this theoretical heaven. One must compare reality with reality, not with some pretty fantasy that better suits the case one wants to make.

care in a profit-making institution at a cost of $14.50 a day seems more
treacherous and less human than care in a state institution at $31 a day.
And the confines of the state hospital, for the dispossessed, seem to threaten
effective liberty less vitally than the sidewalks, streets, and cheap hotels of
the completely homeless.[106]

To suggest that the mental hospital is sometimes a defensible—indeed
preferable—solution to the problems posed by mental disorder, and to
argue that compulsory commitment is also an option we should retain, is
not to deny the need to place a sharp check on psychiatric enthusiasms,
since these are no less capable of leading us astray. Indeed, when we debate the merits and demerits of compulsory commitment, we ought constantly to bear in mind that "the real scandal of contemporary public
psychiatry is not the particular section of the mental-health statutes
under which patients get into hospitals, but the alternatives offered to
these supremely weak members of society by our present social arrangements both inside and outside the mental institution." [107]

106. Warren, *Court of Last Resort*, 207. See also J. Rubin, *Economics, Mental Health, and
the Law* (Lexington, Mass.: Heath, 1978); J. F. Borus, "Deinstitutionalization of the Chronically Mentally Ill," *New England Journal of Medicine* 305 (1981): 339–42.
107. Sedgwick, *Psychopolitics*, 180.

CHAPTER THIRTEEN

The Asylum as Community or the Community as Asylum: Paradoxes and Contradictions of Mental Health Care

For several years after I first became interested in the study of madness, the primary focus of my researches was the nineteenth century. Yet my first book dealt with a far more sociologically respectable topic, contemporary mental health policy in the United States and Britain.[1] In substantial measure, this shift occurred because the first publishers I approached were reluctant to publish the somewhat bloated manuscript that constituted my Ph.D. dissertation; and because I lacked sufficient distance from what I had written (not to mention enthusiasm for the task) to take on the job of pruning and reworking it into publishable form. Consequently, I decided to set that manuscript aside temporarily, and to begin work on a new project.

Having tried in *Museums of Madness* to unravel the *origins* of the commitment to the asylum solution, I now found myself urged by friends and colleagues to scrutinize its contemporary demise. I must confess to a certain initial skepticism about claims that so durable an institution was swiftly and certainly en route to the historical scrapheap, but the subject certainly seemed worthy of further investigation. Moreover, I already sensed that there might be some interesting parallels to be explored between contemporary assaults on the therapeutic legitimacy of the mental hospital and a hitherto neglected, almost subterranean strand of criticism of lunacy reform and its products, which had appeared and per-

---

Portions of Chapter 13 originally appeared in Philip Bean, ed., *Mental Illness: Changes and Trends*, 1982, pp. 329–50, and are reprinted here by permission of John Wiley and Sons, Ltd.

1. Andrew Scull, *Decarceration: Community Treatment and the Deviant—A Radical View* (Englewood Cliffs, N.J.: Prentice-Hall, 1977).

sisted even at the height of Victorian optimism and complacency about the value of the asylum solution.

Very early on in my new researches, I was struck by the further parallels between the millennial expectations of the asylum's founders and the equally extravagant claims of the devotees of community care. It is difficult even a decade or two later to recapture the naive optimism of the late 1960s and early 1970s, for we live now in an era filled with denunciations of "the wholesale neglect of the mentally ill, especially the chronic patient and the deinstitutionalized":[2] a period in which we are bombarded with exposés of scandals in the board and care and the nursing home industries, and urged to reconsider our reluctance to countenance the involuntary confinement of street people. But twenty years ago, the optimistic illusion that we had uncovered a solution to the endless difficulties associated with chronic mental disorder had not yet melted away. To the contrary, the emptying of asylums was then hailed as unambiguous evidence of social progress, part of a third "psychiatric revolution"[3] that would finally liberate mental patients from the shackles of the past.

I completed work on *Decarceration* in late 1975. The book offered, unfashionably, a much bleaker assessment of the realities of deinstitutionalization, together with an account of the origins of this far-reaching change in social control styles and practices that was sharply critical of the then conventional pieties others offered on the subject. Since then, historical materials have once more absorbed the bulk of my attentions. From time to time, however, I have been drawn back to the study of contemporary realities. On one such occasion, half a dozen years ago, I wrote a piece comparing the nineteenth-century asylum as an idealized manufactured community with our idealization of twentieth-century "communities" as asylums for those afflicted with mental disorders. What follows is a revision of that essay, expanded to incorporate some discussion of developments in the 1980s.

2. Donald Langsley, "The Community Mental Health Center: Does It Treat Patients?" *Hospital and Community Psychiatry* 31 (1980): 816.
3. The first two being symbolized by the mythical portrait of Pinel freeing the insane from their chains and by the advent of the technology of the couch, marking Freud's invention of the talking cure.

The Asylum as Community
or the Community as Asylum:
Paradoxes and Contradictions
of Mental Health Care

*As we see wing after wing spreading, and story after story ascending, in every
asylum throughout the country, we are reminded of the overgrown monastic system, which entangled so many interests and seemed so powerful that it could defy
all change, but for that very reason toppled and fell by its own weight, never to be
renewed. Asylum life may not come to so sudden an end, but the longer its present
unnatural and oppressive system is maintained, the greater will be the revolution
when it at last arrives.*

—ANDREW WYNTER,
The Borderlands of Insanity

*Some Persons of a Desponding Spirit are in Great Concern about that vast Num-
ber of poor People, who are Aged, Diseased, or Maimed; and I have been desired
to employ my Thoughts what Course may be taken, to ease the Nation of so grievous an Incumbrance. . . . I am not in the least Pain on that Matter; because it is
very well known, that they are every Day dying and rotting, by Cold and Fam-
ine, and Filth and Vermine, as fast as can reasonably be expected.*

—JONATHAN SWIFT,
*A Modest Proposal For Preventing the Children of Poor People in Ireland from Being
a Burden to Their Parents or Country*

Paradoxical as it may seem, any discussion of "community care" for the
mentally ill must begin by paying serious attention to the mental hospital. The current generation of mental health reformers has shown a remarkable tendency to seize on statistics about reductions in the mental
hospital census as a direct measure of the success of their endeavors.
Moreover, their reiterated emphasis on the horrors endemic and inextricably part of the Victorian bins to which earlier generations consigned
the mentally disturbed has helped to legitimize the notion that any
change (though preferably a drastic change) must represent an improvement over what has gone before and to deflect attention away from "the
demise of state responsibility for the seriously mentally ill and the current crisis of abandonment."[1]

Though the prehistory of the asylum can be traced back to medieval
religious foundations (the most widely known example in the English-

---

1. E. Gruenberg and J. Archer, "Abandonment of Responsibility for the Seriously
Mentally Ill," *Milbank Memorial Fund Quarterly* 57 (1979): 498.

speaking world being the monastic foundation of Bethlehem, or Bedlam),[2] its use as a major instrument of public policy has far less ancient
roots. It is instead, the private, profit-making madhouses of eighteenth-
century England[3] and, to a far greater degree, the publicly funded
county asylums and state hospitals of nineteenth-century England and
the United States[4] that mark the advent of an approach to mental illness
based on the physical and symbolic segregation of "lunatics"—their isolation in ever larger specialized and purpose-built institutions designed
to contain and treat them. It is one of the ironies with which the history
of psychiatry abounds that the emergence of the state-sponsored asylum
system was itself the outcome of a vigorous campaign for reform; and
that, as with the current drive to return the mentally ill to the community, their segregation in these places was urged as being vital on both
humanitarian and therapeutic grounds.

During the first half of the nineteenth century, the weight of informed opinion on both sides of the Atlantic embraced an extreme therapeutic optimism. Those who led the crusade to establish state-supported
mental hospitals—people like Dorothea Dix in the United States and
Lord Shaftesbury in England—saw themselves as rescuing the mad
from maltreatment, neglect, and inhumanity, and ushering in a golden
age of kindness, scientifically guided treatment, and cure. In this respect, their self-portrait is indistinguishable from their present-day successors. But for Dix and Shaftesbury, the certain recipe for neglect and
abuse was to leave the mentally disturbed to the mercies of the community. More often than not, the troublesome qualities of the insane would
ensure their confinement in some nonspecialized environment—the
gaol, the workhouse, or the private madhouse—whose structural deficiencies (to say nothing of the qualities of those in charge of those places)
made harsh treatment all but inescapable. Even those not abandoned by
their families were the unfortunate prey of ignorance, if not callous unconcern. The ministrations of the most devoted relatives, however well
meaning, were all too likely to be misconceived, and thus to exacerbate
rather than mitigate the underlying problem. Beyond this, "relatives and
dependents" were "timid, unskilled, and frequently objects of irrita-

2. E. D. O'Donoghue, *The Story of Bethlem Hospital* (London: Fisher and Unwin, 1913).

3. William L. Parry-Jones, *The Trade in Lunacy: A Study of Private Madhouses in England
in the Eighteenth and Nineteenth Centuries* (London: Routledge and Kegan Paul, 1972).

4. Andrew Scull, *Museums of Madness: The Social Organization of Insanity in Nineteenth-
Century England* (London: Allen Lane; New York: St. Martin's Press, 1979), and *Madhouses,
Mad-Doctors and Madmen: The Social History of Psychiatry in the Victorian Era* (Philadelphia:
University of Pennsylvania Press, London: Athlone Press; 1981); Gerald Grob, *The State
and the Mentally Ill* (Chapel Hill: University of North Carolina Press, 1966); idem, *Mental
Institutions in America* (New York: Free Press, 1973); David Rothman, *The Discovery of the
Asylum: Social Order and Disorder in the New Republic* (Boston: Little, Brown, 1971).

tion,"[5] and the home was precisely the environment that had nurtured the disturbance in the first place.[6]

By contrast, the asylum was portrayed as a technical, objective response to the patient's condition, an environment that provided the best possible conditions for recovery. While relieving the community of the turmoil and disorder at least latently present in madness, it provided those suffering from the condition with a sanctuary, respite from a world with which they could no longer cope. Here they would find a home where they would be known and treated as individuals, while their minds were constantly stimulated and encouraged to return to their natural state. Even the architecture and physical setting of the building could make a vital contribution to its success, by avoiding all impressions of confinement, emphasizing cheerfulness, offering an aesthetically pleasing design, and allowing a maximum of organizational flexibility.[7] Coupled with an expertly chosen and carefully supervised staff, this milieu would secure kindly, dedicated and unremitting care, carefully adapted to the needs and progress of the individual case.

On the one hand, therefore, nineteenth-century reformers promoted a vision of the asylum as providing a forgiving environment in which humane care on a large scale was possible and in and through which a very substantial proportion of "lunatics" could be restored to sanity. The converse of this portrait, however, was an elaborate and prolonged campaign to impress others with the gross unsuitability of the family and community as arenas for the treatment of the insane, and with the need to insulate the insane from the pressures of the world. Repeatedly, the reformers used their speeches and memorials to contrast the horrors of these alternative dispositions with idealized portraits of the asylum's beneficence. Harnessing the combined forces of humanity and science, they had protected future generations of the insane from the trials endured by poor Mary Jones, a Welsh lunatic whose family had kept her

> on a foul pallet of chaff or straw . . . in a dark and offensive room over a blacksmith's forge. . . . Here she had been confined for a period of fifteen years and upward. She was seated in a bent and crouching posture on her bed of nauseous and disgusting filth. Near to her person was a cup emptied from time to time into a chamber utensil. This last vessel contained a quantity of feculent matter, the accumulation of several days. By her side were the remnants of some food of which she had partaken. . . . The stag-

5. R. Hill, *A Lecture on the Management of Lunatic Asylums* (London: Simpkin Marshall, 1839), 6.

6. Brislington House, *Prospectus* (Bristol: Privately printed, 1806).

7. Nancy Tomes, "A Generous Confidence: Thomas Story Kirkbride's Philosophy of Asylum Construction and Management," in *Madhouses, Mad-Doctors and Madmen*, ed. Scull, 121–43.

nant and suffocating atmosphere, and the nauseous effluvia which infected it, were all but intolerable.[8]

Yet if the mentally disordered in the latter half of the nineteenth century were no longer subjected to confinement of this sort, the change in
their situation was hardly one the reformers had envisaged. The small,
intimate institution devoted to the cure and humane care of its inmates
proved to be a chimera of its planners' imaginations. By the last third of
the nineteenth century, public asylums on both sides of the Atlantic had
become mammoth institutions, huge custodial warehouses in which the
conditions of the patients' existence departed further and further from
those in the outside world, for their return to which their incarceration
was still ostensibly preparing them. Even gross statistics serve as an accurate indicator of the basic character of these places. The average size of
county asylums in England was little short of a thousand patients by the
end of the century, and, as in the United States, there were several "hospitals of patients and employees of three thousand, four thousand, and
even higher."[9] Necessarily in such vast lunatic colonies, "all transactions,
moral as well as economic, must be done wholesale," as their sheer
"number renders the inmates mere automatons, acted on in this or that
fashion according to the rules governing the great machine."[10]

Thus, for active cruelty the reformers had succeeded in substituting
the "monstrous evils" of "idle monotony." In what typically became "a
mere house of perpetual detention," there was an "utter absence of any
means of engaging the attention of the patients, interesting them in any
occupations or amusements or affording them a sufficient variety of exercise outdoors."[11] Consequently, those who bothered to examine the
inside of the asylum would find "patients in the prime of life sitting or
lying about, moping idly and listlessly in the debilitating atmosphere
of the wards, and sinking gradually into a torpor, like that of living
corpses." Men and women "who have lost even the memory of hope, sit
in rows, too dull to know despair, watched by attendants; silent, grew-
some [sic] machines which eat and sleep, sleep and eat."[12]

8. *Hansard's Parliamentary Debates*, 3d ser. vol. 81 (1845), cols. 185–86.

9. H. Hurd, *The Institutional Care of the Insane in the United States and Canada* (Baltimore:
Johns Hopkins University Press, 1916), 1:401; Scull, *Museums of Madness*.

10. W. A. F. Browne, *The Moral Treatment of the Insane* (London: Adlard, 1864), 18;
John T. Arlidge, *On the State of Lunacy and the Legal Provision for the Insane* (London:
Churchill, 1859), 107.

11. House of Commons, *Select Committee on the Operation of the Lunacy Law* (1877),
396–97 and 388.

12. Silas Weir Mitchell, *Address Before the American Medico-Psychological Association* (Philadelphia, 1894), 19; Massachusetts State Board of Charities, *Annual Report* (1867), 4:xl;
Henry Maudsley, *The Physiology and Pathology of the Mind* (New York: Appleton, 1871), 427.

In the face of the growing crisis of institutional legitimacy to which these conditions ultimately gave rise, the early twentieth century witnessed a further round of reform, one designed to reinvigorate the asylum and restore it to its original curative function. David Rothman [13] has recently dissected the American period of this second generation of reforms, those of the so-called progressive era, and shown how vast the gap between rhetoric and reality remained, how little, in fact, was changed, despite the ostensibly new emphasis on flexibility, discretion, and the carefully adapted treatment of the individual case. Indeed, the failure of this episode to produce more than cosmetic "improvements," such as the relabeling of asylums as mental hospitals, had already been documented indirectly by that explosion of sociological studies of the mental hospital as "total institution" that marked the 1950s and 1960s. (Since that body of research plays an important, yet controversial, role in the community care movement, I shall discuss it at more length shortly.)

More vividly, and for a wider audience, the same basic message was periodically reiterated in journalistic exposés of the deficiencies of the mental hospitals. Perhaps best-known of the latter genre, certainly in the United States, was Albert Deutsch's *The Shame of the States*. Although Deutsch was certainly no foe of institutional psychiatry, here the wheel seems once more to come full circle, with descriptions of the inmate circumstances bearing an almost eerie resemblance to the ones the original generation of reformers had proffered as irrefutable evidence of the need for an asylum system. At Byberry, for example, "the male incontinent ward was like a scene out of Dante's Inferno. Three hundred nude men stood, squatted, and sprawled in this bare room, amid shrieks, groans, and unearthly laughter. Winter or summer, these creatures were never given any clothing at all. Some lay about on the bare floor in their own excreta. The filth-covered walls were rotting away." [14] Scenes he had witnessed elsewhere reminded him, as they did other observers, of nothing so much as the death camps they had recently viewed at Dachau, Belsen, and Buchenwald. [15]

What is remarkable as one looks back on this 200-year "history of reform without change" [16] is how consistently those in charge of the system, indeed society as a whole, sought to deflect attention away from the horrors of the present by resurrecting the tales of the barbarities of the past. Indeed, it is perhaps not too much to claim that one of the main ideological tasks of the history of psychiatry has been to manufacture reas-

[handwritten margin note: In Strategy (Plan) for future]

13. David Rothman, *Conscience and Convenience: The Asylum and Its Alternatives in Progressive America* (Boston: Little, Brown, 1980). See Chapter 10 above for a critique of his account.

14. Albert Deutsch, *The Shame of the States* (New York: Arno, 1973), 49.

15. Cf. H. Orlans, "An American Death Camp," *Politics* 5 (1948), 162–68.

16. Rothman, *Conscience and Convenience*.

surance of this sort, supplying us with a seemingly inexhaustible store of exemplary tales to document the inhumanities of earlier generations and the heroic struggles through which we arrived at our present (relative) state of grace and enlightenment.

The first generation of reformers seized on this splendid collective defense mechanism almost as soon as their visions began to turn sour. As early as 1845, surrounded by clear signs of the collapse of the very things they had previously urged as indispensable to the whole enterprise, they sought solace in the thought that "the worse asylum that can at this day by possibility be conceived, will still afford great protection" to the poor lunatic, when compared to his or her fate if left to the tender mercies of the community.[17] Later in the century, defenders of the asylum system subtly shifted their ground: the standard of comparison by which the "success" of the asylums was to be judged was not the goals that the reformers had set for themselves, but rather the worst conditions the mad had been found in prior to the enactment of protective legislation.[18] And given such a starting point, it was naturally all but impossible *not* to find evidence of improvement, no matter how dismal the reality one confronted.

Ironically enough, in the most recent variant of this by-now-hallowed ploy the negative referent is not the squalor and viciousness of the period before the work of Pinel and Tuke liberated the mad from their chains and secured for them the blessings of treatment in the mental hospital. Nor is it some dark episode in the asylum's history when, notwithstanding the existence of policy based on the best and most honorable intentions, things went temporarily and inexplicably wrong. Rather, the new target of reformist energy, the evil crying out for abolition, is the mental hospital itself. Instead of basking in their role as "the most blessed manifestation of true civilization the world can present,"[19] even the most up-to-date institutions find themselves denounced as harmful and antitherapeutic, and their destruction is urged as "one of the greatest humanitarian reforms and the greatest financial economy ever achieved."[20] Thus, over the past quarter of a century in what must surely rank as an extraordinary reversal of effort, the energy and resources once devoted to giving the illusion of reality to the chimera of the hu-

17. John Thurnam, *Observations and Essays on the Statistics of Insanity* (London: 1845), 104.

18. See the discussions in Scull, *Museums of Madness*, chaps. 3 and 6; and in Nicholas Hervey, "The Lunacy Commission 1845–1860" (Ph.D. dissertation, Bristol University, 1987).

19. George E. Paget, *The Harveian Oration* (Cambridge: Deighton, Bell, 1866), 34–35.

20. Ivan Belknap, *Human Problems of a State Mental Hospital* (New York: McGraw-Hill, 1956), 212. See also W. Mendel, "Dismantling the Mental Hospital," in "Where is My Home?" (National Technical Information Service, Scottsdale, Arizona, 1974, mimeographed); and Thomas Szasz, *The Manufacture of Madness* (New York: Dell, 1970).

mane and curative asylum have instead been employed in the elaboration and documentation of its irredeemable flaws and deficiencies. From
the late 1950s through the mid-1970s a veritable flood of social scientific
research elucidated the baneful effect of confinement in an institution.
The most famous and influential of these studies was undoubtedly Erving Goffman's *Asylums*,[21] though that work in many ways was simply the
most rhetorically persuasive presentation of a widespread scholarly
consensus.

Studies of institutions as diverse as research hospitals closely associated with major medical schools,[22] expensive, exclusive, and well-staffed
private facilities,[23] and undermanned and underfinanced state hospitals[24] all revealed a depressingly familiar picture. Apparently, "life in such
a community tended inexorably to attenuation of the spirit, a shrinking
of capacity, and slowing of the rhythms of interaction, a kind of atrophy."[25] In the light of this research, it now appeared that, so far from
sheltering the disturbed and helping to restore them to sanity, the mental hospital performed "a disabling, custodial function."[26] Moreover, this
conclusion appeared to be the more plausible in the light of the striking
convergences among those working in such widely different settings, for
as Belknap put it, the very "similarity of these problems strongly suggests that many of the serious problems of the state hospital are inherent
in the nature of mental institutionalization rather than simply in the financial difficulties of the state hospitals."[27]

Echoing one of the central themes of this work, major American psychiatrists, particularly those in university settings, began to express fears
that "the patients are infantile . . . because we infantilize them."[28] Instead of being a positive influence, mental hospitals threatened to am-
plify and even produce disturbance. Such ideas also acquired widespread currency on the other side of the Atlantic, where the work of

21. Erving Goffman, *Asylums: Essays on the Social Situation of Mental Patients and Other Inmates* (Garden City, N.Y.: Doubleday, 1961).

22. P. S. Barrabee, "A Study of the Mental Hospital: The Effect of Its Social Structure on Its Functions" (Ph.D. dissertation, Harvard University, 1951).

23. A. H. Stanton and M. S. Schwartz, *The Mental Hospital* (New York: Basic Books, 1954).

24. Belknap, *Human Problems;* H. Dunham and K. Weinberg, *The Culture of the State Mental Hospital* (Detroit: Wayne State University Press, 1960); and Robert Perrucci, *Circle of Madness: On Being Insane and Institutionalized in America* (Englewood Cliffs, N.J.: Prentice-Hall, 1974).

25. M. Miller, "At Hard Labor: Rediscovering the Nineteenth Century Prison," *Issues in Criminology*, no. 9 (1974): 54.

26. R. C. Hunt, "Ingredients of a Rehabilitation Program," *Milbank Memorial Fund Proceedings*, no. 34 (1957), 21.

27. Belknap, *Human Problems*, 232.

28. F. Redlich, Preface to *The Psychiatric Hospital as a Small Society*, by W. Caudill (Cambridge: Harvard University Press, 1958), xi.

men like Duncan McMillan and T. P. Rees, British pioneers of the concept of the open hospital, was held to provide unambiguous support for the notion "that much of the aggressive, disturbed, suicidal, and regressive behavior of the mentally ill is not necessarily or inherently a part of the illness as such but is very largely an artificial by-product of the way of life imposed on them [by hospitalization]."[29] Another British psychiatrist, Russell Barton, even ventured to give this iatrogenic phenomenon the status of a new psychiatric label of its own—"institutional neurosis."[30]

Seen in the context of this general intellectual climate, many of the details of Goffman's arguments in *Asylums* are not in the least original. The importance of his essays lay rather in the skill with which he deployed and then extended conventional wisdom and in the adroitness with which he made use of limited evidence of often dubious validity to advance some extremely general claims. Though the reader is hard-put to recall the fact, Goffman's primary data source is a relatively brief period of field observation in a single hospital, St. Elizabeth's in Washington, D.C., a data base that in other hands would have produced still another ethnography of a particular institution. In this case, however, the outcome is a general delineation of an organizational type to which *all* mental hospitals belong—along with prisons, monasteries, military schools, old-age homes, and concentration camps. Replete with vivid "references to mortifications that disrupt, defile, assault, or contaminate the self,"[31] Goffman's account of these "total institutions" provides a powerful indictment of such places as engines of degradation and oppression, a finely rendered "symbolic presentation of organizational tyranny, and a closed universe symbolizing the thwarting of human possibilities."[32]

Oddly enough, given his interactionist sensibilities, the central feature of the portrait Goffman sketches is an inevitable and powerful structural determinism. By its very nature, the mental hospital (not unlike Dickens' Marshalsea) manufactures the human materials that justify its existence. The crucial factor in forming mental patients is their institution rather than their illness. And their reactions and adjustments, pathological as they might seem to an outsider, are the product of the ill effects of their environment (with all its peculiar routines and deprivations) rather than the natural outcome of an unfolding intra-individual pathology.

As I suggested earlier, there are serious weaknesses in the evidentiary base on which these extraordinary far-reaching claims rest. There is, for

29. Hunt, "Rehabilitation Program," 14.

30. R. Barton, *Institutional Neurosis*, 2d ed. (Bristol: Wright, 1965).

31. C. McEwen, "Continuities and Discontinuities in the Study of Total Institutions," *Annual Review of Sociology* (Beverly Hills, Calif.: Sage, 1980), 147.

32. N. Perry, "The Two Cultures and the Total Institution," *British Journal of Sociology* no. 25 (1974): 353.

example, not even a token attempt in Goffman's work to confront the issue of what explains inmates' presence in the mental hospital in the first place. We are instead supposed to rest content with an unsubstantiated claim that they are the victims of "contingencies," somehow "betrayed" into the institution by their nearest and dearest (for reasons that remain entirely obscure). The "blame" for their situation, then, lies not at all in their own conduct or mental state, but rather in a conspiracy of others to secure their exclusion from society. Likewise, questions of the social location of madness and of the kind of existence to which hospitalization is an alternative are simply passed over in silence. And perhaps most notably of all, there is not even an attempt to generate valid and reliable evidence essential to any credible assessment of the respective contribution of intrapsychic and environmental influences to what he calls the "moral career of the mental patient." As Craig McEwen puts it, "Goffman's analysis has persuaded readers as much by its literary power as by the weight of its evidence"; indeed it relies for its persuasiveness on our willingness to take "literary metaphor as established fact."[33]

Yet there is no shortage of people (and policymakers) willing to make precisely that leap of faith. In the process, the chilling equation of the mental hospital and the concentration camp, originally the hyperbole of muckraking journalists, has now acquired the mantle of academic respectability. Ideologically, this is a development of profound significance, for it has effectively legitimized "community treatment," not by a careful demonstration of its merits (which would require systematic attention to its practical implementation), but by rendering the alternative simply unthinkable. Who, in the circumstances, would even attempt to dispute the claim that "the worst home is better than the best mental hospital"?[34]

It was this climate of opinion that over more than two decades, from the mid-1950s onward, allowed the portrayal of the simple decline in mental hospital censuses and in length of stay in the hospitals as an unambiguous reform and improvement. Measured in this crude yet easily quantifiable way, the "success" of community care in both England and America is easily shown, though the speed and extent of the changes has varied between the two societies. From the earliest years of the state-funded mental hospital system in the nineteenth century a pattern was established in both societies of consistent and almost uninterrupted increase in in-patient population. This remorseless increase was such that in the United States during the first half of the twentieth century, "the public mental hospital population had quadrupled . . . , whereas the gen-

33. McEwen, "Continuities and Discontinuities," 147–48.

34. Elaine Cumming and John Cumming, *Closed Ranks: An Experiment in Mental Health Education* (Cambridge: Harvard University Press, 1957), 55.

eral population had only doubled."[35] In England, the timing of the rise
was somewhat different, with the most spectacular increases coming in
the last half of the nineteenth century, but even here the hospital census
all but tripled between 1890 and 1950.

This pattern of uninterrupted growth was abruptly reversed in the
mid-1950s. First in England, then in the United States, the in-patient
census began to fall. As Table 1 shows, the population of English mental
hospitals had decreased from little short of 150,000 in 1954 to some
75,000 in 1980. In the United States, the decline began two years later,
and from a maximum of approximately 560,000 had fallen to only
171,500 some twenty years later, and to 132,000 by 1980 (Table 2).
Allowing for population growth, of course, the break with historical
trends was even more dramatic than these data would indicate. In the
United States, for example, had the size of the hospital population relative to the total population remained constant (and historically the tendency was for it to rise faster than the general population), by 1975 the
mental hospitals would have contained some three-quarters of a million
people.

As comparison of Tables 1 and 2 reveals, once the in-patient census
began to decline, it did so each and every year in both countries. This
common experience is the more remarkable given that both societies
were also experiencing a simultaneous and sharp increase in *admissions*
to mental hospitals. Between 1955 and 1968, admissions to mental hospitals in England and Wales rose from 78,586 per year to 170,527; and
although admissions dipped to 162,864 in 1970, this was still more than
twice the number admitted in 1955. The rise in admissions has been
equally steady and of similar magnitude in the United States. Whereas
approximately 185,000 were admitted to mental hospitals in 1956, by
1970 the figure was 393,000 (although, once more, there was a slight decline after this). Statistically speaking, therefore, the decline in mental
hospital populations reflects a policy of greatly accelerated discharge. In
the United States, for example, whereas, in 1950, the average stay in a
state mental hospital was over twenty years, by 1975, it was no more than
seven months.

Still, if deinstitutionalization has shared certain features in the two societies, even the gross statistics in Tables 1 and 2 suggest that there have
also been important divergences. In both England and the United States,
during the first ten years of declines in their hospital populations the
dips were consistent but relatively small. But while the English in-patient
population continued a mostly steady 2 or 3 percent per annum de-

35. Joint Commission on Mental Illness and Health, *Action for Mental Health* (New
York: Basic Books, 1961), 7.

TABLE 1   Resident Population of Mental Hospitals
in England and Wales, 1951–80

Year	Number Resident	Year	Number Resident*
1951	143,200	1966	121,600
1952	144,600	1967	118,600
1953	146,600	1968	116,400
1954	148,100	1969	105,600
1955	146,900	1970	103,300
1956	145,600	1971	103,000
1957	143,200	1972	100,000
1958	142,800	1973	94,000
1959	139,100	1974	90,000
1960	136,200	1975	87,000
1961	135,400	1976	83,800
1962	133,800	1977	80,800
1963	127,600	1978	78,200
1964	126,500	1979	76,500
1965	123,600	1980	75,200

SOURCES: Figures for 1951–60 from E. M. Brooke, "Factors in the Demand for Psychiatric Beds," *The Lancet*, 8 December 1962, 1211 (by permission). Figures for 1961–70 supplied by the Department of Health and Social Security (DHSS). Figures for 1971–80 from DHSS, *Health and Personal Social Services Statistics for England* (London: HMSO, 1982).
Note: All figures are rounded.
*Figures for 1971–80 are for average daily number of in-patients, rather than for total patients resident as of 31 December.

crease, its American counterpart began to decline much more rapidly. The major source of the difference lies in the treatment of the senile and the mentally ill elderly. In England, persons over 65 do not constitute a disproportionate fraction of those discharged from mental hospitals.[36] Beginning in the latter 1960s, however, the contrary is true in the United States. Between 1969 and 1974 alone, the number of patients over 65 in state and county mental hospitals nationwide fell by 56 percent, from 135,322 to 59,685.[37] In individual states, the decline was steeper yet. In 1968, a memorandum from the New York state commissioner of mental hygiene ordered the implementation of more restrictive admissions of the elderly, leading to a fall in hospital cases from 78,020 to 34,000 by

36. Anthony Clare, *Psychiatry in Dissent* (London: Tavistock, 1980), 433, estimates that, at the end of the seventies, there were still more than 50,000 patients in British mental hospitals over the age of sixty-five.

37. Senate Special Committee on Aging, Subcommittee on Long-Term Care, 94th Cong., 2d sess., 1976, *Nursing Home Care in the United States: Failure in Public Policy*, Support Paper no. 7, *The Role of Nursing Homes in Caring for Discharged Mental Patients*, Committee Print, 719.

TABLE 2   Resident Population in State and County Mental Hospitals
in the United States, 1950–80

Year	Number Resident	Year	Number Resident
1950	512,500	1966	452,100
1951	520,300	1967	426,000
1952	532,000	1968	400,700
1953	545,000	1969	370,000
1954	554,000	1970	339,000
1955	558,000	1971	309,000
1956	551,400	1972	276,000
1957	548,000	1973	255,000
1958	545,200	1974	215,600
1959	541,900	1975	191,400
1960	535,000	1976	171,500
1961	527,500	1977	159,500
1962	515,600	1978	153,500
1963	504,600	1979	140,400
1964	409,400	1980	132,200
1965	475,200		

SOURCES: National Institute of Mental Health (NIMH), *Trends in Resident Patients, State and County Mental Hospitals, 1950–1968* (Washington, D.C.: Department of Health, Education, and Welfare, 1972); idem, "Provisional Patient Movement and Administrative Data State and County Mental Hospital Inpatient Services," Mental Health Statistical Note, no. 114 (Washington, D.C.: Department of Health, Education, and Welfare, 1975); Biometry Branch, NIMH.
Note: All figures are rounded.

1973, a decrease of 64 percent in five years. As Table 3 (page 320) shows, other states were even more "successful" than this.

As I shall discuss at greater length later, this pattern of accelerated discharge both reflects and depends on some broad differences in the practical implementation of deinstitutionalization in England and the United States. I have pointed out that one major ideological defense of the decanting of patients from mental hospitals has been the essentially negative one that life in a state-run "total institution" was so irredeemably awful that the mere absence of its deforming, dehumanizing pressures must be an improvement. Some of the deinstitutionalization's supporters have been content with this claim to be guided by a belated recognition of "the limits of benevolence"[38] and have argued that this round of reform rests on a prudent recognition of the need to concentrate on avoiding harm rather than doing good.[39] In most quarters, however, the movement back to the community has involved the invocation

38. Willard Gaylin et al., *Partial Justice* (New York: Knopf, 1974).
39. Rothman, *Conscience and Convenience*.

of millennial claims not very different from those that accompanied its predecessors in the history of psychiatric reform. In Paul Rock's apt phrase, most of the advocates of community treatment have sought to picture the community as a kind of "secular Lourdes providing inexpensive redemption" [40] to the lame, the halt, the morally unfit, and the mentally maimed.

Gliding silently over the reality of the increasingly segmented, isolated, and atomized existence characteristic of late capitalist societies, those active in promoting the community approach to serious forms of mental disorder argued that the very locus of treatment could prove therapeutic. By not segregating the mentally ill from the rest of us, the community approach would help to keep them integrated with their neighbors, and even where those linkages had already been strained or fractured, would more readily permit a reestablishment of social ties with "normal" society. Instead of the passive and dependent behavior nourished by institutional existence, community care would restore independence and initiative. Possibly with some assistance from an outpatient clinic located at a general hospital or, in the United States, from one of the new community mental health centers, patients would find their needs provided for with minimal disturbance to their existing living arrangements and in ways that preserved and protected their basic social capacities.

To an extraordinary extent, however, expectations like these rested upon *a priori* reasoning rather than empirical demonstration; and, as Kirk and Thierren have pointed out, the notion that they even remotely correspond with actual outcomes is simply a myth, "reflecting more the intentions and hopes of community mental health than the uncomfortable realities." [41]

In the midst of all the excitement about the replacement of the mental hospital and the breathless proclamations about the virtues of the community, few people noticed the degree to which the new programs remained castles in the air, figments of their planners' imaginations. Nor did many appear to realize, for some considerable time, that despite all the rhetoric on both sides of the Atlantic about "better services for the mentally handicapped" (the title of an official statement of British policy),[42] the reality was the much darker one of retrenchment or even elimination of state-supported programs for victims of severe and chronic forms of mental disorder. As Peter Sedgwick put it, with pardonable sarcasm, "The reduction in the register of patients . . . has been

40. Paul Rock, personal communication to the author, November 1975.

41. S. Kirk and M. Thierren, "Community Mental Health Myths and the Fate of Formerly Hospitalized Mental Patients," *Psychiatry* 38 (1975): 217.

42. Department of Health and Social Security [England], *Better Services for the Mentally Handicapped*, Cmd. 4683 (1971).

achieved through the creation of rhetoric of 'community care facilities' whose influence over policy in hospital admission and discharge has been particularly remarkable when one considers that they do not, in the actual world, exist."[43]

Sooner or later, however, any audience becomes disenchanted with a shell game in which there is no pea. For almost a quarter century, there was a remarkable dearth of "major research projects of academic respectability that [showed] either the extent of the need or the extent of the failure" of mental health policy.[44] But more recently, the implementation of community care has finally begun to attract more critical attention, much of it journalistic, but some of it (belatedly) from scholarly sources.[45] In consequence, it is now generally conceded that, on both sides of the Atlantic, a policy of deinstitutionalization was implemented with little or no prior consideration of such basic issues as where the patients who were released would end up; who would provide the services they needed; and who would pay for those services.[46] What is perhaps more surprising, the massive reassignment of patients has continued in the face of continuing lack of attention to these matters, with the predictable consequences I shall discuss shortly.

Given the general emphasis on the therapeutic value of reintegration into the community, and leaving to one side the fact that "the belief in the value of reintegration has been devoid of any systematic analysis of what constitutes a relevant community,"[47] one might have "expected that, by now, a substantial body of research would have been built up to demonstrate the advantages that accrue when the educational, occupational, domestic, and protective functions of mental hospitals are taken over by alternative agencies. In fact, such studies [as exist] . . . have been,

43. Peter Sedgwick, "Psychiatry and Liberation" (Paper, Leeds University, 1981), 9.

44. Kathleen Jones, "Deinstitutionalization in Context," *Milbank Memorial Fund Quarterly* 57 (1979): 557.

45. R. Reich and L. Siegal, "Psychiatry Under Siege: The Mentally Ill Shuffle to Oblivion," *Psychiatric Annals* 3 (1973): 37–55; F. Arnhoff, "Social Consequences of Policy Toward Mental Illness," *Science* 188 (1975): 1277–81; Kirk and Thierren, "Community Mental Health Myths"; Andrew Scull, "The Decarceration of the Mentally Ill: A Critical View," *Politics and Society* 6 (1976): 173–212; idem, *Decarceration: Community Treatment and the Deviant—A Radical View* (Englewood Cliffs, N.J.: Prentice-Hall, 1977); idem, "Deinstitutionalization and the Rights of the Deviant," *Journal of Social Issues* 37, no. 3 (1981): 6–20; idem, "A New Trade in Lunacy: The Recommodification of the Mental Patient," *American Behavioral Scientist* 24 (1981): 741–54; Senate Special Committee on Aging, *Role of Nursing Homes;* J. Wolpert and E. Wolpert, "The Relocation of Released Mental Patients into Residential Communities," *Policy Sciences* 7 (1976): 31–51; General Accounting Office, *The Mentally Ill in the Community: Government Needs to Do More* (Washington, D.C.: Government Printing Office, 1977); E. Bassuk and S. Gerson, "Deinstitutionalization and Mental Health Services," *Scientific American* 238 (1978): 46–53; S. Rose, "Deciphering Deinstitutionalization," *Milbank Memorial Fund Quarterly* 57 (1979): 429–60.

46. General Accounting Office, *Mentally Ill*, 39.

47. Kirk and Thierren, "Community Mental Health Myths," 213.

in the main, descriptive rather than experimental, and are rarely epidemiological in nature, so that it is difficult to know how far the results can be generalized."[48] For example, the study of Pasamanick and his associates[49] which is often cited as demonstrating the feasibility of maintaining schizophrenics in the community, deals only with those who are members of intact families, who, as we know, form only a very small percentage of long-term mental patients. Moreover, a subsequent follow-up study with even these patients produced much less favorable findings, possibly the result of the failure of the authorities to maintain adequate funding for the program.[50] On the other side of the equation, we also lack thoughtful and careful analysis, based on a sufficiently representative sample of ex-patients, of the social and economic costs of maintaining such people in the community—defining cost in the broadest sense and moving beyond a narrow concern with fiscal costs to the state to incorporate a consideration of human as well as monetary costs to the patients, their families, and the community at large.

Ex-patients, and those who would formerly have been sent to mental hospitals (for many jurisdictions have sharply cut back the criteria justifying commitment), are to be found, of course, in a wide variety of settings, and attempting to generalize about their situations is necessarily a hazardous business. The problem is intensified by "the paucity of follow-up studies whose data can be generalized and compared and that trace the movement of discharged patients through the labyrinth of psychiatric facilities and living conditions after their release."[51] And it is, of course, still more acute when one is discussing more than one country. Among state mental health bureaucrats, ignorance about the fate of their former charges is often so great that they may not even know where the discharged patients are to be found.[52] A recent American study, for example, discovered with disconcerting regularity that "information on what happened to former mental hospital patients and residents in institutions for the retarded was generally not available. Follow-up of released patients was generally haphazard, fragmented, or nonexistent."[53]

48. John Wing, "Planning and Evaluating Services for the Chronically Handicapped Psychiatric Patients in the United Kingdom," in *Alternatives to Mental Hospital Treatment*, ed. L. I. Stein and M. A. Test (New York: Plenum, 1978), 240.

49. Benjamin Pasamanick, Frank Scarpitti, and Simon Dinitz, *Schizophrenics in the Community: An Experimental Study in the Prevention of Hospitalization* (New York: Appleton-Century-Crofts, 1967).

50. Ann E. Davis, Simon Dinitz, and Benjamin Pasamanick, *Schizophrenics in the New Custodial Community: Five Years After the Experiment* (Columbus: Ohio State University Press, 1974).

51. Bassuk and Gerson, "Deinstitutionalization," 50.

52. As I shall suggest later, this ignorance may not be wholly accidental.

53. General Accounting Office, *Mentally Ill*, 95.

One thing is certain: the overwhelming majority of them are not being serviced by the new community mental health centers. The existence of several hundred of these federally sponsored centers in the United States has fostered the comforting notion, particularly among overseas observers,[54] that those discharged from state hospitals have simply been transferred to a setting that provides a more modern and effective way of delivering treatment. Such assumptions are quite natural. (After all, the patients are allegedly being discharged to receive "community treatment," and the community mental health centers are one of the few places where community treatment is conceivably being dispensed.) Nevertheless, they are also quite mistaken. Even if one disregards the centers' uneven geographical distribution and their current fiscal problems, it remains the case that neither their ideology nor their most common services are "directed at the needs of those who have traditionally resided in state psychiatric institutions."[55] From the outset, those running the new centers have displayed a pronounced preference for treating "'good patients' [rather] than chronic schizophrenics, alcoholics or senile psychotics"[56]—in other words, precisely a desire not to treat the patients being discharged from state institutions. Unsurprisingly, therefore, studies show "no large consistent relationship between the opening of centers and changes in state hospitals resident rates."[57] Indeed, National Institute of Mental Health data demonstrate that "public mental hospitals accounted for fewer referrals to community mental health centers [less than 4 percent] than any other referral source reported, except for the clergy."[58] Partly as a consequence, community health centers "have no direct bearing on the bulk of publicly funded mental health care in the public sector."[59]

Nevertheless, some of those discharged from mental hospitals have unambiguously benefited from the shift in social policy. Victims of an earlier tendency toward what the Wolperts have called "overhospitalization,"[60] they have experienced few problems obtaining employment and housing, maintaining social ties, and so forth, blending all but impercep-

54. Jones, "Deinstitutionalization."

55. Kirk and Thierren, "Community Mental Health Myths," 210; see also Franklin D. Chu and Sharland Trotter, *The Madness Establishment: Ralph Nader's Study Group Report on the National Institute of Mental Health* (New York: Grossman, 1974).

56. R. O. Rieder, "Hospital, Patients and Politics," *Schizophrenia Bulletin* 11 (1974): 11.

57. C. Windle and D. Scully, "Community Mental Health Centers and the Decreasing Use of State Mental Hospitals," *Community Mental Health Journal* 12 (1976): 11.

58. General Accounting Office, *Mentally Ill*, 95.

59. Rose, "Deciphering Deinstitutionalization," 44. On this issue, see also Steven Sharfstein, "Will Community Mental Health Survive in the 1980s?" *American Journal of Psychiatry* 135 (1978): 1363–65; and R. L. Okin, "The Future of State Mental Health Programs for the Chronic Psychiatric Patient in the Community," ibid., 1355–58.

60. Wolpert and Wolpert, "Relocation."

tibly into the general population. Such benign outcomes are, however, far from constituting the norm.

Rather as one might expect, among those with more noticeable continuing impairment, ex-patients placed with their families seem on the whole to have fared best. Even here, there have been costs, sometimes serious costs. John Wing has recently expressed "surprise" that, in view of the greatly increased likelihood of someone with schizophrenia living at home instead of in a hospital, so little research is being done on the problems experienced by their relatives.[61] His own work, and that of his associates, has provided us with much of what little data we do possess on this subject and demonstrates that "the burden on relatives and the community was rarely negligible, and in some cases it was intolerable."[62] A good deal of the distress and misery has remained hidden because of families' reticence about complaining—a natural tendency, but one that has helped sustain a false optimism about the effects of the shifts to community treatment. As George Brown puts it, "relatives are not in a strong position to complain—they are not experts, they may be ashamed to talk about their problems and they have come to the conclusion that no help can be offered which will substantially reduce their difficulties."[63] (Such conclusions may have a strong factual basis, in view of the widespread inadequacies or even absence of after-care facilities and the reluctance, often refusal, of the authorities to countenance rehospitalization.) The new policy has thus unquestionably seen "a considerable burden being placed on the health, leisure, and finances of the families [involved]."[64] The evidence may not be sufficient yet to warrant Arnhoff's claim that "the consequences of indiscriminate community treatment may often have profound iatrogenic effects. . . . We may be producing more psychological and social disturbance than we correct."[65] But at the very least, we must recognize that "if . . . state policy is to shift more responsibility on to 'the family,' then the physical and psychological burdens on individuals will increase disproportionately."[66]

61. Wing, "Planning and Evaluating Services," 245.

62. J. K. Wing and G. W. Brown, *Institutionalism and Schizophrenia* (Cambridge: Cambridge University Press, 1970), 192. See the early study by Jacquelyn Grad de Alcaron and Peter Sainsbury, "Mental Illness and the Family," *The Lancet* i (March 9, 1963): 544–47; and C. Creer and J. K. Wing, *Schizophrenia at Home* (London: Institute of Psychiatry, 1974).

63. G. W. Brown, et al., *Schizophrenia and Social Care* (London: Oxford University Press, 1966), 59.

64. J. K. Wing, "How Many Psychiatric Beds?" *Psychological Medicine* 1 (1971): 189.

65. F. Arnhoff, "Social Consequences," 1277.

66. Ian Gough, *The Political Economy of the Welfare State* (London: Macmillan, 1979), 92. For example, as Richard Lamb has pointed out, the relative with primary responsibility for the patient (usually female) often "cannot leave the house even to go shopping without getting someone to watch the patient. The relatives may not only become jailers, but, in effect, be in jail themselves" (H. Richard Lamb, *Treating the Long-Term Mentally Ill: Beyond Deinstitutionalization* [San Francisco: Jossey-Bass, 1982], 92).

Their public silence and lack of protest notwithstanding, more research into these families' situations is clearly essential. Yet even without
that additional research, we know that one consequence of the new policies is all but certain: "community care," in this form at least, means tying
down women in traditional servicing roles for their disabled kinfolk. To
put it another way, in the absence of "genuine, socially funded resources
of community care, [attempts] to loosen the tyranny of the mental institution [proceed at the price of] re-enforcing an archaic sexual division
of labour." [67]

Yet whatever the difficulties encountered by these ex-patients and
their families, they pale by comparison with the experiences of the
greater number of ex-patients who have no families or whose families
simply refuse to accept responsibility for them. Particularly in the United
States the precipitous decline in mental hospital populations from the
mid-1960s onwards has been matched by an equally dramatic upsurge in
the numbers of psychiatrically impaired residents of nursing homes.
This trend is particularly marked among, but not confined to, the aged
mentally ill. Table 3 suggests how rapid and complete the elimination of
the elderly from American state hospitals has been. That the majority of
them have simply been transferred from one institutional setting to another is suggested by the fact that between 1963 and 1969 the number of
nursing home inmates with mental disorders virtually doubled, [68] and
evidence from the National Center for Health Statistics shows a further
48 percent increase through mid-1974, from 607,400 to 899,500. [69] Data
from the National Institute of Mental Health show that by the mid-
1970s, nursing homes had become the "largest single place of care for
the mentally ill," absorbing 29.3 percent of the direct costs associated
with coping with them. [70] More than 50 percent of these nursing home
residents were placed in facilities with more than a hundred beds, and
more than 15 percent in "homes" with more than 200 beds. [71]

These numbers alone might cause one to suspect that "the return of
patients to the community has, in many ways, extended the philosophy
of custodialism to the community rather than ending it at the gates of
the hospital." [72] But there is a growing volume of more direct evidence
that demonstrates the "ghettoization of the returning ex-patients along
with other dependent groups in the population; the growing succession
of inner city land use to institutions providing services to the dependent

67. Sedgwick, *Psychopolitics*, 239–41.
68. National Institute of Mental Health, "Patterns in Use of Nursing Homes by the
Aged Mentally Ill," *Statistical Note* no. 107 (June 1974), 2.
69. General Accounting Office, *Mentally Ill*, 11.
70. Ibid.
71. Ibid., 16.
72. Kirk and Thierren, "Community Mental Health Myths," 212.

TABLE 3   In-patients over 65 in State Mental Hospitals
in Selected States

State	1969	1974	Reduction (%)
Alabama	2646	639	76
California	4129	573	86
Illinois	7263	1744	76
Massachusetts	8000	1050	87
Wisconsin	4616	96	98

SOURCE: Senate Special Committee on Aging, *Role of Nursing Homes,* 719.

and needy . . . the forced immobility of the chronically disabled within deteriorated urban neighborhoods . . . areas where land use deterioration has proceeded to such a point that the land market is substantially unaffected by the introduction of community services and their clients."[73] The 1977 General Accounting Office study of deinstitutionalization reported "a general tendency to place formerly institutionalized persons in those nursing homes where the quality of care was poorer and safety standards not complied with as rigidly as in other nursing homes. . . . Generally speaking, the more mental patients there were in a facility, the worse the conditions."[74] Despite their titles, these places frequently provided neither nursing nor a home. In the words of an Oregon Task Force, "a typical day for a mentally ill person in a nursing home was sleeping, eating, watching television, smoking cigarettes, sitting in groups in the largest room, or looking out the window [*sic*]; there was no evidence of an organized plan to meet their needs."[75] To make matters worse, state agencies typically provide few or no follow-up services, and little in the way of effective supervision or inspection. In the absence of such controls and lacking the bureaucratic encrustations of state enterprises, nursing home operators have found ways to pare down on even the miserable subsistence existence characteristic of state institutions.

Of course, many discharged mental patients of all ages end up in other, perhaps still less salubrious settings—board-and-care homes and so-called welfare hotels. In Philadelphia, for example, a Temple University study revealed that some 15,000 ex-patients were living in approximately 1,500 boarding homes in the city. In New Jersey, a whole new industry has sprung up, utilizing the huge, cheap, run-down Victorian hotels in formerly fashionable beach resorts as accommodation for several thousand more discharged mental patients. In New York, there have been repeated media exposés of the massive concentrations of ex-

73. Senate Special Committee on Aging, *Trends in Long-Term Care,* Hearings, pts. 12 and 13, 92d Cong., 1st sess. 1971, 1213.
74. General Accounting Office, *Mentally Ill,* 13–14.
75. Cited in ibid., 15–16.

inmates in the squalid single-room occupancy welfare hotels of the upper west side of Manhattan and in the Long Island communities surrounding Pilgrim and Central Islip state hospitals. Many of the boarding homes in the latter area, in a pattern which is becoming all too familiar, were opened by those formerly employed by the state hospitals.[76] In Michigan, the pattern is depressingly similar:

> Many of the foster care homes serving the mentally disabled were in inner-city areas with high crime rates, abandoned buildings, sub-standard housing, poor economic conditions, and little or no recreational opportunities. Of a total of 378 community placement residences in Detroit serving the mentally disabled, 165 were located in the inner-city, with 101 on one street. State officials attributed this to the availability of large homes at relatively low prices . . . and to restrictive zoning which limits after-care homes to the older, run-down sections of the city. Although the number of mentally disabled in these facilities was not known, it has been estimated to be several thousand. The only service being provided many released mentally ill patients was medication.[77]

Such developments have not occurred without implicit and explicit state sponsorship and encouragement. In New York State, the scandals associated with the connections between the board-and-care industry and the political establishment eventually forced a full-scale inquiry and subsequent prosecutions.[78] Pennsylvania, with remarkable foresight, repealed its provisions for inspecting boarding homes the same year (1967) it began "a massive deinstitutionalization program aimed at moving patients out of mental hospitals into community programs."[79] Hawaii faced a massive shortage of beds in licensed boarding homes when it adopted a policy of accelerated discharge. The problem was resolved, with unusual bureaucratic flexibility, through "the proliferation, with the explicit encouragement of the state mental health division, of unlicensed boarding homes for the placement of ex-hospitalized patients."[80] Nebraska at first shied away from such a laissez-faire approach, deciding apparently that some form of state oversight was called for. Accordingly, in a splendidly original variant on the ancient practice of treating the mad like cattle, the state placed licensing and inspection of the board-and-care homes in the hands of its state Department of Agriculture. Subsequent citizen complaints about the resulting conditions led to the

76. See A. Mesnikoff, "Barriers to the Delivery of Mental Health Services: The New York City Experience," *Hospital and Community Psychiatry* 29 (1978): 373–78.

77. General Accounting Office, *Mentally Ill*, 18.

78. See the *New York Times*, 18, 21, 22 January, 4, 5, 6 February 1975; and Charles Hynes, *Proprietary Homes for Adults: Their Administration, Management, Control, Operation, Supervision, Funding, and Quality* (New York: Deputy Attorney General's Office, 1977).

79. *Philadelphia Inquirer*, 21 September 1975.

80. Kirk and Thierren, "Community Mental Health Myths," 211.

SOCIAL ORDER / MENTAL DISORDER

withdrawal of licenses, but not the *patients*, "from an estimated 320 of these homes, leaving them without state supervision or regulation."[81] Missouri simply noted the existence of some "755 unlicensed facilities in [the] State housing more than 10,000 patients"[82] and continued to dispense the state funds on which their operators depended. And still other states, like Maryland and Oregon, opted for perhaps the safest course of all—no follow-up of those they released, and hence a blissful official ignorance about their subsequent fate.[83]

Such systematic academic research as has been done on conditions in board-and-care facilities (and again the research is noticeable mainly by its absence) confirms the picture. Lamb and Goertzel concluded that "it is only an illusion that patients who were placed in board and care homes are 'in the community.' . . . These facilities are for the most part like small long-term state hospital wards isolated from the community. One is overcome by the depressing atmosphere, not because of the physical appearance of the boarding home, but because of the passivity, isolation, and inactivity of the residents."[84] Kirk and Thierren use remarkably similar language to describe their findings in Hawaii: "Many ex-patients are placed in 'ward-like' environments where they are supervised by ex-state hospital staff, and they participate in a state hospital routine, albeit now 'in the community.' But many of these former patients do not even have the limited involvement provided by a day hospital. They spend the majority of their time in a boarding home which promotes dependency, passivity, isolation and inactivity."[85]

In the United States over the past quarter century, with the wholesale assistance of federal funds—Supplemental Security Income (SSI), Medicaid, Medicare, and so forth—mental patients have been transformed into a commodity from which various professionals and entrepreneurs extract a profit. The consequence has been the emergence of a new "trade in lunacy"[86] that in many ways bears a remarkable resemblance to the private madhouses that were employed to deal with the mentally disordered and distracted in eighteenth-century England. In that earlier period, anyone could enter this business, and there was no regulation of conduct, with the result that gross exploitation and maltreatment of patients were commonplace. As critics at the time pointed out, in such "trading speculations [operated] with a view to pecuniary profit . . . the extent of the profit must depend on the amount that can be saved out of

81. General Accounting Office, *Mentally Ill*, 19.
82. Senate Committee on Aging, *The Role of Nursing Homes*, 724.
83. General Accounting Office, *Mentally Ill*, 95.
84. R. Lamb and V. Goertzel, "Discharged Mental Patients: Are They Really in the Community?" *Archives of General Psychiatry* 24 (1971): 29–34.
85. Kirk and Thierren, "Community Mental Health Myths," 212.
86. Parry-Jones, *Trade in Lunacy*.

the sum paid for the board of each individual."[87] Proprietors must therefore "have a strong tendency to consider the interests of the patients and their own at direct variance."[88] Given free entry into the business and the difficulties associated with the inspection and supervision of a multitude of operations, the least scrupulous were likely to be the most successful, and appalling results were all but structurally guaranteed. So it proved: It was precisely the abuses to which this system was prone that led to a campaign for reform and to the establishment of England's state mental hospitals.[89]

Again the cycle is repeating itself. We now live in a period, also hailed as an era of reform, when anyone can open a boarding home for mentally ill patients discharged from the state system. Once more the mentally disturbed are at the mercy of speculators who have every incentive to warehouse their charges as cheaply as possible, since the volume of profit is inversely proportional to the amount expended on the inmates.[90]

At the beginning of this chapter, I alluded to the case of Mary Jones, one of a number of "exemplary tales"[91] the nineteenth-century reformers used to point out the horrors of the nonasylum treatment of the insane. Contrary to their expectations, horrors of a virtually identical sort continued to be generated by the mental hospitals they succeeded in establishing.[92] Recent investigations suggest that they continue unabated in the new community settings. I must confess that beyond a certain point I have difficulty calibrating human misery, but certainly the condition of a

87. Commissioners in Lunacy, *Further Report Relative to the Haydock Lodge Lunatic Asylum* (London: Spottiswoode and Shaw, 1847), 14.

88. S. W. Nicoll, *An Enquiry into the Present State of Visitation in Asylums for the Reception of the Insane* (London: Harvey and Darnton, 1828), 2–3.

89. Cf. Scull, *Museums of Madness*.

90. Thus some ex-patients find themselves housed in "converted mobile homes, or renovated chicken coops" (Senate Special Committee on Aging, *Role of Nursing Homes*, 753. The committee cited some examples of the profits to be made: One partnership, on a turnover of just over $1,000,000, reported a profit of more than $300,000. A second enterprise, spending 58 cents per inmate per day on food, made $185,000 profit a year on revenues of $400,000, and in the space of ten years, the partners' equity grew from $10,000 to $250,000 (ibid., 765). A Chicago home with 188 beds yielded a combined return of $185,248 in a single year on an initial investment of $40,000. The report on a state inspection of the latter home provides some insight into how these spectacular rates of return were achieved. The inspectors found the third floor to be in a deplorable condition. "Urine saturated beds and floor areas. The stench permeated the area. This team also found broken plumbing, peeling plaster, inadequate food" (Senate Committee on Aging, *Trends in Long-Term Care, Hearings*, pts. 12 and 13, 1239, 1256). One result of this situation has been, as Senator Percy pointed out, "the tremendous boom in issues on the stock exchange in facilities for the elderly" (ibid., 1219).

91. Goffman, *Asylums*.

92. For a contemporary example, see Wendell Rawls, Jr., *Cold Storage* (New York: Simon and Schuster, 1980).

Mrs. Bond, an ex-patient found in an Illinois nursing home seems to differ little if at all from that of her Welsh counterpart of the mid-nineteenth century. As the Senate Committee on Aging reported:

> Mrs. Bond was covered with decubiti (bed sores) from the waist down, that decubiti on the hips were the size of grapefruit and bones could be seen; that the meatus and the labia were so stuck together with mucous and filth that tincture of green soap had to be used before a Foley Catheter could be inserted; that her toes were a solid mass of dirt which stuck together and not until they had been soaked in TID for three (3) days did the toes come apart; that body odor was most offensive; edema of feet, legs, and left hand.[93]

On a less lurid level, we possess a handful of studies that systematically compare the social functioning and clinical condition of hospitalized chronic patients with those of their counterparts in quasi-institutional community settings. "From both American and Canadian studies we have reports that fewer of the [hospitalized] patients were incontinent, fewer took no part in bathing, more were able to bathe without help, fewer took no responsibility for their own grooming, more dressed without assistance, fewer failed to dress and remain in hospital gowns, and more had money available and were capable of making occasional purchases."[94] More dramatically, a number of studies appear to demonstrate a close correlation between the relocation of chronic patients and sharp increases in their mortality rates.[95]

Intended as a cheap alternative to the state hospital, the ramshackle network of board-and-care homes and welfare hotels stand as an indictment of contemporary American mental "health" policy. They constitute perhaps the most extreme example of what has become the new orthodoxy, an "almost unanimous abdication from the task of proposing and securing any provision for a humane and continuous form of care

93. Senate Special Committee on Aging, Role of Nursing Homes, 756.

94. L. Epstein and A. Simon, "Alternatives to State Hospitalization for the Geriatric Mentally Ill," American Journal of Psychiatry 124 (1968): 955–61; R. Swan, "A Survey of a Boarding Home Program for Former Mental Patients," Hospital and Community Psychiatry 24 (1973): 485–86.

95. Cf. R. Marlowe, "When They Closed the Doors at Modesto," in State Mental Hospitals: What Happens When They Close? ed. Paul P. Ahmed and Stanley C. Plog (New York: Plenum, 1976), 83–96; C. Aldrich and E. Mendkoff, "Relocation of the Aged and Disabled: A Mortality Study," Journal of the American Geriatrics Society 11 (1963): 105–94; K. Jasman, "Individualized Versus Mass Transfer of Nonpsychotic Geriatric Patients from the Mental Hospital to the Nursing Home," Journal of American Geriatrics Society 15 (1969): 280–84; E. Markus, M. Blenker, and T. Downs, "The Impact of Relocation upon Mortality Rates of Institutionalized Aged Persons," Journal of Gerontology 26 (1971): 537–41; but for contrary findings, see E. Markson and J. Cumming, "The Post-transfer Fate of Relocated Patients," in State Mental Hospitals: What Happens When They Close? ed. Ahmed and Plog, 97–110.

for those mental patients who need something rather more than short-term therapy for an acute phase of their illness."[96] Here, ecologically separated and isolated from the rest of us, the most useless and unwanted segments of our society can be left to decompose quietly and, save for the occasional media exposé, all but invisibly.

In view of the depths of the misery and maltreatment associated with recent American mental health policy, Kathleen Jones' claim that "so far the United States has made a much better job of the business of deinstitutionalization"[97] would, if accurate, constitute an even more damning indictment of British practice than she perhaps intended. Apparently what led her to make this unfortunate assertion was the combination of a relatively intimate knowledge of the failures of British policies with a rather naive acceptance at face value of the claims made by American advocates of deinstitutionalization. And certainly at the level of rhetoric, Americans have by and large been the more active and shameless. Practically, however, the British experience has not (yet?) been quite as awful.

In part the British record is better because deinstitutionalization has simply not been as rapid or far-reaching as in America. In general, the shift away from the mental hospital in both societies has been powerfully influenced by fiscal considerations, the savings realizable by substituting neglect for even minimal custodial care.[98] In the United States, however, these pressures have been magnified by the fragmentation of the political structure. Care of the mentally ill has traditionally been a responsibility of the states, but deinstitutionalization has been promoted by the states' ability to transfer most of the costs of community support to the federal level. (The causal linkage is particularly plain in the case of the mass discharges of the elderly beginning in the late 1960s.)[99] In the absence of this additional incentive, the rush to empty mental hospitals has been somewhat less headlong in Britain.

Ex-patients there have also for the most part been spared the excesses associated with the new trade in lunacy.[100] The chains of private board-and-care homes and the dilapidated welfare hotels, now so large a part of American mental health "services," have few precise British equiva-

96. Sedgwick, *Psychopolitics*, 213.

97. Jones, "Deinstitutionalization," 567.

98. Scull, *Decarceration;* Rose, "Deciphering Deinstitutionalization"; D. N. Sheehan and J. Atkinson, "Comparative Cost of State Hospitals and Community Based in-patient Care in Texas," *Hospital and Community Psychiatry* 25 (1974), 242–44; J. Murphy and W. Datel, "A Cost-Benefit Analysis of Community Versus Institutional Living," *Health and Community Psychiatry* 25 (1976): 165–70; Rieder, "Hospitals, Patients, and Politics."

99. See the analysis in Paul Lerman, *Deinstitutionalization and the Welfare State* (New Brunswick, N.J.: Rutgers University Press, 1982).

100. Scull, "Deinstitutionalization."

lents.[101] In part, this situation probably reflects the somewhat lower numbers of chronic patients discharged. Undoubtedly too, it also mirrors the more entrepreneurial character of American capitalism and the greater legitimacy accorded to the process of the privatization of state and welfare services [102] in a society still wedded to the myth of "free enterprise."

All these qualifications notwithstanding, the British experience with community care remains dismal and depressing in its own right. As Peter Sedgwick points out,

> In Britain no less than in the United States, "community care" and "the replacement of the mental hospital" were slogans which masked the growing depletion of real services for mental patients; the accumulating numbers of impaired, retarded and demented males in the prisons and common lodging houses; the scarcity not only of local authority residential provisions for the mentally disabled but of day care centers and skilled social work resources; the jettisoning of mental patients in their thousands into the isolated helpless environment of their families of origin, who appealed in vain for hospital admission (even for a temporary period of respite), for counselling or support, and even for basic information and advice.[103]

Kathleen Jones is not unaware of these catastrophic failures masquerading under the official guise of a "revolution" in psychiatric care. It is her awareness of the failures that prompts her bitter comparison of British policy with an idealized, indeed mythological portrait of American practices. For her, much of the blame can be apportioned to administrative lapses. In particular, the reorganization of the British National Health Service in 1973, which eliminated any distinctive organization for the mental health services, left "no administrative focus, no forum for policy debate, and no impetus to personal development. The result is that the British services are now fragmented and to a large extent the personnel are demoralized." [104]

But while poor morale and administrative chaos have certainly contributed to worsening the situation, they are scarcely the major sources of the current difficulties. More centrally important is the absence of the

101. Note, however, an estimate, made almost a decade and a half ago, that there were 27,000 men and 2,000 women living in common lodging houses, hostels, and shelters, and at least another 1,000 sleeping in the streets (D. Tidmarsh, "Secure Hospital Units," *British Medical Journal*, 2 November 1974, 216). See also G. Edwards et al., "Census of a Reception Centre," *British Journal of Psychiatry* 114 (1978): 1031–39. There has also been a sizable shift of the mentally disturbed into the prison system, though the precise dimensions of this change remain uncertain.

102. Steven Spitzer and Andrew Scull, "Privatization and State Control: The Case of the Private Police," *Social Problems* 25 (1977): 18–29.

103. Sedgwick, *Psychopolitics*, 193–94.

104. Jones, "Deinstitutionalization," 565–66.

necessary infrastructure of services and financial supports without which talk about community care is simply a sham. During 1973–74, for example, while 300 million pounds was spent on the mentally ill still receiving institutional treatment, a mere 6.5 million pounds was spent on residential and day care services for those "in the community." Local authority spending on residential facilities for the mentally ill was a derisory 0.04 percent of their total expenditure.[105] Three years later, 116 out of 170 local authorities did not provide a single residential place for the elderly mentally infirm.[106] And more recently still, the intensifying fiscal crisis of the Thatcher-Reaganite years has simply reinforced the existing conservative hostility to social welfare services and made the prospect of providing even minimal levels of supportive services still more remote.[107]

It should be starkly apparent, though, that our collective reluctance to make a serious and sustained effort to provide a humane and caring environment for those manifesting grave and persistent mental disturbance has far deeper roots than the callousness of our contemporary political leadership. The personal disorganization and defective social skills of the sufferers themselves preclude their forming an effective pressure group in their own behalf. In any event, "the stigma attaching still to their various disabilities and illnesses usually prevents most of them from asserting a group identity in public, for purposes of demonstration or financial appeal,"[108] while their social marginality and dependency are likely to detract from whatever efforts they *do* make. Worse still, chronic psychotics exhibit persistent dependency, and it is unlikely that even the best programs of treatment will produce "recoveries" on any very large scale.

The idea that we bear a collective moral responsibility to provide for the unfortunate—indeed, that one of the marks of a civilized society is its determination to provide *as of right* certain minimum standards of living for all its citizens—has never secured widespread acceptance in the United States. Ideologically, this is a society dominated by the myth of the benevolent "invisible hand" of the marketplace and by a correspondingly amoral individualism. Moreover, in the last decade and a half, this ideology, always congenial to the privileged, has enjoyed a striking resurgence on the other side of the Atlantic. There is little place

105. Sedgwick, *Psychopolitics*, 251.
106. Ibid., 105, citing *The Guardian* (London), 13 January 1976.
107. For a similar bleak assessment of the prospects, see Clare, *Psychiatry in Dissent*, 434–35. The dilemmas confronted by those concerned for the fate of the mentally ill thus remain terrible. They are not, however, *pace* Professor Kathleen Jones ("Scull's Dilemma," *British Journal of Psychiatry* 141 [1982], 221–26), mine alone.
108. Sedgwick, *Psychopolitics*, 222.

(and less sympathy) within such a worldview for those who are excluded from the race for material well-being by chronic disabilities and handicaps—whether physical or mental disease, or the more diffuse but cumulatively devastating penalties accruing to those belonging to racial minorities or living in dire poverty.

The punitive sentiments directed against those who must feed from the public trough extend only too easily to embrace those who suffer from the most severe forms of psychiatric misery. Those who seek to protect the long-term mental patient from the opprobrium visited on the welfare recipient may do so by arguing that the patient is both dependent and *sick*. But I fear this approach has only a limited chance of success. After all, despite two centuries of propaganda, the public still resists the straightforward equation of mental and physical illness. Moreover, the long-term mental patient in most instances will not get better and often fails to collaborate with his or her therapist to seek recovery. Such blatant violations of the norms governing access to the sick role in our societies [109] make it unlikely that chronic schizophrenics will be extended the courtesies and exemptions accorded to the conventionally sick. Instead, even those incapacitated by psychiatric disability all too often find themselves the targets of those who would abolish social programs because they consider any social dependency immoral.

Symptomatic of the status of the chronically mentally ill as the ultimate outsiders is the retreat even of organized psychiatry from any attempt to deal with their problems. Ironically, it was by capturing control in the nineteenth century of the new state-run establishments for the seriously mad that psychiatry both established itself as a profession and ensured medical hegemony in the treatment of mental disorder. But in the long run, this core patient population became a liability rather than an asset. It was, after all, overwhelmingly drawn from the lower classes; it bore the additional stigma of being composed of wards of the state; and psychiatrists discovered that, notwithstanding the extravagant claims of the founders of their enterprise, it was largely beyond the reach of their therapeutic armamentarium. The development, from the late nineteenth century onwards, of a bifurcated profession, saw the creation of a group of higher-status practitioners who increasingly concentrated on an office practice offering a more treatable, more affluent clientele.[110]

But even this expansion of the psychiatric territory only mitigated the

109. See Talcott Parsons, *The Social System* (New York: Free Press, 1951).

110. Cf. Bonnie Blustein, "New York Neurologists and the Specialization of American Medicine," *Bulletin of the History of Medicine* 53 (1979): 170–83; Barbara Sicherman, "The Uses of a Diagnosis: Doctors, Patients, and Neurasthenia," *Journal of the History of Medicine and the Allied Sciences* 32 (1977): 33–54; idem, "The Quest for Mental Health in America" (Ph.D. dissertation, Columbia University, 1967); Andrew Scull, "The Social History of Psychiatry in the Victorian Era," in *Madhouses, Mad-Doctors, and Madmen*, ed. Scull, 5–32.

socially contaminating effects of overly close association with an impoverished, clinically hopeless clientele. Hence, perhaps, the alacrity with which the majority of the profession has handed over the task of coping with the chronically psychotic to the operators of nursing homes, boarding houses, and welfare hotels. Psychiatric involvement with such unrewarding cases can now be reduced to the occasional prescription of psychoactive drugs to be dispensed by others, thus providing a bare semblance of "medical" attention. And with these miracles of modern psychopharmacology to hand, our contemporary madhouse keepers possess a restraint with which to subdue their charges, less blatant than the chains and straitjackets employed by their counterparts two centuries ago, and, in consequence, all the more desirable.

Some fifteen years ago, George Brown and his colleagues claimed that "the acid test of a community service lies in whether it can meet the needs of the seriously handicapped persons who used, in the old days, to become long-stay mental hospital inmates."[111] By even the most generous interpretation of subsequent events, British and American policies have failed to meet that test. Nor should this occasion much surprise. Many of "the most basic needs of the mentally disabled—above all, the needs for housing, for occupation, and for community—are not satisfied by the market system of resource allocation which operates under capitalism."[112] Nor is it realistic to suppose they will be. In this most profound sense, then, Peter Sedgwick is surely correct when he concludes that "the crisis of mental health provision . . . is simply the crisis of the normal social order in relation to any of its members who lack the wage based ticket of entry into its palace of commodities."[113]

111. Brown et al., *Schizophrenia*, 10.
112. Sedgwick, *Psychopolitics*, 239.
113. Ibid.

SELECTED BIBLIOGRAPHY

BOOKS

Abdy, E. S. *Journal of a Residence and Tour in the United States of North America.* 3 vols. London: Murray, 1835.

An Account of the Rise and Progress of the [Frankford] Asylum, Proposed to Be Established near Philadelphia for the Relief of Persons Deprived of the Use of Their Reason. Philadelphia: Kimber and Conrad, 1814.

Alexander, Franz, and S. Selesnick. *The History of Psychiatry: An Evaluation of Psychiatric Thought and Practice from Prehistoric Times to the Present.* New York: Harper and Row, 1966.

Allen, Matthew. *Cases of Insanity, with Mental, Moral and Philosophical Observations upon Them.* London: Swire, 1831.

———. *Essay on the Classification of the Insane.* London: Taylor, 1837.

American Friends Service Committee. *Struggle for Justice.* New York: Hill and Wang, 1971.

Arlidge, John T. *On the State of Lunacy and the Legal Provision for the Insane.* London: Churchill, 1859.

Arnold, Thomas. *Observations on the Nature, Kinds, Causes, and Prevention of Insanity.* 2d ed., 2 vols. London: Phillips, 1806.

Bakewell, Samuel Glover. *An Essay on Insanity.* Edinburgh: Neill, 1833.

Bakewell, Thomas. *The Domestic Guide in Cases of Insanity.* Stafford: For the author, 1805.

———. *A Letter to the Chairman of the Select Committee on the State of Madhouses, to Which Is Subjoined Remarks on the Nature, Causes, and Cure of Mental Derangement.* Stafford: Chester, 1815.

Bardach, Eugene. *The Skill Factor in Politics.* Berkeley: University of California Press, 1972.

Barton, R. *Institutional Neurosis.* 2d ed. Bristol: Wright, 1965.

Battie, William. *A Treatise on Madness.* London: Whiston and White, 1758.

Becher, John Thomas. *An Address to the Public on the Nature, Design, and Constitu-*

tion of the General Lunatic Asylum near Nottingham. Newark, Nottinghamshire: Ridge, 1811.

Becker, Howard S. *Outsiders: Studies in the Sociology of Deviance.* Glencoe, IL: Free Press, 1963.

Belknap, Ivan. *Human Problems of a State Mental Hospital.* New York: McGraw-Hill, 1956.

Bell, Charles. *Essays on the Anatomy of Expression in Painting.* London: Longman, 1806.

Bellers, J. *Proposals for Raising a College of Industry.* London: T. Sowle, 1696.

Bellot, H. H. *University College London, 1826–1926.* London: University of London Press, 1929.

Bingham, Nathaniel. *Observations on the Religious Delusions of Insane Persons . . . with Which Are Combined a Copious Practical Description . . . of Mental Disease, and of Its Appropriate Medical and Moral Treatment.* London: Hatchard, 1841.

Blackmore, Sir Richard. *Treatise of the Spleen or Vapours.* London: Pemberton, 1724.

Bloomingdale Asylum. *Annual Reports.* 1818–60.

Bond, Earle D. *Dr. Kirkbride and His Mental Hospital.* Philadelphia: Lippincott, 1947.

Bowditch, Nathaniel I. *A History of the Massachusetts General Hospital.* Boston: Privately printed, 1851.

Braginsky, B., D. Braginsky, and K. Ring. *Methods of Madness: The Mental Hospital as a Last Resort.* New York: Holt, Rinehart, and Winston, 1969.

Brière de Boismont, Alexandre. *On Hallucinations: A History and Explanation.* London: Renshaw, 1859.

Briggs, Asa. *The Making of Modern England.* New York: Harper and Row, 1965.

Brook, Charles W. *Battling Surgeon.* Glasgow: Strickland, 1945.

Brooks, Alexander D. *Law, Psychiatry, and the Mental Health System.* Boston: Little, Brown, 1974.

Brougham, Henry. *The Life and Times of Henry Brougham by Himself.* London: Blackwood, 1871.

Brown, G. W., M. Bone, B. Dalison, and J. K. Wing. *Schizophrenia and Social Care.* London: Oxford University Press, 1966.

Browne, William Alexander Francis. *What Asylums Were, Are, and Ought to Be.* Edinburgh: Black, 1837.

———. *The Moral Treatment of the Insane: A Lecture.* London: Adlard, 1864.

Brydall, John. *Non Compos Mentis; or, The Law Relating to Natural Fools, Mad Folks, and Lunatick Persons.* London: Cleave, 1700.

Bucknill, J. C. *The Care of the Insane and Their Legal Control.* London: Macmillan, 1880.

Burgh, J. *Political Disquisitions.* Vol. 3. London: Dilly, 1775.

Burnett, C. M. *Insanity Tested by Science, and Shown to Be a Disease Rarely Connected with Organic Lesion of the Brain, and on That Account Far More Susceptible of Cure than Has Hitherto Been Supposed.* London: Highley, 1848.

Burrows, George Man. *Cursory Remarks on a Bill Now in the House of Peers for Regulating of Madhouses, . . . with Observations on the Defects of the Present System.* London: Harding, 1817.

———. *An Inquiry into Certain Errors Relative to Insanity.* London: Underwood, 1820.

————. *Commentaries on the Causes, Forms, Symptoms, and Treatment, Moral and Medical, of Insanity*. London: Underwood, 1828.

Busfield, Joan. *Managing Madness: Changing Ideas and Practice*. Wolfeboro, N.H.: Longwood Publishing Group, 1986.

Bynum, W. F., Roy Porter, and Michael Shepherd, eds. *The Anatomy of Madness: Essays in the History of Psychiatry*. 2 vols. London: Tavistock, 1985.

Carroll, Lewis. *Through the Looking Glass, and What Alice Found There*. New York: Peter Pauper Press, 1941.

Castel, Françoise, Robert Castel, and Anne Lovell. *The Psychiatric Society*. New York: Columbia University Press, 1982.

Castel, Robert. *L'Ordre psychiatrique: L'Âge d'or d'aliénisme*. Paris: Minuit, 1976. English trans.: *The Regulation of Madness: Origins of Incarceration in France*. Berkeley: University of California Press; Oxford: Polity Press, 1988.

Chadwick, Edwin. *Report on the Sanitary Conditions of the Labouring Population of Great Britain*. London: Clowes, 1842.

Chesler, Phyllis. *Women and Madness*. Garden City, N.Y.: Doubleday, 1972.

Cheyne, George. *The English Malady: or, A Treatise of Nervous Diseases of All Kinds*. London: Wisk, Ewing and Smith, 1733.

Clare, Anthony. *Psychiatry in Dissent*. 2d ed. London: Tavistock, 1980.

Clark, Sir James. *A Memoir of John Conolly, M.D., D.C.L.* London: Murray, 1869.

Clarkson, L. A. *The Pre-Industrial Economy in England, 1500–1750*. London: Batsford, 1971.

Combe, Andrew. *Observations on Mental Derangement: Being an Application of the Principles of Phrenology to the Elucidation of the Causes, Symptoms, Nature, and Treatment of Insanity*. Edinburgh: Anderson, 1831.

Commissioners in Lunacy. *Further Report Relative to the Haydock Lodge Lunatic Asylum*. London: Spottiswoode and Shaw, 1847.

Connecticut Assembly. *Report of the Committee for Locating a Site for a Hospital for the Insane Poor*. New Haven: Babcock and Wildman, 1840.

Connecticut State Medical Society. *Report of a Committee . . . Respecting an Asylum for the Insane, with the Constitution of a Society for Their Relief*. Hartford: Bowles and Frances, 1821.

Conolly, John. *An Introductory Lecture Delivered in the University of London, October 2, 1828*. London: Taylor, 1828.

————. *An Inquiry Concerning the Indications of Insanity, with Suggestions for the Better Protection and Care of the Insane*. London: Taylor, 1830. Facsimile ed., ed. Richard A. Hunter and Ida Macalpine. London: Dawsons, 1964.

————. *The Construction and Government of Lunatic Asylums and Hospitals for the Insane*. London: Churchill, 1847.

————. *A Letter to Benjamin Rotch, Esquire, Chairman of the Committee of Visitors, on the Plan and Government of the Additional Lunatic Asylum . . . About to Be Erected at Colney Hatch*. London: Churchill, 1847.

————. *The Treatment of the Insane Without Mechanical Restraints*. London: Smith, Elder, 1856.

————. *A Study of Hamlet*. London: Moxon, 1863.

Cooper, David. *The Grammar of Living*. Hardmondsworth: Penguin, 1974.

Coulter, Jeff. *Approaches to Insanity*. Oxford: Martin Robertson, 1973.

Cox, Joseph Mason. *Practical Observations on Insanity: In Which Some Suggestions Are Offered Towards an Improved Mode of Treating Diseases of the Mind . . . to*

Which are Subjoined, Remarks on Medical Jurisprudence as Connected with Diseased Intellect. London: Baldwin and Murray, 1806.

———. *Practical Observations on Insanity.* 3d ed. London: Baldwin and Underwood, 1813.

Creer, C. and J. K. Wing. *Schizophrenia at Home.* London: Institute of Psychiatry, 1974.

Crichton-Browne, Sir James. *Victorian Jottings.* London: Etchells and MacDonald, 1926.

Cruden, Alexander. *The London Citizen Exceedingly Injured; or, A British Inquisition Displayed.* London: Cooper and Dodd, 1739.

———. *The Adventures of Alexander the Corrector, with an Account of the Chelsea Academies, of the Private Places of Such as Are Supposed to Be Deprived of the Use of Their Reason.* London: For the author, 1754.

Cullen, William. *First Lines in the Practice of Psychic.* Edinburgh: Bell and Bradfute, 1784.

Cumming, Elaine, and John Cumming. *Closed Ranks: An Experiment in Mental Health Education.* Cambridge: Harvard University Press, 1957.

Dain, Norman. *Concepts of Insanity in the United States, 1789–1865.* New Brunswick, N.J.: Rutgers University Press, 1964.

———. *Disordered Minds.* Williamsburg, VA: Colonial Williamsburg Foundation, 1971.

Darwin, Erasmus. *Zoonomia; or, The Laws of Organic Life.* 2 vols. London: Johnson, 1796.

Davis, A., S. Dinitz, and B. Pasamanick. *Schizophrenics in the New Custodial Community: Five Years After the Experiment.* Columbus: Ohio State University Press, 1974.

Davis, David Brion. *The Problem of Slavery in the Age of Revolution.* Ithaca: Cornell University Press, 1975.

Defoe, Daniel. *Augusta Triumphans.* London: Roberts, 1728.

De la Rive, G. *Lettre adressée aux rédacteurs de la Bibliothèque britannique sur un nouvel établissement pour la guérison des aliénés.* Geneva: For the Author, 1798.

Deporte, Michael V. *Nightmares and Hobbyhorses: Swift, Sterne, and Augustan Ideas of Madness.* San Marino, CA: Huntington Library, 1974.

Deutsch, Albert. *The Shame of the States.* New York: Arno, 1973.

Dickens, Charles. *American Notes.* London: Penguin, 1972.

———. *Charles Dickens' Uncollected Writings from Household Words,* ed. Harry Stone. Bloomington and London: Indiana University Press, 1968.

Digby, Anne. *Madness, Morality, and Medicine: A Study of the York Retreat, 1796–1914.* Cambridge: Cambridge University Press, 1985.

Disraeli, Benjamin. *Sybil; or, The Two Nations.* London: Davies, 1927.

Dix, Dorothea. *Memorial Soliciting a State Hospital for . . . Pennsylvania.* Harrisburg: Lescure, 1845.

———. *Memorial Soliciting an Appropriation for the State [of Kentucky].* Lexington: Hodges, 1846.

———. *Memorial to the Senate and House of Representatives of the State of Illinois.* Springfield: State Printer, 1847.

———. *Memorial Soliciting a State Hospital for . . . Alabama.* Montgomery: Office of the Advertizer, 1849.

————. *Memorial Soliciting Adequate Appropriations for the Construction of a State Hospital for the Insane in the State of Mississippi.* Jackson: Fall and Marshall, 1850.

Dobb, M. *Studies in the Development of Capitalism.* New York: International Publishers, 1963.

Doerner, Klaus. *Madmen and the Bourgeoisie.* Oxford: Basil Blackwell, 1981.

Donzelot, Jacques. *The Policing of Families.* New York: Pantheon, 1980.

Dunham, H., and K. Weinberg. *The Culture of the State Mental Hospital.* Detroit: Wayne State University Press, 1960.

Dwyer, Ellen. *Homes for the Mad: Life Inside Two Nineteenth-Century Asylums.* New Brunswick, N.J.: Rutgers University Press, 1987.

Eaton, Leonard K. *New England Hospitals, 1790–1833.* Ann Arbor: University of Michigan Press, 1957.

Eddy, Thomas. *Hints for Introducing an Improved Mode of Treating the Insane in Asylums.* New York: Samuel Wood, 1815.

Edinburgh Royal Lunatic Asylum. *A Short Account of the Rise, Progress, and Present State of the Lunatic Asylum at Edinburgh.* Edinburgh: Neill, 1812.

Ellis, William Charles. *A Letter to Thomas Thompson, Esq., M.P., Containing Considerations on the Necessity of Proper Places Being Provided by the Legislature for the Reception of All Insane Persons and on Some of the Abuses Which Have Been Found to Exist in Madhouses, with a Plan to Remedy Them.* Hull: Topping and Dawson, 1815.

————. *A Treatise on the Nature, Symptoms, Causes, and Treatment of Insanity, with Practical Observations on Lunatic Asylums, and a Description of the Pauper Lunatic Asylum for the County of Middlesex at Hanwell, with a Detailed Account of Its Management.* London: Holdsworth, 1838.

Ennis, Bruce. *Prisoners of Psychiatry.* New York: Harcourt, Brace, Jovanovich, 1972.

Erikson, Kai. *Wayward Puritans.* New York: Wiley, 1966.

Evans, Charles. *An Account of the Asylum for the Relief of Persons Deprived of Their Reason near Frankford, Pennsylvania.* Philadelphia: Rakestraw, 1846.

Evans, Robin. *The Fabrication of Virtue: English Prison Architecture, 1750–1842.* Cambridge: Cambridge University Press, 1982.

Falconer, William. *A Dissertation on the Influence of the Passions upon Disorders of the Body.* London: Dill, 1788.

Fallowes, Thomas. *The Best Method for the Cure of Lunaticks, with Some Account of the Incomparable Oleum Cephalicum Used in the Same, Prepared and Administered by Tho. Fallowes, at His House in Lambeth-Marsh.* London: For the Author, 1705.

Faulkner, Benjamin. *Observations on the General and Improper Treatment of Insanity.* London: Reynell, 1789.

Ferriar, John. *Medical Histories and Reflections.* Vol. 2. London: Cadell and Davies, 1795.

Fletcher, R. *Sketches from the Casebook to Illustrate the Influence of the Mind on the Body, with the Treatment of Some of the More Important Brain and Nervous Disturbances.* London: Longman, 1833.

Forster, Thomas. *Observations on the Phenomena of Insanity.* London: Underwood, 1817.

Foucault, Michel. *Madness and Civilization: A History of Insanity in the Age of Reason.* New York: Pantheon, 1965.

———. *The Order of Things: An Archeology of the Human Sciences.* New York: Pantheon, 1970.

———. *The Archeology of Knowledge.* New York: Pantheon, 1972.

———. *Histoire de la folie à l'âge classique.* New ed. Paris: Gallimard, 1972.

———. *Discipline and Punish: The Birth of the Prison.* New York: Pantheon; London: Allen Lane, 1977.

———. *The History of Sexuality.* Vol. 1: *An Introduction.* New York: Pantheon, 1978.

———. *Power/Knowledge: Selected Interviews and Other Writings, 1972–1977.* London: Harvester, 1980.

Fox, E. L. *Brislington House, an Asylum for Lunatics Situated near Briston, Lately Erected by Edward Long Fox, M.D.* Bristol: For the Author, 1806.

Fox, Richard. *So Far Disordered in Mind.* Berkeley: University of California Press, 1978.

Freidson, Eliot. *Professional Dominance: The Social Structure of Medical Care.* New York: Atherton, 1970.

———. *Profession of Medicine: A Study in the Sociology of Applied Knowledge.* New York: Dodd, Mead, 1970.

Friends' Asylum. *Account of the Present State of the Asylum for the Relief of Persons Deprived of the Use of Their Reason.* Philadelphia: Brown, 1816.

———. *Annual Reports.* 1818–60.

———. *Rules for the Management of the Asylum, Adopted by the Board of Managers, First Month 20th, 1840.* Philadelphia: Rakestraw, 1840.

Gay, Peter. *The Enlightenment: An Interpretation.* Vol. 2: *The Science of Freedom.* New York: Knopf, 1969.

Gaylin, Willard, et al. *Partial Justice.* New York: Knopf, 1974.

———. *Doing Good: The Limits of Benevolence.* New York: Pantheon, 1978.

Gilman, Sander, ed. *The Face of Madness: Hugh W. Diamond and the Origins of Psychiatric Photography.* New York: Brunner-Mazel, 1976.

Goffman, Erving. *Asylums: Essays on the Social Situation of Mental Patients and Other Inmates.* Garden City, New York: Doubleday, 1961.

Goldstein, Jan. *Console and Classify: The French Psychiatric Profession in the Nineteenth Century.* Cambridge: Cambridge University Press, 1987.

Gough, Ian. *The Political Economy of the Welfare State.* London: Macmillan, 1979.

Granville, J. Mortimer. *The Care and Cure of the Insane.* 2 vols. London: Hardwicke and Bogue, 1877.

Gregory, John. *A Comparative View of the State and Faculties of Man with Those of the Animal World.* London: Dodsley, 1765.

Grob, Gerald. *The State and the Mentally Ill: A History of Worcester State Hospital.* Chapel Hill: Univerity of North Carolina Press, 1966.

———. *Mental Institutions in America: Social Policy to 1875.* New York: Free Press, 1973.

———. *Mental Illness and American Society, 1875–1940.* Princeton: Princeton University Press, 1983.

Guislain, J. *Traité sur l'aliénation mentale et sur les hospices des aliénés.* Amsterdam: Hey, 1826.

Gusfield, Joseph. *Symbolic Crusade: Status Politics and the American Temperance Movement.* 2d ed. Urbana: University of Illinois Press, 1986.

Hall, Basil. *Travels in North America in the Years 1827 and 1828.* 2d ed. Edinburgh: Cadell, 1830.

Hallaran, William Saunders. *An Inquiry into the Causes Producing the Extraordinary Addition to the Number of Insane.* Cork, Ireland: Edwards and Savage, 1810.

———. *Practical Observations on the Causes and Cure of Insanity.* Cork, Ireland: Hodges and M'Arthur, 1818.

Halliday, Andrew. *A General View of the Present State of Lunatics and Lunatic Asylums in Great Britain and Ireland, and in Some Other Kingdoms.* London: Underwood, 1828.

Hallywell, Henry. *Melampronea; or A Discourse of the Polity and Kingdom of Darkness.* London: Printed for Walter Kettilby, 1681.

Harper, Andrew. *A Treatise on the Real Cause and Cure of Insanity.* London: Stalker, 1789.

Haslam, John. *Observations on Madness and Melancholy,* 2d ed. London: Callow, 1809.

———. *Medical Jurisprudence as It Relates to Insanity, According to the Law of England.* London: Hunter, 1817.

Hexter, J. H. *Reappraisals in History.* 2d ed. Chicago: University of Chicago Press, 1978.

Higgins, Godfrey. *The Evidence Taken Before a Committee of the House of Commons Respecting the Asylum at York; with Observations and Notes, and a Letter to the Committee.* Doncaster, Sheardown, 1816.

Hill, George Nesse. *An Essay on the Prevention and Cure of Insanity.* London: Longman, et al., 1814.

Hill, Robert Gardner. *A Lecture on the Management of Lunatic Asylums and the Treatment of the Insane.* London: Simpkin Marshall, 1839.

———. *A Concise History of the Entire Abolition of Mechanical Restraint in the Treatment of the Insane.* London: Longman, et al., 1857.

———. *Lunacy: Its Past and Present.* London: Longman, Green, et al., 1870.

Hobsbawm, Eric J. *Industry and Empire.* Harmondsworth: Penguin, 1969.

Hobsbawm, Eric J., and George Rude. *Captain Swing: A Social History of the Great English Agricultural Uprising of 1830.* Harmondsworth: Penguin, 1969; New York: Norton, 1975.

House of Commons. *Report of the Select Committee on Criminal and Pauper Lunatics.* London, 1807.

———. *Reports of the Select Committee on Madhouses.* London, 1815–16.

———. *Report of the Select Committee on the Care and Treatment of Lunatics.* London, 1859–60.

———. *Report of the Select Committee on the Operation of the Lunacy Law.* London, 1877.

House of Lords. *Minutes of Evidence Taken Before the Select Committee of the House of Lords on the Bills Relating to Lunatics and Lunatic Asylums.* London, 1828.

Howard, J. *The State of the Prisons.* Warrington: Egres, 1778.

Hunter, Richard, and Ida Macalpine. *Three Hundred Years of Psychiatry, 1535 to 1860: A History Presented in Selected English Texts.* London: Oxford University Press, 1963.

Hurd, Henry. *The Institutional Care of the Insane in the United States and Canada.* 4 vols. Baltimore: Johns Hopkins University Press, 1916–17.

Hynes, Charles. *Proprietary Homes for Adults: Their Administration, Management, Control, Operation, Supervision, Funding, and Quality.* New York: Deputy Attorney General's Office, 1977.

Ignatieff, Michael. *A Just Measure of Pain: The Penitentiary in the Industrial Revolution, 1750–1850.* New York: Pantheon, 1978.

Irish, David. *Levamen Infirmi, or, Cordial Counsel to the Sick and Diseased.* London: For the Author, 1700.

Jacobi, Maximilian. *On the Construction and Management of Hospitals for the Insane.* London: Churchill, 1841.

Jacobs, James. *Stateville: The Penitentiary in Mass Society.* Chicago: University of Chicago Press, 1977.

Joint Commission on Mental Illness and Health. *Action for Mental Health.* New York: Basic Books, 1961.

Jones, Kathleen. *Lunacy, Law and Conscience, 1744–1845: The Social History of the Care of the Insane.* London: Routledge and Kegan Paul, 1955.

———. *Mental Health and Social Policy, 1845–1955.* London: Routledge and Kegan Paul, 1960.

King, Anthony D., ed. *Buildings and Society: Essays on the Social Development of the Built Environment.* London and Boston: Routledge and Kegan Paul, 1980.

Kittrie, Nicholas A. *The Right to Be Different: Deviance and Enforced Therapy.* Baltimore: Johns Hopkins University Press, 1972.

Knight, Paul Slade. *Observations on the Causes, Symptoms, and Treatment of Derangement of the Mind.* London: Longman, 1827.

Lamb, Richard. *Treating the Long-Term Mentally Ill: Beyond Deinstitutionalization.* San Francisco: Jossey-Bass, 1982.

Leifer, Ronald. *In the Name of Mental Health: Social Functions of Psychiatry.* New York: Aronson, 1969.

Leigh, Dennis. *The Historical Development of British Psychiatry.* London: Pergamon Press, 1961.

Lerman, Paul. *Community Treatment and Social Control.* Chicago: University of Chicago Press, 1975.

———. *Deinstitutionalization and the Welfare State.* New Brunswick, N.J.: Rutgers University Press, 1982.

A Letter to the Shareholders and Council of the University of London on the Present State of That Institution. London: Taylor, 1830.

Light, Donald. *Becoming Psychiatrists.* New York: Norton, 1980.

Little, Nina F. *Early Years of the McLean Hospital.* Boston: Countway Library of Medicine, 1972.

Locke, John. *Educational Writings.* London: Cambridge University Press, 1968.

Loudon, Irvine. *Medical Care and the General Practitioner; 1750–1850.* Oxford: Clarendon Press, 1986.

Lovejoy, A. O. *The Great Chain of Being.* New York: Harper, 1960.

Lukes, Steven. *Power: A Radical View.* London: Macmillan, 1974.

———. *Essays in Social Theory.* New York: Columbia University Press, 1977.

Lyell, Katherine M., ed. *Memoir of Leonard Horner, Edited by His Daughter.* 2 vols. London: Women's Printing Society, 1890.

Macalpine, Ida, and Richard A. Hunter. *George III and the Mad Business.* London: Allen Lane, 1969.

MacBride, David. *A Methodical Introduction to the Theory and Practice of Physick.* London: Strahan, 1772.

MacDonald, Michael. *Mystical Bedlam: Madness, Anxiety, and Healing in Seventeenth-Century England.* Cambridge: Cambridge University Press, 1981.

Macfarlane, Alan. *Origins of English Inidividualism.* Oxford: Basil Blackwell, 1978.

MacGill, Stevenson. *On Lunatic Asylums.* Glasgow: For the Glasgow Asylum Committee, 1810.

Mackenzie, Henry. *The Man of Feeling.* London: Cadell, 1771.

Malament, B. C., ed. *After the Reformation.* Philadelphia: University of Pennsylvania Press, 1980.

Malthus, Thomas R. *An Essay on the Principle of Population.* London: Johnson, 1798.

———. *An Essay on the Principle of Population.* 6th ed. London: Murray, 1826.

Mantoux, Paul. *The Industrial Revolution in the Eighteenth Century.* London: Jonathan Cape, 1928.

Marcus, Steven. *Engels, Manchester, and the Working Class.* New York, Vintage, 1974.

Marshall, Dorothy. *The English Poor in the Eighteenth Century.* London: Routledge, 1926.

Marshall, Helen E. *Dorothea Dix: Forgotten Samaritan.* Chapel Hill: University of North Carolina Press, 1937.

Marx, Karl. *Capital.* Vol. 1. New York: International Publishers, 1967.

———. *Karl Marx: Selected Writings.* Ed. David McLellan. London: Oxford University Press, 1977.

Massachusetts State Board of Charities. *Annual Reports.* 1867–80.

Maudsley, Henry. *The Physiology and Pathology of Mind.* London: Macmillan, 1867.

———. *The Pathology of Mind.* London: Macmillan, 1879.

Mayne, Zachary. *Two Dissertations Concerning Sense, and the Imagination, with an Essay on Consciousness* (1728). Facsimile ed., ed. René Wellek. New York: Garland, 1976.

Mayo, John, and T. Mayo. *Remarks on Insanity.* London: Underwood, 1817.

Mayo, Thomas. *An Essay on the Relation of the Theory of Morals to Insanity.* London: Fellowes, 1834.

———. *Medical Testimony and Evidence in Cases of Lunacy.* London: Parker, 1854.

McGovern, Constance. *Masters of Madness: Social Origins of the American Psychiatric Profession.* Hanover, N.H.: University Press of New England, 1985.

Mead, Richard. *Medical Precepts and Cautions.* London: Brindley, 1751.

Meyer, Adolf. *The Collected Papers of Adolf Meyer.* Ed. Eunice E. Winters. Baltimore: Johns Hopkins University Press, 1952.

Mill, John Stuart. *Essays on Politics and Culture.* Garden City, N.Y.: Doubleday, 1963.

Millingen, J. G. *Aphorisms on the Treatment and Management of the Insane, with Considerations on Public and Private Lunatic Asylums, Pointing out the Errors in the Present System.* London: Churchill, 1840.

Mitchell, Silas Weir. *Wear and Tear; or, Hints for the Overworked.* Philadelphia: Lippincott, 1871.

———. *Fat and Blood.* 3d rev. ed. Philadelphia: Lippincott, 1884.

———. *Address Before the American Medico-Psychological Association.* Philadelphia,

1894. Reprinted from *Journal of Nervous and Mental Diseases* 21 (1894), 413–37.

Mitford, Jessica. *Kind and Usual Punishment: The Prison Business.* New York, Knopf, 1973.

Monahan, John. *The Clinical Prediction of Violent Behavior.* Washington, D.C.: Government Printing Office, 1981.

Monro, Henry. *Remarks on Insanity: Its Nature and Treatment.* London: Churchill, 1850.

Monro, John. *Remarks on Dr. Battie's Treatise on Madness.* London: Clarke, 1758.

Morison, Alexander. *Outlines of Lectures on the Nature, Causes, and Treatment of Insanity.* Ed. Thomas C. Morison. London: Longman et al., 1825; 4th ed. 1848.

Morris, Norval. *The Future of Imprisonment.* Chicago: University of Chicago Press, 1974.

Myers, Charles S. *Shellshock in France.* Cambridge: Cambridge University Press, 1940.

Neville, William B. *On Insanity, Its Nature, Causes, and Cure.* London: Longman et al., 1836.

Nicoll, S. W. *An Enquiry into the Present State of Visitation in Asylums for the Reception of the Insane.* London: Harvey and Darnton, 1828.

Nightingale, Florence. *Cassandra.* Old Westbury, N.Y.: Feminist Press, 1979.

Nisbet, William. *Two Letters to the Right Honourable George Rose, M.P., on the Reports at Present Before the Honourable House of Commons on the State of Madhouses.* London: Cox, 1815.

Nottingham Lunatic Asylum. *The Articles of Union Entered into and Agreed upon Between the Justices of the Peace for the County of Nottingham; the Justices of the Peace for . . . the Town of Nottingham; and the Subscribers to a Voluntary Institution; for the Purpose of Providing a General Lunatic Asylum.* Newark: Ridge, 1811.

Nye, Robert. *Crime, Madness, and Politics in Modern France.* Princeton: Princeton University Press, 1984.

O'Donoghue, E. D. *The Story of Bethlem Hospital.* London: Fisher and Unwin, 1913.

Paget, George E. *The Harveian Oration.* Cambridge: Deighton, Bell, 1866.

Pargeter, William. *Observations on Maniacal Disorders.* Reading: For the Author, 1792.

Parkin, John. *On the Medical and Moral Treatment of Insanity, Including a Notice on the Establishment for the Treatment of Nervous and Mental Maladies: Manor Cottage, King's Road, Chelsea, Established in 1780.* London: Martin, [1843?].

Parry-Jones, William L. *The Trade in Lunacy: A Study of Private Madhouses in England in the Eighteenth and Nineteenth Centuries.* London: Routledge and Kegan Paul; Toronto: University of Toronto Press, 1972.

Parsons, Talcott. *The Social System.* New York: Free Press, 1951.

Pasamanick, Benjamin, Frank Scarpitti, and Simon Dinitz. *Schizophrenics in the Community: An Experimental Study in the Prevention of Hospitalization.* New York: Appleton-Century-Crofts, 1967.

Pascal, Blaise. *Oeuvres Complètes.* Paris: Gallimard, 1954.

Pattison, Granville Sharp-, and Nathaniel Chapman. *Corresondence Between Mr Granville Sharp-Pattison and Dr Nathaniel Chapman.* 3d ed. Philadelphia: Webster, 1821.

Paul, Sir George Onesiphorous. *Suggestions on the Subject of Criminal and Pauper Lunatics.* Gloucester: For the Author, 1806.

————. *Address to the Subscribers to the Gloucester Lunatic Asylum.* Gloucester: For the Author, 1810.

————. *Observations on the Subject of Lunatic Asylums.* Gloucester: Walker, 1812.

Peers, Edgar A. *Elizabethan Drama and Its Mad Folk.* Cambridge: Heffer, 1914.

Percival, Thomas. *Medical Ethics.* Manchester: Johnson and Bickerstaff, 1803.

Perfect, W. *Select Cases in the Different Species of Insanity, Lunacy or Madness, with the Modes or Practice as Adopted in the Treatment of Each.* Rochester: Gillman, 1787.

————. *A Remarkable Case of Madness, with the Diet and Medicines Used in the Cure.* Rochester: For the Author, 1791.

Perrot, Michelle, ed. *L'Impossible prison.* Paris: Seuil, 1980.

Peterson, M. J. *The Medical Profession in Mid-Victorian London.* Berkeley: University of California Press, 1978.

Pfohl, S. *Predicting Dangerousness.* Lexington, MA: Heath, 1978.

Pinel, Philippe. *A Treatise on Insanity.* Trans. D. D. Davis. Sheffield: Cadell and Davies, 1806. Facsimile ed., ed. Paul Cronfield. New York: Hafner, 1962.

Pliny, Earle. *The Curability of Insanity: A Series of Studies.* Philadelphia: Lippincott, 1887.

Polanyi, Karl. *The Great Transformation.* Boston: Beacon, 1957.

Pollard, S. *The Genesis of Modern Management.* Harmondsworth: Penguin, 1965.

Pomerantz, S. I. *New York—An American City, 1783–1803.* New York: Columbia University Press, 1938.

Porter, Roy. *Mind Forg'd Manacles: A History of Madness in England from the Restoration to the Regency.* London: Athlone Press, 1987.

On the Present State of Lunatic Asylums, with Suggestions for Their Improvement. London: Drury, 1839.

Prichard, James Cowles. *A Treatise on Insanity and Other Disorders Affecting the Mind.* London: Sherwood, Gilbert and Piper, 1835.

————. *On the Different Forms of Insanity in Relation to Jurisprudence.* London: Bailliere, 1842.

Rawls, Wendell, Jr. *Cold Storage.* New York: Simon and Schuster, 1980.

Reade, Charles. *Hard Cash: A Matter-of-Fact Romance.* London: Ward, Lock, 1864.

Reid, John. *Essays on Insanity, Hypochondriacal and Other Nervous Affections.* London: Longman et al., 1816.

Reynolds, F. *The Life and Times of F. Reynolds, Written by Himself.* London: Colburn: 1826.

Roberts, David. *Victorian Origins of the British Welfare State.* New Haven: Yale University Press, 1960.

Robinson, Nicholas. *A New System of the Spleen, Vapours, and Hypochondriack Melancholy.* London: Bettesworth, Innys, and Rivington, 1729.

Rothman, David. *The Discovery of the Asylum: Social Order and Disorder in the New Republic.* Boston: Little, Brown, 1971.

————. *Conscience and Convenience: The Asylum and Its Alternatives in Progressive America.* Boston: Little, Brown, 1980.

Rothman, David, and Sheila M. Rothman. *The Willowbrook Wars.* New York: Harper and Row, 1984.

Rowley, William. *A Treatise on Female, Nervous, Hysterical, Hypochondriacal, Bilious, and Convulsive Diseases with Thoughts on Madness, Suicide, Etc.* London: Nourse, 1788.

Rush, Benjamin. *Medical Inquiries and Observations upon the Diseases of the Mind.* Philadelphia: Kimber and Richardson, 1830.

——. *The Letters of Benjamin Rush.* Ed. L. H. Butterfield. Princeton: Princeton University Press, 1951.

Russell, William L. *The New York Hospital: A History of the Psychiatric Service, 1771– 1936.* New York: Columbia University Press, 1945.

Salmon, William. *A Compleat System of Physick, Theoretical and Practical.* London: For the Author, 1686.

Scheff, Thomas. *Being Mentally Ill: A Sociological Theory.* Chicago: Aldine, 1966.

Schur, Edwin. *Radical Non-intervention.* Englewood Cliffs, N.J.: Prentice-Hall, 1975.

Scull, Andrew. *Museums of Madness: The Social Organization of Insanity in Nineteenth-Century England.* London: Allen Lane; New York: St. Martin's Press, 1979.

——.*Decarceration: Community Treatment and the Deviant—A Radical View.* 2d ed. Oxford: Polity Press; New Brunswick, N.J.: Rutgers University Press, 1984.

Scull, Andrew, ed. *Madhouses, Mad-Doctors, and Madmen: The Social History of Psychiatry in the Victorian Era.* Philadelphia: University of Pennsylvania Press; London: Athlone Press, 1981.

Sedgwick, Peter. *Psychopolitics.* London: Pluto Press; New York: Harper and Row, 1982.

Seymour, Edward J. *Observations on the Medical Treatment of Insanity.* London: Longman et al., 1832.

Sheils, W., ed. *The Church and Healing.* Oxford: Basil Blackwell, 1982.

Shortt, S. E. D. *Victorian Lunacy: Richard M. Bucke and the Practice of Late Nineteenth-Century Psychiatry.* Cambridge: Cambridge University Press, 1986.

Showalter, Elaine. *The Female Malady: Women, Madness, and English Culture, 1830–1980.* New York: Pantheon, 1985; London: Virago, 1987.

Shyrock, Richard Harrison. *The Development of Modern Medicine.* Philadelphia: University of Pennsylvania Press, 1936.

Skene, Alexander. *Medical Gynecology.* New York: Appleton, 1895.

Skey, F. C. *Hysteria.* 2d ed. London: Longmans et al., 1867.

Skultans, Veida. *English Madness: Ideas on Insanity, 1580–1890.* London: Routledge and Kegan Paul, 1978.

Smith, Adam. *The Wealth of Nations.* New York, Modern Library, 1937.

Smith, Roger. *Trial by Medicine: Insanity and Responsibility in Victorian Trials.* Edinburgh: Edinburgh University Press, 1981.

Snape, Andrew. *A Sermon Preach'd Before the Lord Mayor, the Alderman, Sheriffs, and Gouvenours of the Several Hospitals of the City of London, April 16, 1718.* London: Bowyer, 1718.

Soloman, H. *Public Welfare, Science and Propaganda in Seventeenth Century France.* Princeton: Princeton University Press, 1972.

Some Particulars of the Royal Indisposition of 1788 to 1789, and of Its Effects upon Illustrious Personages and Opposite Parties Interested by It. London: Printed for the Editor by R. Taylor, 1804.

Southcomb, Lewis. *Peace of Mind and Health of Body United.* London: Cowper, 1750.

Sprigge, S. S. *The Life and Times of Thomas Wakley.* London: Longman, Green, 1899.

Spurzhiem, J. G. *Observations on the Deranged Manifestations of the Mind, or Insanity.* London: Baldwin, Craddock, and Joy, 1817.

Stanton, A. H., and M. S. Schwartz. *The Mental Hospital: A Study of Institutional Participation in Psychiatric Illness and Treatment.* New York: Basic Books, 1954.

Stark, William. *Remarks on the Construction of Public Asylums for the Cure of Mental Derangement.* Glasgow: Hedderwick, 1810.

Stone, Lawrence. *The Causes of the English Civil War.* New York: Harper and Row, 1969.

Swift, Jonathan. *The Legion Club.* London: Bathurst, 1736.

————. *Gulliver's Travels.* New York: Modern Library, 1958.

Szasz, Thomas. *Law, Liberty, and Psychiatry.* New York: Macmillan, 1963.

————. *Ideology and Insanity.* New York, Doubleday, 1970.

————. *The Manufacture of Madness.* New York: Dell, 1970.

————. *The Second Sin.* Garden City, N.Y.: Doubleday, 1972.

————. *The Myth of Mental Illness: Foundation of a Theory of Personal Conduct.* Rev. ed. New York: Harper and Row, 1974.

Thompson, E. P. *The Making of the English Working Class.* New York: Vintage Books, 1963.

————. *The Poverty of Theory and Other Essays.* New York: Monthly Review Press, 1978.

Thompson, J. D., and G. Goldin. *The Hospital: A Social and Architectural History.* New Haven: Yale University Press, 1975.

Thurnam, John. *Observations and Essays on the Statistics of Insanity, Including an Inquiry into the Causes Influencing the Results of Treatment in Establishments for the Insane: To Which Are Added Statistics for the Retreat near York.* London: Simpkin Marshall, 1845.

Tomes, Nancy. *A Generous Confidence: Thomas Story Kirkbride and the Art of Asylum Keeping, 1840–1883.* Cambridge: Cambridge University Press, 1984.

Trollope, Anthony. *The Small House at Allington.* London: Oxford University Press, 1980.

Tuke, Daniel Hack. *The Moral Management of the Insane.* London: Churchill, 1854.

————. *Chapters in the History of the Insane in the British Isles.* London: Kegan Paul and Trench, 1882.

————. *Reform in the Treatment of the Insane.* London: Churchill, 1892.

Tuke, Samuel. *Description of the Retreat: An Institution near York for Insane Persons of the Society of Friends* (1813). Facsimile ed., ed. Richard A. Hunter and Ida Macalpine. London: Dawsons, 1964.

————. *A Letter to Thomas Eddy of New York on Pauper Lunatic Asylums.* New York: Samuel Wood, 1815.

University of London. *Second Statement by the Council of the University of London Explanatory of the Plan of Instruction.* London: Longman, 1828.

Uwins, David. *A Treatise on Those Disorders of the Brain and Nervous System, Which Are Usually Considered and Called Mental.* London: Renshaw and Rush, 1833.

Valenstein, Elliot S. *Great and Desperate Cures: The Rise and Decline of Psychosurgery and Other Radical Treatments for Mental Illness.* New York: Basic Books, 1986.

Waln, Robert, Jr. *An Account of the Asylum for the Insane . . . near Frankford.* Philadelphia: Kite: 1825.

Warren, Carol A. B. *The Court of Last Resort: Mental Illness and the Law.* Chicago: University of Chicago Press, 1982.

Weber, Max. *The Protestant Ethic and the Spirit of Capitalism.* London: Allen and Unwin, 1930.

Willis, Francis. *A Treatise on Mental Derangement.* London: Longman, et al., 1823; 2nd ed., 1843.

Willis, Thomas. *The Practice of Physick: Two Discourses Concerning the Soul of Brutes.* London: Dring, Harper, and Leigh, 1684.

Wing, J. K. *Reasoning About Madness.* London: Oxford University Press, 1978.

Wing, J. K. and G. W. Brown. *Institutionalism and Schizophrenia.* Cambridge: Cambridge University Press, 1970.

Woolf, Leonard. *Beginning Again: An Autobiography of the Years 1911–1918.* New York: Harcourt, Brace, Jovanovich, 1972.

Wyman, Rufus. *A Discourse on Mental Philosophy as Connected with Mental Disease, Delivered Before the Massachusetts Medical Society.* Boston: Office of the Daily Advertiser, 1830.

Wynter, Andrew. *The Borderlands of Insanity.* London: Hardwicke, 1875.

Zilboorg, Gregory. *A History of Medical Psychology.* New York: Norton, 1941; paperback ed., 1967.

Unpublished Doctoral Dissertations

Barabee, Paul, "A Study of the Mental Hospital: The Effect of Its Social Structure on Its Functions." Ph.D. diss., Harvard University, 1951.

Bynum, William. "'Time's Noblest Offspring': The Problem of Man in the British Natural Historical Sciences." Ph.D. diss., University of Cambridge, 1974.

Clark, Michael. "'The Data of Alienism': Evolutionary Neurology, Physiological Psychology, and the Reconstruction of British Psychiatric Theory, c. 1850– c. 1900." D.Phil. diss., Oxford University, 1982.

Dowbiggin, Ian. "The Professional, Sociopolitical, and Cultural Dimensions of Psychiatric Theory in France, 1840–1900." Ph.D. diss., University of Rochester, 1986.

Evans, Robin, "'A Rational Plan for Softening the Mind': Prison Design, 1750– 1842: A Study of the Relationship Between Functional Architecture and Penal Ideology." Ph.D. diss., Essex University, 1974.

Goldstein, Jan Ellen. "French Psychiatry in Social and Political Context: The Formation of a New Profession, 1820–1860." Ph.D. diss., Columbia University, 1978.

Hervey, Nicholas. "The Lunacy Commission, 1845–1860, with Special Reference to the Implementation of Policy in Kent and Surrey." Ph.D. diss., Bristol University, 1987.

MacKenzie, Charlotte. "A History of Ticehurst Asylum." Ph.D. diss., University of London, 1987.

Pitts, John. "The Association of Medical Superintendents of American Institutions for the Insane, 1844–1892: A Case Study of Specialism in American Medicine." Ph.D. diss., University of Pennsylvania, 1978.

Pressman, Jack David. "Uncertain Promise: Psychosurgery and the Development of Scientific Psychiatry in America, 1935 to 1955." Ph.D. diss., University of Pennsylvania, 1986.

Sicherman, Barbara. "The Quest for Mental Health in America, 1880–1917." Ph.D. diss., Columbia University, 1967.

Stone, Martin. "The Military and Industrial Roots of Clinical Psychology in Britain, 1900–1945." Ph.D. diss., London School of Economics, 1985.
Tomes, Nancy Jane. "The Persuasive Institution: Thomas Story Kirkbride and the Art of Asylum Keeping, 1841–1883." Ph.D. diss., University of Pennsylvania, 1978.

Articles

Aldrich, C., and E. Mendkoff. "Relocation of the Aged and Disabled: A Mortality Study." *Journal of the American Geriatrics Society* 11 (1963): 105–94.
Arnhoff, F. "Social Consequences of Policy Toward Mental Illness." *Science* 188 (1975): 1277–81.
Bassuk, E., and S. Gerson. "Deinstitutionalization and Mental Health Services." *Scientific American* 238 (1978): 46–53.
Beard, George M. "The Influence of Mind in the Causation and Cure of Disease: The Potency of Definite Expectation." *Journal of Nervous and Mental Diseases* 4 (1877): 429–34.
Beck, A. T. "The Reliability of Psychiatric Diagnosis: 1. A Critique of Systematic Studies." *American Journal of Psychiatry* 119 (1962): 210–16.
Blomberg, Thomas. "Diversion and Accelerated Social Control." *Journal of Criminal Law and Criminology* 68 (1977): 274–82.
Blustein, Bonnie Ellen. "'A Hollow Square of Psychological Science': American Neurologists and Psychiatrists in Conflict." In *Madhouses, Mad-Doctors, and Madmen*, ed. Andrew Scull, 241–70. Philadelphia: University of Pennsylvania Press, 1981.
Borus, J. F. "Deinstitutionalization of the Chronically Mentally Ill." *New England Journal of Medicine* 305 (1981): 339–42.
Briggs, A. "The Language of 'Class' in Early Nineteenth-Century England." In *Essays in Labour History*, ed. Asa Briggs and John Saville, 43–73. London: Macmillan, 1960.
Bynum, William F. "Rationales for Therapy in British Psychiatry, 1780–1835." In *Madhouses, Mad-doctors, and Madmen*, ed. Andrew Scull, 35–57. Philadelphia: University of Pennsylvania Press, 1981.
Bynum, William F., and M. Neve. "Hamlet on the Couch." In *The Anatomy of Madness*, 2 vols., ed. W. F. Bynum, Roy Porter, and Michael Shepherd, vol. 1, 289–304. London: Tavistock, 1985.
Castel, Robert. "Moral Treatment: Mental Therapy and Social Control in the Nineteenth Century." In *Social Control and the State*, ed. Stanley Cohen and Andrew Scull, 248–66. New York: St. Martin's Press, 1981.
Chapman, L. J., and J. P. Chapman. "Illusory Correlations as an Obstacle to the Use of Valid Psycho-Diagnostic Signs." *Journal of Abnormal Psychology* 74 (1969): 271–80.
Chase, J. "Where Have All the Patients Gone?" *Human Behavior* (1973): 14–21.
Clark, Michael. "The Rejection of Psychological Approaches to Mental Disorder in Late Nineteenth-Century British Psychiatry." In *Madhouses, Mad-Doctors, and Madmen*, ed. Andrew Scull, 271–312. Philadelphia: University of Pennsylvania Press, 1981.
Cohen, Stanley. "The Punitive City: Notes on the Dispersal of Social Control." *Contemporary Crises* 3 (1979): 339–63.

Dain, Norman, and Eric T. Carlson. "Milieu Therapy in the Nineteenth Century: Patient Care at the Friends' Asylum, Frankford, Pennsylvania, 1817–1861." *Journal of Nervous and Mental Disease* 131 (1960): 284–85.

Digby, Anne. "Moral Treatment at the Retreat, 1796–1846." In *The Anatomy of Madness*, ed. W. F. Bynum, Roy Porter, and Michael Shepherd, vol. 2, 52–72. London: Tavistock, 1985.

Dohrenwend, Bruce P., and Barbara S. Dohrenwend. "Sex Differences and Psychiatric Disorders." *American Journal of Sociology* 81 (1976): 1447–54.

Dowbiggin, Ian. "French Psychiatry, Hereditarianism, and Professional Legitimacy, 1840–1900." In *Research in Law, Deviance, and Social Control*, vol. 7, ed. Andrew Scull and Steven Spitzer, 135–65. Greenwich, CT.: JAI Press, 1985.

———. "Degeneration and Hereditarianism in French Mental Medicine, 1840–1890: Psychiatric Theory as Ideological Adaption." In *Anatomy of Madness*, ed. W. F. Bynum, Roy Porter, and Michael Shepherd, vol. 1: 188–232. London: Tavistock, 1985.

———. "French Psychiatric Attitudes Toward the Dangers Posed by the Insane ca. 1870." In *Research in Law, Deviance, and Social Control*, vol. 9, ed. Andrew Scull and Steven Spitzer, 87–111. Greenwich, CT: JAI Press, 1988.

Ennis, Bruce, and Eugene Litwack. "Psychiatry and the Presumption of Expertise: Flipping Coins in the Courtroom." *California Law Review* 62 (1974): 693–753.

Epstein, L. and A. Simon. "Alternatives to State Hospitalization for the Geriatric Mentally Ill." *American Journal of Psychiatry* 124 (1968): 955–61.

Fessler, A. "The Management of Lunacy in Seventeenth-Century England." *Proceedings of the Royal Society of Medicine, Historical Section* 49 (1956): 901–7.

Fox, Richard. "Beyond 'Social Control': Institutions and Disorder in Bourgeois Society." *History of Education Quarterly* 16 (1976): 203–7.

Frank, Justin A. "Non-restraint and Robert Gardiner Hill." *Bulletin of the History of Medicine* 41 (1967): 140–60.

Goldstein, Michael. "The Politics of Thomas Szasz: A Sociological View." *Social Problems* 27 (1980): 570–83.

Grad de Alcaron, Jacquelyn, and Peter Sainsbury. "Mental Illness and the Family." *The Lancet* i (March 9, 1963): 544–47.

Grob, Gerald. "Samuel B. Woodward and the Practice of Psychiatry in Early Nineteenth-Century America." *Bulletin of the History of Medicine* 36 (1962): 420–43.

———. "Welfare and Poverty in American History." *Reviews in American History* 1 (1973): 43–52.

———. "Rediscovering Asylums: The Unhistorical History of the Mental Hospital." *Hastings Center Report* 7, no. 4 (1977): 33–41.

Harris, Ruth. "Murder Under Hypnosis: In the Case of Bompard—Psychiatry in the Courtroom in Belle Epoque Paris." In *The Anatomy of Madness*, ed. W. F. Bynum, Roy Porter, and Michael Shepherd, vol. 2, 197–241. London: Tavistock, 1985.

Hervey, Nicholas. "Advocacy or Folly: The Alleged Lunatics' Friend Society, 1845–63." *Medical History* 30 (1986): 245–75.

Hunter, Richard A., and Ida Macalpine. "Dickens and Conolly: An Embarrassed Editor's Disclaimer." *Times Literary Supplement* 11 (August 1961): 534–35.

Ignatieff, Michael. "State, Civil Society and Total Institutions: A Critique of Recent Social Histories of Punishment." In *Social Control and the State,* ed. Stanley Cohen and Andrew Scull, 75–105. New York: St. Martin's Press, 1981.
————. "Total Institutions and the Working Classes: A Review Essay." *History Workshop Journal* 15 (1983): 169–72.
Ingleby, David. "Mental Health and Social Order." In *Social Control and the State,* ed. Stanley Cohen and Andrew Scull, 141–88. New York: St. Martin's Press, 1981.
Jacyna, Steven. "Somatic Theories of Mind and the Interests of Medicine in Britain, 1850–1879." *Medical History* 26 (1982): 233–58.
Jasman, K. "Individualized Versus Mass Transfer of Nonpsychotic Geriatric Patients from the Mental Hospital to the Nursing Home." *Journal of the American Geriatrics Society* 15 (1969): 280–84.
Johnson, Richard. "Educational Policy and Social Control in Early Victorian England." *Past and Present* 49 (1970): 96–119.
Jones, Kathleen. "Scull's Dilemma." *British Journal of Psychiatry* 141 (1982): 221–26.
Kaplan, Leonard V. "State Control of Deviant Behavior: A Critical Essay on Scull's Critique of Community Treatment and Deinstitutionalization." *Arizona Law Review* 20 (1978): 189–232.
Kirk, S., and M. Thierren. "Community Mental Health Myths and the Fate of Former Hospitalized Patients." *Psychiatry* 38 (1975): 209–17.
Lamb, H., and V. Goertzel. "Discharged Mental Patients—Are They Really in the Community?" *Archives of General Psychiatry* 24 (1971): 29–34.
Langsley, Donald. "The Community Mental Health Center: Does It Treat Patients?" *Hospital and Community Psychiatry* 31 (1980): 815–19.
Lewis, Aubrey. "Henry Maudsley: His Works and Influence." *Journal of Mental Science* 97 (1951): 259–77.
MacDonald, Michael. "Insanity and the Realities of History in Early Modern England." *Psychological Medicine* 11 (1981): 11–25.
————. "Religion, Social Change and Psychological Healing in England." In *The Church and Healing,* ed. W. J. Sheils, 101–26. Oxford: Basil Blackwell, 1982.
————. "The Secularization of Suicide in England, 1660–1800." *Past and Present* 3 (1986): 50–100.
Markson, E., and J. Cumming. "The Post-Transfer Fate of Relocated Patients." In *State Mental Hospitals: What Happens When They Close?* ed. Paul P. Ahmed and Stanley C. Plog, 97–110. New York: Plenum, 1976.
Markus, E., M. Blenker, and T. Downs. "The Impact of Relocation upon Mortality Rates of Institutionalized Aged Persons." *Journal of Gerontology* 26 (1971): 537–41.
Marlowe, R. "When They Close the Doors at Modesto." In *State Mental Hospitals: What Happens When They Close?* ed. Paul P. Ahmed and Stanley C. Plog, 83–96. New York: Plenum, 1976.
Maudsley, Henry. "The Alleged Increase of Insanity." *Journal of Mental Science* 23 (1877): 45–54.
————. "Sex in Mind and in Education." *Fortnightly Review* 15 (1874): 466–83.
McCandless, Peter. "Liberty and Lunacy: The Victorians and Wrongful Confinement." In *Madhouses, Mad-Doctors, and Madmen,* ed. Andrew Scull, 339–62. Philadelphia: University of Pennsylvania Press, 1981.

McEwen, Craig. "Continuities in the Study of Total and Non-Total Institutions." *Annual Review of Sociology* 6 (1980): 143–85.

McKendrick, N. "Josiah Wedgwood and Factory Discipline." *Historical Journal* 4 (1961): 30–55.

Mesnikoff, A. "Barriers to the Delivery of Mental Health Services: The New York City Experience." *Hospital and Community Psychiatry* 29 (1978): 373–78.

Messinger, Sheldon. "Confinement in the Community." *Journal of Research in Crime and Delinquency* 13 (1976): 82–92.

Midelfort, H. C. Erik. "Madness and Civilization in Early Modern Europe: A Reappraisal of Michel Foucault." In *After the Reformation*, ed. B. C. Malament, 247–65. Philadelphia: University of Pennsylvania Press, 1980.

Monahan, John, and David Wexler. "A Definite Maybe: Proof and Probability in Civil Commitment." *Law and Human Behavior* 2 (1978): 37–42.

Morgan, David. "Explaining Mental Illness." *European Journal of Sociology* 15 (1975): 262–80.

Morse, Stephen J. "A Preference for Liberty: The Case Against the Involuntary Commitment of the Mentally Disordered." *California Law Review* 70 (1982): 54–106.

Muraskin, William. "The Social Control Theory in American History: A Critique." *Journal of Social History* 9 (1976): 559–65.

Murphy, J., and W. Datel. "A Cost-Benefit Analysis of Community Versus Institutional Living." *Health and Community Psychiatry* 25 (1976): 165–70.

Nathanson, Constance. "Illness and the Feminine Role: A Theoretical Review." *Social Science and Medicine* 9 (1975): 57–62.

Orlans, H. "An American Death Camp." *Politics* 5 (1948): 162–68.

Perry, Nicholas. "The Two Cultures and the Total Institution." *British Journal of Sociology* 25 (1974): 345–55.

Philips, David. ""A Just Measure of Crime, Authority, Hunters and Blue Locusts': The Revisionist History of Crime and the Law in Britain, 1750–1850." In *Social Control and the State*, ed. Stanley Cohen and Andrew Scull, 50–74. New York: St. Martin's Press, 1981.

Phillips, Derek. "Rejection: A Possible Consequence of Seeking Help for Mental Disorder." *American Sociological Review* 28 (1963): 963–73.

Porter, Roy. "Being Mad in Eighteenth-Century England." *History Today* (December 1981): 42–48.

———. "Shutting People Up." *Social Studies of Science* 12 (1982): 467–76.

———. "The Rage of Party: A Glorious Revolution in English Psychiatry?" *Medical History* 27 (1983): 35–50.

Quen, Jacques. "David Rothman's *Discovery of the Asylum.*" *Journal of Psychiatry and the Law* 2 (1974): 105–20.

Ray, L. J. "Models of Madness in Victorian Asylum Practice." *European Journal of Sociology* 22 (1981): 229–64.

Reich, R., and L. Siegal. "Psychiatry Under Siege: The Mentally Ill Shuffle to Oblivion." *Psychiatric Annals* 3 (1973): 37–55.

Rose, Stephen. "Deciphering Deinstitutionalization: Complexities in Policy and Program Analysis." *Milbank Memorial Fund Quarterly* 57 (1979): 429–60.

Rosenberg, Charles. "The Crisis of Psychiatric Legitimacy: Reflections on Psychiatry, Medicine, and Public Policy." In *American Psychiatry: Past, Present, and*

Future, ed. G. Kriegman et al., 135–48. Charlottesville, VA: University Press of Virginia, 1975.

Rothman, David. "Social Control: The Uses and Abuses of the Concept in the History of Incarceration." In *Social Control and the State,* ed. Stanley Cohen and Andrew Scull, 106–17. New York: St. Martin's Press, 1981.

Rovner-Pieczenik, Roberta. "Labeling in an Organizational Context: Adjudicating Felonies in an Urban Court." In *The Research Experience,* ed. M. P. Golden, 447–64. Itasca, IL: Peacock, 1976.

Salomon, A. "Max Weber's Methodology." *Social Research* 1 (1934): 157.

Scott, Francis. "English Country Asylums." *Fortnightly Review* 26 (1879): 114–43.

Scott, Robert A. "The Construction of Stigma by Professional Experts." In *Deviance and Respectability,* ed. J. D. Douglas, 255–290. New York: Basic Books, 1970.

Scull, Andrew. "The Decarceration of the Mentally Ill: A Critical View." *Politics and Society* 6 (1976): 173–212.

———. "Mad-Doctors and Magistrates: English Psychiatry's Struggle for Professional Autonomy in the Nineteenth Century." *European Journal of Sociology* 17 (1976): 279–305.

———. "Madness and Segregative Control: The Rise of the Insane Asylum." *Social Problems* 24 (1977): 338–51.

———. "Community Corrections: Panacea, Progress, or Pretense?" In *The Politics of Legal Informalism,* ed. Richard Abel, vol. 1, 99–118. New York: Academic Press, 1981.

———. "Deinstitutionalization and the Rights of the Deviant." *Journal of Social Issues* 37 (1981): 6–20.

———. "Desperate Remedies: A Gothic Tale of Madness and Modern Medicine." *Psychological Medicine* 17 (1987): 561–77.

Scull, Andrew, and Diane Favreau. "'A Chance to Cut Is a Chance to Cure': Sexual Surgery for Psychosis in Three Nineteenth-Century Societies." In *Research in Law, Deviance, and Social Control,* vol. 8, ed. Steven Spitzer and Andrew Scull, 3–39. Greenwich, CT: JAI Press, 1986.

———. "The Clitoridectomy Craze." *Social Research* 53 (1986): 243–60.

Sedgwick, Peter. "Mental Illness *Is* Illness." *Salmagundi* 20 (1972): 196–222.

Sharfstein, Steven. "Will Community Mental Health Survive in the 1980s?" *American Journal of Psychiatry* 135 (1978): 1363–65.

Sheehan, D. N., and J. Atkinson. "Comparative Cost of State Hospitals and Community Based In-patient Care in Texas." *Hospital and Community Psychiatry* 25 (1974): 242–44.

Sicherman, Barbara. "The Uses of a Diagnosis: Doctors, Patients, and Neurasthenia." *Journal of the History of Medicine and the Allied Sciences* 32 (1977): 33–54.

Smith, Roger. "The Boundary Between Insanity and Criminal Responsibility in Nineteenth-Century England." In *Madhouses, Mad-Doctors, and Madmen,* ed. Andrew Scull, 363–84. Philadelphia: University of Pennsylvania Press, 1981.

Smith-Rosenberg, Carroll, and Charles Rosenberg. "The Female Animal: Medical and Biological Views of Woman and Her Role in Nineteenth-Century America." *Journal of American History* 60 (1973): 332–56.

Spitzer, R. L., and J. Fleiss. "A Re-analysis of the Reliability of Psychiatric Diagnosis." *British Journal of Psychiatry* 125 (1974): 341–47.

Spitzer, Steven, and Andrew Scull. "Privatization and State Control: The Case of the Private Police." *Social Problems* 25 (1977): 18–29.

Stone, Martin. "Shellshock and the Psychiatrists." In *The Anatomy of Madness*, ed. W. F. Bynum, Roy Porter, and Michael Shepherd, vol. 2, 242–71. London: Tavistock, 1985.

Sudnow, David. "Normal Crimes: Sociological Features of the Penal Code in a Public Defender Office." *Social Problems* 12 (1965): 255–76.

Swan, R. "A Survey of a Boarding Home Program for Former Mental Patients." *Hospital and Community Psychiatry* 24 (1973): 485–86.

Szasz, Thomas. "Involuntary Psychiatry." *University of Cincinnati Law Review* 44 (1976): 347–65.

Thompson, E. P. "The Moral Economy of the English Crowd in the Eighteenth Century." *Past and Present* 50 (1971): 76–136.

Tomes, Nancy Jane. " A Generous Confidence: Thomas Story Kirkbride's Philosophy of Asylum Construction and Management." In *Madhouses, Mad-Doctors, and Madmen*, ed. Andrew Scull, 121–43. Philadelphia: University of Pennsylvania Press, 1981.

Walk, Alexander. "Lincoln and Non-restraint." *British Journal of Psychiatry* 117 (1970): 481–95.

Walton, John. "Lunacy and the Industrial Revolution: A Study of Asylum Admissions in Lancashire, 1848–50." *Journal of Social History* 13 (1979–80): 13–18.

———. "The Treatment of Pauper Lunatics in Victorian England: The Case of Lancaster Asylum, 1816–1870." In *Madhouses, Mad-Doctors, and Madmen*, ed. Andrew Scull, 166–97. Philadephia: University of Pennsylvania Press, 1981.

———. "Casting Out and Bringing Back in Victorian England: Pauper Lunatics, 1840–1870." In *The Anatomy of Madness*, 2 vols. ed. W. F. Bynum, Roy Porter, and Michael Shepherd, vol. 2, 132–46. London: Tavistock, 1985.

Warren, Carol. "Electroconvulsive Therapy: 'New' Treatment of the 1980s." In *Research in Law, Deviance, and Social Control*, vol. 8, ed. Steven Spitzer and Andrew Scull, 41–55. Greenwich, CT: JAI Press, 1986.

Wexler, David B. "Mental Health Law and the Movement Toward Voluntary Treatment." *California Law Review* 62 (1974): 671–92.

Wing, John K. "Institutionalism in Mental Hospitals." *British Journal of Social and Clinical Psychiatry* 1 (1962): 38.

———. "Planning and Evaluating Services for the Chronically Handicapped Psychiatric Patients in the United Kingdom." In *Alternatives to Mental Hospital Treatment*, ed. L. I. Stein and M. A. Test, 240. New York: Plenum, 1978.

Wolpert, J., and E. Wolpert. "The Relocation of Released Mental Patients into Residential Communities." *Policy Sciences* 7 (1976): 31–51.

Yarrow, M., C. S. Schwartz, H. S. Murphy, and L. C. Deasy, "The Psychological Meaning of Mental Illness in the Family." *Journal of Social Issues* 11 (1955): 12–24.

INDEX

Compositor: G&S Typesetters, Inc.
Text: 10/12 Baskerville
Display: Baskerville
Printer: Maple-Vail Book Mfg. Group
Binder: Maple-Vail Book Mfg. Group